Kurt Lewin

Jean Piaget

Gregor J. Mendel

Edward B. Titchener

Ivan P. Pavlov

Max Wertheimer

TOPICS
IN THE
HISTORY
OF
PSYCHOLOGY
Volume 1

TOPICS
IN THE
HISTORY
OF
PSYCHOLOGY
Volume 1

Edited by

Gregory A. Kimble
Duke University

Kurt Schlesinger
University of Colorado

LEA LAWRENCE ERLBAUM ASSOCIATES, PUBLISHERS
1985   Hillsdale, New Jersey   London

Lawrence Erlbaum Associates, Inc., Publishers
365 Broadway
Hillsdale, New Jersey 07642

Library of Congress Cataloging in Publication Data
Main entry under title:

Topics in the history of psychology.

Includes indexes.
1. Psychology—History. I. Kimble, Gregory A.
II. Schlesinger, Kurt.
BF95.T67   1984   150'.9   84-24709
ISBN 0-89859-311-5 (v.1)
ISBN 0-89859-312-3 (v.2)

Printed in the United States of America

Contents

Contents of Volume 2

Preface

In writing the history of any field of inquiry, there are two important decisions to make: where in time to begin and where to end. At one end of the time scale, speculations about psychological processes go back to classical Greek philosophy and beyond. For centuries thereafter, the treatment of psychological subject matter remained largely in the domain of other disciplines, especially philosophy, where it became inextricably interwoven with epistemology. The chapters of this book tend to glance only briefly at these philosophical antecedents, to review the basic concepts and principles that early investigators were to take for granted. They tend then to move to the end of the last century when the systematic study of psychological processes began.

At the other end of the time scale, every subfield of psychology has been undergoing extremely rapid growth and change, especially during the last two decades. Before that, there had been a fairly gradual evolution of experimental methods, theoretical concepts, and empirical issues. More recently, however, the dominant trends in the field have changed significantly as new approaches gained ascendency. These developments were accompanied by an explosive spurt in new research. Even when the substantive problems remained the same, they were often reformulated, described in a new language, and attacked by new methods. How the old concepts and methods relate to the new is a topic of continuing debate, and sometimes controversy.

A great deal of what has been happening in the most recent years is still too new and controversial to be placed in historical perspective. As Boring wrote, "It is a nice question as to when the past becomes history, as to how old it needs to be before a first stable perspective of it can be limned" (1942, p. iii). The editors invited the contributors to these volumes to end their coverage at a point in time when their respective fields seemed to have been characterized by coherence and closure. For most of them this meant a point in time during the third quarter of this century, which brings us to the threshold of the current era and avoids the controversies of today.

Even within this truncated temporal span, many of the contributors of these volumes describe the work of the earliest years in greater detail than that of the later years. Inevitably, the questions that were asked first and the methods that were developed first set the agenda for a long time to come. Of course, the treatment has been highly selective throughout, with the selection of earlier work guided as much as possible by later developments. To quote Boring again, "Strange as it may seem, the present changes the past" (1950, p. ix).

The volumes of this work consist of nineteen chapters. Seventeen were written by psychologists expert in a particular branch of our field. For this reason, the book as a whole is not organized chronologically, as reflected in our title *Topics in the History of Psychology*. The first chapter in each of the volumes are the editors' attempts to remedy this deficiency. The first volume covers the areas of conditioning and learning, human learning and memory, sensory and perceptual processes, comparative psychology, and physiological psychology. Volume 2 covers the history of behavioral genetics, psychological testing, developmental psychology, drives and motives, sleep and dreaming, psychotherapy, psychopathology, personality theory and social psychology.

In developing this work, the editors had a particular concept in mind which we hoped would make these volumes appropriate as a textbook for a particular course. Psychology is a vast and incoherent field. In spite of this, it is our experience that students and teachers alike yearn for some type of capstone course that will put psychology in perspective. Historical perspective is the obvious candidate. The chapters in this book provide it for most of the important topics in our field.

The problem with a book that mainly provides perspective is that the liberalities of the twentieth-century university curriculum leave students unacquainted with the basic subject matter for which perspective is provided. This leads us, finally, to the description of a course which we believe should be required of all serious senior majors in psychology and would be very appropriate for beginning graduate students. This course would be based on this work supplemented by any of a dozen or so large encyclopedic introductory books that are currently available. These books are of a remarkably high quality; they present the current thinking which our volumes do not, and, most importantly, they change with changes in methods, concepts, data and interpretation. Exposure to the history of a topic, together with a picture of where that history has lead, strikes us as about as useful an integrating experience as we can provide our students.

Gregory A. Kimble
Kurt Schlesinger

TOPICS
IN THE
HISTORY
OF
PSYCHOLOGY
Volume 1

1

A Brief Introduction to a History of Psychology

Kurt Schlesinger
Department of Psychology and Institute for Behavioral Genetics
University of Colorado

In 1971 I had the honor of escorting a very famous scientist across the campus of the University of Colorado to the lecture auditorium in which he was going to speak. It was a beautiful spring day, and we were having a delightful conversation. With enthusiasm, the Nobel Laureate was telling me about the incredible potency of a particular pheromone. Calculations had yielded results consistent with the hypothesis that a single molecule of the pheromone was sufficient to excite the appropriate receptor in an insect. This, he told me, was similar to the calculations of Hecht, Shlaer, and Pirenne (1942) indicating that one quantum of light is sufficient to trigger the response of a single rod receptor. Quite suddenly our visitor stopped, his discourse ending in mid-sentence, and with some agitation he pointed to the inscription etched over the entrance to our library. "Who knows only his own generation remains always a child." Cicero had touched a raw nerve. The rationalization etched in granite, actually a slab of exposed concrete, should be erased. Why? Because scientists should not read history; it is counter-productive. Scientific problems should be approached naively, with the simplicity and creativity of a child. In science, historical "truths" should not be revered, they should be discarded gleefully in the light of new discoveries. New evidence is the life-blood of the scientist. We had started walking again and my response was cut short as we entered the auditorium, where we were soon treated to an excellent lecture.

Given the chance I would have responded with a text taken from Crutchfield and Krech (1962) who, in a guide to the understanding of the history of psychology, point to the following difference between many of the natural sciences and psychology: The history of physics, chemistry, biology, etc. is taught by historians, historians of science to be sure, who are not themselves primarily working scientists. This is different in psychology. In most colleges and universities a "History of Psychology" class is offered as an integral part of the undergraduate curriculum, and successful completion of work in this course is often a requirement for graduation. The course is offered within the department, and the instructor is a working psychologist whose specialty is probably not the history of psychology. Why is there this difference? Crutchfield and Krech offer several reasons, one of which is that academic psychology is a relatively new discipline and the individuals teaching the course are close enough to the beginnings of the field (or in fact are part of the history themselves) to be (1) interested in history, and (2) competent to teach it. Crutchfield and Krech offered this assessment some 20 years ago, and one cannot help but wonder whether this evaluation is as valid today as it was then. My own impression is that history of psychology courses, offered within departments of psychology, will soon become a thing of the past. Students interested in this area will have to go to history of science departments to take a course probably titled "A History of the Social and Behavioral Sciences." Whether such an event, if it occurs, will be a healthy development for our field, or its students, remains to be seen; but some of us will miss "the good old days" when we could tell our students that "psychology has a long past, but only a short history," and that as an academic and scientific discipline experimental psychology is only 100 years old.

The two volumes of this work titled *Topics in the History of Psychology* consist of 16 chapters, each written by an expert in a particular branch of psychology. As such, it represents separate accounts of the development of 16 areas within our discipline. Such an organization presents several difficulties: (1) In its entirety, the book is not organized chronologically. The two introductory chapters are meant to remedy this deficiency. (2) As a consequence of this organization there is some redundancy. In the view of the editors this redundancy is a virtue because, to pick a single example, Thorndike's contributions to the areas of learning and memory, drives and motives, comparative psychology, clinical psychology, etc. receive somewhat different and more appropriate emphases within the contexts of the various areas. (3) Each chapter is written by a different individual, by a person who is very much a part of the history being discussed. This is as it should be, except that the psychologists writing these accounts were too modest, in most cases greatly underestimating their own contribution to the history of their specialty.

This chapter consists of a very brief overview of the areas of (1) conditioning and learning, (2) human learning and memory, (3) sensory and perceptual processes, (4) comparative psychology, and (5) physiological psychology.

THE BEGINNINGS

Speculations concerning the nature of human and even animal behavior have very ancient origins. Human beings began domesticating dogs some 10,000 years ago. The Babylonians speculated about the etiology of epilepsy and were among the first to localize specific sensory and motor functions. The Egyptians performed rather crude forms of brain surgery, sometimes with the specific intent to modify or change behavior, procedures which we refer to as psychosurgery today. However, it is in the works of the Greek philosophers that we first begin to see the emergence of what in modern terms would be called real theories concerning human behavior. More specifically, it is in ancient Greece that we find the origins of association theory, the beginnings of the nature-nurture controversy, speculations concerning sensory and perceptual functions, and the first systematic attempt at the formulation of a theory of organic evolution based on an "internal perfecting principle."

Within the context of research concerning learning and memory we must credit Aristotle with the development of the first theory of learning. Although Aristotle did not specifically speak about associations, referring rather to a succession of ideas (Postman, Chapter 2, this volume), he concluded that ideas were generated in consciousness based on four principles: contiguity, similarity, contrast, and succession. Without doubt these four principles form the substance of the epistemological system known as British associationism, fundamentally important to the development of modern psychological thinking.

From the point of view of modern work on sensory and perceptual processes, the Greek origins are important because it is in the work of Alcmaeon, Plato, and Aristotle that speculations concerning the location of sensory receptors have their origins. Also, lists of sensory qualities were first proposed. Perhaps most importantly, it is here that we see the beginnings of questions that address sensory functions and how these are translated into perceptions of the world around us. For example, Plato's emanation hypothesis had the eye emitting streams of rays that probe the objects of regard. Aristotle rejected this hypothesis, but his own view was not very helpful; he believed that the soul takes on the form of a seen object, as wax takes the impression of a ring. With respect to the chemical senses, the Greeks could not explain the lack of a correlation between rates of decay of odoriferous substances and odor intensity, a question that was to puzzle Newton in the seventeenth century (Bartoshuk, Cain, & Pfaffman, Chapter 6, this volume).

The origins of physiological psychology can also be traced to Greek beginnings. For example, Alcmaeon, working in the fifth century B.C., recognized the brain as the seat of all the human intellectual faculties. This point of view was not universally accepted. Aristotle, for example, thought that the heart was the repository of all sensory experience and, thus, mediated our behavior. Hippocrates' writings on epilepsy, mental disorders, and especially his theory of bodily humors are important antecedents in the history of biological psychology.

Finally, from the point of view of comparative psychology, the Greeks, and especially Aristotle, are our intellectual predecessors because of their attempts at classifying species, their attempts at arranging life along a continuum of complexity, and their interests in explaining organic evolution in terms of independent creations and an internal perfecting principle, through which every species strove to perfection at its level of complexity. In his *History of Animals* Aristotle offered descriptions of the psychological capacities of animals of various species, using these to point to the unique position of *Homo sapiens* in his scala naturae.

THROUGH THE MIDDLE AGES AND RENAISSANCE

With the fall of Rome, Western intellectual development entered a period of stagnation. In the writings of this period independent thought was replaced by appeals to *authoritative sources,* Aristotle and Hippocrates became dogma, truths could be discovered by deductive reasoning from ancient sources, and, most important of all, empirical research, particularly anatomical studies, was discouraged and sometimes punished. Science, if it existed at all, survived in the hands of Arabic scholars. In the works of Muslim philosophers the idea of visual rays emanating from the eyes surfaced again, and was again rejected. The observation that strong sources of light result in persistent afterimages was recorded, and speculations concerning the point-for-point representation of visual images, on the cornea to be sure, were made (Riggs, Chapter 5, this volume). With respect to the sensory qualities of taste, Avicenna, writing *circa* 1000 A.D., spoke of five taste qualities, inventing the idea of an insipid quality that represented no, or zero, taste.

The emergence of the Renaissance, a period of history spanning the fourteenth to sixteenth century, brought about enormous changes in the intellectual climate of the Western world. The developments that occurred during this period changed the course of intellectual history; the causes that resulted in these changes in intellectual history have puzzled historians for centuries. One thing seems clear; many factors, political, economic, religious, etc., contributed to the decline and eventual disappearance of what has been referred to as the *Dark Ages.*

The fall of the feudal system changed politics and economics for all time. The Protestant Reformation produced the same results vis-a-vis religion. The work of Kepler, Copernicus, and Galileo created modern science as we know it today, and changed man's philosophy of man forever. Not that appeals to authority had been defeated for all eternity, witness the trial of Galileo at the time and even the Stokes trial many centuries later, but an unstoppable retreat of beliefs in superstition had begun. At the time, this culminated in the works of Francis Bacon, and his advocacy of empirical research as a method for discovering the truth. The Copernican revolution, the empiricism of Bacon, and the art of the Renaissance remain unsurpassed jewels in our intellectual and artistic heritage.

Alchemy produced no gold, but resulted in the development practical chemistry. Harvey discovered the circulation of blood in 1628, one of the truly great discoveries in biology. In 1542 Fernal wrote the first text on physiology since Galen. Not only were telescopes and microscopes invented, but also eye glasses were manufactured; camera obscura were produced, lacking only shutters and film, but the idea that these were the mechanical equivalents of the eye was not recognized. Kepler recognized that the optical image is inverted and reversed, and Scheiner (1579–1650) saw it as such when he cut away the opaque back of an eyeball.

DESCARTES: GIANT OF THE SEVENTEENTH CENTURY

René Descartes' contributions to our history are immense. His seminal insights in mathematics, physics, philosophy, and psychology are so great that he will always remain one of the giants of Western intellectual history. Descartes' psychology was so original that to call him the founder, or father, of modern psychology would hardly be an exaggeration. Descartes initiated a conceptual revolution, a change in canonical form, that was to dominate psychology well into the mid-twentieth century. Sharpless (1982) has called this canonical form, this prescribed standard form of thinking, *iatrophysics*, because physical and mechanical systems were used as models to account for behavior. Listen to Descartes. . . .

> All the most active, vigorous and finest particles of the blood tend to run into the cavities of the brain, inasmuch as the arteries which carry them are those which come in the straightest line of all from the heart and, as you know, all bodies in motion tend, as far a possible, to continue their motion in a straight line. (De l'Homme)

In proposing the concept of the reflex arc, Descartes moved the agent responsible for behavior (motion) from the head (soul) to the external world. Animal behaviors were responses to external events, stimuli. The energy necessary for behavior comes from within, but the precipitating cause is external, physical energy that impinges on the organism in the form of stimuli. Stimuli are *reflected* by the brain to the appropriate muscles to cause behavior. If one were to ask an Aristotelian "why is it that smoke rises?," the answer would be that it is in the nature of smoke to rise. Descartes and Galileo, and all Western scientists since them, would have responded differently; namely, that some external agent causes smoke to rise. Herein lies the genius of the seventeenth century; the philosophy exemplified by Descartes represents the first major change in causative thinking since the Greek philosophers. Descartes was quite wrong in almost every detail of his physiological description of the reflex arc. This does not detract in the least from his contributions. Pavlov and Sherrington were much more sophisticated in their knowledge of physiology. Nevertheless, they made the reflex arc their model of behavior, and their reflex arcs were purely Cartesian since they followed strict iatrophysical canonical forms. Sigmund Freud and the young Konrad Lorenz, to cite only two other examples, were also strict iatrophysicists.

Descartes made many other important contributions within the context of the history of psychology. Here we can only list some of them: (1) He invented a method, the so-called method of universal doubt, to study the mind. (2) His arguments for dualism raised the mind-body problem in a novel and poignant way. (3) His study of sensory processes and perception led him to discuss the point-to-point representation of retinal images on the brain. He did not recognize the optic chiasm as a decussation, and speculated that the pineal gland put two distinct images together to form a single perception (Riggs, Chapter 5, this volume). (4) Finally, and in large measure as a reaction against Cartesian nativism and rationalism, Descartes stimulated a philosophical reaction resulting in what we today call British Associationism.

BRITISH ASSOCIATIONISM

British associationism, or empiricism, refers to the collective work of a group of philosophers from Hobbes to Mill and Spencer, to ideas that developed over a period of some 300 years. Descartes held that certain basic ideas were innate, the *doctrine of innate ideas,* although he did acknowledge that experience must play some role in shaping our mind. Not so the British empiricists. For them experience is the sole source of all knowledge. John Locke (1690), for example, wrote "Let us suppose the Mind to be, as we say, white paper, void of character, without any ideas. How comes it to be furnished? Whence has it all the materials of reason and knowledge? To this I answer, in one word, from Experience."

The notion that all ideas come from experience, sensory experience, presents certain problems. After all, our eyes and ears can only supply us with sensations, not organized ideas. On the other hand, our mind is not a disorganized jumble of sensations; ideas are organized into meaningful units. How is this organization achieved? The British empiricists proposed that some imaginary "mental string" held together the sensations, or the "image" of sensations, that in their aggregate form an idea. These mental strings were formed by *associations.* Any two sensations that shared certain features, say any two sensations that occur together, contiguously, will become associated. Once two sensations are associated, the occurrence of one will evoke the memory of the other. According to these philosophers, associations are also formed between successive sensations. Thus, the ordering of ideas is also explained by associations.

Many laws of association were formulated. The two most important laws were (1) *contiguity,* which was central, and (2) *similarity,* accepted by some and rejected by others of the associationists. There were other mechanisms that resulted in associations—for example, contrast. Thomas Brown is remembered for his list of so-called secondary laws of association, including duration, liveliness, frequency, and recency, that were assumed to determine the strength of associations.

The impact of the British empiricists was profound, and their thinking remains important today. As Kimble (Chapter 2, this volume) has pointed out, and according to the associationists, adult mental life is a record of history, and what is studying the history of an individual except studying learning and memory. From this follows the importance of the field of learning and memory as a subject of psychological investigation. As Postman (Chapter 3, this volume) has said, two questions derived from the British associationists are of special concern to psychologists. These are: (1) what are the relationships between experienced events that are conducive to associations, and (2) what determines the persistence, or strength, of associations? As we shall see, from this follows more or less directly Wundt's idea that the proper subject matter for a science of psychology should be an analysis of the mind into its constituent elements and the manner in which these elements are connected.

OUR IMMEDIATE PREDECESSORS

In this section we shall briefly trace the contributions of individuals, some primarily psychologists others not, whose work contributed to the establishment of psychology as an independent academic discipline. Many contributions to knowledge made during the eighteenth and nineteenth centuries bear on this point. This discussion is organized into ideas and research as these are pertinent to the areas of psychology discussed in this volume.

Learning and Memory.   By the late nineteenth century the intellectual climate was such that modern work on learning and memory could begin. The Zeitgeist was ripe because, to quote Kimble (Chapter 2, this volume), ". . . dominant decisions had been made concerning the nature of man and how to study behavior." These decisions were both methodological and philosophical. Methodologically, empiricism was dominant, and the tool for studying behavior was to be observation. Materialism had triumphed over vitalism; the reflex arc, now buttressed by the discoveries of Bell and Magendie, was accepted as the fundamental unit of behavior. Darwin's theory of natural selection added a new dimension to investigations of reflex arcs, in that they were seen as having adaptive value. Within the domain of psychology, associationism had won its battle against rationalism, and contiguity was viewed as the single most important feature in the analysis of learning and memory. In all areas, and because of the impressive progress in the natural sciences, psychologists were now ready to imitate the methods used in the physical sciences. Given that empiricism, materialism, associationism, and elementalism (Kimble, Chapter 2, this volume) had carried the day, the stage was set for what was to come: Wundt, Ebbinghaus, Pavlov, and Thorndike created modern psychology.

Sensation and Perception.   What is the minimun change, for example, in light energy that will produce a just perceptible change in brightness? Whatever the answer to this question might be, such minimum changes are called thresholds, and thresholds measure a relationship between physical stimuli and subjective experience. The small physical difference between two lights that a subject can just notice would define the *difference threshold* for that subject. The *absolute threshold,* a special case of the difference threshold, would be the minimum amount of light necessary for a subject to just detect the presence of the stimulus.

E. H. Weber, working in the early part of the nineteenth century, was the first to note an important property of thresholds. This discovery was that the magnitude of the difference threshold varied as a function of the physical magnitude of the standard. The higher the energy level of the standard, the greater was the difference between the standard and the comparison stimuli necessary for subjects to notice a difference. Weber expressed this relationship in terms of the following mathematical formula: $\Delta I = KI$, where ΔI is the difference in energy between the standard and comparison stimuli that can be perceived 50% of the time; I is the energy level of the standard stimulus; and K is a constant, Weber's fraction, that depends on particular perceptual (for example, brightness) and physical (light-energy) dimensions.

In 1860 Fechner published *Elemente der Psychophysik,* and with it the philosophical and methodological foundations for an experimental psychology had been developed. Fechner believed that sensation cannot be measured (cf., Stevens, 1975). All we know is whether a sensation is present or absent, or whether two sensations are the same or different. However, stimuli can be measured, and it is therefore possible to determine the stimulus values necessary to produce a particular sensation, and the stimulus values necessary to produce differences in sensations. Based on much experimental evidence Fechner proposed his law, Namely $S = k \log R$, which, together with the methods of limits, of constant stimuli, and of average errors, was to become the cornerstone of an independent psychology.

The other nineteenth-century giants most important within the context of the history of research on sensory and perceptual processes are Helmholtz and Hering. The trichromatic theory of color vision, or the Young-Helmholtz theory as it is sometimes called, recognizes that visual sensation depends on waves of all frequencies. Since it is impossible to conceive the retina as containing elements sensitive to all frequencies, the theory states that the retina contains elements sensitive to the three principal colors—red, yellow, and green. Hering rejected this theory, substituting his own opponent-process theory to account for the phenomenological appearance of colors (although, contrary to what is sometimes written, he did not reject the Young-Helmholtz theory as it pertained to color mixture).

Physiological Psychology. During the eighteenth century scientists were fascinated by electricity, although research was handicapped by the rather primitive methods available to generate it (friction), store it (the Leyden jar was invented around midcentury), and measure it (the metallic leaf electroscope). Nevertheless, Galvani caused movement by connecting the leg of a frog to two dissimilar metals, concluding that it was caused by *animal electricity.* Volta showed that the movement was in fact caused by electricity generated when the leg was connected to the metals, but the idea that nervous activity was caused by electricity was generally accepted. The experimental evidence to support this idea was produced in experiments conducted by Carlo Matteuci and Emile du Bois-Reymond in the nineteenth century. The difference in electrical potential across the nerve membrane was measured. Du Bois-Reymond recorded the action potential, and within a few years Helmholtz had succeeded in measuring the velocity of nerve impulses. Further developments in neurophysiology followed rapidly when Gasser and Erlanger introduced the cathode-ray oscilloscope into physiology laboratories. Nevertheless, by the end of the nineteenth century the stage was set for the next important discoveries, those of Cajal and Golgi, whose contributions to neuroanatomy are as important today as they were then. The neuron doctrine remains the central theorem of physiological psychology, as indeed it does of the neurosciences more generally speaking. Work on the chemistry of the brain was beginning. Sir Charles Sherrington wrote his enormously influential *The Integrative Action of the Nervous System* in 1906, making the unit of analysis of the nervous system the reflex arc. The integrative action of the nervous system is to be understood by studying how simple reflexes are compounded according to their interactions, namely excitation and inhibition. The fact that the activity of the brain is electrical in nature was first discovered when Richard Caton measured the electrocorticogram in 1875; Hans Berger measured similar waves with surface electrodes in 1929.

The history of localization of function in the brain can be dated with the publication of a truly remarkable paper that Sir Charles Bell published in 1811. Some modern historians (see Diamond, Chapter 8, this volume) see this paper as the origin of the modern neurosciences. Bell's most important discovery was the observation that spinal nerves divide into two roots before they enter the spinal cord. Touching the ventral root with a knife produced movement, whereas touching the dorsal root did not. From this Bell deduced that sensory and motor nerve fibers were distinct in a peripheral nerve. At approximately the same time, Francois Magendie made the same discovery independently. It is for this reason that we call this fact the Bell-Magendie Law. Gall and Spurzheim's phrenology followed and flourished in spite of government edicts prohibiting its practice.

Pierre Flourens invented the ablation technique and applied it to his studies of the cerberal cortex, noting that ". . . not only do all perceptions, all volitions, in a word, all intellectual functions reside exclusively in this organ, but they reside there coextensively and without being separable from each other." In 1861 Paul Broca presented the case of Tam to a meeting of the Paris Anthropological Society. The world was ready for what Diamond has called "changes in the concept of the sensory pathway."

Comparative Psychology. Civilizations everywhere have always been interested in animal behavior for both practical and "academic" reasons. Nevertheless, two giants of nineteenth-century biology developed the theories that made modern comparative psychology possible. These two individuals were Charles Darwin and Gregor Mendel. In 1859 Darwin published his monumental *On The Origin of Species,* in which the basic tenets of evolutionary theory were set forth, in a form that Darwin referred to as "my abstract." The major theme of the book was the contention that species were not immutable. To make this point Darwin used an impressive amount of data from three sources: the fossil record, similarities in the morphology of existing species, and evidence of change resulting from domestication. Using these data Darwin concluded that (1) phenotypic variation is a fact of biological life, (2) there is a struggle for existence, and (3) natural selection functions to select more fit individuals. Since organisms vary in nearly all morphological and physiological traits, natural selection acts to select individuals with adaptive variations and to eliminate individuals with traits that detract from fitness. Fitness is defined as the number of offspring an individual produces. From the point of view of psychology, it is important to point out that behavioral traits also contribute to fitness, and that behaviors that have this attribute will be selected for; natural selection does not distinguish between behavior and morphology, fitness is what counts. In 1874 Darwin published *The Descent of Man,* in which the behavioral differences between human beings and other organisms are described as quantitative rather than qualitative. Thus, scientific investigations of animal behavior can make important contributions to our understanding of human beings.

Romanes immediately tried to discover behaviors that demonstrated this evolutionary continuity. Unfortunately, Romanes' data were largely anecdotal, and there was the additional difficulty of rather fanciful interpretations. C. Lloyd Morgan published *An Introduction to Comparative Psychology* in 1894, and will remain famous for what has since been known as Morgan's Canon . . . "In no case may we interpret an action as the outcome of the exercise of a higher psychical faculty, if it can be interpreted as the outcome of the exercise of one which stands lower in the psychological scale." What followed was Jacques Loeb's theory of tropisms, an attempt to explain all behavior in terms of physical stimuli that impinge on an animal. H. S. Jennings refuted this theory by showing that past experience is also important in determining the behaviors of organisms, even organisms as simple as protozoans.

The science of genetics was "born" in 1865 when the Augustinian monk Gregor Mendel published the results of his plant hybridization experiments. His findings were totally ignored for almost 30 years. The reasons for this indifference are manyfold, but one reason was that biologists did not understand the mechanisms that would explain his results. By the turn of the century, the cytological basis of cell reproduction was sufficiently well understood, and geneticists began to see the relationship between these two types of research. In 1903 the great American geneticist Sutton published a paper titled *The Chromosomes in Heredity,* explaining Mendel's data in cytological terms. From the point of view of psychology the developments in genetics are important because they suggested that genetic variables could be used to explain individual differences in behavior. The details of these developments are discussed in Volume 2.

WILHELM WUNDT

It is customary to say that academic psychology was born in 1879. Why? This birthday is usually chosen because it was in 1879 that Wilhelm Wundt, professor of philosophy at Leipzig, converted his laboratory, originally established for demonstration purposes, into the first institute for research in experimental psychology. For the first time in history, here was a place to which students could come for the explicit purpose of studying psychology and conducting psychological research. Because psychology is so firmly established as a part of the modern university curriculum, it is difficult to imagine that it was not until the 1870s that colleges began to offer formal courses in this field. During this decade two such laboratories were established. One of these was in Germany, as we have just seen, and the other was William James' demonstration laboratory at Harvard. James' operation remained a demonstration laboratory, whereas Wundt's establishment became an institute, and it is for precisely this reason that 1879 is usually chosen as the birthday of psychology, and Wundt is considered our father.

Wundt's experimental contributions were enormous; he was an extraordinarily productive individual. Wundt published approximately 500 research papers and books. According to one calculation, this output approximated 60,000 printed pages. Strangely enough Wundt is best remembered not for these experimental contributions, but because of his systematic ideas concerning what the subject matter of psychology should be and how this subject matter should be studied.

Borrowing from the associationists, and especially from John Stuart Mill, Wundt reasoned that the whole of an idea is both more *and* less than the sum of its parts. Ideas concerning things come about through mental chemistry. The parts of an idea, the elements, are lost when the idea itself, the compound, is formed. The job of psychology is to analyze ideas, with the purpose of discovering the constituent elements. Ideas are a subjective creation of the mind. Wundt's mental chemistry is to be studied as follows: First, the sensations themselves, their intensity and quality, should be studied. Next, psychologists should study how these sensations are combined to form perceptions and ideas. Then, we should study how these perceptions and ideas are stored in memory. Finally, we should study the attributes of these perceptions and ideas; these attributes are intensity, and spatial and temporal organization. All this is to be accomplished by using the techniques of mental chronometry and introspection.

Wundt's ideas resulted in the formation of a school of thought called *structuralism*. As the title implies, the goals of structuralism are to dissect the mind into its constituent elements, to practice a mental chemistry. Titchener, one of Wundt's most famous students and the psychologist who brought structuralism to the United States, counted 32,820 discriminable colors, 11,600 discriminable tones, etc. Wundt's philosophy was also strongly opposed by many psychologists with other ideas about what a scientific psychology should be all about, and these counter reactions resulted in the formation of several other "schools of psychology." These schools of psychology were to be of great importance during the next 50 years.

SCHOOLS OF PSYCHOLOGY

Structuralism.   As we have just seen, structuralism was the first so-called school of psychology. Structuralists were interested in describing the "generalized human mind" in terms of the elements which made it up—sensations, images, and affects. Not only were the irreducible elements of consciousness to be discovered, but synthesis, or the process by which elements of the mind were put together to form more complex aspects of consciousness, was also to be studied.

Functionalism.   The first serious challenge to the ideas of the structuralists was an American invention called functionalism. This school of psychology was developed by William James at Harvard, James R. Angel and John Dewey at the University of Chicago, and Edward L. Thorndike and Robert S. Woodsworth at Columbia. In very general terms, it was the contention of the functionalists that mental chemistry should not be the major preoccupation of psychologists. Rather, psychologists should study what functions consciousness serves. In more modern terms we would say that the functionalists were interested in the adaptive value of behavior. They did not reject the emphasis which the structuralists had placed on studying consciousness, nor did they reject introspection as a method.

Behaviorism.   By far the greatest challenge to both structuralism and functionalism was another American invention called behaviorism, identified most strongly with the work of John B. Watson. He rejected both the subject matter that interested structuralists and functionalists alike, consciousness, and intro-spection as a method of investigation. Watson argued that the private mental life of individuals cannot be the subject matter of an objective science. The only variables that could be objectively analyzed and quantitatively measured were overt responses, that is, behavior. Responses were elicited by stimuli, and be-haviorism also became known as S-R psychology. The goals of psychology were to study the relations between stimuli and responses, and to discover the laws that govern their associations.

Behaviorism was to triumph over the other schools, especially in the United States. If you were to knock on the door of an academic psychologist's office in the 1930s, the chances were better than nine out of ten that you would be answered by a behaviorist. Not that all behaviorists were alike; they ranged in view from Watson's type to "muscle twitch" psychology to Edward Tolman's "molar behaviorism" (see, for example, Kimble, Chapter 2, this volume).

Gestalt Psychology.   During the late nineteenth and early twentieth century, another school, Gestalt psychology, emerged to challege both structuralism and behaviorism. Gestalt psychology, as a school of thought was developed in Ger-many by Max Wertheimer, Kurt Koffka, and Wolfgang Kohler. All three of these psychologists migrated to the United States, greatly influencing psychol-ogy in this country. The major thesis of the gestalt psychologists was the argu-ment that the analysis of the mind as practiced by both the structuralists and behaviorists was in error because experience and behavior were "wholes," with properties that were unequal to the sum of their parts. Patterns, or form, are an inherent property of perceptions, and perceptual gestalten are isomorphic with physical gestalten (Dember & Bagwell, Chapter 7, this volume). According to this view it made no sense to study the mind in terms of its constituent elements, sensations, ideas, and emotions; rather, what was necessary was to study the interactions of these elements forming complex wholes. The major influence of the gestalt psychologists was on research in sensory and perceptual processes, but their impact was also felt in work on learning and memory.

Psychoanalysis.   Although originally developed as a method for treating neurotic patients, psychoanalysis became a much grander theory, an attempt to explain human behavior in its entirety. Psychoanalysis became a theory of per-sonality, a theory of motivation, and a theory of development; its impact on academic psychology was profound, and this influence is detailed in Volume 2.

PAVLOV, THORNDIKE, AND EBBINGHAUS

As we now proceed to summarize the contributions of Ivan Pavlov (1848–1936), Edward Thorndike (1874–1949), and Herman Ebbinghaus (1850–1909), we have lost our chronological thread. In a strict sense the work of these three giants of our field predates the establishment of nearly all the "schools of psychology" discussed in the preceding section. In fact, both behaviorism and functionalism built on the works of these early pioneers. Nevertheless, we discuss them here as direct antecedents to the learning theorists whose ideas were central within the psychology that developed between approximately 1920 and 1950.

Pavlov. Although Pavlov never thought of himself as a psychologist, and despite the fact that he had a rather low opinion of psychology as it was practiced at the turn of the century, his impact on our discipline is enormous and cannot easily be summarized, As Kimble (Chapter 2, this volume) has pointed out, he not only discovered classical conditioning, but described very nearly all of the basic phenomena associated with this form of learning. Conditioned reflexes provided a means of extending all we knew about reflex mechanisms into a new realm, learning. Here was a tool for studying learning with techniques other than introspection, precisely what the behaviorists wished to accomplish. Learning, so clearly a faculty of the mind, could now be studied with very scientific methods; Cartesian dualism was no longer a viable philosophy. The connections of Pavlov's work to British associationism are rather obvious; two stimuli, the conditioned and unconditioned stimuli, were presented contiguously and became associated. But more, the strength of associations could also be measured in terms of the amount of salivation, the latency to salivate, the frequency of salivation, etc.

Thorndike. Thorndike's experimental and theoretical contributions were within the framework of the functionalist tradition. His early experimental work is as well known as Pavlov's. Theoretically he differed from Pavlov in a number of respects: He thought that learning occurred through the strengthening of S-R, rather than S-S, connections. Since the latencies at which Thorndike's experimental subjects solved puzzle boxes decreased slowly over trials, he reasoned that learning occurs gradually, a principle known as the *law of exercise.* Finally, Thorndike placed great emphasis on reinforcement, S-R connections being strengthened by rewards and weakened by punishment, a principle known as the *law of effect.* As Thorndike performed more and more experiments, especially as he began to study human learning, his theoretical position changed. The importance of the law of exercise was downgraded. Perhaps more fundamental were changes in the law of effect. The importance of punishment was also downgraded; the effects of punishment were seen as increasing response variability, rather than as weakening S-R connections.

Ebbinghaus. As Postman (Chapter 3, this volume) has pointed out, Ebbinghaus did for higher mental processes what Fechner had done for sensory and perceptual processes. Reasoning that memories could not be measured directly, he developed the methods of savings to measure retention. In looking for the appropriate type of material that could be used in studies of human memory, he invented the nonsense syllable. Given nonsense syllables and the method of savings, Ebbinghaus went on to discover a large number of facts: He was the first to describe the forgetting curve. He discovered that learning varies as a function of the length of the list and the meaningfulness of the material; that retention, within limits, varies as a function of the number of repetitions; etc. G. E. Müller, working in Gottingen, continued the tradition of studying human memory. Here, many other methodological developments were made, including the invention of the memory drum, the paired-associate method, etc. Research in this laboratory led to discovering the role of grouping, associations to position, the importance of distribution of practice (Jost's 1st and 2nd laws), and so forth.

THE LEARNING THEORISTS

When we speak about "the learning theorists" we have in mind the collected works of a group of American psychologists, the most important of whom were Edward C. Tolman (1886–1959), Clark L. Hull (1884–1952), Kenneth W. Spence (1907–1967), and Edwin R. Guthrie (1886–1959). B. F. Skinner's research is equally important, although it is difficult to include him in this list, because he rejected the deductive approach so important in the work of the other learning theorists. The work and ideas of these theorists were to dominate psychology from roughly the 1920s through the 1950s, and their many contributions are discussed in detail by Kimble (Chapter 2, this volume).

The work of these men was inspired by the objectivism that is the central core of behaviorism, and by the methods that became available when Pavlov's work became known in the United States. Philosophically, these theorists were greatly influenced by what has been called logical positivism, and especially by the operationism of Percy Bridgman as set forth in his book *The Logic of Modern Physics* (1927). The basic idea was that concepts, even mentalistic concepts, could be given operational definitions by their relationship to observable behaviors. Hull, Spence, Tolman, and Guthrie all tried to explain learning and memory in animals with "chains of concepts linking independent with dependent variables." There were grand controversies concerning (1) place versus response learning, (2) the importance of habits versus expectancies, S-R as contrasted with S-S associations, (3) continuity versus noncontinuity, and (4) whether reinforcement is both a necessary and sufficient condition for learning, to name only a few. The theoretical differences between these individuals, especially the differences between Hull and Spence on the one hand and Tolman on the other hand, resulted in the publication of important research papers that supported or refuted one or the other of many theoretical constructs. It was a very exciting time.

B. F. Skinner differed from his contemporaries in many ways. He was far less interested in theory. He rejected the deductive approach. He was not interested in speculating about the physiological underpinnings of any of his constructs. The Skinner box, the use of individual animals, and the cumulative record were quite different from the mazes, group differences, and learning curves that interested Hull, Tolman, etc. What was studied were rates of responding; the behavior of organisms was totally determined by variables such as the number of reinforcements, their quality, and the schedules at which rewards and punishments were administered.

"Higher mental processes" such as delayed response learning, double alternation learning, Umweg behavior, etc. were also being studied. Wolfgang Kohler's research on learning in higher primates is of great importance in this context since it suggested that acquisition might not be a continuous process, that certain kinds of learning might depend on "insights."

Within the domain of human learning and memory, important theoretical and empirical contributions were being made at approximately the same time, although much of the work in this area continued in the functionalist tradition initiated by Ebbinghaus. The details of this research are discussed by Postman in Chapter 3. Here we can only highlight some of these developments. Robinson (1932) clearly articulated the idea that the laws governing associations should be defined as functional relations that connect the strength of associations to conditions of acquisition. McGeoch (1936) standardized the methods and measures used in studying human learning and memory, changed the emphasis to investigations of both learning and memory, distinguished between incidental and intentional learning, and was among the first to differentiate immediate and long-term memory. Hull's (1935) miniature theory attempting to account for serial learning stimulated much research. According to Hull, each presentation of an item in a serial list increases both the excitatory and inhibitory potential for that item, the difference being the effective excitatory potential. The theory predicts the serial position effect, the advantages of distributed over massed practice, and the occurrence of reminiscence. Hovland's empirical research on distributed versus massed practice and his work on reminiscence derive directly from Hull's theory. Gibson's theory (1940) also generated a good deal of research. According to this theory, successful performance depends on adequate discrimination, the result of reinforcing correct responses. Generalization impairs acquisition. The research of Postman and Underwood represents the zenith of research on human learning and memory within the functionalist tradition.

SENSORY AND PERCEPTUAL PROCESSES

The first half of the twentieth century produced enormous advances in our understanding of sensory and perceptual processes. In the area of vision, for example, Hecht proposed that all psychophysical phenomena could be understood on the basis of the bleaching of visual pigments. This idea, although a great oversimplification, generated an enormous amount of research. The best example is the paper by Hecht, Shlaer, and Pirenne (1942), which demonstrated that under perfect conditions a single photon of light was sufficient to trigger the response of one rod. In 1938 Granit and Svaetichin (see Granit, 1947) were the first to use microelectrodes to produce extracellular recordings from ganglion cells in the retina. Hartline and Graham (1932) discovered receptive fields in the retina, and Kuffler (1953) demonstrated center-surround antagonism in visual processes.

In the 1930s, Lord Adrian began his research on olfaction; he recorded neural responses in the olfactory bulb and in the pyriform cortex. The basic experimental questions that this research addressed were whether there were a limited number of functional types of cells, and whether olfactory information traveled along labeled lines. The answer was negative; the nervous system encodes odor information in terms of complex patterns. Stereochemical theories were developed suggesting that the shape and size of molecules determined their odors (Troland, 1930). Pfaffman's research on the chorda tympani remains a "classic"; recording from this nerve, he discovered that there were three types of fibers that responded to different tastes. Cohen, Hagawara, and Zotterman (1955) discovered a fourth type of fiber, a so-called "water fiber," found in animals of some species and not in organisms of other types. Finally, it was in the 1930s that Richter introduced the two-bottle preference test and began to study the hedonic properties of tastes.

PHYSIOLOGICAL AND COMPARATIVE PSYCHOLOGY

The first half of the twentieth century witnessed important discoveries that changed the face of these two areas of psychology. One field in which enormous progress occurred was in understanding how nerve cells communicate with each other and with muscles and glands. Working in the 1920s Loewi and Dale showed that the vagus nerve does not affect the activity of the heart directly; rather the nerve affects the heart by releasing a chemical substance, acetylcholine, to which the heart responds. Since that time, many other neurotransmitters have been discovered. Since synaptic transmission is often chemical in nature, neuroscientists have learned how to use drugs to alter the flow of information between nerve cells. This has resulted in great advances in our understanding of many behaviors, and in the establishment of a new area of study called "psychopharmacology."

Many other significant advances occurred during this period. W. R. Hess stimulated the diencephalon in freely behaving animals and discovered the importance of the hypothalamus in regulating many vegetative functions. In the late

1940s Magoun and Moruzzi discovered what had hitherto been the terra incognito of the brain, the reticular system. What Morruzzi and Magoun discovered was that the reticular system controlled the general level of excitability of the entire nervous system. Finally, in the early 1950s, two psychologists, James Olds and Peter Milner, discovered a phenomenon called "self-stimulation." These investigators discovered that there exist within the brain areas that animals actively seek to stimulate. Here, perhaps, was the biological substrate of reinforcement.

Research in comparative psychology progressed at a rapid pace during the early parts of this century. As psychologists became more and more interested in learning and memory processes, organisms of fewer and fewer species found their way into psychological laboratories. Beach lamented this fact in a wonderful article titled "The Snark is a Beejum" (1960). Nevertheless, research in comparative psychology continued; this work is best exemplified in Beach's important work on historical, experiential, and organismic determinants of sexual behavior. Scott's and Nissen's attempts at classifying behavior deserve a place in history, since comparing behavior across phyletic levels requires such classifications. The influence of the European ethologists, especially von Frisch, Lorenz, and Tinbergen, cannot be overestimated. Their emphasis on evolutionary determinants of behavior and their methods of studying behavior in natural environments has had a lasting impact on comparative psychology.

THE RECENT PAST

In this chapter I have tried to trace the history of psychology from its ancient origins to approximately 1950. Of necessity, this history is a bare skeleton; however, the various chapters of this volume provide much meat. Now it is time to bring the reader up to date, to speak of the developments that have taken place in the recent past. Since it is fair to say that we have learned more about behavior in the last 30 years than we learned in the preceding 3000, such an attempt at a summary is very difficult. To pick just two examples: Three types of cone receptors have been discovered, giving us the mechanistic underpinnings to explain Helmholtz's trichromatic theory of color vision. In addition, recent discoveries have shown that there exist so-called *opponent neurons* that increase their rate of firing maximally to one wavelength and decrease their firing maximally to the presentation of another. The opponent responses of these neurons correspond to Hering's theoretical idea of opposing red-green and yellow-blue processes in color vision. In a word, we can now say that we understand color vision.

During and immediately after World War II, important new developments occurred in the engineering sciences. Machines had been developed that transformed information into decisions, in the same sense that previous machines had changed energy into work. As control systems of this kind (computers, steering machines, etc.) became ever more complex, it became necessary to develop a new mathematics to describe their behavior. Thus, under the leadership of individuals such as von Neuman, Wiener, and others, cybernetics and the information sciences were born. These developments had profound effects on all of psychology because the mind (brain) is, after all, the best example of a machine that transforms information into decisions. Until the 1950s, psychologists had used variations of the doctrine of reflex action to describe behavior. Now a new way of thinking about behavior was possible. This way of thinking about behavior has little to do with reflexes; it involves computer analogies, complex control systems, set points, error signals, and so forth. Within physiological psychology, this new way of thinking about the behavior of organisms involves a new view of how the brain works, namely as multiple and interacting control systems all packed into our heads. In the area of sensation and perception the emergence of signal detection theory can be traced to these developments. So can the new emphasis on attentive processes, and the "new look" that stresses the importance of emotional states on our view of the world. In the domain of learning and memory, as well as in psycholinguistics, the computer, the idea of control systems, and the general theories of the information sciences have made possible a new way of looking at these behaviors, a new look we call *cognitive psychology*. Comparative psychology seems less influenced by these developments, but here too a new way of looking at behavior has emerged in the form of a theory known as *sociobiology*.

What will happen when the possibilities presented by these new ways of looking at behavior have been exhausted? Given the biases of this psychologist, ". . . it is possible, just possible, that the next new way of looking at things, the next set of canonical forms, will come from study of the brain itself" (Sharpless, 1982).

REFERENCES

Beach, F. A. The snark is a beejum. *American Psychologist,* 1960, *35,* 1–18.

Bridgman, P. W. *The logic of modern physics.* New York: Macmillan, 1927.

Crutchfield, R. S., & Krech, D. Some guides to the understanding of the history of psychology. In L. Postman (Ed.), *History of selected research topics.* New York: Knopf, 1962.

Cohen, M. J., Hagawara, S., & Zotterman, Y. The response spectrum of taste fibers in the cat: A single fiber analysis. *Acta Physiologica Scandinavica,* 1955, *33,* 316–332.

Darwin, C. *On the origin of species by means of natural selection, or the preservation of favoured races in the struggle for life.* London: John Murray, 1859. (New York: Appleton, 1869)

Darwin, C. *The descent of man and selection in relation to sex.* London: John Murray, 1871. (New York: Appleton, 1873)

Gibson, E.J. A systematic application of the concepts of generalization and differentiation to verbal learning. *Psychological Review,* 1940, *47,* 196–229.

Granit, R. *Sensory mechanisms of the retina.* New York: Oxford University Press, 1947.

Hartline, H. K., & Graham, C. H. Nerve impulses from single receptors in the eye. *Journal of Cellular and Comparative Physiology*, 1932, *1*, 227–295.

Hecht, S., Shlaer, S., & Pirrenne, M. H. Energy, quanta and vision, *Journal of General Physiology*, 1942, *25*, 819–840.

Hull, C. L. The conflicting psychologies of learning—a way out. *Psychological Review*, 1935, *42*, 491–516.

Kuffler, S. W. Discharge patterns and functional organization of mammalian retina. *Journal of Neurophysiology*, 1953, *16*. 37–68.

McGeoch, J. A. The vertical dimensions of mind. *Psychological Review*, 1936, *43*, 107–129.

Morgan, C. L. *Introduction to comparative psychology*. New York: Scribner's, 1894.

Robinson, E. S. *Association theory today*. New York: Century, 1932.

Sharpless, S. K. Historical concepts in the study of brain and behavior. In P. M. Groves & K. Schlesinger, *Biological psychology*. Dubuque: W. C. Brown, 1982.

Sherrington, C. S. *The integrative action of the nervous system*. New York: Scribner's, 1906. (New edition, Cambridge: Cambridge, 1947).

Stevens, S. S. Psychophysics: Introduction to its perceptual, neural, and social prospects. New York: Wiley, 1975.

Troland, L. T. *The principles of psychophysics: Vol. II: Sensation*. New York: Van Nostrand, 1930.

2 Conditioning and Learning

Gregory A. Kimble
Duke University

The scientific study of the psychology of learning originated in the late nineteenth century in three very different parts of the world. In Russia the great physiologist, Ivan Petrovich Pavlov turned from work on digestion to the investigation of classically conditioned reflexes; in America, Edward Lee Thorndike did his early studies of animal intelligence that were somewhat complex versions of what later came to be called instrumental or operant conditioning; in Germany, Hermann Ebbinghaus invented the nonsense syllable and began his self-inflicted studies of human verbal learning and memory. In this chapter we shall review the history that grew out of the first two of these contributions. Chapter 3 describes the history that began with Ebbinghaus.

SETTING THE METHODOLOGICAL STAGE

To appreciate the history of conditioning and learning one must understand the scholarly climate in which this study emerged. By the end of the nineteenth century dominant decisions had been made about human nature and how to know it. We say "dominant" because there were objections then as there are now to dominant themes. But the most influential scholars in those days had taken a stand in favor of certain methodological "isms" that specified the framework within which the psychology of learning developed: **empiricism, elementism, associationism,** and **materialism.**

Empiricism

The most important ideas determining the nature of the emerging scientific study of learning were put forth by the British Empiricists over a period of some 300 years, from about 1600 to about 1900. All of the methodological principles mentioned above appeared in their writings. Possibly the most basic of these was the proposal that knowledge comes from experience with the world. This idea has two closely related consequences. The first is that it carries a directive as to the nature of scientific procedures: they must be based upon observation rather than opinion, intuition or authority.

The second is more closely related to the psychology of learning. John Locke put the position in its most quotable form. The mind of the child, he said, is a blank slate (*tabula rasa*) upon which experience writes. Adult mental life is merely the record of the previous history of the individual. Although today we recognize such statements as too radically empiricistic, they legitimized the study of the individual's history of experience, one way of considering the process of learning.

Elementism

The major goal of the British Empiricists was to understand the mind or consciousness. In their striving toward such understanding they relied upon the method of analysis which had achieved such success in physical science, especially chemistry. Consciousness, they held, consisted of mental elements. These were ideas, each of which corresponded to a unit of experience, and were, therefore, sensory or perceptual in nature. This conception led to efforts to determine the number of mental elements that existed—to discover a psychological "periodic table." The question of how these elements were combined to recreate consciousness as we know it was answered in terms of associationism, which in the words of John Stuart Mill, was the essential process of the new "mental chemistry."

Associationism

The assignment of this basic role to association and attempted descriptions of the process led to the formulation of several sets of proposed laws of association. The law proposed most often was a **law of contiguity** which states that associations are most easily formed between experiences that occur closely together in time and space. Other suggested laws of association were those of *similarity, contrast, vividness, frequency,* and *recency.* Although they are seldom, if ever, called laws, these conceptions have survived and appear in discussions of learning and memory today.

Materialism

Although some of the British Empiricists interpreted the sensory elements in terms of physicalistic "vibrations" in the brain, the most significant materialistic themes were developed in the field of biology. René Descartes (1596–1650), sometimes called the father of physiology, made modest beginnings. He developed the view that the material human body is controlled by an immaterial soul. Descartes believed that the site of this interaction was the pineal gland which, under the direction of the soul, controlled the flow of animal spirits through nervous tubules to determine bodily actions. Among Descartes' contributions was a clear statement of the concept of reflex. Later on in the history of our topic, reflexes were to become an alternative to sensations as the fundamental elements out of which psychological processes are built.

In the course of this history there were two developments that had a particular significance for the study of learning. The first was the independent discovery by Sir Charles Bell (1774–1842) in England and Francois Magendie (1783–1855) in France that there is a segregation of function in the nervous system at the level of the spinal cord. Sensory nerves enter by way of the dorsal roots and motor fibers exit by way of the ventral roots. The importance of this discovery is related to the concepts of elementism and associationism discussed earlier. Now a new stimulus-response form of associationism became possible. A century later the question of whether associative learning involves stimuli and responses or sensations (the *ideas* of the British Empiricists) had become the focus of bitter dispute.

In the meantime, Charles Darwin (1809–1882) had published his theory of evolution and had added a new perspective to the developing materialistic view of behavior, the concept that it is adaptive. This was the second development in biology of significance for the psychology of learning that was mentioned earlier. Later on, the functionalists were to make the concept of the adaptive value of mental processes central to their theory.

RUSSIAN REFLEXOLOGY

The founding father of Russian reflexology was Ivan Michailovich Sechenov (1829–1905). The details of his writings show that, at least in those days, the dominant intellectual themes in Russia were the same as in the West. On *empiricism,* Sechenov (1935) maintained that ". . . 999/1000 of the contents of the mind depends upon education in the broadest sense, and only 1/1000 depends on individuality" (p. 335). The features of *elementism* and *materialism* were closely related to each other. Sechenov nominated the reflex as the elementary unit of behavior, and this was a materialistic proposal. Sechenov was quite specific on the point that all behavior was built up of reflexes piece-by-piece. In addition he accepted Darwin's proposal that reflexes are adaptive, calling attention to the way in which the reflexes of blinking, sneezing, and coughing expelled injurious foreign objects from the body. Finally, Sechenov supported *associationism* as the mechanism by which the creation of complex behavior is accomplished, and described the process of association as one in which the proprioceptive stimulus

FIG. 2.1.   Dog with esophageal fistula and gastric fistula (Asratyan, 1949).

produced by a first reflex is connected to the stimulus that elicits a second reflex. Thus Sechenov's associationism was stimulus-stimulus (S-S) association. All of these ideas were to become a part of Pavlovian theory.

Ivan Petrovich Pavlov and Classical Conditioning

The basic idea behind the study of conditioning seems to have suggested itself during Pavlov's earlier work on digestion for which he received the Nobel Prize in 1904. In much of this work Pavlov used dogs with esophageal and stomach fistulae as shown in Figure 2.1. In the condition illustrated, these animals "ate" the food provided for them but it never reached the stomach. In spite of this the stomach secreted gastric juice much as it would have had the food been eaten normally. This could only mean that the taste of food and/or the acts of chewing and swallowing were stimulating gastric secretion, presumably by connections through the brain.

Conditioning Experiments

With this simple but brilliant insight Pavlov turned to his studies of salivation which was much easier to measure than gastric activity. All that was necessary was to make a minor incision in a dog's cheek and to bring the parotid gland outside the cheek to allow the measurement of the amount of salivation secreted. As is well known, Pavlov did his conditioning experiments on dogs prepared in this way. In these experiments, Pavlov (1927) discovered most of the basic phenomena of learning, which there is room here only to list(see Kimble, 1961, pp. 44–108 for a more complete description): *acquisition, extinction, spontaneous recovery, higher-order conditioning,* the *generalization of excitation and inhibition, differential conditioning, summation, external inhibition, conditioned inhibition,* and *inhibition of delay.*

The general character of these phenomena has suggested to many psychologists that Pavlovian conditioning is of significance only for simple behavior in simple organisms. Pavlov, himself, did not see it that way. He believed that the mechanisms of conditioning could explain the most elaborate features of human behavior. We turn now to some of the most important of these applications.

Context effects.   Evidence for the subtlety and complexity of the conditioning process came from studies which showed that the general environment made important contributions. For example, the same conditioned stimulus could act as the signal for very different responses in different rooms or at different times of the day. In one experiment, a metronome ticking at a given rate was the stimulus for a salivary response based on food in the morning but for a flexion response based on shock to the paw in the afternoon. These experiments, showing a transfer of function for the same stimulus from one general situation to another, were referred to as demonstrations of **trans-switching.** Related, but even more dramatic, phenomena came under the heading of what Pavlov called **dynamic stereotypes.** In one demonstration a series of conditioned stimuli was presented to the dog in a conditioning experiment in the same sequence, day after day. Following such training, it was found that any alteration in the order or timing of the stimuli disrupted conditioning. The general point was that the details of the patterning of stimuli exercised important control over the conditioned response (Bogoiavlensky, 1957).

Language, Thought, and Understanding.   Pavlov considered language to be an exclusively human talent, but he reduced it to mechanistic terms. The most important aspect of his account was a distinction between first and second signalling systems. The **first signalling system** was the familiar system in which the conditioned stimulus was a signal for the unconditioned stimulus. The signals in the **second signalling system** were signals of signals: words were taken as signals for ordinary conditioned stimuli and one another.

Pavlov believed that the second system grew out of the first. Initially, words are associated with (conditioned to) physical stimuli and have a fairly specific meaning. In time, however, words acquire a ''comprehensiveness'' which (a) increases with experience and (b) will vary from person to person, depending upon the connections that are formed between words and other events. In other terms, Pavlov was saying that individual words have many meanings and that there are individual differences in these meanings.

According to Pavlov, words also had peculiar properties that were not characteristic of the physical stimuli of the first signalling system. For one thing, their connections are much less temporary; they show little tendency to extinguish. For another, words show a kind of semantic organization. In an illustrative experiment, a conditioned response in human subjects was established to the names of six birds (*swallow, hawk, hen, owl, dove, turkey*). The response did not generalize to other bird names (*sparrow, crow, goose, robin*), but it did elicit a response to the word *bird* when it was presented. This *elective generalization* creates a *sudden coupling* of certain verbal terms and others. Pavlov believed that these connections are the elements of understanding and that the sudden character of the process captures the essence of insight.

Conclusion

Pavlov's Huxley Lecture, delivered at the Charing Cross Hospital in London in 1906, on the scientific investigation of the psychical faculties in animals appeared in *Science* and became available to Western Psychology. Details of Pavlov's experiments were summarized 3 years later in a review by Yerkes and Morgulis. This information did not, however, lead to any immediate replications of Pavlov's work in America. There are probably several reasons for this. For one thing, World War I was soon to begin, and the psychologists who did basic research in peace time turned to such applied problems as the assessment of intelligence in military recruits. Even after the war, however, there was little or no research in the Pavlovian tradition in America. A minor problem was that American investigators had difficulty with Pavlovian techniques of collecting saliva. A more important point was that other methods had developed and, without recognizing that there might be an important difference, American investigators had turned to a variety of instrumental, or operant, conditioning procedures.

What, then, was Pavlov's contribution to the psychology of learning? From a later perspective, there appear to have been two contributions. The first was a factual one. Most of the conditioning phenomena discovered by Pavlov turned out to be general ones that appeared in other forms of learning. Thus Pavlov contributed knowledge out of which psychology hoped to create a scientific account of human and animal behavior. The second contribution was that Pavlov's method provided an alternative to the introspectionistic psychology that was dominant in those days, but seemed inappropriate to psychology as it was developing.

AMERICAN FUNCTIONALISM

In early twentieth century America, the leader of experimental psychology was Edwin Bradford Titchener (1867–1927) whose thinking was in the tradition of the British Empiricists. He identified the subject matter of psychology as the mind or consciousness and its most important method as **introspection.** The purpose of this method was to analyze the content of consciousness into its elements. The general idea was that these elements were the basic building blocks of the mind, the units of its structure. Hence the position was called **structuralism.**

As early as 1884, in an article in *Mind* entitled "On Some Omissions of Introspective Psychology," William James was writing in a vein that was very critical of structural psychology. The difference between James' position and that of the structuralists was basic. Whereas the structuralists presented a picture of mind as composed of static content, James spoke of a "stream of consciousness," made up of substantive terms that are "stopped over" for an instant, only to give way to transitive "moments of flight." One difficulty with introspective psychology is that it cannot handle these moments of flight. For to introspect upon them is to stop them, to make them substantive and to lose the very object of introspection. Directing the light of introspection against the stream of thought is like turning up the gas lamp to see how the darkness looks.

A related criticism made by James in the same article, and by many others elsewhere, was that an awareness of our subjective states modifies them. We have all had the experience of examining a mood of joy or anger only to find ourselves a little less joyous or a bit less angry. Particularly the emotions, but to a degree all mental states, present this problem for the introspective method.

A third criticism that James had for the structuralists involved their obsession with analysis: "What God has joined together, they resolutely and wantonly put asunder." This, James considered to be the root of all structuralistic evil. Typically, as James saw it, structuralism analyzed the unanalyzable and then indulged itself in the meaningless exercise of trying to synthesize the original object of analysis. James gave this procedure short shrift in the observation that two pinks (the products of analysis) do not make one scarlet (the mental state with which the analysis began).

There were also other dissatisfactions with the structuralist position, particularly with the introspective method. Psychology was developing an interest in child development, mental disorder, and animal behavior. Introspection was peculiarly unsuited to the study of any of these areas. In the face of such pressures, a new psychology began to take form in which the ideas of Darwin played a central role. This new psychology stressed the adaptive value of mental processes and asked about their functions, hence its name, **functionalism.**

The Basic Tenents of Functionalism

James Rowland Angell (1869–1949) put the functionalist position before psychology in 1907 in a paper entitled "The Province of Functional Psychology." He presented functionalism as a return to established themes in psychology from which structuralism had briefly strayed. In the writings of Angell and the other important functionalists, Harvey Carr (1863–1954), John Dewey (1859–1952), and Robert Woodworth (1869–1962), functionalism developed as more of an attitude or general orientation than a well defined school. Some of the features of their orientation were the following:

Mental processes have two aspects, a structural one and a functional one. It is important to develop a psychology of both. Upon analysis it turns out that some psychological phenomena (e.g., idea, image) are more structural in nature; others (e.g., attention, thinking) are more functional. The basic error of structuralism lay precisely in the fact that it limited its interest to just one of these aspects. Since functionalism concerned itself with both of them, it was broader than the structural psychology with which it competed.

Functionalism was also broader in another way. As mentioned earlier, the basic functionalist question is the question of the adaptive value of the mental processes, the question of what they are for. This concern for the functions of mental processes led easily to a tolerance for applied psychology and an interest in mental tests, educational psychology, child development, and psychopathology. It also laid the foundation for a new view of psychology which took *behavior,* rather than the mind, to be the basic subject matter of the field.

Taking the cue from Darwin, seeing mental activity as involved in the struggle for survival and as showing an adaptive function, led easily to an interest in learning. Well ingrained habits and reflexes were seen as automatic ways of adapting to the routine requirements of existence. Functioning automatically they allowed the mind to free itself for higher activities, coming down to these everyday matters only in moments of conflict or decision. In the language of maze learning, which came on the scene at about the same time as functionalism did, "consciousness arises at a choice-point."

OPERANT (INSTRUMENTAL) CONDITIONING AND SELECTIVE LEARNING

The study of animal learning developed in the functionalist context. Although we shall single out Edward Lee Thorndike as the individual in early American psychology whose contributions now seems greatest, it is important to mention one other influence that helped to shape the developing study of conditioning and learning. In 1899 W. S. Small at Clark University built a replica of the Hampton Court maze and studied the ability of rats to learn it. This rat-in-maze methodology was an essential aspect of the psychology of learning for the next two or three decades. Today the concept appears to have been a bad one. Not only did it give psychology a bad name among undergraduates, it also led to programs of research that were largely unproductive. On the one hand, maze learning is so complex that it is hard to understand. On the other hand, the study of just one species, the rat, limited the generality of the little that was ever learned with the aid of this method.

The maze learning experiments were early examples of **instrumental learning** because the rat had to make certain definite responses in order to receive the food in the goal box. This is the hallmark of such learning: the responses are instrumental (in the words of Hilgard and Marquis [1940]) to the receipt of reward. Thorndike's studies, begun before the turn of the century, were the most important historical examples of instrumental learning or, as Skinner later called it, **operant conditioning.**

Thorndike

Edward Lee Thorndike (1874–1949) was born in Williamsburg, Massachusetts, the son of a Methodist minister. He entered Wesleyan University in 1891 where he studied the standard classical curriculum and graduated with honors and a *Phi Beta Kappa* key in 1895. During his undergraduate career Thorndike had read William James and, impressed by James' deep understanding of psychology, went to Harvard as a graduate student intending to study with James.

At Harvard Thorndike began his research career with a study of telepathy that never got off the ground. Then, as would happen most places now, the faculty objected and Thorndike turned to a study of the intelligence of chicks. This research ran into a different kind of problem. There was no animal lab available to Thorndike at Harvard. He tried to do his work in his rooming house but his landlady objected. He transferred his project to William James' basement and worked there for a while, an unsatisfactory solution to the problem. Beset with all these difficulties, and now, short of funds, Thorndike finally transferred to Columbia in 1897, to take a fellowship with James McKeen Cattell. He received the Ph.D. degree in 1898, following which he took a teaching job at Western Reserve. He returned to Columbia as an instructor in the Teachers College in 1899 and remained there until his death 50 years later.

The Laws of Learning

For the purpose of this record, Thorndike's most important work was that which he carried out for the doctorate where he investigated selective learning in a variety of species including cats, dogs, chicks, fish, and monkeys. His most famous experiments were carried out with cats learning to escape from a "puzzle box" of the type shown in Figure 2.2 to obtain release and a bit of food as a reward. In the apparatus in the illustration the response required of the cat was to press a treadle. In other versions the cat learned to turn a latch, to pull a string, or to perform one or more other responses. The major data in Thorndike's experiment were from 13 cats and 3 dogs. It is probably safe to say that never in the history of psychology has so much controversy arisen from such a modest basis in fact. The controversy was, of course, not about the facts but about three points of interpretation (Thorndike, 1911).

Stimulus-response Connectionism. Two of these three controversial items were stated as formal laws. The third was not. This last was the concept that learning consisted of stimulus-response (S-R) connections rather than the association of ideas, as the British Empiricists had suggested, or stimulus-stimulus

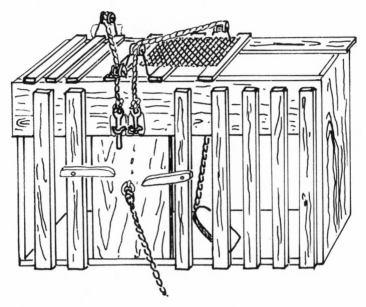

FIG. 2.2.   One of Thorndike's famous puzzle boxes. In this one the cat had to
press the treadle to be released from the box. (Thorndike, 1911)

(S-S) connections, as Pavlov believed. The S-R position was so essential to the
statement of Thorndike's two major laws, however, that there never was any
doubt as to where Thorndike stood on the issue.

The Law of Effect.   Thorndike (1911) believed that reward and punishment
played a critical role in learning and stated that belief as follows:

> The **Law of Effect** is that: Of several responses made to the same situation, those
> which are accompanied or closely followed by satisfaction to the animal will, other
> things being equal, be more firmly connected with the situation, so that, when it
> recurs, they will be more likely to recur; those which are accompanied or closely
> followed by discomfort to the animal will, other things being equal, have their
> connections with that situation weakened, so that, when it recurs, they will be less
> likely to occur. The greater the satisfaction or discomfort, the greater the strength-
> ening or weakening of the bond. (p. 244)

The law of effect came under immediate attack on two main fronts. There
were those who claimed that the law could not be universally true. How, these
critics asked, do reward and punishment play any part when we happen to
remember (and therefore must have learned) that there is a mail box along the
route we normally take when we walk to work? Others objected on methodological grounds claiming first that the term ''satisfier'' was unscientifically subjec-

tive and that the law of effect was circular. The circular argument went this way: The law of effect proposes that S-R connections are strengthened because a response is followed by a satisfier; but how does one know that an event is a satisfier? By its ability to strengthen S-R connections. This comes down to S-R connections being strengthened because S-R connections are strengthened. The fact and its explanation are the same thing, logically circular and unacceptable as scientific explanation.

These latter objections should never have been raised. On the page following the statement of the Law of Effect, Thorndike made the concept of satisfier what we would now call an intervening variable and also broke the circle by giving an independent definition of a satisfier: "By a satisfying state of affairs is meant one which the animal does nothing to avoid, often doing such things as attain and preserve it" (p. 245). Eventually most psychologists who accepted a version of the law of effect also accepted this way of stating the logical situation.

The Law of Exercise.   Thorndike's third controversial proposal was the law of exercise, stated as follows:

> The **Law of Exercise** is that: Any response to a situation will, other things being equal, be more strongly connected with the situation in proportion to the number of times it has been connected with that situation and to the average vigor and duration of the connection." (p. 244)

What made the law of exercise controversial was the explicit statement that learning is gradual rather than sudden or insightful.

Later Developments.   By the early 1930s Thorndike had modified his position considerably. The law of exercise was repealed (1932) largely on the basis of the observation that repetition appeared to produce no increase in the strength of strong connections. The law of effect was modified (e.g., 1932) but also strengthened. The modification was one that enhanced the importance of reward and minimized the importance of punishment in learning. This was because a variety of experimental demonstrations seemed to indicate that an annoying aftereffect did not weaken the tendency that produced it. The strengthening of the law of effect took the form of a statement that *any* S-R connection could be strengthened by a satisfying aftereffect.

The statement that *any* connection could be strengthened by reward carried an important proviso, however. Thorndike had noted that the responses an animal learned often seemed "natural" to the situation and "relevant" to the animal's wants. They somehow "belonged" to the learning situation. According to Thorndike, such responses were easier than others for animals to acquire and specifically could be learned with a greater delay of satisfaction than unnatural or irrelevant responses. Thirty years later this **law of belongingness** was to receive full confirmation in studies of learned aversions to tastes.

Although Thorndike proposed other laws of learning and although the modifications of the basic laws were important, his most major contribution was the clear statement of three fundamental propositions about learning: It consists of S-R connections; it occurs gradually; it depends upon reinforcement (reward and punishment). These ideas were to become central to certain later theories of learning as well as the main objections to those theories advanced by their critics.

BEHAVIORISM

Behaviorism may be said to have been launched with the publication of Watson's 1913 paper, entitled "Psychology as a Behaviorist Views It." As usual, however, many of the important concepts had been developed by others and possibly earlier. In this case, one of the most significant early figures was a Russian contemporary of Pavlov.

Bekhterev

Vladimir M. Bekhterev (1857–1927) began his systematic investigation of "association-reflexes" during the winter of 1906–1907. In his experimental work, he used human subjects as well as dogs to study the conditioning of withdrawal and respiratory responses evoked by electric shock. Bekhterev's *Objective Psychology*, describing this work, appeared serially from 1907 to 1912, published, of course, in Russian. By 1913, however, Bekhterev's work had been translated into French and German, languages with which the psychologists of the West were familiar, a knowledge of these two languages being required in all American doctoral programs. The translations of Bekhterev's work were widely read by American investigators, and most of them adopted his motor methods rather than the salivary method of Pavlov.

Even more important that Bekhterev's experimental contribution was his more basic methodological contribution. This took the form of a strong case for the exclusive use of objective observation, which Bekhterev made with the aid of the now familiar "Man from Mars" metaphor. Suppose, he argued, that you are a creature from another planet, that you arrive somehow on earth, and that you get interested in the activities of the species called Man. After a period of informal observation, you decide that you will try to develop a science of these activities. What methods would you have at your disposal? Being from another world, you could not possibly rely upon your intuitions, for they depend too much upon your own experience. This rules out the major method which psychology tends to use too much. You could not interview these beings, because you do not know how to communicate with them. That eliminates another common method. Finally, you realize there there are available to you only two kinds of materials: the things these people do (responses) and the situations in which these responses occur (stimuli). If you could find dependable relationships between the responses and the stimuli in whose presence they occur, that would be a science of Man's behavior. It was such a program that Bekhterev and, almost simultaneously, Watson urged as the appropriate method for psychology.

Watson

John Broadus Watson (1878–1958) was born near Greenville, South Carolina. He received Bachelor and Master degrees from Furman University. After that, he went to the University of Chicago to study philosophy. There the great functionalist psychologist, James Rowland Angell, soon turned his interest to psychology, particularly animal psychology. Watson's doctoral dissertation, entitled *Animal Education* (cf. Thorndike's *Animal Intelligence*) was published in 1903. Watson moved to the Johns Hopkins University in 1908, where he remained for the rest of his academic career.

The program of research associated with Watson's name that attracted most scientific attention was on the problem called the **sensory control of the maze,** in which the basic question was this: What contributions do each of the sensory departments make to the rat's mastery of the maze habit? The method of attempting to answer this question was systematically to deprive the rat of sight, hearing, smell, and tactile sensitivity provided by the vibrissae and to measure maze performance. The results of decades of such work can be described briefly. Loss of any sensory department interferes with maze learning; the more senses that are lacking, the greater the impairment, but the loss of all the senses mentioned above still leaves the rat capable of learning the maze, albeit slowly.

By the middle to late 1940s, when the last of these studies was done, the options had been reduced to two: either the rat somehow learns the maze with its mind, a proposition the behavists could not accept, or else it uses kinesthetic information provided by the muscles used in running the maze. The problem of the ''sensory control of the maze'' had become the problem of the **kinesthetic control of the maze.**

The method of tackling this problem goes back to the discoveries of Bell and Magendie, mentioned earlier. Since sensory information enters the spinal cord dorsally, it is possible in theory (though very difficult in surgical practice) to deprive rats of this final possible sensory representation of the maze habit. These studies were done, largely under the direction of Walter S. Hunter, at Brown University. These were never entirely conclusive, however, and psychology lost interest in the issue before it was firmly settled.

Another of Watson's studies (with Rosalie Rayner), his conditioning of the boy Albert to fear a white rat, turned out to have a more lasting importance. It led to certain of the methods of behavioral therapy still used today and described elsewhere in this book.

It was not Watson's experimental work that was so significant, however. It was his theoretical work which came to be called behaviorism. The important systematic point in this theorizing was an extreme environmentalism. Watson's most quoted statement sums up this aspect of his position very well:

> Give me a dozen healthy infants, well-formed, and my own specified world to bring them up in and I'll guarantee to take any one of them at random and train him to become any type of specialist I might select—doctor, lawyer, merchant-chief and, yes, ever beggarman and thief, regardless of his talents, penchants, tendencies, abilities, vocations and race of his ancestors. (1925, p. 104)

In his presidential address to the American Psychological Association in 1915, Watson put forth the conditioned reflex as the agent for such training. Watson rejected all psychological concepts that seemed to him to be "subjective." He didn't care much for the concept of reinforcement employed by Pavlov, let alone Thorndike's theory of satisfiers. He substituted for the law of effect a principle of recency, according to which connections are formed on the basis of temporal continguity. He reduced pleasure to a matter of stimuli originating in peripheral erogenous zones and thought to implicit subvocal speech. Such treatments were what led Tolman to criticize Watson for creating a "muscle-twitch psychology."

Watson left academic psychology in the early 1920s after a scandalous (for those days) divorce, initiated by his wife on the grounds of adultery with Rosalie Rayner. He went into advertising, but continued to promote behaviorism, chiefly in popular writing. He was an effective writer and probably did more to influence lay opinions than those of his colleagues in psychology. Although the behavioristic theme was to increase in importance, Titchener's structural psychology was still the most important school when Watson bowed out.

An End and A Beginning

When Titchener died in 1927, the professional gossip of the next year or two centered on the question of his successor: Who was to replace Titchener as the leader of experimental psychology in the years to come? The two most promising candidates for that role appeared to be E. G. Boring, one of Titchener's most distinguished students, and K. S. Lashley, later to emerge as a giant in the field of physiological psychology, but seen back then as a behaviorist of the Watsonian persuasion.

As it turned out, neither man achieved the prominence predicted for him. For, out of the blue in 1929 there came a paper, by a former applied psychologist who had just moved from the University of Wisconsin to Yale, that was to upset all the odds. The psychologist was Clark Leonard Hull; the title of his paper was "A Functional Interpretation of the Conditioned Reflex." This article propelled Hull into the position of *the* leading experimental psychologist. The reason for Hull's instant eminence was that, better than anyone else, he brought together the themes and methods that had been prominent in the past half century. For the conditioned reflex, the basic explanatory concept of behaviorism, Hull had asked the functionalist question: What is the adaptive significance of this phenomenon? For the next few decades, which might be dated from 1929 to 1959—from the publication of Hull's paper just mentioned to the publication of Hull's last book, *A Behavior System*—psychology was dominated by a new set of themes. These dates saw the rise and fall of a set of theories of learning which bound another significant era in the history of psychology.

METHODOLOGICAL BACKGROUND

Watson's behavioristic proclamation now appears to have had its greatest impact as a negative statement. It told psychology what it must not do: it must not deal with anything mentalistic. The cost of attempting to comply with Watson's program was enormous. Psychology lost its mind, its will, and its consciousness. It received a cold Watsonian stare of disapproval if it thought, made a judgment, experienced an emotion, had an attitude, or even paid attention. Watson created this unpsychological psychology by reducing the basic subject matter to stimuli and responses defined in a very narrow way. Stimuli were such things as rays of light of different wave lengths, sound waves of different amplitude, length, phase and combinations, and gaseous particles of such small diameters that they affect the membrane of the nose. Responses were such things as muscle contractions and glandular secretions.

The most effective critic of this position was E. C. Tolman. In a paper entitled "A New Formula for Behaviorism," published in 1922, Tolman proposed a liberalization of the concepts of stimulus and response. Presenting himself as still a behaviorist he substituted the concepts of *stimulating agency* for stimulus and *behavior act* for response:

> The stimulating agency may be defined in any standardized terms, those of physics, of physiology, or of common sense, and it constitutes the independent, initiating cause of the whole behavior phenomena. . .
> . . . The behavior act is simply the name given the final bits of behavior as such. The behavior act together with the stimulating agency constitutes the fundamentals upon which the rest of the system is based. . . it is they alone which. . . tell us all that we know of . . . an organism's mentality (even when that organism is another human being who can introspect).

Later on, Tolman and others would refer to this type of psychology, in which the concepts of situation or stimulating agency and behavior were the basic terms, as a *molar behaviorism*. Such a system was adopted by almost all behavioristic psychologists as more attractive and more realistic than Watson's *molecular* ("muscle-twitch") *behaviorism*. This is a point that deserves clearer understanding than it has received. The critics of behaviorism, almost without exception, resurrect the dead horse of Watsonian behaviorism and beat it in their destructions of behaviorist psychology.

Operationism

In several papers published in the next half dozen years Tolman sought to show how such mentalistic concepts as instinct, emotion, sensory quality, ideas, insight, consciousness and purpose (all discarded by Watson) could be retained in a behavioristic psychology. A few key sentences, not in sequence, from Tolman's treatment of purpose will serve to illustrate the procedure.

> When one observes an animal performing, one knows nothing concerning possible "contents" of the latter's "mind" and to assume such contents seems to us to add nothing to one's description. One does, however, see certain aspects of the behavior itself which are important and for which the term "purpose" seems a good name.
>
> When an animal is learning a maze, or escaping from a puzzle box, or merely going about its daily business of eating, nest building, sleeping and the like, it will be noted that in all such performances a certain *persistence until* character is to be found. Now it is just this *persistence until* character which we will define as purpose.
>
> . . . We, being behaviorists, *identify* purpose with such aspects . . . and there is no additional explanatory value, we should contend, in making the further assumption that such responses are accompanied by a mentalistic something, also to be known as "purpose."

In this statement, Tolman was saying that this aspect of persistence until (a goal was reached) in the behavior of an animal could provide an objective definition of the purpose of the animal to achieve that goal. This is the essential idea of the movement called **operationism,** which psychology was to discover in the writings of the Harvard University physicist, Percy Bridgman (1927). Unobservables, for example mentalistic concepts, are acceptable in science if they can be given **operational definitions** that relate them to observables. In physical science these operations are usually operations of measurement. In psychology they more frequently are statements of the objective bases used to introduce an unobservable into our scientific vocabulary. The impact of operationism on the psychology of learning was enormous. For the next two decades, the most deadly sin a psychologist could commit was to fail to define his terms operationally.

Hypothetico-Deductive Method

Operationism deals with the factual aspects of science. An important development was also occurring on the theoretical front. This was an application of the deductive methods of physics in psychology. The first important spokesman for this position was Clark L. Hull. Modeling himself on Newton, Hull undertook the ambitious task of developing a deductive theory of the phenomena of learning. As Newton had done in his *Principia,* Hull's plan was to assemble a set of basic laws that would serve as postulates or basic *hypotheses* in a *deductive* system. The theorems deduced from these postulates would constitute the essential proof or disproof of the system. This strategy was widely accepted and came to be known as the **hypothetico-deductive method.**

Taxonomies of Learning

By the late 1920s (see, Konorski & Miller, 1937) a number of psychologists had recognized an important operationally defined difference between the Pavlovian and Thorndikean experiments. In the Thorndikean case, there is a contingent relationship between responses and reinforcement. The cat receives food if, but only if, it pulls the string or makes some other specified response. In the Pavlovian case, no such contingency exists. The dog receives food at a specified time after the presentation of the CS whether or not it salivates. Although the expressions Pavlovian conditioning and Thorndikean learning were sometimes used to refer to these different procedures, it became more conventional to refer to the former as classical or respondent conditioning and to the latter as instrumental or operant. Hilgard and Marquis (1940) popularized the classical-instrumental terminology. B. F. Skinner (1938) suggested the respondent-operant distinction.

It is important to note that these different procedures provide *operational definitions* of two different methods of conditioning. They say nothing about differences in underlying processes. The important question, of course, involves this latter point: Do classical and instrumental operations produce different forms of learning? A good many psychologists claimed that they did. The important proposed distinctions are summarized in Table 2.1.

TABLE 2.1
Proposed Differences between Pavlovian and Thorndikean Learning

	Pavlovian Procedure	Thorndikean Procedure
Procedural distinction	No contingency between response and consequence	Response-Consequence contingency
Type of response	Elicited by US reflexive involuntary	Emitted without discoverable stimulation, voluntary
Neural mechanisms	Autonomic nervous system	Skeletal nervous system
Essential law of learning	Contiguity	Reinforcement (effect)
What is learned	S-S connections expectancies preparatory responses	S-R connections habits

The differences summarized in Table 2.1 have now been the object of experimental work for half a century. The two specific dey questions suggested by the materials in the Table have been the following: (1) Is it possible to obtain instrumental conditioning of elicited, reflexive responses of the autonomic nervous system? For example, can the galvanic skin response of a human subject be conditioned by making reward contingent upon the appearance of such a response? (2) Can emitted "voluntary" skeletal responses be conditioned classically? For example, can the key pecking response of a pigeon be conditioned by the mere pairing of a light and the presentation of food? Although the returns are not all in, the tentative answer to both of these questions seems to be "yes." Kimmel (e.g., 1973) has provided a number of demonstrations of instrumental conditioning of the GSR. The phenomenon of *autoshaping* to be considered later is often presented as a case of classical conditioning of an emitted response. Such results mean, in short, that the classical-instrumental distinction may be a purely definitional one.

Varieties of Instrumental Learning

In their influential book, *Conditioning and Learning,* Hilgard and Marquis first made the distinction between classical and instrumental conditioning and then went on to distinguish among four different types of the latter form of learning: (1) *reward training* (Skinner box experiments where a rat receives food for pressing a bar), (2) *escape training* (a rat learns to run off an electrified grid when the shock comes on), (3) *avoidance training* (given a signal that shock is about to come on, the rat leaves the grid before the shock appears), and (4) *secondary reward training.* Early experiments on secondary reward training were those of Wolfe (1936) and Cowles (1937). In these experiments chimpanzees first learned to deposit tokens about the size of poker chips into a vending machine ("chimp-o-mat") to obtain a bit of fruit. Later on the subjects would perform a series of other tasks for which the reward was a token. The token was a *secondary reward* because its value as a reward was learned. Food itself was a *primary reward.*

Hilgard and Marquis arrived at their classification by thinking in terms of the effects of primary rewards and punishments in situations where they were either present or absent. Thus, reward training was produced in situations where the primary reward was present but the secondary reward training occurred when it was absent. Escape training occurred where the primary punisher (shock) was present. Avoidance training occurred where it was absent.

In his revision of Hilgard and Marquis' *Conditioning and Learning,* Kimble (1961) also proposed a four-fold classification of types of instrumental conditioning, but on a partially different basis. He defined the types in terms of reward and punishment again, but his second defining variable was whether the specified response led to the presence or absence of a reward or punishment. This classification resulted in four types of instrumental conditioning: (1) **reward training**—if the response occurs, reward occurs, (2) **omission training**—if the response occurs reward is withheld, (3) **punishment training**—if the response occurs, punishment occurs, and (4) **avoidance training**—if the response occurs, punishment is withheld. All of these procedures are probably familiar to the reader except, perhaps, omission training.

Omission training has not been widely studied, although it is of some interest because it is the experimental analogue of the procedure in which a parent withholds a reward in attempting to get a child to give up undesirable behavior. In an experiment on this topic, a dog might first be trained to lift a paw to obtain food. In the next stage, food would be withheld if the dog lifts its paw, but presented if the dog fails to lift its paw. An interesting effect of this procedure is that the animal learns the opposite of the original response, in this case an extension of the leg.

More recent taxonomies of learning have built on this last one, adding another dimension, whether or not a signal indicates the beginning of a trial. This added variable creates eight types of instrumental learning produced by all combinations of whether or not a signal is used, whether reward or punishment is used as a reinforcer, and whether the response produces the reinforcer or eliminates it. Notice that the primary-secondary distinction has disappeared. All of these form of instrumental learning are summarized in Table 2.2.

TABLE 2.2
Eight Varieties of Instrumental Learning

Type	Signal Available	Effect of Response on Reinforcer	Type of Reinforcer	Effect on Response
Reward training	no	produces	reward	strengthened
discriminated reward training	yes	produces	reward	strengthened
escape training	no	eliminates	punishment	strengthened
discriminated* escape training	yes	eliminates	punishment	strengthened
omission training	no	eliminates	reward	weakened**
discriminated omission training	yes	eliminates	reward	weakened**
punishment training	no	produces	punishment	weakened**
discriminated punishment training	yes	produces	punishment	weakened**

*More traditionally called avoidance training.
**Opposed reaction strengthened.

Higher Mental Processes

Many of the early taxonomies of learning covered procedures that were much more elaborate than those just presented. Some of the more interesting ones are described briefly in the following sections.

The Delayed Reaction. In their most frequent form, experiments on the **delayed reaction** went as follows: An animal watched while the experimenter put a desirable bit of food under one of two cups. Then the experimenter lowered a screen that obscured the two containers from view. After an amount of time that varied from trial to trial, the screen was raised and the animal lifted one cup or the other, a response that indicated whether it could remember where the food had been placed. The measure of interest in these experiments was the amount of time that could elapse before the animal lost the correct response.

One question which the delayed reaction attempted to answer concerned the ordering of animal species in terms of their abilities to bridge these temporal gaps. Under roughly comparable conditions, human subjects were superior to other species which followed in the order: rhesus monkey, gibbon, marmoset, raccoon, and cat. These results, of course, raised the further question of the processes used to span the delay. To say that an animal uses its intelligence or mental powers for such purposes is obviously not satisfactory. Hilgard and Marquis (1940) offered a more behavioristic alternative. They proposed that the sight of food might elicit an anticipatory response which has the potential to lead the animal to approach food. This response could be conditioned to the cup under which food was placed even though an actual approach to the food was impossible. On tests when the approach was permitted, the sight of the cup would elicit the anticipatory reaction which, in turn, would lead to an overt reaction of approach.

Double-alternation.   A second method used to investigate the higher mental processes in animals tested subjects in the **double-alternation maze.** Such mazes required the mastery of a sequence of right (R) and left (L) turns that could be symbolized RRLLRRLL, etc. Double-alternation mazes were constructed in the spatial and temporal forms illustrated in Figure 2.3. The spatial form of the maze proved to be unsatisfactory because it was difficult to remove all external cues. The temporal maze avoided this problem by requiring different responses to the same stimuli at different times. The subject began in the central alley. To receive food it had to go through the maze four times on a single trial, turning right at the choice point on the first two runs and left on the second two. Rats were usually unable to solve the double-alternation problem. Raccoons, dogs, monkeys, and children all solved it.

Umweg.   The **umweg** (round about) problem required the animal to turn away from a goal and circumvent a barrier in order to reach it (see Figure 2.4). One interesting result obtained in such studies was that a very attractive reward

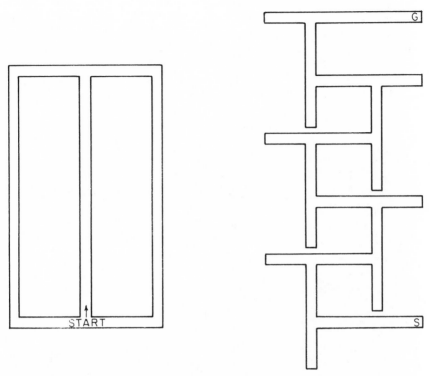

FIG. 2.3.   Two forms of the double-alternation maze. The left-hand maze is a temporal maze; the righthand maze is a spatial maze.

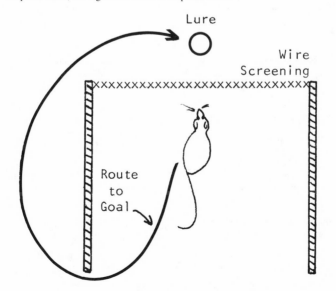

FIG. 2.4.   An example of the Umweg Problem

or a very high level of motivation interfered with mastery. Since a moderate level of motivation was required for such learning, this suggested that the relationship between performance and motivation might be nonmonotonic, an inverted U-shaped function. Yerkes and Dodson (1908) were probably the first to obtain this result, although with electric shock and discrimination learning. For this reason the inverted U relationship was sometimes called the *Yerkes-Dodson law*.

Insight.   Some psychological theorists, most frequently the Gestalt psychologists, proposed that the solution to the Umweg problem required a reorganization of the perceptual field of the learner. The animal came to see a new set of relationships among the elements of the world. This interpretation was put forth most effectively by Wolfgang Kohler. As is too well known to recount in detail here, Kohler (1925) made observations of tbe problem solving of chimpanzees and was impressed with the fact that the apes seemed to solve the problems suddenly and that these solutions occurred when they had an insight into the nature of the problem. For example, one chimpanzee suddenly solved the problem of raking in a banana outside its cage when it "saw" that joining two hollow tubes together could make the tool required to do this.

Conclusion

While this work was going on, the psychology of learning was developing delusions of grandeur. Although Hull had put the point most strongly, the whole field (except for Skinner) had accepted the view that the road to progress lay in the development of deductive treatments of learning. This meant that the right scientific strategy was to discover the elementary laws of learning which then could be put together to account for complex behavior. On this ground, research on complex learning gave way to simpler studies involving single-unit T-mazes, straight alleys, the Skinner box, and eyelid conditioning. The theories of learning, to which we turn now, were grounded in research of that type.

HULL AND SPENCE

Pavlov died in 1936. By the same date Thorndike had left the field of his early work and had moved into educational psychology where he was the most significant individual on the scene. The vacuum left by the departure of these giants was destined to be filled by Clark L. Hull and Kenneth W. Spence. Although these men disagreed on many specific points of interpretation, their goals were so much the same that the position they represented came to be called the Hull-Spence theory. To set the historical record straight, it may be worth two sentences to mention that Spence was not a student of Hull. He was a student of Robert M. Yerkes (at Yale where Hull held a faculty appointment) and did his dissertation on a problem of visual acuity in the chimpanzee.

Biographical

Clark L. Hull (1884–1952) was born on a farm in New York State, but he moved with his family to Michigan at a very early age. Hull's undergraduate work was at Alma College and the University of Michigan. He received the Ph.D. degree at the age of 34 from the University of Wisconsin, having been slowed up in his career first by a temporary decision to become a mining engineer and then by poliomyelitis. During his lifetime Hull made important contributions in three areas: applied psychology, hypnosis and suggestibility, and learning theory. As mentioned earlier, Hull began his study of learning with his important paper which gave a functionalist interpretation of the conditioned reflex. Subsequent papers turned to the treatment of a variety of forms of learning, some of which will be covered in the next section. A decade of such work led finally to the publication of *Principles of Behavior* (1943), the Hullian contribution treated most extensively in this chapter.

Kenneth W. Spence (1907–1967) was born in Chicago, Illinois, but he moved with his family to Montreal, Canada, at the age of four. Spence received his Bachelor's and Master's degrees from McGill. He then transferred to Yale where he received the Ph.D. in 1933. After a period at the Yale Laboratories of Primate Biology in Orange Park, Florida, and a one-year appointment at the University of Virginia, Spence moved to the State University of Iowa, arriving in 1938. In 1942 he became Head of the department, a position he retained for over 20 years. In 1964 he moved to the University of Texas in Austin, three years before his death.

Even while he was still at Yale, Spence's work began to be associated with that of Hull. In 1932 Spence published a paper on the order of elimination of blinds in maze learning which involved ideas essential to the goal-gradient hypothesis. At the Orange Park Laboratories, Spence did his work on discrimination learning which was taken over by Hull in his 1943 account of that process. After arriving at Iowa, Spence carried on an extensive correspondence with Hull in connection with Hull's manuscript of the book, *Principles of Behavior*. This interaction had a significant impact on the final content of the book.

Early Work

Hull's most important early work in learning represented an attempt to analyze complex behavior in terms of the principles of conditioning. The analysis of certain aspects of maze learning with the aid of the concepts of **habit-family hierarchy** and the **goal-gradient hypothesis** was typical. The idea essential to the concept of habit-family hierarchy was that in most situations where there is a goal to be attained, the organism has at its disposal several different responses (*a habit-family*) to use to attain that goal. At the same time, however, these habits vary in strength (*form a hierarchy*). The strength of the habit determines the probability that it will be used.

One of the most straightforward applications of this concept was to explain trial and error learning. Hull saw the process as a matter of reordering the strengths of the various habits in the hierarchy. Since the situation is a learning situation, the strongest habit cannot be the correct one. For such learning to occur, this strongest incorrect habit must be weakened and a habit that is initially weaker must be strengthened. The mechanisms put forth to accomplish these effects were reinforcement and extinction. In an early paper on the habit-family hierarchy, Hull (1934) used these ideas to explain the occurrence of errors in a multi-unit maze. For example, one of the strongest habits in the animal's hierarchy is that of approaching goals once their location is recognized. This leads to errors made by entering goal-pointing blind alleys and difficulty in elimination of these errors.

Even earlier, Hull (1932) had presented the *goal-gradient hypothesis* this way, ". . . The goal reaction gets conditioned the most strongly to the stimuli preceding it, and other reactions get conditioned to their stimuli progressively weaker as they are more remote (in time or space) from the goal." In this statement Hull conceived of any behavioral situation as capable of being analyzed into a series of S-R links. He then proposed that the strength of the connections was a function of the distance of the particular link in time or distance from the goal. Hull used the goal-gradient hypothesis to explain a dozen different features of maze learning. The most important of these involved speed of running and the order in which blind alleys are eliminated in maze learning.

Principles of Behavior

The most influential Hullian theory appeared in 1943 in a book entitled *Principles of Behavior*. In this book, Hull presented what he believed to be the fundamental laws of all behavior and an organization of these principles into a formal deductive system. Although the theory was expressed mathematically and also had a neurophysiological component, its enduring contribution can be presented as a chain of hypothetical processes that connected stimuli on the one hand with responses on the other. As this statement suggests, Hull was clearly in the camp of the S-R theorists.

Habit Formation. The central concept in Hull's theory was that of **habit,** which he defined in Thorndikean terms. Habits were (1) stimulus-response connections which (2) developed gradually (3) as a result of reinforcement. This last assumption was Hull's version of the law of effect. Hull proposed that reinforcement consisted in a process of **drive reduction:** food is reinforcing for a hungry organism because it reduces the drive of hunger.

For Hull, stimulus generalization was also a part of the process of habit-formation. Hull recognized that stimulus situations would vary slightly trial by trial and that an organism could never learn anything unless habits generalized to these different stimuli.

Performance. An important aspect of Hull's theory was an acceptance of the learning-performance distinction. *Learning* he conceived as a permanent product of previously reinforced pairings of stimuli and responses. *Performance* was the manifestation of these products in behavior. The concept of *drive* allowed Hull to take a first step toward an explanation of an organism's ability to make use of what it has learned.

The most interesting aspect of Hull's treatment of drive was that he made it exclusively a performance variable which gave habits the energy required to produce performance, but which played no role in learning. Given a level of drive sufficient to produce responding and to make a reinforcer such as food reinforcing, learning should be the same at all drive levels. This prediction received support in a number of drive-shift experiments (see Figure 2.5) In these experiments, different groups of subjects began training under two or more different levels of drive. This produced differences in performance; the stronger the drive the better the performance. In a second stage of the experiments, a portion of the animals in each group were switched to higher or lower levels of drive. The result favoring Hull's theory was that under the new drive level the subjects behaved as if they had been trained at that drive level from the beginning. Differential drive levels, in other words, had no differential effect on learning.

Inhibition. Following the lead of Pavlov, Hull included an inhibitory concept in his theory to account for extinction, spontaneous recovery, discrimination

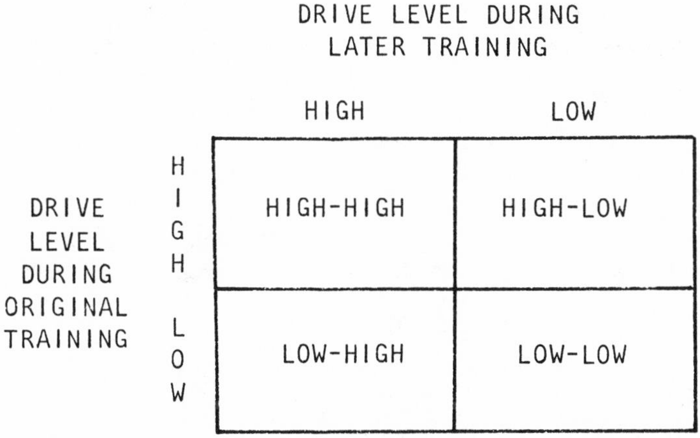

DRIVE LEVEL DURING
LATER TRAINING

		HIGH	LOW
DRIVE LEVEL DURING ORIGINAL TRAINING	HIGH	HIGH-HIGH	HIGH-LOW
	LOW	LOW-HIGH	LOW-LOW

FIG. 2.5. Design of a typical experiment intended to determine whether motivation affects learning. Animals are first trained on two different drive levels (rows in the Figure). Then each of these two groups is divided (represented by the columns in the Figure). Half of the subjects continue under the original condition of drive; the other half are switched to the alternative condition. The performance of interest is that occurring following the switch. If performance differs for the two groups *trained* under different drives, then motivation affects learning.

learning, and the like. Hull proposed that two inhibitory mechanisms were required to account for various inhibitory phenomena. The first of these, **reactive inhibition,** developed with the occurrence of every response whether reinforced or not and dissipated with rest or non-responding . Hull considered reactive inhibition to be a fatigue-like state with motivational properties. This latter assumption meant that the dissipation of inhibition would be reinforcing because it was drive-reducing. With reinforcement thus provided, Hull argued that non-responding could be conditioned to the stimuli in any situation. In this way Hull deduced the existence of a second form of inhibition, **conditioned inhibition,** which added to the effects of reactive inhibition. Both forms of inhibition reduced the level of performance.

These ideas bought a great deal for Hull in the way of interpretation of experimental data. The theory predicted that performance under distributed practice would be superior to performance under massed practice, that extinction would occur with the development of inhibition, and that spontaneous recovery would occur with rest as a result of the dissipation of inhibition. Since part of the inhibitory process was a habit, the theory also predicted that spontaneous recovery would not restore performance to its complete pre-extinction level. Conditioned inhibition would continue to suppress it. Results of experiments supported all of these predictions.

Response Evocation.   Hull developed two final concepts that were required in order to account for certain details of performance. The first of these was a concept of **oscillation.** On the basis of several lines of evidence, Hull assumed that response tendencies varied randomly from moment to moment. Second, Hull introduced a concept of **threshold** which these tendencies had to exceed if a learned response were to occur. Hull used these ideas to explain the facts that sometimes many reinforcements had to occur before the appearance of the first learned response and that frequently learning curves showed an initial period of positive acceleration.

Summary of Hull-Spence Theory.   As we mentioned earlier, it is useful to think of the Hull-Spence theory as a chain of concepts connecting a set of independent variables with a set of dependent variables. Figure 2.6 displays the links in this chain. An important thing to notice is just the general structure of the theory as a serial chain of concepts describing the mechanisms thought to take place between the independent variables on the left and the dependent (response) variables on the right. Some important questions to ask about the theory concern its obvious complexity: Can a theory so elaborate be manageable? Is it realistic? Answering the second question first: Unfortunately it begins to appear that behavior is at least that complexly determined. But manageable is something else. The increasing cumbersomeness of Hull's theory, as it was revised in later versions, was one of the important factors leading to the downfall of the theory.

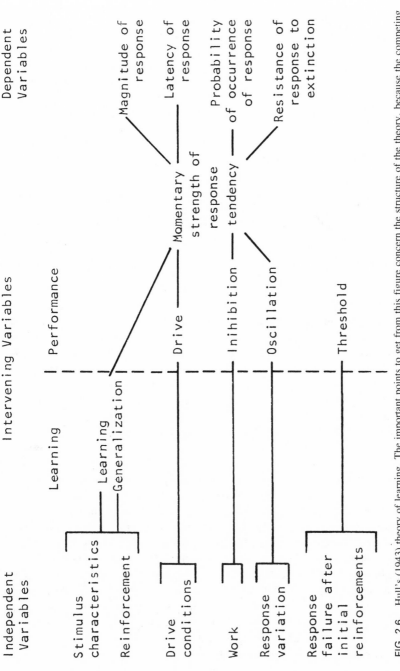

FIG. 2.6. Hull's (1943) theory of learning. The important points to get from this figure concern the structure of the theory, because the competing theories had very similar structures as will emerge in Figures 2.7., 2.11, and 2.12. Note that Hull's theory is of the intervening variable variety and that it incorporates a distinction between learning and performance.

47

TOLMAN

In the 1940s the theory which stood as the main alternative to Hull's was that of Tolman. Edward Chace Tolman (1886–1959) was born in West Newton, Massachusetts, the younger brother of Richard Chace Tolman, the famous physical chemist and physicist. Tolman received a Bachelor of Science degree from MIT and the M.A. and Ph.D. degrees from Harvard. After a year as an instructor at Northwestern University, Tolman moved to the University of California at Berkeley, where he remained for the rest of his life.

Tolman's most important theoretical statement was contained in his 1938 paper, *The Determiners of Behavior at a Choice Point.* In this paper Tolman presented the outline of a theory designed to answer the simple question: What accounts for the probability that a rat will turn to the left at an intersection in a T maze? The answer, he claimed, would be in terms of the effects of a set of independent variables. In quasi-formal terms, $P_{BL} = f_1(x_1, x_2 \ldots x_n)$; that is, the probability of left-turning behavior will be a function (f_1) of the values of the independent variables x_1, x_2 to however many there are (x_n).

Tolman identified ten variables as probably among the most important. Six of these were environmental variables: maintenance schedule or drive (M), the appropriateness of the goal object (G), types of stimuli provided (S), types of responses required (R), nature and number of trials (we will use the symbol N, although Tolman called it $\Sigma[OBO]$), and pattern of maze units (P). The other four were individual difference variables: heredity (H), age (A), previous training (T), and special endocrine, drug, or vitamin conditions (E). Thus, Tolman's f_1 function would be: $P_{BL} = f_1(M, G, S, R, N, P, H, A, T, E)$.

Although this statement may seem complex enough already, Tolman introduced further complexities, claiming that even the more elaborate expression was surely an oversimplification. To illustrate just one of the complicating aspects, Tolman maintained that the individual difference variables interacted with each of the environmental variables and would influence the effect of each. Anticipating a more explicit later statement by Feigl (1945), Tolman saw that he could simplify things by breaking the f_1 function down into two sub-functions with the aid of **intervening variables.** His specific proposal was to introduce these intervening variables as functions (f_2) of the independent variables and then to relate them to behavior by a third set of functions (f_3). Tolman did not attempt to state these functions quantitatively but, instead, presented them in the diagram presented in Figure 2.7. This figure is similar to Figure 2.6 and makes the very important point that the theories of Tolman and Hull were not dissimilar in structure. The main points of disagreement were in the positions Tolman and Hull took on certain experimental questions.

Expectancy Versus Habit.   Although Tolman called himself a behaviorist and in 1938 set his goal as that of explaining a simple item of behavior, he did

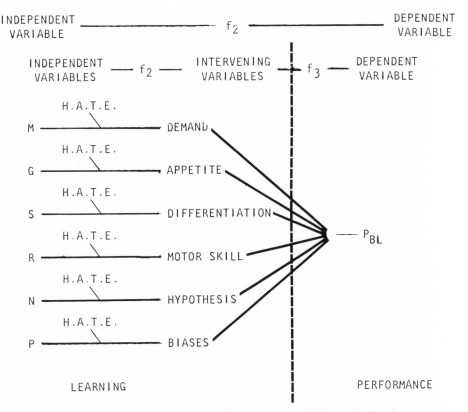

FIG. 2.7. Tolman's (1938) theory. The independent variables are listed at the top of the figure. The theory itself has the same major features as Hull's theory depicted in Figure 2.6.

not think of learning in terms of *stimulus-response connections or habits.* He spoke instead of the development of *knowledge, expectations, cognitions,* or *stimulus-stimulus associations.* What a rat running a maze actually learns, he sometimes said, is a knowledge of what leads to what in this situation. More specifically (to show why the theory was a stimulus-stimulus theory), Tolman proposed that the rat learns that given such and such a first stimulus it will arrive at such and such a second stimulus, if it performs a particular response. This contrasts sharply with the theories of Hull and Thorndike, who proposed that learning involves the formation of stimulus-response associations.

One experimental test of these alternative interpretations was in a series of experiments with rats designed to compare **place learning** and **response learning.** Tolman, Ritchie, and Kalish (1947) reported a typical study of this type using the maze shown in Figure 2.8. This maze differs from most mazes in that it has two starting points, S_1 and S_2. In the experiment, rats sometimes began their trial at S_1 and sometimes at S_2.

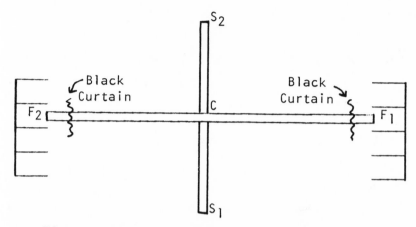

FIG. 2.8.   Apparatus for the study of place and response learning. S_1 and S_2 are starting points. Rats began some trials at S_1 and others at S_2. F_1 and F_2 show the locations of goal boxes containing food. Under conditions of place learning, food was always in the same place, day, F_1. In response learning, food was shifted from F_1 to F_2 so the animal always had to make the same response (right or left), depending upon the starting point. (Tolman, Ritchie, & Kalish, 1946)

There were two groups of rats in the study. One group, a response-learning group, had to learn to make a right turn, no matter which was the starting point. If they began at S_1, they had to go to F_1 to be fed; if they began at S_2, they had to go to F_2. The other group was a place-learning group which was always reinforced in the same place, say F_1, without respect to the starting point.

The latter, place-learning, group mastered the maze very much more rapidly than the response-learning group. Whereas the average rat in the response-learning group did not meet the criterion of 10 successive correct runs in 72 trials, the place-learning group met this criterion in only 2 trials. Obviously the place-learning conditions favored learning in a way the response-learning conditions did not. Again, the simplest form of S-R theorizing failed to predict the outcome.

More sophisticated versions of S-R theorizing, however, suffer no embarrassment from the place-learning experiments. It is easy to see that if the rat were to learn a generalized approach to the stimuli marking the location of food it could probably master the place-learning problem quite easily. Support for such an account came from data which show that when there are no distinctive features in the environment to identify the location of food, animals resort to response learning.

Reward Versus Incentive

The second Thorndikean point upon which Tolman and Hull disagreed had to do with the role played by reward in learning. As we have seen, Hull made reinforcement the essential condition of *learning*. Tolman, on the other hand, believed that cognitions could develop without reward just on the basis of experience with successions of stimuli in the environment. For him, reward was a *performance* variable. It functions as an *incentive* and simply provides the learner with a good reason for producing responses that it has learned. The **latent-learning** experiment was designed to provide evidence for such an interpretation.

The reference latent-learning experiment is that of Tolman and Honzik (1930) in which rats ran a maze for 10 days with (control group) or without (one experimental and one control group) reward. On the eleventh day reward was introduced for the experimental group previously run without reward. The results of this experiment showed that the introduction of reward on the eleventh day led to an immediate decrease in the number of errors in the group treated this way. This last observation is the most direct kind of evidence for the existence of latent learning. It was as if the rats in this group had *learned* considerably more about the maze than their previous *performance* indicated, and all that was required to make them show it was an adequate reason (incentive). The crux of such an interpretation is in the assumption that reinforcement has its effects on performance rather than on learning.

S-S versus S-R Associations

One line of experimentation in favor of Tolman's stimulus-stimulus position was the phenomenon of **sensory preconditioning.** These studies proceeded in three stages: (1) two neutral stimuli were presented together for many trials; (2) one of the stimuli then became the conditioned stimulus paired with an unconditioned stimulus; (3) finally, there was a test with the second stimulus. If this stimulus now elicited a response, the interpretation was that the paired presentations in stage 1 had produced a stimulus-stimulus association between the two neutral stimuli. Obviously there would not be much point in describing such experiments if they had not come out positively.

The case for pure stimulus-stimulus associations was not so strong as this may suggest, however. The diagram in Figure 2.9 gives a stimulus-response interpretation of the process by showing what might theoretically happen at each stage of the experiment where the neutral stimuli are a tone and a light, and the unconditioned stimulus is a shock which produces flexion as the unconditioned response.

The important point to note is that CS_2 actually does produce a response that is conditioned to the tone in stage 1 of the experiment. The lower case r is a common notation in the literature on the psychology of learning to represent a covert response, in this case perhaps a partial blink or pupillary constriction. Note that this fractional response has a consequence in the form of proprioceptive stimulation (s), perhaps kinesthetic feedback.

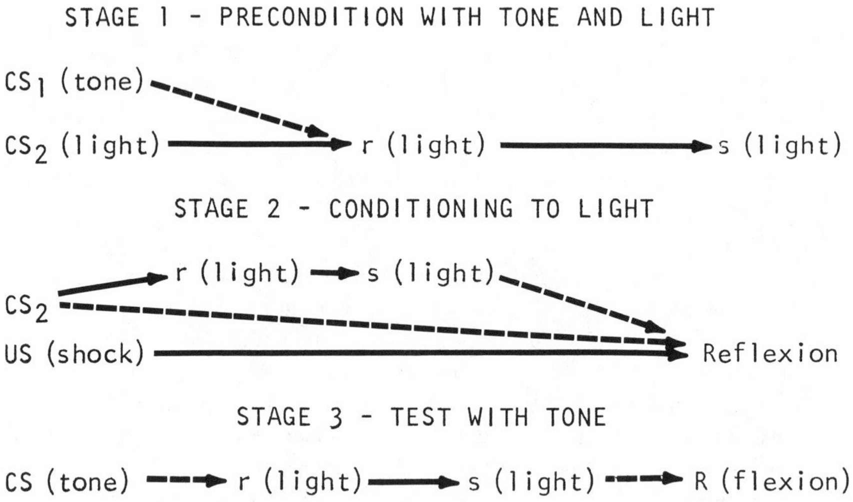

STAGE 1 - PRECONDITION WITH TONE AND LIGHT

CS₁ (tone)

CS₂ (light) ────────► r (light) ────────────► s (light)

STAGE 2 - CONDITIONING TO LIGHT

r (light) ──► s (light)

CS₂

US (shock) ──────────────────────────────► Reflexion

STAGE 3 - TEST WITH TONE

CS (tone) ──► r (light) ──► s (light) ──► R (flexion)

FIG. 2.9. An S-R explanation of the phenomenon of sensory preconditioning.

In stage 2, according to this theory, both CS₂ and s serve as stimuli to which flexion gets conditioned. This means that in stage 3 the tone elicits r→s, and s elicits the conditioned response. This mechanism, incidentally, is perhaps the best example available of a process of **mediation** which S-R psychologists frequently used to explain mentalistic phenomena.

Continuity versus Noncontinuity

A final point of disagreement between Tolman and certain other theorists was that Tolman at least sometimes believed that learning occurred suddenly (insightfully), whereas Hull in particular had argued that learning is a gradual process. In this difference of opinion, Hull took the continuity position; Tolman took the noncontinuity position. One set of experiments designed to evaluate these two positions was the **discrimination reversal** experiments.

In these studies rats were run in a simple, single-choice apparatus, perhaps a T-maze where they had to learn to go to a black alley rather than a white one. Trial by trial the black and white alleys were shifted randomly from the right side of the apparatus to the left. For the rat, the mastery of such a discrimination is not easy. It performs at a chance level for a long *presolution period* before it begins to respond to the positive stimulus. The continuity and noncontinuity theories had different accounts of what went on during the presolution period. The noncontinuity position was that the animal entertained a series of *hypotheses* during this period, for example, "go left," "go right," "first go left then go right," "choose white," "choose black." All of these except for the last two would lead to reinforcement 50% of the time, whenever black and the choice based on the hypothesis happened to coincide. An important element of the noncontinuity position was that testing a wrong hypothesis had no effect upon the strength of a tendency to choose the black side of the maze. The continuity theorists made the opposite assumption, namely, that chance reinforcements following a response to the correct stimulus add an increment to the strength of the tendency to respond to this stimulus again. The concept of hypothesis did not appear in these accounts.

The test of these alternatives involved the discrimination reversal experiment. If positive and negative stimuli were switched during the presolution period, this manipulation, according to the noncontinuity theorists, should have no effect. According to the continuity theorists, the reversal should slow up mastery of the discrimination, because it would be necessary for the animal to unlearn the developing habit to go to the now incorrect stimulus. Many experiments of the type just described were carried out between 1930 and 1950. The preponderance of results favored continuity theory. That is, reversing the contingency of reinforcement slowed up mastery of the discrimination (Krechevsky, 1932; Spence, 1940, 1945).

GUTHRIE

Edwin R. Guthrie (1886–1959) was an S-R theorist who reduced the learning process to the simplest possible formula. As Guthrie saw it, what happens in any learning situation is this: The organism makes a variety of responses. If one of these responses produces a significant change in the situation or removes the animal from it, that response is the one that will occur upon a later occurrence of the same situation. Rewards and punishments have nothing to do with the process except that they are ways of producing dramatic changes in the situation (Guthrie, 1935).

Act Versus Actone

Guthrie was the only important learning theorist of the period under discussion to retain the Watsonian molecular form of behaviorism. Whereas other theorists concentrated on behavior **acts** defined in terms of such environmental consequences as reaching the end of a maze or pressing a bar, Guthrie emphasized the detailed movements, **actones,** which occurred as an organism performed the response being learned.

Guthrie did very few experiments. His most important one, done in collaboration with G. P. Horton, made the argument for this approach fairly convincingly. In this experiment, cats learned to escape from a puzzle box by tilting a pole in the center of the apparatus. The response also operated a camera which took a picture of the behavior as it occurred. The ''data'' of the experiment were

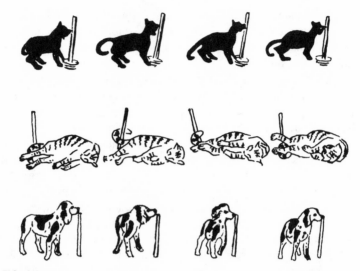

FIG. 2.10.   Tracings of the responses of two cats and one dog on successive escapes from the puzzle box. Note the great degree of similarity of the successive responses. From Guthrie and Horton (1946).

sequences of pictures of the animals making the escape response on successive trials in the experiment. Tracings of these pictures obtained on such a series appear in Figure 2.10. As you can see, the details of the cats' movements do, in fact, remain quite constant trial by trial.

Although this part of Guthrie's theory received support from this investigation, such results were not enough to lead to general acceptance of the position. This is because the act-versus-actone aspect was not one of the issues central to the theoretical dispute. We turn now to the issues that counted for more.

Contiguity Versus Reward.   Guthrie rejected Thorndike's law of effect and offered in its place a law of contiguity. All that is necessary for learning to take place is for a response to occur in the presence of a stimulus. Under those circumstances, the association is automatic.

This aspect of Guthrie's theory did not fare well when subjected to experimental tests. Several experimenters showed that animals failed to learn a response if they were removed from the apparatus immediately after making it or if the response changed the situation, for example, by turning the room lights on or off. Although these procedures produce important changes in the situation, learning was either slow or nonexistent, or else it was easy to detect the existence of a reward.

Continuity Versus Noncontinuity.   The second major assumption in Guthrie's theory was that the S-R association was complete after just one pairing.

Guthrie, like Tolman, was a noncontinuity theorist. Guthrie approached the issue from a different angle, however. Faced with the fact that learning as it actually happens is usually gradual and not sudden, Guthrie proposed that this is because learning situations do not repeat themselves exactly trial by trial. The learner must attach the response to all of these variations of the situation before learning is complete. In this way, he argued, what seems to be gradual learning is really many one-trial learnings to make a response to what are actually somewhat different situations.

Later, Estes (1950) was to make such an interpretation central to a **statistical theory of learning.** In this theory, Estes treated the stimulus side of learning as a large, but finite, collection of stimulus elements, comprising a stimulus population. On any given trial, only a sample of the stimuli in the population is assumed to be present. Those which are present are conditioned to the response on that trial. After the first trial, the stimulus sample on later trials will consist of some stimuli which have been previously conditioned to the response and some which have not. With continued practice, the number of stimulus elements not condi-

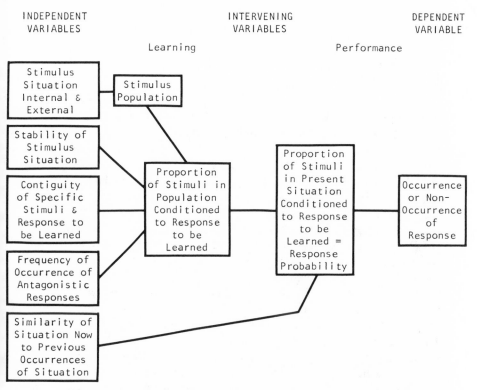

FIG. 2.11.   Guthrie's Theory as interpreted by Estes. The structure is of the same general kind as Hull's Theory (Fig. 2.6) and Tolman's (Fig. 2.7).

tioned to the response will diminish, and the number which have been conditioned will increase, until the entire population of stimuli has been conditioned to the response. Assuming that the proportion of previously conditioned stimuli present in the sample on any trial represents the probability that a conditioned response will occur on that trial leads to the prediction of a gradual increase in response probability with practice. The exact form of the function will depend upon the trial-to-trial variability in the stimulus situation. If the situation is perfectly controlled so that the sample of stimuli is exactly the same from trial to trial, one-trial learning should occur. In a general way, this prediction is that learning will be more rapid in a very constant situation than it will be in a highly variable one. There is considerable reason to accept this idea as a valid one. We know from Pavlov's work, for example, that extraneous stimuli disturb the course of acquisition through external inhibition. In order to guard against the effects of uncontrolled disturbances of this sort, Pavlov eventually had to build a laboratory carefully shielded from outside stimulation.

Figure 2.11, is a diagram of Guthrie's theory, as developed by Estes. Comparison reveals that it has much in common with the theories of Hull and Tolman presented earlier.

SKINNER

A final important psychologist who presented the first detailed statement of his position in this period was B. F. Skinner. In his book, *Behavior of Organisms,* Skinner (1938) described the results of a series of experimental studies of the bar-pressing behavior of rats, begun in 1930. Skinner offered an approach to the study of learning and to learning theory that differed sharply from that of the other theorists: (1) He rejected the hypothetico-deductive method, proposing instead to determine the quantitative properties of behavior and, through induction, to establish the laws of behavior. (2) He came out against physiological hypotheses, claiming that the gains from such approaches were far outweighed by "all the misdirected experimentation and bootless theorizing that have arisen from the same source." (3) He studied behavior in a free responding situation, whereas all of his opponents were attempting to understand how learning proceeded trial by trial. (4) He concentrated on the behavior of individual organisms, whereas other psychologists studied groups of individuals, the larger the group the better. (5) He presented his data unorthodoxly, in the form of cumulative records produced on a kymograph as the rats pressed the lever in the Skinner box. Kenneth Spence, who could be very caustic in his comments, probably caught the mood of most learning theorists when, in his courses, he sometimes asked, "How can we be expected to take him seriously when he doesn't even know how to draw a learning curve?"

The irony of it all is that by 1975 or so Skinner had come to be recognized as the most important psychologist of his era because of his consistent adherence to a concept with which his earlier contemporaries agreed. This was the concept that behavior is *determined,* a position that was expressed most forcefully in Skinner's controversial publication, *Beyond Freedom and Dignity.* There he took the position that everything we do and everything we are is controlled by our history of rewards and punishments. Even what we say we do "on purpose" or "through an act of personal will" is actually an expression of what we have been rewarded or punished for doing or not doing in the past.

Skinner "Theory"

Skinner sometimes (e.g., 1950) argued that theories of learning are unnecessary and claimed not to have one. In fact he used very few intervening variables—drive and emotion were the main ones—and he limited his treatment to an analysis of two measures of behavior, the number of responses emitted in extinction and the rate of responding under a variety of circumstances.

As a shorthand for the first of the aspects of behavior, Skinner spoke of a **reflex reserve,** the store of unreinforced responses that the organism had available to emit in extinction. The size of the reflex reserve depends upon the number of reinforcements the organism has received, the quality and quantity of such reinforcements and, most importantly, the schedule on which the reinforcements were delivered.

Schedules of Reinforcement. The pattern of trials or responses on which a learner receives or does not receive reinforcement is called a **schedule of reinforcement.** At the extremes are continuous reinforcement where reinforcement occurs after every response and extinction where it never does. In between, it is possible to identify numerous schedules of partial or intermittent reinforcement. One of Skinner's important contributions was a systematic investigation of many of them (Ferster & Skinner, 1957).

The most basic schedules of partial reinforcement are defined either in terms of numbers of responses or in terms of their timing. The first of these are **ratio schedules,** where reinforcement occurs after some number of responses. The second are interval schedules, where reinforcement occurs for the first response after a specified period of time.

The number of responses or the amount of time involved in a schedule may be either *variable* or *fixed.* Combining these bases for defining schedules yields four varieties: **variable interval, variable ratio, fixed interval,** and **fixed ratio.** In the variable schedules, reinforcement occurs after some average number of responses or minutes, but the exact number changes from reinforcement to reinforcement. In the fixed schedules, the number of responses or minutes is always the same.

Ratio schedules lead to rapid rates of responding in which as many as several hundred unreinforced responses may occur prior to the reinforced one. In fixed ratio schedules, there is often a long pause after the reinforced response before responding resumes. Variable ratios produce a steadier rate of responding.

Fixed interval schedules produce a pattern of responding often called a **fixed interval scallop.** Early in the interval responding is slow, but, as time passes, rate of responding picks up and is greatest at the moment when the reinforced response occurs. Variable interval schedules produce low but very stable rates of responding and are often used in studies to determine the effects of other variables, such as the administration of a drug.

Other schedules of reinforcement put rate requirements on performance. For example, reinforcement may occur only if the organism performs at a slow rate or a fast one. Organisms learn to respond slowly or rapidly under such contingencies. Still other, more complex, schedules can be produced by combining the basic schedules in various ways. A discussion of such schedules can be found in Ferster and Skinner (1957).

By comparison with continuous reinforcement, extinction following partial reinforcement is very slow. This **partial-reinforcement effect (PRE)** has been the object of a considerable amount of theoretical conjecture. It now appears to be explainable in terms of a theory that relies on two assumptions: (1) Traces of nonreinforcement are a part of the stimulus complex that comes to control responding. Nonreinforcement in extinction creates these same stimuli, thus supporting the response. (2) The discrimination between acquisition and extinction is easier following continuous reinforcement that following partial reinforcement. The omission or reinforcement in extinction following continuous reinforcement creates a different situation, and the learned response loses strength through generalization decrement. To return to Skinner's theory, however, it will be sufficient to note that the effect of partial schedule is to enlarge the reflex reserve, the number of responses available in extinction.

Drive and Punishment.   An important form of support for the concept of reflex reserve came from the results of studies of levels of motivation during acquisition and mild punishment early in extinction. These results can be summarized very quickly: neither variable had an effect upon the total number of responses obtained in extinction; that is, the size of the reflex reserve remained the same. However, there frequently was an impressive effect upon the *rate* at which this fixed total of responses was emitted. To take the most famous case, an apparatus that delivered a slight slap to the paw of the rat whenever it pressed the bar, during the first 10 minutes of extinction, slowed up responding considerably. The number of responses produced by the rat before extinction was completed was the same as for an unpunished animal, however. Punishment had affected rate of responding but not the size of the reflex reserve (Estes, 1944).

Subsidiary Reserve.   Other observations, of which the phenomenon of spontaneous recovery is a good example, forced Skinner to develop a concept that was a bit more theoretical than anything mentioned so far in this account. In the bar pressing situation, spontaneous recovery appears as a small flurry of rapid responses that occurs when extinction begins again after a rest. After that, performance settles down to something more like the pre-rest rate until all of the responses in the reserve have been exhausted. The brief period of rapid responses suggested to Skinner that there might be a "secondary," "momentary" or **subsidiary reserve** where responses are stored for a while just prior to their

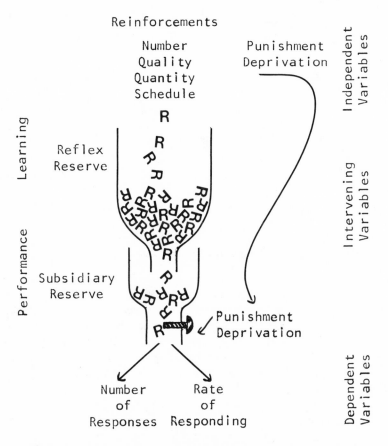

FIG. 2.12.   Skinner's "Theory." Although I (GAK) never saw him do it, I have heard that Skinner at one time drew sketches like this to represent his theory, but without the control indicated by the handle labeled "punishment/deprivation." I included it because the theory requires it. As Clarence Graham remarked after seeing one of Skinner's drawings (it is said) "Fred, what your system needs is a sphincter."

emission. These responses can be emitted faster than they can be replaced by additional responses from the basic reserve. The various aspects of Skinner's concept can be summarized in a diagram of the type that appears (with apologies to Skinner) in Figure 2.12. It is important to mention that, except for the hypothetical plumbing, this representation leaves Skinner's theory with a certain resemblance to those of Hull, Tolman, and Guthrie.

DECLINE AND FALL

The period just discussed has sometimes been called the Age of Grand Theory in the psychology of learning, for two reasons mentioned earlier. First, although the classical theories were formulated and tested in terms of simple learning, behind the scenes there was always the presumption that these theories could be applied to all behavior. That is, they were grand in scope. The theories were also grand in their estimation of where the psychology of learning stood in its history, the presumption in this case being that most of the basic laws of learning had already been discovered and all that remained was the minor problem of resolving the few systematic issues that separated the major theorists. Disillusionment came more quickly than the classical theorists could possibly have anticipated. By the middle of the century it had become clear that the classical theories of learning were limited in scope and that the state of our scientific knowledge was pre-Gallilean rather than post-Newtonian, as Hull and others had thought. This reevaluation laid the ground for major changes in the field.

The "Cognitization" of Learning Theory

The most fundamental mistake of the Grand Theories had been to underestimate the extent to which the characteristics of the organism affect the progress of learning. Both individual and species differences were involved, and the tradition out of which the classical theories came had not prepared them to cope with such factors. This was a tradition that embraced the concept of "standard man." Although this tradition acknowledged the existence of individual differences, it gave more importance to what it hoped would be the universal laws of behavior.

Equipotentiality Versus Preparedness. An extreme example of this position assumed the complete generality of the conditioning process. For example, Kimble (1956), commenting on research related to this point, held that "a great deal of such research may be summarized by saying that it indicated that just about any activity of which the organism is capable can be conditioned, and these responses can be conditioned to any stimulus that the organism can perceive" (p. 195).

Kimble should have known better. As early as 1930, C. W. Valentine had reported being unable to repeat Watson's demonstration of fear conditioning in children, using a pair of opera glasses instead of a white rat as the conditioned stimulus. It was well-known laboratory lore that training a rat to press a bar or a pigeon to peck a key to turn off shock was next to impossible. More formal evidence along these lines was soon to accumulate to prove that the assumption of *equipotentiality* is wrong: animals are *prepared* to form certain associations and counterprepared to form others (Seligman & Hager, 1972).

For example, rats are prepared to form associations between novel tastes and a subsequent experience of sickness. In one experiment, rats were made sick by x-radiation after they had sampled saccharin-flavored water from a drinking bottle. In subsequent tests they avoided the sweet solution. Comparable procedures designed to establish an association between a visual-auditory stimulus and nausea were unsuccessful. On the other hand, the visual-auditory stimulus was easy to condition to an avoidance response based on shock. This is to say that the rat is prepared to form an association between sickness and taste or between pain and visual-auditory stimuli. It is *counterprepared* to form associations between sickness and visual-auditory stimulation or pain and taste (Garcia & Koelling, 1966).

The phenomenon of **autoshaping** provides a particularly impressive demonstration of the importance of preparedness. If a hungry pigeon is shown a lighted key for a few seconds before grain is delivered by a food magazine, the pigeon comes to peck the key without any special training. Pigeons are so thoroughly prepared to peck for food that they teach (shape) this response to themselves (auto) (Brown & Jenkins, 1968).

The significance of the rejection of the assumption of equipotentiality is far-reaching. On the one hand it means that the universal laws of learning put forth by the grand theorists are not universal. They are pretty flimsy material out of which to construct a general theory. At the same time, the concept of preparedness opens anew the possibility that there may be capabilities for which the human organism is uniquely prepared to develop. Language is the clearest example. Although investigators have had impressive success in teaching chimpanzees to perform language-like behavior, even more impressive is the difficulty of such training. The human 2-year-old picks up language effortlessly and without any special program of training. For the chimpanzee it takes intensive tutelage. It is as if the human being is prepared to develop linguistic skill in a way that the chimpanzee is not.

Relativity of Reinforcement.   One very important point where the Grand Theories gave too little credit to the organism was in their description of the operations of reinforcers. A common position was that reinforcement was an automatic process that took place outside the realm of consciousness. Support for such a position came from early studies of *verbal conditioning* which seemed to show that people could be led, without awareness, to increase the frequency with which they used plural nouns or personal pronouns, if the experimenter rewarded such responses with a mild expression of approval—saying "mmhmm" in an unemotional tone of voice. Later results (e.g., Spielberger, Levin, & Shepard, 1962) showed that this interpretation was in error on two counts: (1) Subjects did not increase their use of the reinforced responses unless they were aware of the relationship between their behavior and that of the experimenter. (2) Moreover, even if they were aware of the relationship, the effectiveness of the reward depended on whether or not the subject saw reinforcement as important. In this last point particularly, the significance of the learner's contribution comes through clearly.

Related work was contributing to an emphasis on this point in other ways. Premack (e.g., 1965), for example, showed that a given state of affairs may or may not be reinforcing, depending upon which aspect of an organism's behavior is being reinforced. Others were able to show that the reinforcing value of a given reinforcer depended upon the context in which it appeared. A standard reward is less rewarding following a series of larger rewards than following a series of smaller ones. All of this evidence was gradually forcing the psychology of learning to the conclusion that learners make comparisons, judge the significance of events, and in general contribute a cognitive component to the process of reinforcement.

A FORCE FOR CHANGE

As the psychology of learning gradually assimilated these lessons it took on an appearance that sounds more like Tolman's S-S expectancy position than Hull's S-R habit position. The transition just discussed has sometimes been presented as if this is a good way to describe it. There is a sense in which this is true, but it would be wrong to say that the psychology of learning has given up Hull and accepted Tolman. If nothing else, this would be because the theories of Tolman and Hull were so similar in structure. What has happened is more basic. It relates to the issue of objectivism which has come up before in this history.

Looking back, it now appears that strict operationism represented a necessary stage in the development of our field. Prior to the acceptance of this position, psychology had been far too subjective to become an experimental science. Watson had led a movement away from such subjectivism, but he went too far. Too many topics of interest were banished from the field.

Even in Watson's day there were those, most notably Tolman, who attempted to bring mentalistic-sounding concepts back into psychology by means of what amounted to operational definitions. In a general way, the operational point of view did nothing more than insist that unobservable terms be defined in ways that relate them to observables. From there it proceeded to a further insistence that concepts defined in this way must have a relationship to behavior. In this way these concepts became what are called **intervening variables** that stand between observable antecedent conditions on the one hand and behavior on the other. The diagram below serves to summarize this point:

Antecedent Conditions——Mentalistic Concepts——Behavior
Independent Variables——Intervening Variables——Dependent Variables

Obviously there is nothing in this formula to exclude mentalistic concepts. In fact, the whole point of it is to admit unobservables. But the damage had been done. In mid-century American psychology it would have cost a career to publish on mind, consciousness, volition, or even imagery. Established opinion seemed to maintain that such terms were somehow irretrievably subjective in a way that "habit," "drive," or even "expectation" were not. In addition to its feature of illogicality, this stance led to a period of pretty dreary science because most of the interesting topics seemed to be beyond the pale.

Eventually the psychology of human learning and memory, which had been wrestling with the same problems (see Chapter 3, volume 1), came to the rescue. It did so by making an unanswerable case for the importance of certain mentalistic concepts. In the face of facts, prejudicial opinion had to yield.

This work involving mentalistic concepts fits the intervening variable model quite comfortably, although it deals with such concepts as organization, context effects, and imagery. Take the concept of imagery, for example, as it applies to the behavior of subjects learning lists of materials with the aid of the mnemonic device called the **method of loci.** In this method subjects are instructed to form images of the items to be remembered, seeing them placed in specific locations in some familiar place. Then, to recall them, the subject takes an imaginary trip through the terrain where the items have been placed, identifying each item in turn. With a little practice using this method subjects can remember almost all of a list of 30–40 items (Ross & Lawrence, 1968).

For our purposes here the importance of all this is that the concept of "image" emerges as a perfectly respectable intervening variable. Filling in the diagram used previously the status of the concept is like this:

Independent Variable——Intervening Variable——Dependent Variable
Instructions to Imagine————Image————Ease of Learning

As this diagram shows, the concept intervenes between the instructions on the antecedent side and ease of learning on the behavioral side. Although it took nearly half a century, Tolman's point has finally received the attention it should have had in the beginning.

CONCLUSION

Although the concept of association was familiar to Aristotle, the experimental study of conditioning and simple learning did not begin until the late 1900s. Initial progress was very rapid, however. By the turn of the century Pavlov had discovered many of the phenomena of classical conditioning and Thorndike had done his early studies of instrumental learning. Thorndike had also put forward an S-R, continuity, reinforcement account of the learning process that was to set the stage for controversy for the next half century.

The explanations of learning advanced by Pavlov and Thorndike both fit the general methodological scheme that had evolved from British empiricistic philosophy and European physiology. Both were empirical, in that they used the experimental method and presented objective, even quantitative data. Both were elementistic in that they analyzed their subject matter into simple units—reflexes to be conditioned, stimuli and responses to be connected. They were associationistic in that each built a psychology of learning in which connections among elements was a basic process. They were both physiologically oriented and, therefore, materialistic in outlook.

In spite of this nearly perfect match to the methodological spirit of the times, the psychology of learning remained at the periphery of scientific psychology for the first quarter of the century, for a number of reasons. For one thing, in America where the psychology of learning found a comfortable home, experimental psychology was dominated by the tradition of Titchener. The most important research was in the area of the sensory processes and perception. J. B. Watson, who might have led the psychology of learning to a position of prominence, left the field after his divorce. Moreover even Watson's behavioristic psychology lacked one feature that had to be incorporated before the psychology of learning would come fully into its own. The history of the field as this century entered the '30s identified this feature.

A landmark publication in this history was Hull's 1929 paper, "A Functional Interpretation of the Conditioned Reflex." This article made Hull the most important psychologist of learning in the world. The key to Hull's instant eminence was the word "functional" in the title of his paper. Even before Watson, a new school of psychology had been gaining adherents. This school, called Functionalism, took a theme from Darwin and concerned itself with the purposes or the functions of mental processes. Functionalism appealed to the practical American mind. It was Hull's combination of this view with the objective approach of Pavlov that caught the fancy of so many psychologists in the field of learning.

To say that Hull was the leading figure in the psychology of learning is not to say that he had no competitors. He had many, as well as one most powerful supporter, in the person of Kenneth W. Spence. The three most important individuals in the opposition were Tolman, Guthrie, and Skinner. Each of these men—even Skinner—developed theories that seemed quite different from Hull's theory at that time. All of them used different concepts and advocated different laws of learning and Skinner had more basic differences at the level of methodology. In retrospect, all of these positions look very similar in structure. All of them took the intervening variable approach; all of them made a learning-performance distinction; all of them dealt with similar variables and phenomena.

The intervening variable approach to psychology was the result of the most important methodological development of the twentieth century—the nearly universal acceptance of logical positivism, especially operationism, as the appropriate philosophy of science for psychology. The impact of the operational movement was enormous. It affected the types of research being done, standards of editorial review, what appeared in the textbooks and what was taught in the classroom. So powerful was this influence that by 1940 psychology had invented an eighth deadly sin. In addition to greed, lust, the misuse of chi-square, and the rest there now was added the failure to define one's variables operationally.

The domination of psychology by operationism from about 1940 to about 1960 was both good news and bad news for the field. The good news was that it fostered an objectivism that was badly needed in the psychology of learning; the bad news was that operationism, applied in the tradition of Watson, led to an exclusion from the field of too much that was interesting and important. By 1980 or so, one of psychology's major accomplishments had been a liberalization of operationism so that such topics as consciousness, imagery, and even volition had become acceptable subjects for study. With this relaxation of the operational regulations, and the roughly simultaneous demise of the grand theories, the psychology of learning is now entering the second century of its official existence. It does so in high spirit and the expectation of great accomplishment in the next phase of its history.

REFERENCES

Angell, J. R. The province of functional psychology. *Psychological Review*, 1907, *14*, 61–91.
Asratyan, E. A. *I. P. Pavlov, his life and work*. Moscow: Foreign Languages Publishing House, 1949.
Bekhterev, V. M. *La psychologie objective*. Paris: Alcon, 1913.
Bogoiavlensky, D. N. The psychology of understanding. In B. Simon (Ed.), *Psychology in the Soviet Union*. Stanford, CA: Stanford University Press, 1957.
Bridgman, P. W. *The logic of modern physics*. New York: Macmillan, 1927.
Brown, P. L. & Jenkins, H. M. Auto-shaping of the pigeons key-peck. *Journal of the Experiment Analysis of Behavior*, 1968, *11*, 1–8.
Bykov, K. *The cerebral cortex and the interval organs*. Moscow: Foreign Languages Publishing House, 1959.
Cowles, J. T. Food-tokens as incentives for learning by Chimpanzees. *Comparative Psychology Monographs*, 1937, *14*, No. 71.
Egger, M. D., & Miller, N. E. Secondary reinforcement in rats as a function of information value and reliability of the stimulus. *Journal of Experimental Psychology*, 1962, *64*, 97–104.
Estes, W. K. An experimental study of punishment. *Psychological Monographs*, 1944, *47*, No. 263.
Estes, W. K. Toward a statistical theory of learning. *Psychological Review*, 1950, *57*, 94–107.
Feigl, H. Operationism and scientific method. *Psychological Review*, 1945, *52*, 250–259.
Ferster, C. B. & Skinner, B. F. *Schedules of reinforcement*. New York: Appleton-Century-Crofts, 1957.
Garcia, J., & Koelling, R. Relation of cue to consequence in avoidance learning. *Psychonomic Science*, 1966, *4*, 123–124.
Guthrie, E. R. *The psychology of learning*. New York: Harper, 1935.

Guthrie, E. R., & Horton, G. P. *Cats in a puzzle box.* New York: Rinehart, 1946.

Hilgard, E. R., & Marquis, D. G. *Conditioning and learning.* New York: Appleton-Century-Crofts, 1940.

Hull, C. L. A functional interpretation of the conditioned reflex. *Psychological Review,* 1929, *36,* 498–511.

Hull, C. L. The goal gradient hypothesis and maze learning. *Psychological Review,* 1932, *39,* 25–43.

Hull, C. L. The concept of habit—family hierachy and maze learning. *Psychological Review,* 1934, *41.* Part I, 33–52; Part II, 134–152.

Hull, C. L. *Principles of behavior.* New York: Appleton-Century-Crofts, 1943.

Hull, C. L. *A behavior system.* New Haven: Yale University Press, 1952.

James, W. On some omissions of introspective psychology. *Mind,* 1884, *9,* 1–26.

Kimble, G. A. *Principles of General Psychology.* New York: Ronald, 1956.

Kimble, G. A. *Hilgard and Marquis conditioning and learning.* New York: Appleton-Century-Crofts, 1961.

Kimmel, H. D. Instrumental conditioning. In *Electrodermal activity in psychological research.* New York: Academic Press, 1973.

Köhler, W. *The mentality of apes.* New York: Harcourt-Brace, 1925.

Konorski, J., & Miller, S. On two types of conditioned reflex. *Journal of General Psychology,* 1937, *16,* 264–272.

Krechevsky, I. "Hypotheses" versus "chance" in the pre-solution period in sensory discrimination-learning. *University of California Publications in Psychology,* 1932, *6,* 27–44.

Moore, B. R., & Stuttard, S. Dr. Guthrie and *Felis Domesticus* Or: Tripping over the cat. *Science,* 1979, *205,* 1031–1033.

Pavlov, I. P. The scientific investigation of the psychical faculties or processes in the higher animals. *Science,* 1906, *24,* 613–619.

Pavlov, I.P. *Conditioned reflexes* (Trans. G. V. Anrep). London: Oxford University Press, 1927.

Premack, D. Reinforcement theory. In M. R. Jones (Ed.), *Nebraska Symposium on Motivation: 1965.* Lincoln: University of Nebraska Press, 1965.

Razran, G. The observable unconscious and the inferrable conscious in current Soviet psychophysiology: interoceptive conditioning, semantic conditioning and the orienting reflex. *Psychological Review,* 1961, *68,* 81–147.

Ross, J., & Lawrence, K. A. Some observations on memory artifice. *Psychonomic Science,* 1968, *13,* 107–108.

Sechenov, I. M. *Selected works.* Moscow: State Publishing House, 1935.

Seligman, M. E. P., & Hager, J. L. (Eds.) *Biological boundaries of learning.* New York: Appleton-Century-Crofts, 1972.

Skinner, B. F. *The behavior of organisms.* New York: Appleton-Century-Crofts, 1938.

Skinner, B. F. Are theories of learning necessary? *Psychological Review,* 1950, *57,* 193–216.

Skinner, B. F. *Beyond freedom and dignity.* New York: Alfred A. Knopf, 1971.

Small, W. S. An experimental study of the mental processes of the rat. *American Journal of Psychology,* 1899–1900, *11,* 133–164.

Spence, K. W. The order of eliminating blinds in maze learning by the rat. *Journal of Comparative Psychology,* 1932, *14,* 9–27.

Spence, K. W. Continuous versus non-continuous interpretations of discrimination learning. *Psychological Review,* 1940, *47,* 271–288.

Spence, K. W. An experimental test of the continuity and non-continuity theories of discrimination learning. *Journal of Experimental Psychology,* 1945, *35,* 253–266.

Spielberger, C. D., Levin, S. M., & Shepard, M. C. The effects of awareness and attitude toward reinforcement on the operant conditioning of verbal behavior. *Journal of Personality,* 1962, *30,* 106–121.

Thorndike, E. L. *Animal intelligence*. New York: Macmillan, 1911.

Thorndike, E. L. *The fundamentals of learning*. New York: Teacher's College, 1932.

Tolman, E. C. A new formula for behaviorism. *Psychological Review*, 1922, *29*, 44–53.

Tolman, E. C. the determiners of behavior at a choice point. *Psychological Review*, 1938, *45*, 1–41.

Tolman, E. C., & Honzik, C. H. Introduction and removal of reward, and maze learning in rats. *University of California Publications in Psychology*, 1930, *4*, 257–275.

Tolman, E. C., Ritchie, B. F., & Kalish, D. Studies in spatial learning. V. Response learning vs. place learning by the non-correction method. *Journal of Experimental Psychology*, 1947, *37*, 385–392.

Valentine, C. W. The innate bases of fear. *Journal of Genetic Psychology*, 1930, *37*, 394–419.

Watson, J. B. *Animal education*. Chicago: University of Chicago Press, 1903.

Watson, J. B. Psychology as the behaviorist views it. *Psychological Review*, 1913, *20*, 158–177.

Watson, J. B. *Behaviorism*. New York: Norton, 1925.

Watson, J. B., & Rayner, R. Conditioned emotional reactions. *Journal of Experimental Psychology*, 1920, *3*, 1–14.

Wolfe, J. B. Effectiveness of token rewards for chimpanzees. *Comparative Psychology Monographs*, 1936, *12*, No. 60.

Yerkes, R. M., & Oodson, J. D. The relation of the strength of a stimulus to rapidity of habit-formation. *Journal of Comparative Neurology and Psychology*, 1908, *18*, 459–482.

Yerkes, R. M., & Morqulis, S. The method of Pavlov in animal psychology. *Psychological Bulletin*, 1909, *6*, 257–273.

3 Human Learning and Memory

Leo Postman[1]
University of California, Berkeley

The experimental study of human learning and memory began a few years earlier than the studies of conditioning and learning described in the previous chapter. They were initiated not long after Wilhelm Wundt's founding of the first psychological laboratory in 1879 and represented a line of experimental investigation that Wundt believed to be impossible. This radical position followed logically from Wundt's definition of the data and methods of psychology. The data were the givens of immediate experience, and the method was introspection. Experimental psychology must study the conditions that influence the state of consciousness. Accordingly, the work of the new laboratory concentrated on sensation, perception, reaction time, and attention. As for the higher mental processes, Wundt held that they were to be examined by the historical method, an undertaking that he saw as the task of a separate discipline of folk psychology. If Wundt had prevailed, the experimental study of memory would not have become part of the new psychology. He did not prevail, however, because one independent investigator refused to be bound by prejudgments on the scope of psychological experimentation. This investigator was Hermann Ebbinghaus.

EBBINGHAUS

In tracing Ebbinghaus' intellectual history, Boring (1950, p. 387) tells us that during a sojourn in France the young German philosopher happened upon a copy of Fechner's *Elements of Psychophysics* in a second-hand bookstore in Paris. It

---

[1] I am grateful to Dorothy Postman for her assistance in the preparation of this chapter.

appears that he was impressed with the power of the psychophysical methods and with the success that had already been achieved in their application to the measurement of sensation. No comparable progress, however, had been made in the experimental analysis of the higher mental processes. Thus, he set out to do for memory what the psychophysicists had done for sensation. He reported the results of his efforts in his classical treatise, *Ueber das Gedächtnis* (*On Memory*), which was published in 1885.

Experimental Method

The task which Ebbinghaus (1885/1913) set for himself was to establish quantitative laws of memory which would describe variations in retention as a function of experimentally controlled conditions. This task presented enormous difficulties when it was seen in terms of the dominant psychological ideas of the 1880s. Degree of retention could not be assessed by introspection. Furthermore, material in memory that is inaccessible to consciousness at one time may become accessible at some later time. To solve these problems, Ebbinghaus decided to measure the strength of memories indirectly. The procedure was to learn a set of materials to a criterion of complete mastery and then to relearn it to the same criterion after an interval of time. The reduction in the number of repetitions, or the amount of time, required for relearning as compared to original learning could then be used as an index of the degree of retention. That is, retention was scaled in terms of the amount of work saved in relearning. This procedure came to be known as the **method of savings.**

The experimental procedure Ebbinghaus chose for his investigation was serial memorization of lists of **nonsense syllables.** The serial task was an obvious choice for studying the acquisition and retention of successive associations. Accepting the prevailing philosophical assumptions about the nature of mental processes, Ebbinghaus viewed association by contiguity as a basic principle of memory.

But why nonsense syllables? Ebbinghaus believed that nonsense series offered three major advantages as materials for memorization. First, as compared to prose or poetry, he considered the nonsense material to be relatively simple and homogeneous, free of the many "disturbing" influences—associations and emotional reactions—that are called forth by meaningful text. Ebbinghaus was careful to note, however, that nonsense syllables had not turned out to be as simple and homogeneous as one might have hoped. "These series exhibit very important and almost incomprehensible variations as to the ease and difficulty with which they are learned. It even appears . . . as if the differences between sense and nonsense material were not nearly as great as one would be inclined *a priori* to imagine" (p. 23). Thus, Ebbinghaus anticipated the later finding that nonsense syllables vary widely in meaningfulness, and hence in difficulty, according to the degree to which they approximate familiar letter sequences in the language. They had, however, other advantages as well. In addition to their relative homogeneity, they provided a practically unlimited supply of lists composed of comparable elements. Finally, they made it possible to vary the amount of material to be memorized in a simple and straightforward fashion, without the disturbances of meaning that arise when one attempts to segment prose passages or poetry.

Ebbinghaus was his own subject. His standard procedure was to read each series aloud repeatedly at a rate of 2/5 sec. per syllable, paced by a metronome or by the ticking of his watch. The readings were continued until, given the first syllable, the series could be recited without hesitation and with the consciousness of being correct. Attempts at reciting the series by heart were made when considered appropriate. If a hesitation occurred during the recitation, the rest of the series was read through again. Speed of learning and relearning was measured in terms of the amount of time, or the number of repetitions, required to reach the point of an errorless recitation.

Results of the Experiments

In all of the experiments, the effects of reptition on the acquisition or retention of serial lists were investigated. Retention was always measured by the method of savings.

Speed of Learning as a Function of List Length.   Varying the number of syllables in the list, Ebbinghaus found that he usually could reproduce a series of seven (and occasionally eight) items after a single reading. Beyond this point, the number of repetitions required for complete mastery increased at a sharply accelerated rate as a function of list length. Thus, it took an average of 16.6 trials to memorize a list of 12 syllables, and 30 trials for a list of 16 syllables. The function continued to rise, though somewhat less sharply as the list was made still longer.

To emphasize the steepness of the function relating learning time to the number of syllables in the list, Ebbinghaus presented for purposes of comparison the results he obtained when memorizing (in English) stanzas from Byron's poem "Don Juan." Each stanza contained 80 syllables, but the mean number of repetitions to criterion was only eight. Extrapolating the function for nonsense syllables, he estimated that it would have taken him from 70 to 80 repetitions to master a series of comparable length. He viewed this as a demonstration of the "extraordinary advantage which the combined ties of meaning, rhythm, and a common language give to material to be memorised" (p. 51).

Ebbinghaus did not comment further on the results of these experiments, but from the vantage point of history we can say that in this first study he discovered three basic phenomena of memory. First, there is the **length-difficulty relationship** that he set out to measure, a relationship that has remained a matter of

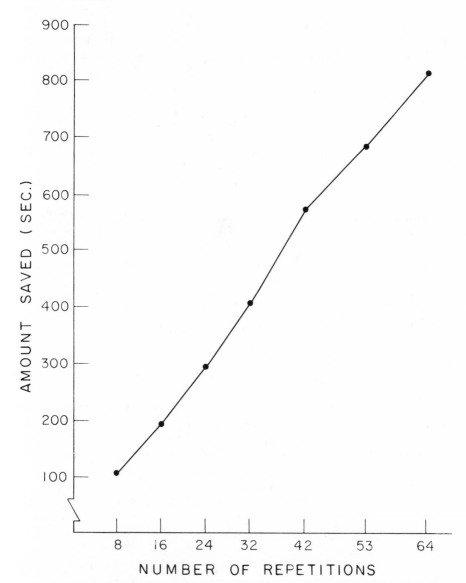

FIG. 3.1.   The effect of frequency on retention. The figure shows amount of time saved in relearning lists of nonsense syllables after 24 hours as a function of the number of repetitions in original learning. Data from Ebbinghaus (transl. 1913), p. 56.

theoretical interest ever since because it reflects the capacity limitations of the memory system. Second, his ability to reproduce up to seven items in serial order after a single presentation exemplifies the **immediate memory span,** an index that was to be defined explicitly a short time later. Third, he demonstrated the powerful effects of **meaningfulness** on speed of learning.

Retention as a Function of the Number of Repetitions.   In the next study, Ebbinghaus focused on the central theme of his inquiry—the nature of the relationship between the frequency of repetitions during acquisition and subsequent retention. Underlying Ebbinghaus' approach to this problem was the concept of associative strength, although he did not actually use this phrase. If associative strength varies continuously as a function of the frequency of repetitions, so should retention. Thus, there should be a measurable effect on retention even if original learning stopped short of the criterion of perfect recitation, and retention should increase with the amount of practice beyond the criterion.

The frequency with which lists of 16 syllables were repeated was varied over a wide range. The lists were relearned to a criterion of one perfect recitation 24 hours later. The amount saved as a function of the number of repetitions in original learning is plotted in Figure 3.1. The relationship is linear, i.e., the amount saved is proportional to the frequency of repetitions. The average saving per repetition represented about 30% of the work required in original learning. The linear relationship shown in Figure 3.1, however, held only within limits. In supplementary experiments Ebbinghaus found that increases in the frequency of repetitions eventually yielded diminishing returns.

These results firmly established **frequency** of repetition as a major determinant of retention. They also made it clear that measures of retention are sensitive to practice effects that cannot be detected during acquisition. Thus, overlearning retards the course of forgetting. It is safe to say that the orderly and powerful effects of repetition demonstrated by Ebbinghaus helped to lay the foundation for the subsequent ascendancy of strength theory.

The Forgetting Curve.   Ebbinghaus began his chapter on "retention and oblivescence as a function of time" with a brief review of some of the historical speculations about the causes of forgetting—that ideas gradually fade, or are repressed and sink below the threshold of consciousness, or gradually disintegrate. He found all such speculations wanting because they eluded precise definition and lacked empirical support. He preferred to forgo theorizing, at least for a while, and devote his efforts instead to determining the temporal course of forgetting, whatever the underlying processes might be.

To obtain the data necessary for plotting the curve of forgetting, Ebbinghaus learned lists of 13 syllables to a criterion of two perfect recitations and then relearned them to the same criterion after one of seven retention intervals—20 minutes, 1 hour, 9 hours, 1 day, 2 days, 6 days, or 31 days. In Figure 3.2 the

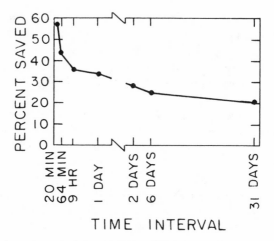

TIME INTERVAL

FIG. 3.2.   Ebbinghaus' forgetting curve. Percentage of time saved in relearning
lists of nonsense syllables is plotted as a function of the length of the retention
interval. Data from Ebbinghaus (transl. 1913), p. 76.

percentage of time saved in relearning, which is used as the index of the amount
retained, is plotted against the length of the retention interval. This is Ebbinghaus' classical **forgetting curve,** which continued to be reproduced in textbooks for many years to come. The curve drops precipitously at first (more than
40% is forgotten after 20 minutes), then more slowly, and finally levels off. The
losses are very heavy indeed, reaching 66% after 24 hours. The leveling off at
the longer intervals, however, suggests that forgetting would become complete
only after an indefinitely long time. Although Ebbinghaus fitted an equation to
the curve, he cautioned that it was only a shorthand statement of the results,
"which have been found but once," and might not hold for other individuals.

Ebbinghaus' doubts about the generality of the numerical values he obtained
were justified. In subsequent studies, the course of forgetting was found to vary
widely as a function of many variables, including the type of material and the
method of measurement, although negatively accelerated declining functions
proved fairly common. To anticipate the most important limitation of Ebbinghaus' results, it later became clear that the extraordinarily fast rate of forgetting shown by Ebbinghaus reflected massive **interference** from the many similar
lists he had learned.

Retention as a Function of Repeated Learning.   In this study, Ebbinghaus
presented further evidence for the effects of overlearning on retention. Lists of
nonsense syllables were learned to criterion and then relearned, again to criterion, on each of the next 5 days. The same procedure, extending over 4 days, was
used with six stanzas of Byron's "Don Juan." On each day, then, the point of
one correct reproduction was reached. Speed of relearning increased pro-

gressively from day to day. That is, the more often a list had been relearned, the less forgetting occurred during the immediately following 24-hour period. The earlier results regarding the effects of frequency of repetitions on retention were thus confirmed. The most important and far-reaching conclusion, however, was suggested by a comparison of the repetition effects observed in the two experiments.

In the earlier experiment, all repetitions on a given list were *massed,* i.e., occurred in immediate succession. In the later experiments, the repetitions associated with successive relearnings were *distributed,* separated by 24-hour intervals. It was possible, therefore, for Ebbinghaus to inquire into the relative effectiveness of **massed and distributed practice** in producing a given level of retention. Using speed of relearning after 24 hours as the measure of retention, he found distributed practice far superior. For 12-syllable series, 38 distributed repetitions were equivalent to 68 massed repetitions.

Ebbinghaus noted that distributed learning is a commonplace procedure in the classroom but did not pursue the theoretical implications of this finding. Yet there is a basic puzzle here. On the face of it, there is more opportunity for forgetting between successive practice periods when repetitions are distributed than when they are massed. Hence, there must be a positive factor associated with distribution or a negative factor with massing; or both may obtain.

Remote Associations. In his final study, Ebbinghaus focused on the nature of the associative connections that are formed among the members of a series as a result of repetition. The hypothesis he set out to test was that ''. . . the associative threads, which hold together a remembered series, are spun not merely between each member and its immediate successor, but beyond intervening members to every member which stands to it in any close temporal relation'' (p. 94). The strength of the associative connection may be expected to vary inversely with the distance between the members of the series. Being strongest, the successive associations are normally dominant; hence, remote associations are unlikely to emerge spontaneously and to be observed directly.

To demonstrate the existence of **remote associations** and to determine the function relating associative strength to degree of remoteness, Ebbinghaus devised the **derived-list paradigm.** Under this procedure, the acquisition of a derived list is substituted for the relearning of an unchanged list. In a derived series, the items remain the same but their order is systematically rearranged. Items that were separated by *n* intervening members in the original list are now placed in adjacent positions. For example, given an original list in which the successive items are numbered 1 through 16, by skipping one position the following derived series is generated:

1, 3, 5, 7, 9, 11, 13, 15, 2, 4, 6, 8, 10, 12, 14, 16

If remote associations are formed between nonadjacent items during original learning, the acquisition of the derived list should be facilitated because the remote associations have now become the prescribed successive ones.

In his experiments, Ebbinghaus worked with original lists of 16 syllables. To vary degree of remoteness, he skipped either 1, 2, 3, or 7 intervening items. To obtain a baseline for measuring the savings attributable to remote associations, he added a condition in which syllables from the original lists were arranged in random order, except for the first and last positions that were left unchanged. In learning the derived lists 24 hours after the original ones, Ebbinghaus found that the percentages of savings decreased in an orderly fashion as the degree of remoteness of the original associations increased. The control lists yielded no savings at all. Supplementary experiments with derived lists yielded evidence for the development of **backward** as well as **forward associations.** At a given degree of remoteness, the forward associations were clearly the stronger. Ebbinghaus concluded that associations are, indeed, formed between nonadjacent members of a series, and that the strength of such associations varies inversely with their degree of remoteness. He thought that these results had important implications for a general theory of association: The development of remote associations favors "a more rapid growth, a richer differentiation, and a many-sided ramification of the ideas which characterize the controlled mental life" (p. 109).

With the chapter on remote associations, Ebbinghaus ended his treatise. We have described his experiments in considerable detail because in the aggregate they did become the first "paradigm" of memory research. Not only had he demonstrated that memory could be measured, but he had also opened up important new avenues for the analysis of associative processes. Thus, he was well justified in choosing as the motto for his treatise, "From the most ancient subject we shall produce the newest science."

G. E. MÜLLER AND THE GÖTTINGEN LABORATORY

In spite of the strictures of Wundtian systematists, the Zeitgeist had been ready for Ebbinghaus. Within a few years after publication of his treatise, experimental studies of memory began to appear at a rapid rate. In these early developments, if there is any one individual that can be considered as Ebbinghaus' direct successor, it was Georg Elias Müller. Müller and his associates at Göttingen continued and extended Ebbinghaus' work, progressively expanding both the methodology and the range of experimental problems.[2] Müller was much more of a theorist than Ebbinghaus, and he did not hesitate to go well beyond his empirical data in formulating general principles of memory.

---

[2]For a previous review of Müller's work, see Murray (1976)

Methodological Innovations

In the interest of objectivity the roles of experimenter and subject were now separated. However, the number of subjects in any given experiment remained quite small, usually two or three, and sometimes only one. Typically, each subject was given extensive practice in the experimental task and tested repeatedly under several conditions. Thus, the use of highly experienced subjects remained the rule.

Standardization of Experimental Conditions. To standardize the conditions of learning, a mechanical exposure device was constructed for presenting a series of syllables at a constant rate. The device consisted of a drum that rotated behind a screen. The syllables were exposed one after the other through a window in the screen. This apparatus was the first **memory drum.** Improved in many ways over the years, the memory drum has remained a standard piece of laboratory equipment to the present.

Rules for the construction of lists of nonsense syllables were developed, with a view to reducing the large variations in difficulty that Ebbinghaus had noted. Some of the rules specified constraints on the duplication of letters (formal intralist similarity); other rules were designed to control meaningfulness in the formation of associative connections.

The method of recitation to be used on study trials was standardized as well. The subject read the series in a trochaic rhythm. A trochee is a metrical unit or foot consisting of two syllables, the first of which is accented and the second unaccented. Thus, the series was divided into a sequence of pairs of syllables; during recitation, the first member of each pair was stressed and the second member remained unstressed.

Paired-Associate Method. The segmentation of a serial list into trochees made it possible to measure recall of individual items by the **paired-associate method:** the accented syllable of a given foot was presented as a cue, and the unaccented syllable was the required response. The latencies of the subject's responses were measured routinely. The paired-associate procedure was first used by Calkins (1894, 1896), but it was in Müller's laboratory that it was thoroughly explored.

The introduction of the paired-associate method of measuring recall represented an important change in orientation toward the assessment of retention. Ebbinghaus had limited himself to measures of savings because he wanted to use a continuous scale of memory strength, a scale that would be sensitive to the retention of items that could not be reproduced after a given interval of time as well as those that could. When the method of paired associates is used, the question is whether the strength of association between two items, A and B, is great enough to permit the recall of B given A. Thus, it was recognized that the effects of past training can be evaluated in different ways, and that alternative indices may be expected to vary in sensitivity.

In the sections that follow, we review some of the major empirical and theoretical contributions of Müller and his students. Most of the experimental results come from the classical investigations of Müller and Schumann (1894), and Müller and Pilzecker (1900). When this work is considered, it is rather surprising to find how many later, and indeed current, developments originated or were at least partly anticipated at this early stage.

The Role of Grouping

Ebbinghaus had been interested in determining "the influence of the mere repetitions upon the natural memory" (p. 25); therefore, he attempted to make the process of memorization as passive as possible. Müller and his associates set out to investigate systematically the effects of active **grouping** on the pattern of associations formed during serial learning. The groupings they studies were the trochaic feet within a list. Their results consistently showed that within-foot associations were clearly stronger than associations linking the second member of one trochee with the first member of the next trochee. For example, in some of their experiments, the subject was presented with either the initial (accented) or terminal (unaccented) member of a trochaic foot as a cue on the test of retention. To both types of cues, the other member of the same foot was the most likely response, representing a forward association to the initial syllable, and a backward association to the terminal syllable. Temporally adjacent items from the preceding or following foot were given occasionally, but the probabilities of such backward and forward associations were quite low. The picture that emerges is quite different from that suggested by Ebbinghaus' results: rhythmic organization carried far greater weight than either temporal succession or the direction of the associative connection.

Association to Position

Once the powerful influence of rhythmic grouping on serial memorization had been demonstrated, Müller went on to ask whether the subject learns the locations of subgroups (feet) within a series. The method of derived lists was used to answer this question. In the test phase, intact feet from two original lists were alternated. Under one condition, the pairs from each list appeared in the same ordinal positions as during original learning. Under the second condition, the pairs were displaced, although their relative order was preserved. Only the first condition yielded a substantial amount of saving. The implication, of course, is that each subgroup had become associated with a specific location in the series.

Thus, successful recall was shown to require grouping and knowledge of the location of items. Yet it is a curious historical fact that this work had little direct influence on the development of research on serial learning. Rather, the point of reference remained Ebbinghaus' formulation of serial learning as entirely a matter of associative chaining, with a network of remote associations superimposed on the connections between successive items. It is only recently that Ebbinghaus' principle of associative chaining was seriously challenged (cf. Young, 1968). Interestingly enough, association to position and subjective grouping have recently emerged as important alternative hypotheses about the process of serial learning, hypotheses that were developed independently without harking back to Müller's work.

Distribution of Practice

Ebbinghaus had noted that savings were higher when the acquisition trials were distributed rather than massed but failed to explore the implications of this finding. The problem was soon taken up by Jost (1897) in Müller's laboratory. After convincing himself that fatigue or loss of efficiency under conditions of massed learning was not responsible for the effect, Jost hit on the idea that the functional properties of an association depended on its age. To explain the increase in savings produced by the spacing of repetitions, he formulated what came to be known as **Jost's first law:** "If two associations are of equal strength but of different age, a new repetition has a greater value for the older one." In this context, "strength" refers to availability as reflected in recall rather than to an attribute of the memory trace. Distribution of practice, then, is beneficial because the intervals between practice periods allow the associations to age and thus enhance the effectiveness of repetitions.

Jost proposed a **second law** relating the age of an association to retention, primarily in order to account for Ebbinghaus' finding that savings increase with repeated learning: "If two associations are of equal strength but of different age, the older declines less with time." The fact that retention losses over time are rapid at first and then become more and more gradual is in accord with this principle. An item that is recallable immediately after the end of learning has a much higher probability of being forgotten after a given delay than does a recallable item that was learned some time ago. The principle also received presumptive support from the finding that the latency of reproducible associations increases directly as a function of age.

Jost's laws became widely known and for many years continued to be considered as general principles of retention. In retrospect, the importance of Jost's work lies in the fact that it brought the problem of distribution of practice into sharp focus. His laws were essentially reformulations of empirical findings and had little explanatory value. As McGeoch (1942) noted later, the age of an association "is a temporal abstraction . . . and cannot itself be a determining condition. Not age itself, but what age brings or means is the determiner . . ." (p. 142).

Associative and Reproductive Inhibition

In the course of the experiments on rhythmic grouping, it was discovered that learning was more difficult when members of an earlier list were paired with new items than if all items were new. This finding led to the formulation of a principle of **associative inhibition:** the existence of an association between two items (A-B) makes it more difficult to form a new association between either item and a new one (A-D or B-D).

A systematic investigation of the effects of interference between successive pairs was undertaken by Müller and Pilzecker. Their experimental arrangements will sound quite familiar to the modern reader. (For convenience of exposition, we shall refer to stimulus-response pairs; Müller and Pilzecker spoke of the accented and unaccented syllables of trochaic feet.) The subject first learned an original series comprised of A-B associations. These were followed by "post-series" that included both A-D and C-D (control) associations. All the stimulus terms from the two series were then presented, in random order, and the subject was instructed to report the appropriate response terms. When two different responses had been learned to the same stimulus (A-B, A-D), both were to be reported. Such factors as the relative frequency of repetition of the two lists and the length of the retention interval were varied.

The main findings will also sound familiar. When two responses were learned to the same stimulus, both the first and the second associates were recalled less frequently and with longer latencies than were corresponding control items. The decrements were greater for the first-list than the second-list associations. When both associates were recalled (Doppeltreffer), the more recent one was likely to be given first, even though it had been learned less well.

In their theoretical analysis, Müller and Pilzecker distinguished between **associative inhibition** (generative Hemmung) and **reproductive inhibition** (effectuelle Hemmung). The former refers to the interfering effect of an old association (A-B) on the acquisition of a new one (A-D); the latter refers to interference at recall reflecting competition (Concurrenz) between alternative responses. The activation of A-B during the acquisition of A-D was identified as an important source of associative inhibition; the fact that B is in a state of readiness may have an inhibitory effect, even if the earlier response does not actually intrude.

It is apparent that the procedures in these experiments—the successive acquisition of different responses to the same stimuli followed by a test of cued recall—anticipated the main features of what later became the standard paradigm for the measurement of **retroactive inhibition.** There is an interesting historical twist here. As will be noted presently, Müller and Pilzecker were also the first to define and measure retroactive inhibition, but they interpreted it as a process quite different from reproductive inhibition. Much later, reproductive inhibition in the sense of response competition came to be considered the major mechanism of retroaction.

Retroactive Inhibition

Discovery of the Phenomenon.   In Müller and Pilzecker's experiments, subjects frequently had to learn two lists in immediate succession. On one occasion, the subject complained that her memory for the first list had become blurred after she had finished studying the second list. (The subject happened to be Professor Müller's wife, a very experienced and efficient memorizer.) In this serendipitous fashion, the phenomenon of retroactive inhibition was discovered. The appropriate design for measuring the phenomenon was soon implemented. Under the interference condition, the subject learned a second list immediately after the first; under the control condition, the subject rested after learning the first list. The length of the interval between the end of first-list learning and the test of retention for that list was, of course, kept constant. In several experiments, recall was found to be consistently lower under the interference than under the control condition, regardless of whether the retention interval was as short as 6 minutes or as long as 24 hours. The decrements in recall were accompanied by increases in latency.

Perseveration Hypothesis.   In interpreting these results, Müller and Pilzecker advanced what came to be known as the **perseveration theory** of retroactive inhibition. They proceeded from the assumption that after the end of learning the neural activities essential for the **consolidation** of associations persist for a period of time, gradually diminishing in intensity. If an individual engages in strenuous mental activity during the period of perseveration, the process of neural consolidation is disrupted and the associations fail to be established at full strength.

Any demanding mental activity was deemed sufficient to disrupt the process of consolidation. Müller and Pilzecker explicitly rejected explanations based on the similarity of the original and interpolated materials, or competition between items associated to the same serial position in the successive lists. To rule out such alternative interpretations, they used an interpolated activity that bore no relation to the original learning task. Instead of a second list of syllables, a set of complex pictures was presented which the subject had to describe. The amount of retroactive inhibition was comparable to that obtained in the original experiments. Another important implication of the perseveration hypothesis was also tested: the shorter the interval between the end of original learning and the beginning of the interpolated activity the greater should be the retroactive loss. The picture task was introduced either 17 seconds or 6 minutes after the acquisition of a series of syllables; as expected, a subsequent test of recall showed that an immediate interpolated task was more damaging than a delayed one. Thus, the experimental evidence appeared to support the perseveration hypothesis. To anticipate later developments, the results of these critical tests did not prove reproducible, which left the perseveration hypothesis vulnerable to the attacks that were to be mounted on it.

The Role of Recognition in Recall

The relationship between **recall** and **recognition** has been a persistent systematic issue in the experimental analysis of memory. One of Müller's important theoretical contributions was to translate this issue into terms that could be related to the experimental investigation of recall. Müller (1913) took his point of departure from the assumption that a judgment about the correctness of a reproduced item (modale Beurteilung) is an integral part of the recall process, at least when recall is intentional. He then specified the criteria of correctness that are used by subjects in making such judgments. These criteria included the manner in which the target item emerged into consciousness: how promptly, exclusively (i.e., free of competitors), persistently, clearly and elaborately.

Most important from a current theoretical point of view is Müller's analysis of the role of recognition in the judgmental phase of recall. He distinguished three types of recognition that can influence judgments about the correctness of a response: (a) In simple recognition, the target item by itself is experienced as having occurred previously. (b) In pairwise recognition, it is the two members in juxtaposition that appear familiar. (c) In place recognition, the position of an item is identified as being the same as during original learning. The more definite one or the other of these types of recognition, the more confident the subject is in the correctness of the target item.

All the criteria mentioned—the characteristics of the reproduced item and the different forms of recognition—may influence the subject's final judgment in various combinations. Each criterion may be met to a greater or lesser degree, and may be weighted differentially by individual subjects. Subjects also vary in the standards they apply in evaluating the evidence concerning the correctness of a response. Thus the "thresholds of acceptance" vary from one individual to the next. It can be seen that the concept of a **criterion,** in the sense in which the term is used in modern signal-detection theory, is adumbrated here. Today the conception of recall as a two-stage process—memory search followed by a recognition decision (**generation-recognition theory**)—is widely accepted and supported by considerable experimental evidence (cf. Kintsch, 1970).

THE EXPANSION OF EXPERIMENTAL METHODS

Müller and his students began by extending and refining Ebbinghaus' procedures. They soon proceeded to devise different methods in order to attack new problems. The same was happening in other laboratories. These methodological innovations reflected the proliferation of empirical and theoretical questions that began to be investigated; inevitably they also helped to determine the directions of subsequent research.

Method of Retained Members

In serial recitation and on paired-associate tests, correct performance depends on both the retention of the required responses and the integrity of the appropriate associations. Procedures were soon devised to assess each of these components separately. Under the **method of retained members**, the subject reproduces all the items he can, but not necessarily in the order of presentation; the score is based on the number of items reproduced (Binet & Henri, 1894a, 1894b; Kirkpatrick, 1894; Pohlmann, 1906). While fairly popular at first, this method fell into relative disuse for a long time, undoubtedly because theoretical interest continued to focus primarily on associative processes in learning and retention. Renamed the method of free recall, it made a spectacular comeback in the 1950s and 1960s, when it became the preferred vehicle for the study of organizational processes; today it remains one of the most widely used procedures in memory research (cf. Tulving, 1968).

Reconstruction Method

To assess the retention of sequential associations per śe, independently of the availability of the required responses, the **method of reconstruction** was devised. A series of items is presented in a particular order. On the test trial, the items are arranged in a random sequence, and the subject's task is to reconstruct the order in which they had been presented. In the early experiments of Münsterberg and Bigham (1894), the materials were series of numbers, colors, or forms, which were either presented visually or whose names were read to the subjects. Gamble (1909) used nonsense syllables and, interestingly enough, series of odors. Operationally, the test is one of memory for order. It can, and has been, considered a test of associative memory on the assumption that memory for order is based on sequential associations (or possibly associations to serial position).

Memory Span

Ebbinghaus had reported that he could reproduce a series of seven nonsense syllables after a single reading. He considered this result as a limiting case of the length-difficulty relationship. In a study published just 2 years after the appearance of Ebbinghaus' monograph, Jacobs (1887) approached the problem of immediate memory for an ordered series from a different perspective. Jacobs defined as the "span of prehension" (the capacity to register incoming information) the longest series that could be reproduced without error after a single presentation. He was interested in assessing individual differences in this capacity and proceeded to measure the span in school children of different ages. Strings of digits and letters were read to the subjects at a 2-second rate. The subjects repeated the series either orally or in writing. The obtained values of the span ranged from about 5 to about 9. The values were consistently higher for digits than for letters. The average scores increased as a function of age. There was other evidence of individual differences: the best students had the highest spans; girls performed better than boys, although not consistently so.

The **memory span** soon became a very popular measure of memory capacity. The dependence of the span on the type of materials and the conditions of presentation was extensively investigated. (For a review see Blankenship, 1938; an interesting discussion of the early history of the method is given by Murray, 1976.) The major interest was in the span as a measure of individual differences, and in particular of changes in mental ability as a function of age. Eventually, the span became a standard item in tests of intelligence.

Since the span is an average value that does not represent a sharp discontinuity in the function relating length of series to amount recalled, it can be, and has been, measured in many different ways. A relatively early review listed 27 different procedures that had been used to estimate the span (Guilford & Dallenbach, 1925). It is well to keep in mind that the span is not, in fact, a fixed quantity and the operations of measurement used to define it are to some extent arbitrary. These considerations apply with equal force to current uses of the span as an index of the capacity of short-term memory.

Recognition

In tracing the history of the method of recognition, it is important at the outset to distinguish between two lines of development: the use of recognition procedures for measuring the amount retained on the one hand, and for gauging temporal changes in the nature of memory representations on the other.

Measurement of Amount Retained.   The yes-no recognition test was introduced early. On such a test, previously presented items are intermixed with new items; the subject has to decide which items are old and which ones are new. The procedure was used to measure retention of lists composed of discrete units, such as syllables, words, and pictures (Binet & Henri, 1894a; Kirkpatrick, 1894; Smith, 1905; Strong, 1912) A correction for guessing was often adopted. It was assumed that errors represented random guesses; since such guesses could also lead to correct responses, the probability of a false positive response was subtracted from the probability of a correct response.

Recognition was regarded as an easier or more sensitive test of retention than recall. This assumption was supported by experimental findings showing higher recognition than recall after a given amount of training (Fischer, 1909; Kirkpatrick, 1894). This view was later formalized in theories of memory that

related retention to the strength of the memory trace: the threshold of strength
was said to be lower for recognition than for recall (cf. McDougall, 1904).

Temporal Changes.   In an article in *Philosophische Studien,* the organ of
Wundt's laboratory, Wolfe (1886) criticized Ebbinghaus' recently published
studies as representing too complex an approach to the problem of memory.
Tests of recognition, he argued, provide simpler and more sensitive measures of
retention than do tests of reproduction. By recognition he actually meant successive comparison of sensory stimuli. In his own experiments, Wolfe presented
pairs of tones, with the intervals between the two stimuli ranging from 1 to 60
seconds. The two tones were either identical or differed from each other by a few
cycles per second. The subject had to decide whether the second tone was higher

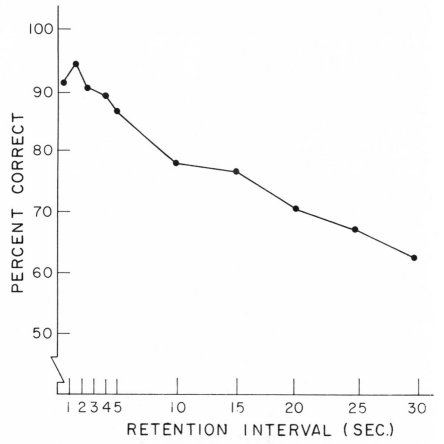

FIG. 3.3.   Forgetting curve for recognition of tones. The curve shows percentage
of correct recognition as a function of the interval between successive presentations of the same tone. Data from Wolfe (1886), p. 552.

or lower than the first. For physically identical stimuli, the equivalent of a forgetting curve is obtained when the probabilities of correct judgments of *same* are plotted against the length of the interstimulus interval.

Figure 3.3 presents an average forgetting curve based on the data of seven subjects, each of whom was tested a large number of times. The general decline in accuracy over time was taken by Wolfe to reflect the fading of the memory image. The curves of individual subjects could be fitted reasonably well by a logarithmic equation quite similar to Ebbinghaus'.

The assumption that recognition decisions are based on memory images did not stand up under careful empirical scrutiny. Bentley (1899) instructed his subjects to make a deliberate attempt to recall an image of the first stimulus and to compare it with the second stimulus before deciding whether or not the two were the same. For judgments based on brightness or color, the subjects were able to call up a memory image in the majority of cases. However, their decisions were only slightly more accurate when the memory image was available than when it was not. Working with tones (as Wolfe had done), Whipple (1901) likewise concluded that correct recognition did not depend on the availability of a memory image. He reported "bewildering" individual variations in the subjects' introspections.

The early psychophysical studies of recognition may be viewed as attempts to find a place after all for the experimental analysis of memory within the introspectionist framework of the Leipzig laboratory. A number of similar studies, in which the course of retention was charted for various stimulus attributes—brightness, visual length and size, weight, pressure, odor, and so on—continued to appear for a number of years. (For summaries of several of these studies see Bentley, 1899; and the recent review by Murray, 1976.)

NEW DIRECTIONS IN EARLY EXPERIMENTAL RESEARCH

The expansion of experimental methods brought with it an early information explosion. However, while the number of empirical investigations grew very rapidly, the prevailing theoretical ideas about memory remained rather static for many years. The validity of the classical laws of association was rarely questioned. Equally pervasive was the view that the degree of retention reflects memory strength. It was also taken as given that memory representations fade or decay over time. While mechanisms of interference had been identified early, they were not seen as playing an important role in the process of forgetting. Nevertheless, there were developments that helped to change and broaden the directions of research in the long run, if not immediately.

We now fill out the picture with a brief survey of some respresentative studies that reflect these developments. This survey brings us up to about the end of the First World War.

Materials and Conditions of Presentation

A great amount of effort was devoted to the evaluation of the effects on retention of the nature of the learning materials and of the modality of sensory stimulation. Much of the work was concerned with immediate or short-term retention. This trend was fostered by the interest of many investigators in memory for "simple" materials (i.e., sensory attributes such as pitch and brightness) on the one hand, and the immediate memory span on the other. The emphasis on immediate retention was similar to that found in much contemporary work on memory. It was only during a long "middle period"—roughly between the two World Wars—that interest in immediate retention largely lapsed.

Meaningfulness and Concreteness. Some of the comparisons among various types of materials revealed differences that have since become familiar. Higher immediate retention was found for meaningful items, such as words and numbers, than for nonsense syllables (Bigham, 1894; Pohlmann, 1906). As Ebbinghaus had already noted, lists of nonsense syllables were remembered less well than stanzas of poetry (Radossawljewitsch, 1907).

The powerful effects of **linguistic context** on the recall of words were demonstrated early by Binet and Henri (1894a, 1894b), who compared immediate retention for lists of unrelated words and for brief textual passages. School children recalled on the average about five of the seven unrelated words. By contrast, of the eight idea units (phrases) in a 14-word passage, 7.9 were recalled correctly. Comparing the percentages of loss in the two cases, Binet and Henri concluded somewhat sanguinely that parts of sentences were recalled 25 times better than unrelated words! Detailed analysis of the recall protocols showed that the units carrying the gist of the passage were most likely to be retained. The authors also noted that both sentence structure and wording were often simplified.

The fact that item **concreteness** favors retention was discovered early. Seeking to determine how memory was influenced by the "kind and intensity of impressions," Kirkpatrick (1894) used three conditions of presentation for 10-item lists: visual, aural, or display of physical objects. Recall was clearly highest for the series of objects, and this advantage became more pronounced when the subjects were retested 3 days later. Other investigators soon reported comparable results (Calkins, 1898; Smith, 1905). Another early finding was that pictures were recognized better than words (Smith, 1905).

Modality Effects. The advantages of concreteness were discovered in experiments that were designed to determine the relative durability of memories established through different kinds of sensory impressions—the visual registration of the written word or physical object, or the sound of the spoken word. The guiding theoretical assumption behind these studies of **modality effects** was that the underlying process of remembering is the revival of past impressions. From this point of view, the modality of sensory stimulation assumed major significance as a potential determinant of the probability of revival.

The questions asked by Münsterberg and Bigham (1894) were typical of those considered in many studies of the modality effect. These investigators wanted to know whether different senses act independently in memory, help each other, or hinder each other. The stimulus materials were colors and numbers, and retention was measured by the method of reconstruction. Performance was higher after visual than after aural presentation (although the difference was reversed when both types of items were included in the series). Retention substantially improved when visual and aural presentation were combined. While the results of such comparisons in subsequent experiments were quite variable, the combination of visual and auditory stimulation was always found to be a favorable condition, although not always superior to the more effective of the two single modes (e.g., Pohlmann, 1906). Adding kinesthetic stimulation by requiring articulation of visually presented items facilitated recall (Cohn, 1897). This positive effect, however, was not always found, e.g., when overt vocalization was added to combined visual and auditory stimulation, presumably overtaxing the individual's attentional capacity (Pohlmann, 1906).

It is useful to bear in mind that interest in these studies centered primarily on differences among modes of sensory stimulation. The role of associatively aroused **imagery** was considered only occasionally. For example, Netschajeff (1900) read to his subjects (school children) words denoting visual objects, sounds, tactile impressions, emotional states, and abstract concepts. Memory for the names of visual objects was highest. In retrospect, one may view such studies as attempts to study the role of associative imagery; however, the distinction between sensory representations and associative imagery was not drawn clearly at that time.

While investigations of modality effects remained popular for years, it was recognized that the results were inherently difficult to interpret. The experimenter could control the sense avenue through which the materials were presented, but the subject remained free to translate the input into other modalities. This objection was given especial force by the widespread assumption that individuals fell into distinct memory types (or ideational types) reflecting preferences for different modalities. A basic distinction was made among visual, auditory, and tactual-motor types, but many individuals were assumed to have "mixed" dispositions. Given such individual variations, differences between conditions of stimulation in any one experiment would be heavily dependent on the distribution of memory types in the sample of subjects.

Forgetting Curves

Following Ebbinghaus' lead, investigators continued to plot curves of forgetting, seeking to determine the basic shape of the function. For sensory stimuli ("simple materials''), a negatively accelerated declining curve was typically obtained, similar to Wolfe's for pitch. Thus, the temporal trends appeared to be similar for "simple" and "complex" materials.

A striking feature of Ebbinghaus' own curve was the extremely rapid rate of forgetting. Subsequent investigators who used Ebbinghaus' methods observed heavy but less severe losses (e.g., Radossawljewitsch, 1907; Finkenbinder, 1913). The more recent findings were considered more plausible. "What an unreliable instrument memory would be if it forgot as rapidly as Ebbinghaus believes!" (Meumann, 1913, p. 332). It now seems very likely, of course, that none of the subjects tested later was victimized by the cumulative effects of interference as much as was Ebbinghaus.

The general shape of the forgetting curve appeared to be largely independent of both the type of material and the method of testing. Measuring recognition for lists of common English words over retention intervals ranging from 1 minute to 7 days, Strong (1913) obtained a function that strikingly resembled Ebbinghaus'. Most of the empirical curves could be adequately fitted by a logarithmic equation (cf. Woodworth, 1938, p. 55).

Toward the end of the period we are reviewing, a new problem of interpretation arose: the assumption that retention necessarily declines over time was called into question. In experiments on the retention of poetry by children, Ballard (1913) found increases in performance after intervals ranging from 1 to 5 days. In these experiments, practice was terminated before the material was fully mastered. The subjects were tested immediately and then retested after a delay. The gains observed on the delayed test were attributed by Ballard to a process of **reminiscence,** a process that is antithetical to forgetting and thus can produce a rise in the retention curve. Interestingly enough, he found the amount of reminiscence to be inversely related to chronological age. While admitting that uncontrolled rehearsal might serve to improve retention, Ballard was convinced that it could not account for the entire effect. He was inclined to attribute it to continued neural growth after the end of learning. In view of the length of the intervals over which rises in performance were observed, such a process clearly would involve more than consolidation in Müller's and Pilzecker's sense.

Distinction Between Immediate and Long-Term Retention

An explicit differentiation between **immediate** and **long-term memory** was made surprisingly early. Thus, we find Binet and Henri (1894a) contrasting "la mémoire immédiate de répétition" and "la mémoire de conservation" (p. 10), adding that only the latter is "useful." They also devised a procedure to document this point.

In some of their experiments, the subjects were presented with series of seven-word lists, each of which they reproduced immediately. In addition, however, the subjects were instructed after each block of seven lists to write down all the words they could remember from that block. (This is, of course, the currently popular procedure of measuring final free recall for a series of once presented lists in order to assess amount retained in secondary memory, a procedure reintroduced by Craik in 1970.) Only about a third of the immediately recalled items were reproduced on the final test. Thus, short-term forgetting was rapid. (However, in an ancillary experiment, performance on a final test of recognition was nearly perfect, indicating that forgetting was not complete.) Binet and Henri also reported that in immediate recall most of the outside intrusions were *phonemically* similar to words in the list; on the final test, the similarity was usually *semantic*. The authors suggested that on an immediate test the final items of a list are repeated as sounds; in particular, the last word remains in memory "like an echo" (p. 13). Hence, many errors are phonemic. On the final test, only those words whose meaning has been registered can be recalled; hence most errors are semantic in origin. The concept of **echoic memory** has reappeared in current discussions of information processing. The same is true for the idea that coding is mainly phonemic in primary memory, and semantic in secondary memory.

It is not difficult to find other cases in which the methods of current research on **short-term memory** were anticipated. For example, distractor tasks—reading or listening to passages of text—were used by Bigham (1894) to fill retention intervals ranging from 2 to 60 seconds. Less was retained after filled than after unfilled intervals. Furthermore, the interference was greater when the modality of stimulation remained the same for the memory task and for the distractor activity than when it changed. We also find an early example of the use of a distractor task (mental arithmetic) for the purpose of preventing immediate rehearsal in a study of long-term retention (Strong, 1913).

The fact that the performance of a concurrent task during the presentation of the memory series impairs immediate retention was also well known. One of the first demonstrations was by Münsterberg (1890). His span for letters was substantially reduced when he performed mental arithmetic during the presentation of the series. The major effect was an increase in order errors. In numerous other investigations of the effects of concurrent tasks, the focus was on the limitations of attention and on individuals' ability to cope with distraction. For a review of this work, see Meumann (1913, ch.4).

The idea that immediate and long-term memory are functionally distinct processes was supported by the specificity of memory deficits found in mental patients. Ranschburg (1911) observed cases in which immediate retention was normal while the ability to recall material after a period of delay was greatly impaired. Similar findings were reported by Goldstein (1906). Contemporary proponents of **dual-process theories** of memory have considered specificity of pathological retention deficits as strong evidence for their position.

The nature of the functional differences between short-term and long-term memory received systematic attention only intermittently. In his *Principles of Psychology,* James (1890), of course, had drawn a clear distinction between primary and secondary memory. "An object which is recollected, in the proper sense of the term, is one which has been absent from consciousness altogether, and now revives anew. It is brought back from a reservoir . . . in which it lay buried and lost from view. But an object of primary memory is not thus brought back; it was never lost" (pp. 646 f.). "Memory proper" he designated as secondary. Contemporary theorists who developed their models of memory around the distinction between a short-term and a long-term system returned to James' formulation, and he is much quoted today.

Some years later, Meumann (1913) discussed the differences between "immediate" and "permanent" memory (without referring to James) in terms that likewise have a modern ring. For example, he described immediate retention as "the only form of revival of an impression which takes place without the original impression being crowded out of consciousness." By contrast, permanent retention comes into play "after the original impression has been effaced or forced out of consciousness by other ideas or perceptions" (p. 43). And, "The effect of immediate retention is peculiar in that it lasts only a brief period of time, and that it may readily be obliterated by distracting impressions" (p. 44).

Economy of Learning

Early investigations of learning were often undertaken for the purpose of identifying economical methods of practice.

Distribution of Practice. Distribution effects received sustained attention. Both the amount of work per session and the length of the interval between sessions were varied (Perkins, 1914; Starch, 1912). Of the two modes of distribution the former appeared to be the more effective. The positive effects of distribution were not limited to the memorization of verbal materials; they were equally in evidence in the acquisition of such perceptual-motor skills as typewriting (Book, 1908; Pyle, 1914).

Whole Versus Part Learning. Another question considered to have pedagogical implications was whether the part or the whole method of memorization was more economical. When one is confronted with a lengthy memory task, is it more efficient to continue studying it as a whole or to learn it in parts and then to combine the parts? The initial experiment on this problem was carried out by Steffens (1900), a student of G. E. Müller's. In preliminary observations she found that subjects left to their own devices usually divided the task into parts, occasionally reviewing earlier parts while learning later ones. In the experiment proper, however, these same subjects learned both stanzas of poetry and lists of nonsense syllables somewhat faster under the whole than under the part procedure. Steffens suggested several reasons for the inferiority of the part procedure: effort has to be expended in linking the separately learned parts; neither appropriate positional associations nor remote associations among components of nonadjacent parts can be established. The whole method was also found to be more efficient in some subsequent experiments, especially for practiced subjects. However, as G. O. McGeoch's (1931) review shows, there was considerable variation from one experiment to the next. The enthusiastic claims made for the advantages of the whole method (Meumann, 1913, ch. 6) were not justified.

The Role of Recitation.   Another question with obvious educational implications was brought into the laboratory: when allotted a fixed amount of time for studying a lesson, how much of it should the learner devote to reading the material and how much to recitation. In an early study of this problem, Witasek (1907) found that performance improved as the relative frequency of recitation trials was increased. Just a few years later, Gates (1917) published his classical experiment showing that both immediate and delayed recall of nonsense lists and passages of text increased as a direct function of the proportion of learning time devoted to recitation. Gates saw recitation as aiding the process of acquisition in a number of ways, notably by giving subjects information about their progress and thus permitting them to concentrate on the parts requiring further attention, by providing opportunities for developing a useful organization of the material, and by giving the subjects practice in the act of recalling.

Measurement of Learning

Ebbinghaus plotted the first forgetting curve, but he did not plot the first learning curve. His interest was in retention. In the years that followed, the emphasis remained on the measurement of retention. As interest developed in problems of the economy of learning, speed of acquisition per se came to be treated as a significant dependent variable, for example in comparisons of the whole and part methods. Even so, economy of learning continued to be evaluated primarily by measures of retention. It is not altogether surprising, then, that trial-by-trial changes in performance were not usually recorded in these experiments.

Practice curves, however, were in the meantime being plotted and analyzed in studies of the acquisition of perceptual-motor skills. The classical studies by Bryan and Harter of the acquisition of skill in sending and receiving telegraphic messages were published in 1897 and 1899. Probably the best known result of this investigation was the **plateau** in the practice curve for receiving—a period of little or no improvement preceded and followed by a rising trend. Bryan and Harter interpreted the plateau as reflecting the transition from lower-order habits (processing individual letters and words) to higher-order habits (processing groups of words). There was no visible improvement while the lower-order habits were being perfected and integrated. Thus, the concept of **hierarchical organization,** later to become so important in theories of memory, made an early appearance in the analysis of skills.

Transfer and the Educability of Memory

Early Work on Bilateral Transfer.   As Woodworth (1938) pointed out, "the scientific study of transfer began with our old friends, the psychophysicists" (p. 181). He was referring to the early research on the **bilateral transfer** of perceptual skill, notably to Volkmann's (1858) classical investigation of the two-point threshold (i.e., the sensitivity to the difference between one and two tactual stimuli). During practice trials on a given area of the skin (e.g., left middle finger), the threshold declined progressively. As measured by the difference between pre- and post-tests, the improvement was equally great in the unpracticed symmetrical area (right forefinger), although not in other areas (e.g., forearm). Thus, the concept of transfer was introduced before research on memory began, as was the use of pre- and post-tests for measuring the magnitude of transfer effects.

Ability Training.   When problems of transfer came to be considered in experimental investigations of memory, the question that came to the fore was whether the ability to remember could be improved by practice. This question was rooted in the historical doctrine of **formal discipline** and the theory of mental faculties on which this doctrine was based. The doctrine held that the faculty of memory is educable through exercise, just as are other faculties such as judgment and reasoning.

The doctrine of formal discipline was brought under heavy attack in a landmark investigation by Thorndike and Woodworth (1901). In this study, they assessed the breadth of the transfer effects produced by training on selected task requiring observation and judgment. For example, subjects were given practice, with informative feedback, in estimating the areas of rectangular forms; the same type of judgment was made on the transfer test, but on stimuli differing in size and shape from those used in training. In spite of the similarity of the successive tasks, the transfer effects were small and irregular. To the extent that transfer was found, it appeared to reflect the carrying over from the training experience of quite circumscribed habits and dispositions that remained useful in the test situation. Thorndike and Woodworth concluded that "spread of practice occurs only when identical elements are concerned in the influencing and influenced function" (1901, p. 250).

Thorndike became a vigorous and articulate exponent of the **theory of identical elements** and did not hesitate to urge its application to educational practice. He also attempted to specify the kinds of "elements" whose identity makes transfer possible. "Chief amongst such identical elements of practical importance in education are associations including ideas about aims and ideas of method and general principles, and associations involving elementary facts of experience" (1903, p. 81). Since ideas about aims and general principles were included, the term "element" was not used in a reductionist sense; the intent rather was to insist that transfer effects were inherently circumscribed and dependent on overlap in task components.

Some phenomena of specific negative transfer, in the current sense of the term, were described by Müller and his associates in their studies of associative inhibition. These problems, however, were not pursued systematically until later, when principles of specific transfer based on the relationships of the stimuli and of the responses in successive tasks began to be formulated (Poffenberger, 1915; Wylie, 1919).

The Role of Intent to Learn

Experimenters trained in the tradition of introspectionism probably took it for granted that the "will" to engage in the learning task was essential for successful performance. The importance of the subject's set or "will to learn" became a focus of investigation when a distinction was made equivalent to that between **intentional** and **incidental learning.** For example, in an early study by Poppelreuter (1912) subjects instructed to learn took many fewer trials to master a list of nonsense syllables than did subjects instructed merely to observe the materials.

It is worth noting that when the phrase, "incidental memory," began to be used (Myers, 1913), the reference was to the retention of information to which the subject had not been asked to attend. In Myers' experiment, the subjects' task (what would today be called the orienting task) was to count the number of Os interspersed among other letters printed in color. Their memory was then tested for various features of the display, such as the other letters and their colors, the number of lines on the page, and so on. (The level of retention was generally low.) Thus, the concept of **incidental memory** came to be used in two ways. In its general sense, it referred to retention in the absence of instructions to learn; in a more restricted sense, it referred to the retention of information on which the subject had presumably not focused at the time of input. In much of the later work, interest centered on the role of intent to learn and on the effects of different orienting activities; hence, care was taken that the subject did attend to the target information.

Memory and Testimony

As empirical work on memory got under way, there was no sharp line drawn between pure and applied research. Studies were often carried out in a school setting, and the "pedagogical" implications of experimental results were given considerable attention. Another early area of application was the psychology of testimony. The accuracy of testimony, of course, depends not on the fidelity of memory alone; it is also conditioned by the initial perception of the critical event on the one hand, and by a multitude of factors—motivational and social as well as cognitive—that influence the individual's behavior on the witness stand (cf. Whipple, 1909). Nevertheless, it is the fallibility of memory more than anything else that limits the possibility of accurate testimony. Thus, research in this area was closely tied, both methodologically and conceptually, to the study of remembering.

At the turn of the century, two individuals pioneered in opening up this field of inquiry, defining its objectives and developing its methods—Binet (1900, 1905) and Stern (1902). It was Binet who first called for a "science of testimony" and introduced the picture-description test as an experimental analogue of testimony. The systematic exploration of the field and the development of sophisticated techniques of measurement were largely the work of Stern.

The two major types of experimental procedures were the **picture-test** and the **event-test**. In the former, a picture showing an elaborate scene was presented to the subject for inspection; in the latter, a realistic incident such as a quarrel was enacted by confederates of the experimenter. The tests comprised two phases: (1) In the narrative, subjects gave as full a description as they could of the picture or incident. (2) In the interrogatory (designed to mimic a cross-examination), subjects were asked a series of detailed questions about what they had observed; in answering, they often had to rate their degree of certainty, on a scale ranging from hesitancy to willingness to take an oath. The tests were given either immediately or after varying intervals of time.

Completely correct reports were the exception, even on immediate tests. Some details apparently were not noticed at all or perceived incorrectly. There was clear evidence of selective retention in the reports. The interrogatory typically elicited details that had been omitted from the narrative; however, the information obtained under questioning was less accurate than that produced spontaneously. The accuracy of reports, of course, declined over time, especially in the interrogatory phase.

Developmental changes in the characteristics of testimony were studied extensively. The accuracy of reports increased steadily as a function of age. There were also orderly trends in the qualitative nature of the reports—from disconnected enumerations by the youngest children to the description of object properties and people's activities by older subjects.

FUNCTIONALISM

After the First World War, the center of active research on memory shifted more and more from Germany to America. The developments during the decades between the two wars were thus strongly influenced by American psychologists who put their mark on the field during a new period of expansion and consolidation. They did not represent a well defined movement, but many of the most influential workers during that period shared theoretical attitudes and methodological preferences that can be subsumed under the label of **functionalism.**

Antecedents of Modern Functionalism

As was shown in the previous chapter, functionalism represented an approach to psychology that was profoundly influenced by evolutionary theory; it focused on the role of mental processes in the organism's survival and adjustment to the environment. In sharp opposition to structuralism, the functionalists were concerned "with the effort to discern and portray the typical *operations* of consciousness under actual life conditions, as over against the attempt to analyze and describe its elementary and complex *contents* (Angell, 1907, p. 63) . . . the answer to the question 'what' implicates the answers to the questions 'how' and 'why' " (p. 67). In this spirit the functionalists welcomed the extension of the field to animal behavior, child psychology, and educational psychology. In fact, the functionalist par excellence was E. L. Thorndike whose contributions to animal learning were described in Chapter 2.

As we saw in Chapter 2, Thorndike's theory was a stimulus-response connectionism. Learning consisted in the establishment of such connections, a process that was governed by the laws of effect, exercise, and belongingness (pp. 000). Later on Thorndike (1913) added a **law of disuse** to account for forgetting: "When a modifiable connection is not made between a situation and a response during a length of time, the connection's strength is decreased" (p. 4). Thorndike believed that these basic principles applied to all forms of learning, human as well as animal. With time his research was increasingly devoted to the investigation of his laws with human subjects (1931, 1932, 1935).

In investigations of the **law of effect,** the rewards and punishments were symbolic, announcements of "right" and "wrong" following an individual's response. The associations chosen for study were usually arbitrary. In one typical "Thorndikian situation," the subjects were asked to guess a number from 1 to 10 to each word in a long list; in another situation, the task was to choose among alternative translations of each of a series of words unknown to the subjects. The probabilities of repetition of the same response on a second trial were used to evaluate the changes produced by the symbolic rewards and punishments. In experiments concerned with the **law of exercise,** the frequency of occurrence of connections was manipulated.

The results of these experiments led to important revisions in the laws of learning. With respect to the principle of effect, Thorndike concluded that punishments did not directly weaken stimulus-response connections in the same sense that rewards strengthened them. Punishment was seen as influencing behavior only indirectly—by increasing the variability of behavior and thereby making it more likely that the correct response will be made and strengthened. Thus, the law of effect became a law of reward. The importance of exercise came to be downgraded if not denied altogether. Sheer repetition appeared to strengthen connections slowly at best. Furthermore, for repetition to be useful, another condition had to be met, which Thorndike designated as **belonging**. For example, repetition was found to strengthen the connection between paired words, but not that between the second member of one pair and the first member of the next. By "belonging" Thorndike (1932) meant simply a perception on the part of the individual that "this goes with that;" he cautioned that "there need be nothing logical, or inherent, or unifying in it" (p. 72).

While ready to revise his laws in the light of experimental evidence, Thorndike never wavered in his advocacy of the basic principles of connectionism. He continued to insist that rewards strengthen connections automatically, that the mechanism of effect is "as natural in its action as a falling stone . . . or a hormone in the blood" (1935. pp. 39f.) Nor did he abandon his belief that the entire repertoire of human behavior could be subsumed under the laws of connections. "Any given person . . . is the total of his S-R probabilities" (1943, pp. 23f.).

Influence of Connectionism

Much of Thorndike's experimental work on human learning soon came under heavy attack, in particular his analysis of the role of punishment. The most telling criticisms were methodological (e.g., the use of faulty chance baselines in the evaluation of response probabilities). Controversy continued to center on the question of whether the repetition of rewarded responses reflects the automatic strengthening of connections or the utilization of information by the learner. Today, there is persuasive evidence that symbolic rewards and punishments are effective largely by virtue of their informational value (Buchwald, 1969).

It was Thorndike's general theoretical orientation much more than his substantive experimental findings that had a significant influence on the field of human learning. Connectionism marks the transition from the historical doctrine of association of ideas to the stimulus-response analysis of associative processes. However, Thorndike was not a reductionist, applying the same principles to the acquisition of simple motor movements and of complex cognitive skills. Such pragmatic use of stimulus-response language became characteristic of later workers in the functionalist tradition (cf. McGeoch, 1942, p. 26).

The Modern Functionalists

The most productive and influential investigators of human learning and memory during the period between the two World Wars came out of the functionalist tradition. Unlike Thorndike, they were not systematists. It was their definition of the objectives of experimental analysis and their attitude toward theory that had a pervasive effect on the direction of research. In the sections that follow we consider the characteristics of their approach.

FUNCTIONALISM IN RESEARCH ON LEARNING AND MEMORY

To convey the flavor of the functionalist approach to research on learning and memory, we discuss briefly three historically important publications by psychologists who were its more influential exponents—Robinson, McGeoch, and Melton. Through them we follow a direct line of descent from Angell and the original "school" of functionalism.

The New Associationism

The functionalists were the principal contemporary representatives of the associationist point of view. The concept of association had gradually become detached from its philosophical origins and physiological connotations, without being given a clear new definition. If the principles of association were to serve as a useful framework for the description and analysis of behavior, then they should be restated in a form that is appropriate for contemporary usage. That is what Robinson (1932) set out to do in his book, *Association Theory To-day*.

Robinson began by offering a definition of association that focuses on the core of the concept and bypasses the issues that have surrounded its detailed explication. By association is meant simply "the establishment of functional relations among psychological activities and states in the course of individual experience" (p. 7). Given this definition, the specification of the units that are associated becomes a pragmatic matter. One has to choose units that are likely to enter into significant functional relations.

How are associations stored? In contrast to Thorndike, Robinson saw little value in equating the establishment of associations with neurological changes because such a theory simply "endows the brain with all of the characteristics necessary to explain the observed facts of association" (p. 32). While one should keep an open mind regarding neural hypotheses, it is better for the time being to think of associations as being formed among psychological **dispositions.** A disposition is a capacity to act under appropriate conditions. "The Frenchman's actual possession is a capacity to say Bon jour! when he sees his friend. . . . Such capacities are . . . real as the stubborn presence of a carved inscription on a block of granite" (p. 34). Robinson here appeared to be moving toward a distinction between habit and performance, a distinction that was notably missing in Thorndike's connectionism.

Robinson's book became best known for his discussion of the laws of association, a discussion that marks a self-conscious disengagement from philosophical doctrine. For Robinson, laws of association were no more and no less than functional relations linking associative strength to conditions of acquisition. The general law of association is A = f (x, y, z, ...), where A is associative strength, and x, y, z, etc., are factors that can be shown empirically to be related to associative strength. Within this framework, special laws state the nature of the functional relations that obtain for individual factors.

Robinson's treatise brings out both the strengths and the weaknesses of the associationism of the functionalists. Their main positive contribution was to clear the theoretical air, and to focus directly and exclusively on the pragmatic value of the concept of association in the experimental analysis of learning and memory. Robinson insisted that laws of association should be no more and no less than statements of empirically verifiable functional relations. The overriding emphasis on descriptive functional relations at the expense of theory construction can also be seen as the major weakness of the approach. As Boring (1933) pointed out in a review of Robinson's book, the risk is that the outcome is no more than a "hodge-podge of laws."

The Vertical Dimensions of Mind

Robinson's formula was intended to summarize the factors determining the formation of associations. As he pointed out, another formula would have been needed for retention, including such variables as disuse, interpolated learning, age of associations, and so on (pp. 131 f.). The fact that Robinson chose to develop his system with reference to the laws of fixation rather than the laws of retention was consistent with the functionalists' interest in the broad problem of learning, as distinct from the classical problem of memory. This conceptual shift from "memory" to "learning and memory" was articulated clearly in a landmark paper by McGeoch (1936a), entitled, "The Vertical Dimensions of Mind."

McGeoch began by pointing out that the accepted mode of analysis in early experimental psychology had been **cross-sectional,** i.e., concerned with psychological events occurring at a particular moment or spanning a brief period of time. By contrast, **longitudinal** analysis focuses on vertical organization, i.e., "the conditions under which progressive change of function occurs from before birth to senescence" (p. 108). The time had come, McGeoch argued, to impose vertical order on the multitude of diverse cross-sectional data.

In developing his own description of the flow of psychological events, McGeoch introduced the concept of "vertical dimension," which he defined as "a variable which is present throughout practically all of the life-span and which, by virtue of its continuity must be present to some degree in any discription of psychological events" (p. 108). The two major vertical dimensions of mind are maturation-degeneration and learning-forgetting. His own concern was with the latter, and under this heading he included the phenomena of acquisition, transfer, and retention.

In the body of his paper, McGeoch went on to marshal evidence that learning is not "a special and compartmentalized set of events" (p. 113), but rather pervades a wide rage of psychological functions: perception, ideation and reasoning, motivation, affection, emotion, personality, volition. All of these, when studied horizontally, are just "moments in the flow of learning" (p. 129).

For McGeoch, the most important implications of his analysis were methodological. First, in the search for widely applicable laws of learning, standardization of methods and measuring operations is important, Second, experimental analysis should focus on processes of learning that are likely to play a significant role in the vertical organization of psychological functions. Here McGeoch stressed, rather prophetically, the importance of investigating the relations between incidental and intentional learning, and between immediate memory and more permanent retention. Third, the operations of learning and transfer experiments can be profitably extended to other domains, such as object perception, psychophysical discrimination, reasoning; and also the development of attitudes, emotional reactions, and personality traits. Given these extensions of methodology, learning can become a fundamental dimension in the systematic organization of the facts of psychology.

Melton's Dimensional Analysis of Learning

The concept of vertical dimension implies that the changes effected by learning are quantitative rather than qualitative. As Hilgard (1956, p. 334) points out, functionalists generally preferred continuities over discontinuities or typologies. We find the same emphasis on continuous variation in Melton's (1941, 1950) well known dimensional analysis of learning paradigms.

Studies of learning can be classified on the basis of (a) situational features or experimental arrangements, and (b) the nature of the processes that are assumed to influence performance. Any instance of learning can be defined operationally by specifying its location on these various dimensions.

Three main situational dimensions serve to identify the nature of the responses demanded by the experimental arrangements. These concern the extent to which: (a) part responses must be integrated in order to satisfy the task requirements, as in serial or motor-skill learning; (b) specific reactions must be attached to specific stimuli, as in classical conditioning and paired-associate learning; (c) the subject must react to relationships among stimuli rather than to individual stimuli in isolation, as in experiments on transposition and in the type of investigation made famous by Köhler, where the subject had to invent a tool in order to solve a problem.

Cutting across the situational dimensions are process dimensions. Here the reference is to variations in the following characteristics: (a) the extent to which successful performance depends on discovery of the correct response, with the extremes of the continuum defined by classical conditioning and rote learning on the one hand, and problem-solving tasks on the other; (b) the degree to which the required responses are available in the individual's repertoire, e.g., the appropriate movements in motor learning, the prescribed units in verbal learning, and the relevant categories in concept identification; (c) the relative importance of ideational and motor responses in both the discovery and fixation phases, as exemplified by the contrast between motor and verbal learning; (d) the closeness of the relationship between the required response and the occurrence of a satisfying state of affairs, i.e., the extent to which the principle of effect comes into operation. (The distinction between intentional and incidental learning, which is recognized to be a matter of degree, is included under this last heading.)

When this schema is applied, it becomes clear that the assignment of learning paradigms to mutually exclusive categories can be misleading. For example, as Melton pointed out, rote learning and reasoning differ with respect to the requirement of discovery of the correct response, but they are similar in that they call primarily for verbal and ideational activity. While specific responses are prescribed in rote-learning tasks, conditions requiring discovery can nevertheless be introduced, e.g., rules defining classes of correct responses.

In principle, dimensional analysis encompassed a wide range of learning situations: in practice the intensive exploration of functional relations inevitably came to be restricted to a limited number of experimental paradigms. Given the historical linkage between modern functionalism and association theory, these were primarily the paradigms of associative learning. In the theoretical interpretation of results, there was a corresponding trend toward the construction of miniature systems, i.e., the formulation of principles that provide a detailed explanation of a circumscribed range of phenomena.

In describing the functionalists, Hilgard (1956, p. 334) listed tolerance as one of their distinguishing characteristics. They were not committed to any one behavioral or physiological model. The prevailing attitude toward conditioning theory is a case in point. There was no disposition to adopt the view, first advanced by radical behaviorists, that all associative learning is reducible to classical conditioning. Nevertheless, some of the key principles of conditioning gained wide acceptance as theoretical constructs in the analysis of verbal learning and memory because they proved to be of considerable heuristic value as explanatory devices and as a source of hypotheses.

THE INFLUENCE OF CONDITIONING THEORY

In attempting to extend the principles of conditioning to phenomena observed under other experimental arrangements, it is possible to take one of two approaches. First, one can argue that the phenomena of interest are in fact conditioned responses and that they can be fully understood without reference to any additional concepts. Second, one can assume that the functional relations established in the highly controlled conditioning situation apply to all associations, but that these general laws of association operate in conjunction with other principles in determining behavioral change. It is primarily the latter approach that was taken by Hull when he set out to demonstrate the heuristic value of conditioning principles in the analysis of verbal learning.

Hull's Analysis of Rote Learning

In 1935 Hull published a paper that was to become a classic in the field, ''The Conflicting Psychologies of Learning—A Way Out.'' It was an eloquent plea to psychologists to adopt for their discipline the methods that had proved so successful in the physical sciences—the construction of formal systems permitting the rigorous deduction of theorems that can be subjected to experimental test. To demonstrate that his proposal was indeed feasible, Hull presented a miniature theoretical system designed to account for the phenomena of serial rote learning. It was a highly formal system comprising definitions, postulates, and theorems. A few years later, a revised and greatly expanded version of the system was published in a monograph entitled, ''Mathematico-deductive Theory of Rote Learning'' (Hull, 1940). This was a prohibitively complex treatise, and it is not surprising that few if any subsequent investigators were inclined to work with the formalisms of the system. Nevertheless, some of the basic concepts of the theory gained wide currency, and specific predictions derived from it opened up important new avenues of experimental research.

The core of Hull's theory was an elaboration of a hypothesis originally formulated by Lepley (1934), which drew an analogy between remote associations established in serial learning and trace conditioned responses. In trace conditioning, the offset of the conditioned stimulus and the onset of the unconditioned stimulus are separated by an interval of time. In the course of training, the conditioned response moves closer in time to the onset of the unconditioned stimulus. This increase in latency is assumed to reflect a temporary inhibition of the response (inhibition of delay). By analogy, remote associations are inhibited while the prescribed sequence is produced.

In developing his own model, Hull assumed that the presentation of each item in a serial list establishes a **stimulus trace** which diminishes in intensity as the trial continues. It is to these stimulus traces that subsequent items are associated (''conditioned''). Since the trace of each stimulus persists throughout the series, associations are formed to increasingly complex compounds. Each presentation of the list increases the **excitatory potential** for successive associations, i.e., the correct responses are strengthened. At the same time, however, each presentation also adds to the inhibition falling on the correct responses. Figure 3.4 illustrates the mechanism responsible for the growth in **inhibitory potential.** When the syllable NAR is presented, it becomes conditioned to a compound that comprises the traces of the four preceding items. In order for NAR to be given at

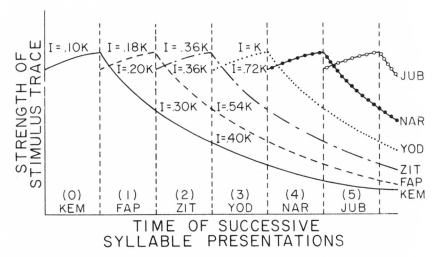

FIG. 3.4. The development of inhibition in serial learning according to Hull's theory. The trace of an item is assumed to decline in strength as the presentation of the list continues. Successive responses are associated to compounds comprising the traces of all preceding items. Inappropriate responses are held in check by inhibition. The diagram shows the amount of inhibitory potential (values of K) generated at each point in the series when the response NAR is learned. From Hull, Hovland, Ross, Hall, Perkins, and Fitch (1940), p. 57.

the appropriate point in the series, two kinds of competing tendencies have to be inhibited: the habit of reading aloud the current item (YOD) and remote associations between NAR and each of the first three items in the series (KEM, FAP, and ZIT). The amount of inhibition that is generated varies inversely with the distance between the response and the preceding items. Of course, there is a different pattern of inhibitory components at each position in the list. For each response, the difference between the excitatory and the inhibitory potential defines the **effective excitatory potential,** which determines the probability and speed of correct performance.

With appropriate quantitative assumptions, the theory can postdict the characteristic bowed shape of the **serial-position curve** of errors, which rises to a peak just past the center of the series and declines thereafter. The initial rise in errors reflects the progressive increase in the number of trace components with inhibitory loadings; the terminal decline occurs because the number of remote associations subject to inhibition declines rapidly as the end of the list is approached.

The excitatory tendencies are assumed to decay more slowly than the inhibitory tendencies. Given this postulate, several important deductions follow. First, serial learning should be faster when practice is distributed than when it is massed. The distribution intervals are advantageous because the dissipation of inhibition outweighs any loss of excitatory strength. Second, following massed practice reminiscence should be observed after relatively short retention intervals. Owing to the differential rates of decay of the excitatory and inhibitory tendencies, the net excitatory potential will increase before it begins to decrease as the retention interval is lengthened. Third, the beneficial effects of distribution, and reminiscence, should be directly related to the amount of inhibition accumulated during practice; hence, they should be greater for the central portion than for the beginning and end of the serial list.

These deductions received early experimental support. Reminiscence in the recall of a serial list after an interval of 2 seconds or less was observed by Ward (1937) and Hovland (1938a, 1938b). As predicted, reminiscence was more pronounced for the central portion of the serial list than for the ends. Again in accord with theoretical expectations, serial lists were learned faster by distributed than by massed practice, with the largest differences in speed of acquisition occurring for the middle of the list. This result is illustrated in Figure 3.5 which is taken from an experiment by Hovland (1938a), the first in a major series of studies in which the implications of the dissipation-of-inhibition hypothesis were systematically tested. Several of his other findings were consistent with deductions from Hull's theory. Hovland's studies are an impressive example of painstaking systematic experimentation. Unfortunately, they are by now largely of historical interest. For reasons that are still not entirely clear, distribution effects in rote learning were later found to be elusive and complexly determined at best (Underwood, 1961). Nor did reminiscence fare any better, becoming notorious as a "now-you-see-it-now-you-don't" phenomenon.

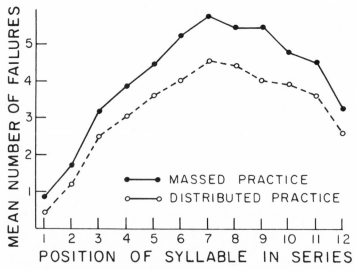

FIG. 3.5.   Distribution effects in serial rote learning. The figure shows mean number of errors made at each serial position under conditions of massed and of distributed practice. From Hovland (1938a), p. 209.

Hull's theoretical ideas, if not his formal system, had a limited but important influence. In particular, the dissipation-of-inhibition hypothesis proved to be of heuristic value, for a time at least, in guiding research on distribution of practice and reminiscence. One obvious weakness of the theory was that it pertained only to serial rote learning, a limitation imposed deliberately in the interest of developing a self-contained and precise miniature formal system. Another weakness was the inadequate treatment of the problem of forgetting. Temporal changes in performance were seen as reflecting the decay of excitatory and inhibitory tendencies, and the role of intertask interference was largely ignored. By contrast, Gibson's theory of verbal learning, which was also based on conditioning principles, placed major emphasis on the analysis of interference processes.

Gibson's Generalization Hypothesis

Gibson's theory was published in 1940 in a paper entitled, "A systematic application of the concepts of generalization and differentiation to verbal learning." Like Hull, Gibson chose to base her theory on laws of conditioning because ". . . the greater the simplicity of the learning, the better are the chances of laying bare mechanisms which operate in all learning" (p. 196).

As the title of the paper implies, the principles of conditioning on which the theory is founded are **generalization** and **differentiation.** The key assumption is that success in verbal learning depends on the establishment of discriminations among the items included in the task. To the extent that generalization occurs among stimuli, discrimination is impaired and acquisition of the correct responses is hindered. For learning to proceed, generalization must be reduced. The reduction of generalization is designated differentiation and is effected by differential reinforcement. That is, differentiation occurs when correct responses are reinforced and generalized responses are not reinforced. In verbal-learning situations, the presentation of the prescribed items serves as the vehicle of differential reinforcement. This argument applies to situations in which each stimulus requires a different response. When stimuli share a common response, generalization facilitates learning.

We now consider some of the major postulates of the theory, and the predictions that follow from them. These predictions are stated for tasks in which each stimulus is associated with a different response.

1. The stronger the generalization tendencies among the stimuli in a list, the greater the amount of reinforced practice required to establish differentiation. Hence, speed of learning should vary inversely with the level of generalization.

2. After the end of learning, differentiation declines over time, and there is spontaneous recovery of generalization. As a result of spontaneous recovery, retention loss should be proportional to the degree of initial gener-

alization, e.g., forgetting should increase as a direct function of intralist stimulus similarity.

3. The more differential reinforcement has been applied during acquisition, the slower will be the spontaneous recovery. It follows that the amount retained after a given interval of time should be directly related to the degree of original learning.

4. The more the stimuli of a first list generalize with the stimuli of a second list, the more repetitions will be required to master the second list, and also the poorer will be the retention of the second list. That is, both negative transfer and proactive inhibition should increase directly with interlist similarity.

5. The more the stimuli of a second list generalize with the stimuli of a first list, the greater will be the retroactive inhibition in the recall of the first list.

In all these cases, facilitation rather than interference is expected when the relevant stimuli require the same rather than different responses.

In the postulates of the theory, **meaningfulness** is treated as a special case of differentiation. Thus, meaning is defined as "a characteristic of a verbal or visual item which serves to differentiate it from other items" (p. 205). Less generalization, therefore, will normally occur among meaningful than among nonsense stimuli. Consequently, meaningful material is expected to be learned faster and to be retained better than nonsense materials, and also to be less susceptible to interlist interference.

For purposes of testing deductions from the theory, degree of generalization between stimulus A and stimulus B was defined empirically, i.e., in terms of the probability that B will elicit a response associated with A. In this fashion, a gradient of generalization can be determined for a standard stimulus. The question of what types of stimulus continua yield generalization gradients was left open. It was taken for granted, however, that scaled similarity and generalization would usually be correlated. Under the empirical definition, degree of generalization could be related to meaningfulness as well as to similarity.

The stimulus materials used by Gibson in her experiments were sets of nonsense figures consisting of a standard and variants that represented different degrees of generalization with respect to the standard. Control figures unrelated to the standards were also used. Choosing stimulus items from this pool, Gibson (1942) found, as predicted, that speed of paired-associate learning was inversely related to the degree of generalization among the stimulus terms. However, no reliable evidence for the expected difference in long-term retention was obtained.

The implications of the theory for transfer and retroaction were investigated in complementary experiments by Gibson (1941) and Hamilton (1943), in which the degree of generalization between the stimuli (nonsense figures) in two successive lists was manipulated systematically. In Gibson's experiment, the nonsense-syllable responses in the two lists were different; in Hamilton's experiment, the responses remained the same. The theory predicts a gradient of interference when the responses are new, and a gradient of facilitation when the responses are old. The trends in speed of transfer learning yielded a rough approximation at best to the expected gradients. The relative transfer effects, both positive and negative, were largest when the stimuli remained the same and smallest when they were unrelated, with two levels of generalization occupying intermediate positions. The absence of differences between the latter, however, was clearly at variance with the theory. The amounts of retroactive inhibition and facilitation obtained on a test of first-list recall were consistent with the transfer results; the gradients were more regular although different in form.

While the experimental tests of the deductions yielded equivocal results, Gibson's analysis nevertheless proved to be an important landmark in the history of contemporary research on verbal learning and memory. Gibson's work was much more influential than Hull's, not only because it was unencumbered by prohibitive formalisms but primarily because it focused on a wider range of fundamental issues. The key concepts of the theory bore directly on the operation of the powerful and ubiquitous factor of item similarity, and thus carried potentially important implications for the analysis of acquisition, transfer, interference, and long-term retention.

DEVELOPMENT OF THE INTERFERENCE THEORY OF FORGETTING

The systematic trends we have been discussing—the functionalist approach to experimental analysis and the formulation of specific hypotheses on the basis of principles of conditioning—are well illustrated in the development of the interference theory of forgetting. It is fair to say that it is in the methodical exploration of interference processes and of their role in forgetting that the functionalists made their most significant substantive contribution. The **interference theory** of forgetting emerged as a consequence of two converging trends: increasing doubts about the validity of the law of disuse, and mounting indications that it was retention rather than the consolidation of the trace that was impaired by interpolated activities.

Rejection of the Law of Disuse

We begin this brief survey of the development of the theory with an important paper published by McGeoch in 1932, entitled "Forgetting and the Law of Disuse." From this paper we learn how and why ideas about the relationship between retroactive inhibition and forgetting had changed since the days of Müller and Pilzecker.

Arguments Against the Law of Disuse. McGeoch's article was both a spirited attack on the law of disuse and an argument for a "positive explanation of forgetting," i.e., an explanation giving major weight to interference processes. His major objections to the law of disuse were as follows: (1) Even as a descriptive statement, the law lacks generality, as witness the spontaneous recovery of conditioned responses and reminiscence. (2) Reliance on disuse, i.e., the passage of time, as an explanatory principle is logically unsound. "Time, in and of itself, does nothing" (p. 359). The same point had been made earlier by others, e.g., Foucault (1913). (3) The amount of forgetting during a fixed interval of time can be influenced systematically by varying the conditions during that interval. It follows that disuse is not a major condition of forgetting. Rather, it must be the interpolated conditions that "constitute at least one major causative factor" (p. 360). This last point is the critical step in the argument, and it is supported by results of experiments on retroactive inhibition.

Interpolated Activities as a Cause of Forgetting. At the time McGeoch wrote this paper, a considerable number of experimental studies on **retroactive inhibition** was in hand which he used to document his conclusion. He referred first of all to the well known experiment by Jenkins and Dallenbach (1924) which showed that the retention of nonsense syllables was considerably higher after a period of sleep than after an equavalent period of wakefulness. The inference, of course, was that interference from the individual's waking activities was a more powerful determinant of forgetting than disuse.

Formal experiments on retroactive inhibition had produced abundant evidence that the amount of retroactive loss depends on the conditions of interpolation. In the spirit of functionalist analysis, the effects of many variables had been explored, including the degree of interpolated learning, the temporal locus of the interpolated activity during the retention interval, and above all the similarity between the original and the interpolated task. McGeoch did not discuss these early results in detail, nor do we do so here. The important point was that the amount of forgetting could be significantly influenced by manipulation of the conditions of interpolation.

McGeoch concluded that "disuse is, as such, utterly unimportant" (p. 364). Thus, he felt justified in advancing the hypothesis that "retroactive inhibition . . . is one of the major necessary conditions of forgetting" (ibid.). As a second condition of forgetting he added change in the stimulating context between acquisition and recall. He felt it necessary to propose this additional factor more on logical than empirical grounds: it must be taken as given that responses are associated not only to focal stimuli but also to the external and internal context.

Transfer Theory of Retroactive Inhibition

If retroactive inhibition is a major determinant of forgetting, what is the mechanism of interference that produces the retention loss? Much of McGeoch's later work focused on this question. The theory he developed (cf. McGeoch, 1936b, 1942) took its point of departure from the proposition that retroactive inhibition is a special case of **negative transfer.** This formulation was in accordance with his and other functionalists' disposition to classify phenomena of learning and memory in terms of experimental operations. The operations used in the measurement of transfer and of retroactive inhibition are clearly continuous; in both cases, the interaction between successive tasks is considered.

Specifically, McGeoch chose the A-B, A-D arrangement (in which different unrelated responses are learned to the same stimuli) as the reference paradigm for negative transfer and retroaction. He identified **response competition** as the common mechanism of interference which operates both during interpolated learning and at the time of recall. Competition between the old (B) and new (D) responses leads to negative transfer; after the new responses have been established, they compete with the old ones on the test of recall. The consequences of competition depend on the relative strengths of the alternative responses. Responses of approximately equal strength are likely to block each other. When the competing response is stronger, it may displace the correct one. Overt intrusions (e.g., substitution of D for B at recall) reflect the momentary dominance of the competing response.

Retroactive losses are thus attributed to **reproductive inhibition:** competition inhibits the reproduction of the appropriate response. An important assumption underlying this interpretation is that ''responses thus inhibited are not necessarily lost from the subject's repertoire'' (McGeoch, 1942, p. 495). That is, the two successive response systems remain independent and intact. This assumption came to be known as the **independence hypothesis.**

Two-Factor Theory

The independence assumption was an essential part of McGeoch's theory because he considered reproductive inhibition as the main, if not the only determinant of retroactive inhibition. Two responses can compete with each other only if they are both potentially available. However, if reproductive inhibition were not the sole mechanism of retroaction, the independence assumption can be relaxed: it need then apply to only that subset of responses that fail to be recalled because of competition. Just such a revision of McGeoch's theory was proposed in a widely known study by Melton and Irwin (1940).

The results that led Melton and Irwin to propose a revision of McGeoch's single-factor theory were obtained in an investigation of the relationship between the degree of interpolated learning and retroactive inhibition. The materials in the experiment were serial lists of nonsense syllables. With degree of original learning held constant, the amount of retroactive loss increased at a negatively accelerated rate as a function of the number of trials on the interpolated list. An application of McGeoch's hypothesis would attribute this trend to increasingly heavy response competition. If so, Melton and Irwin reasoned, overt intrusions

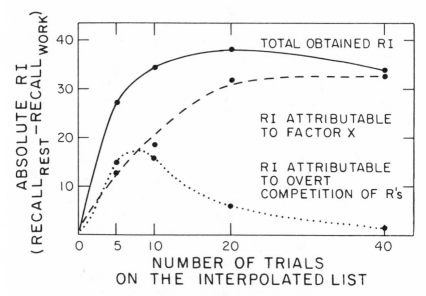

FIG. 3.6.   The two-factor theory of retroactive inhibition. The solid line shows the amount of retroactive inhibition as a function of the degree of interpolated learning. The dashed curves represent theoretical estimates of the relative contributions of unlearning and response competition to the observed retroactive losses. From Melton and Irwin (1940), p. 198.

which directly reflect response competition, should exhibit the same trend. As Figure 3.6 shows, such was not the case. The frequency of intrusions rose to a maximum (when interpolated learning was slightly higher than original learning) and then declined, while the amount of retroactive inhibition continued to increase.

Melton and Irwin concluded that response competition could not account for all the retroactive losses they had observed. There appeared to be a second mechanism, which assumed increasing importance as interpolated learning continued. They labeled this second mechanism "Factor X," and then suggested that it may represent the unlearning or extinction of the first-list associations during second-list learning. The analogy to extinction of conditioned responses appeared appropriate on the assumption that the original responses are elicited as errors during interpolated learning, fail to be reinforced, and thus are extinguished. Responses that escape extinction are subject to reproductive inhibition. Thus, the **two-factor theory** proposed by Melton and Irwin attributes retroactive inhibition to the operation of two mechanisms—**unlearning or extinction** on the one hand, and **response competition** or **reproductive inhibition** on the other. The theoretical functions shown in Figure 3.6 show the estimated contributions of the two factors to the total retroactive losses at different stages of interpolated learning.

The two-factor formulation became the definitive version of the classical interference theory of forgetting and had a profound impact on research in this area for many years. The continuing influence of two-factor theory is attributable in the first place to the fact that it generated important new hypotheses about the conditions of forgetting. As will become apparent shortly, the new deductions stemmed in large measure from the interpretation of unlearning as a process akin to extinction. Equally important in the long run, the theoretical inference that the availability of old associations is reduced during the acquisition of new ones later received strong empirical support. When subjects learn two successive lists conforming to the **A-B, A-D paradigm** and then are asked to reproduce *both* responses to each stimulus on an unpaced test of recall, heavy retroactive losses continue to be obtained (Barnes & Underwood, 1959). The test arrangements— recall of both responses without pressure of time—were designed to eliminate or minimize competition. The failure to recall a substantial proportion of the original responses thus provided direct evidence for unlearning.

Generalization and Interference

The transfer theory of interference was built upon a paradigm of stimulus identity (A-B, A-D). To account for interference between similar tasks, it was necessary to define similarity in terms of shared identical elements (McGeoch, 1942, p. 494). Such a treatment of similarity obviously lacked predictive power. This was a problem of old standing in the development of interference theory. In the 1920s, an attempt by Robinson to determine the empirical function relating interference to task similarity had proved unsuccessful.

As we saw earlier, it was precisely the effects of stimulus similarity that Gibson's generalization hypothesis was designed to explain. Thus, there were two parallel developments: the elaboration of the competition-of-response theory of transfer and retroaction by McGeoch, and Gibson's application to the same phenomena of the principles of generalization and differentiation. Both approaches had generated significant empirical data that awaited integration. That is what Osgood set out to do when he constructed his **transfer and retroaction surface.**

Response Generalization.   Osgood recognized that Gibson's theory was incomplete because it focused exclusively on stimulus generalization and took no account of relationships among responses. In a paper published in 1946, he proceeded to extend the application of the concept of generalization to verbal responses. According to his model, the excitatory strength accruing to a particular word spreads to other words along a dimension of meaningful similarity. The generalization is assumed to be mediated by "meaning reactions" conditioned to the words in the course of the individual's linguistic history. The more similar the meaning reaction to two words, the higher is the degree of response generalization between them. Osgood added the assumption that concurrently with the growth of excitatory potential for a particular meaning reaction there is a build-up of inhibition for the directly opposite or antagonistic meaning reaction, e.g., the reaction representing an antonym. Inhibitory tendencies, like excitatory ones, generalize along dimensions of meaningful similarity. While Osgood (1946, 1948) obtained evidence for response generalization, the gradients were not regular, nor was the inhibition postulate supported.

The Transfer and Retroaction Surface.   Osgood's (1949) surface representing the joint effects of stimulus and of response similarity on transfer and retroaction is shown in Figure 3.7. Variations along the stimulus dimension (from identity through similarity to neutrality) are plotted from front to back; variations along the response dimension (extending all the way from identity to antagonism) are plotted from left to right. The direction and amount of transfer or retroaction are presented on the vertical axis. The specific forms of the functions plotted along the edges were intended to accommodate a wide range of existing empirical findings. Two general principles reflected in the surface are that (a) transfer and retroaction occur only when there is some similarity between stimuli, and (b) the direction and magnitude of the effects are a function of response similarity.

Historically, Osgood's surface was an important forward step in the systematic analysis of transfer and interference. It served to accommodate within a single framework McGeoch's identity paradigm, Gibson's principle of stimulus generalization, and Osgood's own principle of response generalization. This evalua-

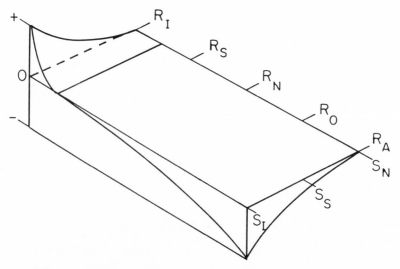

FIG. 3.7.   Osgood's transfer and retroaction surface. From Osgood (1949), p. 140. For explanation, see text.

tion is not seriously diminished by the fact that specific predictions derived from the surface never received strong empirical support. In retrospect, this failure can be seen as inevitable because the analysis considers only the relationships between forward associations in successive tasks. It later became clear that there are other subprocesses that play a significant role in transfer and retroaction, in particular, backward associations and response learning. Surfaces modeled after Osgood's were subsequently constructed for these other subprocesses (Martin, 1965).

Expansion of Interference Theory: Proactive Inhibition

When interference was pitted against disuse as a major determinant of forgetting, the only experimentally established condition of interference was retroactive inhibition. Thus, theories of interference were theories of retroactive inhibition. When another condition of interference—**proactive inhibition**—was discovered (Whiteley, 1927; Whiteley & Blankenship, 1936), it first received relatively little attention. This situation changed with the advent of two-factor theory, which provided a systematic framework for the analysis of the mechanisms of proactive as well as retroactive inhibition. According to the theory, both unlearning and response competition contribute to retroaction. In a proactive situation, however, only one of these factors can come into play. There is no possibility of unlearning because retention is measured for the task learned last; hence, whatever interference is found must be the result of response competition only. It follows that retroactive inhibition must exceed proactive inhibition. This deduction was confirmed by Melton and von Lackum (1941) who compared retroactive losses immediately after the end of interpolated learning with proactive losses after an equivalent brief interval.

The picture turned out to be quite different when progressive temporal changes in retroaction and proaction came to be examined. This work was prompted by Melton and Irwin's suggestion that unlearning has the functional properties of extinction. If so, then unlearned associations should show spontaneous recovery over time, just as do extinguished conditioned responses. Underwood (1948) was the first to recognize this important implication of the unlearning hypothesis: Retroactive inhibition should decrease—recall of the original associations should improve—as the interval from the end of interpolated learning is lengthened. Proactive inhibition should increase concomitantly; as the original associations recover, they enter into effective competition with those acquired later.

Both predictions about temporal changes in the two types of interference have received empirical support. The weight of the evidence supports the conclusion that unlearning is, indeed, a reversible process (see Brown, 1976, for a review). As for proactive inhibition, it does develop over time. What is now in doubt, however, is that these temporal changes are the manifestations of a common underlying process. Mechanisms other than the recovery of competing associations probably play an important role in producing proactive inhibition, e.g., a loss of the ability to differentiate at the time of recall between the most recently learned task and prior ones. Taken literally, the conditioning analogy is surely invalid; viewed in historical perspective, it had considerable heuristic value, if for no other reason than because it focused attention on proactive inhibition as a potentially powerful determinant of forgetting.

Cumulative Proactive Inhibition.   The damaging effects of proactive inhibition on long-term retention can be drastic indeed when interference from multiple prior tasks is allowed to accumulate. Impressive demonstrations of this fact have come from experiments in which the subjects go through successive cycles of learning and later recalling lists in the laboratory. As the experimental sessions continue, speed of acquisition usually increases; in sharp contrast, the amount retained after an interval of time declines progressively. In this situation, then, the rate of forgetting depends much more on the learning activities preceding the critical task than those filling the retention interval. Proactive inhibition here carries greater weight in determining the amount of retention loss than does retroactive inhibition.

Cumulative proactive inhibition provides the explanation for the massive amounts of forgetting observed by Ebbinghaus and many of his successors. Persuasive support for this interpretation was obtained by Underwood (1957) in

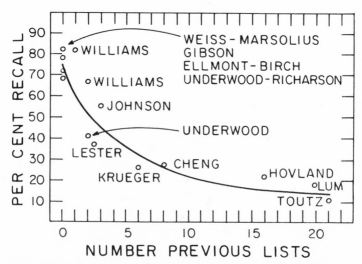

FIG. 3.8.   The effects of cumulative proactive inhibition on the retention of lists learned in the laboratory. Percentage recalled is plotted as a function of the number of prior lists learned in the same experiment. Each point represents a study in which original learning was to a criterion of one perfect recitation, and recall was tested after 24 hours. From Underwood (1957), p. 53.

an analysis of the results of many different experiments that had appeared in the literature over the years. The results of his analysis are shown in Figure 3.8. The percentage of recall for a list learned in the laboratory shows a steady and orderly decline as a function of the number of prior lists learned in the same experiment. A naive subject is likely to retain about 80%, whereas the score of a highly experienced subject may be as low as 20%. This brings us back full circle to the first measurements of forgetting by Ebbinghaus. His famous forgetting curve now carries a very different message.

Underwood's analysis of proactive inhibition marks the culmination of the classical interference theory of forgetting. We leave the theory here. In recent years some basic weaknesses of the theory have become apparent. In particular, attempts to apply the laws of interference established in the laboratory to forgetting outside the laboratory have so far met with little success. There has also been a growing debate about the basic assumptions of the theory, but this is a current controversy and not yet part of history.

GESTALT THEORY OF MEMORY

Experimental research on memory began with the investigations of the acquisition and retention of verbal associations. More than 50 years later, the new theories derived from principles of conditioning still focused on the same class of problems. This is not to say, however, that there were no challenges to the associationistic position in the intervening years. Quite on the contrary, as the "established" doctrine, association theory was the prime target for dissenters from the classical tradition. The most articulate exponents of an opposing point of view were the gestalt psychologists. In the history of ideas about learning and memory, few if any conflicts have been as persistent and apparently irreconcilable as that between associationists and gestaltists.

Principles of Organization

The theoretical conflict is succinctly expressed in the contrast between the *principles of association and organization*. What one side saw as the products of association, the other attributed to organization. Gestalt psychology began as a theory of perception, a revolt against the traditional doctrine that perceptions can be understood as combinations of sensory elements. Perceptions, the theory held, are the outcomes of organizational processes in the brain that are activated by sensory stimulation. The perceptual field is structured, with figures segregated against a ground, because organization tends toward stability. Maximal stability is established when the perceptual forms are "good," i.e., well articulated, simple, and symmetrical.

How a perceptual field is structured depends on the relations among its component parts: Other things being equal, parts that are adjacent are likely to be grouped together, and so are parts that are similar. (Note that the familiar laws of contiguity and similarity surface here as principles of perceptual organization.) Within the constraints of external stimulation, perceptual groupings will exhibit good continuation and closure, i.e., lines and curves will follow their natural course and figures will be closed rather than open. More generally, perceptual organization will conform to the **Law of Prägnanz:** "Psychological organization will always be as 'good' as the prevailing conditions allow" (Koffka, 1935, p. 110), where "good" refers to such properties as simplicity and symmetry.

Trace Theory

Our main interest here, of course, is in the gestalt theory of memory. As the analysis shifts from perception to memory, organization remains the governing principle. The key assumption of the theory is that each perception leaves a *neural trace,* and that the system of traces is governed by the same laws of organization as are the perceptions themselves. This hypothesis has two major implications: (a) The interactions among traces and the temporal changes in the trace system conform to the principles of organization, and in particular to the Law of Prägnanz. (b) The interaction or "communication" of ongoing perceptual processes with memory traces are governed by the same laws of organization. Recall and recognition are the product of process-trace communication.

The theory is stated in very broad terms. In practice, the principles of organization applied to memory phenomena have varied widely from one situation to the next. A good way to gain an understanding of the theory, therefore, is to consider some selected experimental findings that have been offered in its support. In tracing the development of this work, we draw primarily on the writings of Köhler (1929, 1940, 1947) and Koffka (1935).

The Isolation Effect. We consider first the proposition that the memory traces of separate events interact and form new structures in accordance with the principles of organization. One implication of this view is that the traces of homogeneous sequences of elements should be grouped together in the trace field, just as are similar elements in the perceptual field. That is, larger trace fields are formed, in which the individual elements lose their identity. It follows that isolated items in an homogeneous series, i.e., items that differ qualitatively from the remainder of the material, should have a considerable advantage in retention. The traces of such isolated items would not be absorbed into the larger trace field and thus maintain their identity. This hypothesis was tested in a classical study by von Restorff (1933).

In one of her experiments, von Restorff presented to her subjects lists comprising three types of pairs—syllables, geometric figures, and numbers. In any given list, there were six pairs of one type (e.g., syllables) and one pair each of the other two types (e.g., figures and numbers). As expected, the probability of cued recall was far higher for isolated than for crowded items. In further experiments, von Restorff extended her analysis to interlist interference. She showed that the recall of isolated items is greatly reduced if subsequent or prior lists contain a number of units belonging to the same class. These retroactive and proactive losses were attributed to the aggregation of similar traces.

It is important to bear in mind that the effects on memory observed in these experiments were not attributed to perceptual organization at the time of input but rather to dynamic processes in the trace system, specifically the aggregation of traces of similar items. A perceptual explanation was ruled out because the isolated unit appeared in the second or third position in the series, i.e., before a background of homogeneous items had been established. Thus, the locus of isolation must be in the trace system.

While the **isolation effect** is consistent with the gestalt theory of traces, it can also be predicted on the basis of principles of interference. In terms of Gibson's analysis, an isolated stimulus has the advantage that its generalizes less with other items in the list than do the homogeneous stimuli. In fact, Gibson (1940) included the isolation effect among the specific predictions derived from her hypothesis. Gibson, of course, was concerned only with stimulus differentiation, but the argument can be, and has been, extended to response differentiation (Newman & Saltz, 1958). The literature on the von Restorff phenomenon contains numerous attempts to evaluate the gestalt and interference hypotheses, and to pit them against each other. As Wallace's (1965) careful review of this research shows, the empirical findings have been far from consistent and at times contradictory. For present purposes, the important point is that the isolation effect did not constitute decisive evidence for the gestalt hypothesis any more than for the generalization hypothesis.

Temporal Changes in Memory for Form.   Now consider the hypothesis that traces will change progressively over time in accordance with the Law of Prägnanz. Consequently, the trace left by weakly organized percepts should progressively move in the direction of a better form. This prediction, which embodies the key assumptions of the gestalt theory of memory, was tested in a classical investigation by Wulf (1922).

Wulf's stimulus materials consisted of abstract line drawings, all of which violated the principles of simplicity and symmetry. In each of several experimental sessions, a few (two to four) patterns were shown to the subject for 5-10 seconds. Thirty seconds after inspecting a figure, the subject reproduced it. Additional reproductions were obtained from the same subjects after 24 hours, after one week, and occasionally also after 2 months.

In virtually all cases, the reproductions showed changes from the original which Wulf classified under three headings: (a) normalization, (b) pointing, and

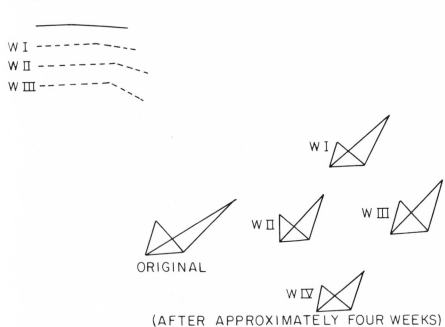

FIG. 3.9. Two of Wulf's figures and successive reproductions (W's) by a subject. Both designs were labeled "envelope." From Ellis (1938), p. 142.

(c) autonomous changes. **Normalization** occurred when the design was altered so as to increase its resemblance to a familiar object. **Pointing** was said to occur when some part or feature of the figures was accentuated. **Autonomous changes** presumably reflected the operation of dynamic forces intrinsic to the design. These classes of change are not mutually exclusive. For example, the designs shown in Figure 3.9 were both designated as an "envelope" by a subject. Each of them was normalized, in one case through pointing (sharpening of the angle), in the other through an increase in symmetry. The latter change could also be reasonably classified as autonomous since symmetry is a principle of organization. To highlight the occurrence of dynamic transformations, Wulf singled out as autonomous those changes that ran counter to normalization. Whatever the nature of the changes in a given figure, Wulf claimed that they were progressive, becoming more pronounced over time.

On the face of it, normalization is not a gestalt principle but on the contrary suggests that associative processes systematically influence retention. Wulf disposed of this difficulty by arguing that familiar objects are usually stable forms. "Pointing" was likewise interpreted as a special case of organizational change: An optimally balanced pattern is sometimes achieved by selective emphasis on a particular aspect of the figure.

It is apparent that Wulf took the validity of the Law of Prägnanz for granted. What constitutes a stable organization was essentially inferred from the subjects' reproductions. Wulf firmly rejected an alternative interpretation of memory changes proposed by Müller. According to Müller, the memory trace becomes progressively less distinct over time. Consequently, qualitative and quantitative differences among parts of the object are obliterated; however, features that receive special attention in perception remain a distinctive part of the trace and are emphasized in recall. Wulf viewed his results as a conclusive refutation of Müller's position because successive reproductions were not characterized by increasing vagueness but rather by the growing salience of structural characteristics of the pattern.

In studying memory for form, Wulf worked with materials to which the principles of perceptual organization apply quite directly, rather than by analogy as in the case of verbal series. Thus, his investigation brought the gestalt theory of memory into sharp focus, and it was probably for this reason that it became the starting point of a long controversy which extended over many years. This controversy centered as much on methodological as on theoretical issues and was given momentum by the demonstration of serious deficiencies in Wulf's experiment. Several major difficulties were brought out in a series of studies by Hanawalt (1937), in which he used Wulf's figures as the stimulus materials. Hanawalt's critical findings included the following:

1. Deviations of the reproductions from the stimulus patterns often do not represent memory changes, but rather have their origin in the initial perceptions, as revealed in subjects' copies of the stimulus figures.
2. A reproduction is a highly fallible index of the state of the trace. Having to choose between changed reproductions resembling their own and the original designs, subjects more often than not preferred the latter.
3. Earlier reproductions systematically influence later ones. As compared to results obtained when separate groups are tested after each interval, repeated testing serves to enhance the number and to reduce the variability of the reproductions. As Woodworth (1938) commented, "We cannot observe the state of a memory trace without letting it act and so strengthening and perhaps distorting it and altering its subsequent history" (p. 91).
4. Even on repeated tests, changes are only occasionally progressive. It may be noted in passing that a reexamination of Wulf's own protocols showed his classification of changes as progressive to be highly debatable in the majority of cases (Woodworth, 1938, p. 89).

Hanawalt's analysis illustrates the empirical uncertainties and the methodological difficulties that have beset experimental tests of the gestalt theory of memory for form. In 1938, after reviewing the already substantial literature available at the time, Woodworth concluded that "Evidence for any progressive change in the direction of better figure is extremely meager, and evidence for real forgetting is abundant" (p. 91).

That is not the end of the story. During the next two decades, persistent attempts were made to overcome the methodological obstacles and to devise an appropriate test of Wulf's hypothesis. To avoid the biases inherent in methods of reproduction, investigators turned increasingly to tests of recognition and to psychophysical procedures such as successive comparison. The history of this research is given in a comprehensive review by Riley (1962), and we do not pursue it here. Suffice it to say that the objective of devising a crucial test of the hypothesis, equally acceptable to proponents and opponents of gestalt theory, proved elusive. With this reservation in mind, it is fair to say that the weight of the evidence remained on the negative side.

Process-Trace Communication

One of the principal tenets of gestalt theory is that laws of organization govern the communication between present perceptual processes and traces. Hence, recognition and recall, which require such communication, are organizational processes sui generis. Specifically, the activation of a trace by a process is considered as a special case of grouping or unit formation in accordance with the principle of similarity. The communication occurs most readily if trace and process are not only similar but also form a distinctive unit, one that stands out as a figure against a homogeneous background.

To demonstrate the influence of such "distinctive similarity" on process-trace communication, Köhler and his associates (Bartel, 1937; Köhler & von Restorff, 1935) carried out a series of experiments on "spontaneous recall," i.e., recall that occurs without any intention on the part of the subject to retrieve past information. They assumed that the degree of distinctive similarity between process and trace is the primary determinant of spontaneous recall, whereas other factors are likely to come into play as well when recall is intentional.

The following experiment by Köhler and von Restorff illustrates the logic of these investigations. In the initial phase of the procedure, the subjects worked on a series of computational problems. The last of these could be solved quickly by application of a familiar formula. Most subjects failed to notice this possibility. After the problem had been worked out, the experimenter mentioned casually that a shortcut had been available. In the second half of the experiment, half the subjects continued to solve arithmetic problems (none of which called for the shortcut), whereas the other half worked on matchstick problems. In the final and critical phase, all subjects were asked to solve a problem to which the shortcut was once again applicable. It was expected that the subjects who had worked with matchsticks would spontaneously recall the shortcut more often than those who had been occupied with additional computational tasks. The degree of distinctive similarity between the process (final test problem) and the trace (information about the shortcut) would be greater in the former than in the latter case. This prediction was borne out. Variants on this procedure yielded comparable results.

Organization and Association

Gestalt psychologists, of course, did not dispute the raw empirical facts of associative learning. However, laws of association were rejected as explanatory principles because they failed to consider the nature of the associated terms. Once account is taken of the relationship between the terms which become connected, the formation of an association must be considered as a special case of organization. The principles of perceptual grouping determine the ease with which the organization is established. The law of contiguity appears to work because proximity is one of these principles. By the same token, similarity of the component terms facilitates organization.

An organized experience leaves an organized trace. From the gestalt point of view, therefore, the existence of an association reflects "coherence within the unitary trace of a unitary experience"(Köhler, 1944, p. 493). Once a trace is contacted through presentation of an appropriate cue, "this excitation will spread more easily within the trace than to other regions of the tissue" (ibid.). This view receives presumptive support if it can be shown that whatever factors make for stability of perceptual organization also favor associative learning. Numerous attempts were made to verify this proposition. To give just one example, Köhler (1944) showed that the ease with which two geometric forms were associated depended on how well they "fitted" each other, i.e., how regular a combination they formed. Such findings, however, are inherently difficult to interpret because the "goodness" of a combination is likely to be correlated with other properties, such as familiarity or ease of naming.

Gestalt psychologists had a very limited impact on the field of human learning and memory. One major reason is that they were inclined to use experiments more as demonstrations than as tests of the validity of their position. Thus, alternative explanations were given little consideration, and the concept of organization was unduly strained in post hoc explanations. Second, and perhaps more important, the findings offered in support of the theory, such as the isolation effect and the temporal changes in memory for form, were amenable to interpretations within the framework of association theory. All this is not to imply that associationists never took doctrinaire stands or engaged in post hoc explanations of their results. However, it is a truism that a weak theory will survive until it is replaced by a stronger one. If association theory was weak, gestalt theory was not sufficiently strong to supersede it.

BARTLETT AND THE CONSTRUCTIVE THEORY OF
MEMORY

While the gestaltists replaced association with organization, much of their research remained within the laboratory tradition of the day. Like their opponents, they were prepared to assume that results obtained with artificial materials in highly controlled situations could yield conclusions applicable to the functioning of the memory system in "real life." This assumption was brought under powerful attack in a classical treatise that appeared in 1932, Bartlett's *Remembering: A Study in Experimental and Social Psychology*. In his research, Bartlett broke sharply with the prevailing methodology of rote learning. His objective was to study the conditions and functions of remembering in the everyday life of the individual; accordingly, he made a concerted effort to employ experimental arrangements that were as naturalistic as possible. In his theoretical analysis, he focused on the role of memory in cognitive functioning and in adjustment to the environment, and on the intimate relationship between intellectual processes and the interests and attitudes of the individual.

Studies of Perceiving and Imaging

A pervasive theme of Bartlett's analysis is the continuity of the processes of perceiving, imaging, and remembering. Thus, perception often involves recall, when the individual fills in gaps in what he has perceived on the basis of prior knowledge. What is remembered, in turn, depends on what has been perceived and is often modified by imagery. Bartlett thought it useful, therefore, to begin his investigations of remembering with experiments on perceiving and imaging.

In the studies of perception, a variety of stimulus materials was used, ranging from simple shapes to complex pictures. After a brief exposure, the subjects drew or described what they had seen. The reproductions and descriptions were rarely perfect. The changes that were introduced depended on the nature of the materials, but in the aggregate they suggested that perceiving is a constructive process. The subject reacts to the stimulus by establishing a setting or scheme into which it can be fitted, a setting that may actually be imaged. The details of the percept then emerge within this scheme, and much of what is reported is actually inferred. Within the overall scheme, some specific details often stand out. The specific changes made by individuals often appeared to reflect their interests and attitudes. To the extent that these personal dispositions persist over time, they may help to determine what is remembered.

The importance of interests and attitudes was even more clearly in evidence in the experiments on imaging, in which subjects were exposed to a series of inkblots and asked to describe what they saw in them. Topics reflecting a prevailing interest or mood often persisted from one stimulus to the next. There were also pronounced individual differences in style. The images of some observers were specific and detailed, those of others rarely had concrete referents. The results of the experiments on perceiving and imaging led Bartlett (1932) to suggest that "it is fitting to speak of every human cognitive reaction—perceiving, imaging, remembering, thinking, and reasoning—as an effort after meaning" (p. 44). The individual tries to make sense of the situation with which he is confronted, to relate it to something else that he knows, to fit it into a pre-existing scheme. Achievement of meaning is thus a constructive activity; in remembering, this activity focuses on a specific past event. The experiments on remembering reported in the book were designed to lay bare some of the ways in which individuals go about the task of reconstructing their earlier experiences.

Experiments on Remembering

In his experiments, Bartlett attempted to use materials that would be intelligible and interesting to the subjects, and which did not require unusual modes of processing. On the tests of retention, all the subject was required to do was to reproduce what he could remember. The data were collected in a rather informal manner; for example, delayed reproductions were obtained not after fixed intervals but whenever an opportunity presented itself. We summarize here two of his studies, the best known of his series, that illustrate well his style of experimenting and his theoretical concerns.

Method of Repeated Reproduction.   We encountered this method before in the studies of memory for form. The subject receives an initial exposure to the stimulus material, and then reproduces it repeatedly at spaced intervals. What is of interest in Bartlett's research is the type of materials he used and the conclusions he drew from the results. The subject studied either a story or an "argumentative prose passage," or a drawing, and gave his first reproduction after 15 minutes. Further reproductions followed after intervals of increasing length (which varied from one subject to the next). Bartlett's objective was to trace the progressive changes that normal individuals introduce into remembered material over time.

The protocols presented in the book all come from reproductions of a North American folk tale, entitled "The War of the Ghosts." It is an allegorical story about the adventures of a young Indian warrior, rather disjointed and enigmatic for a Western reader, with supernatural elements. Bartlett chose this story precisely because of its strange quality and apparent lack of rational order, which were likely to result in substantial transformations.

The expectation that the story would undergo drastic transformations over time was fully borne out. When the reproductions were relatively infrequent, the changes continued to evolve over time and included "omission of detail, sim-

FIG. 3.10. The transformations of a figure in the course of serial reproduction. From Bartlett (1932), pp. 180 f.

plification of events and structure, and transformation of items into more familiar detail'' (Bartlett, 1932, p. 93). When the reproductions were closely spaced, the changes quickly became stereotyped. Outstanding details, although sometimes transformed to conform to the subject's interests and expectations, tended to be highly persistent.

Method of Serial Reproduction.   This is the "rumor method" that had previously been used in investigations of testimony (cf. Whipple, 1909). Subject A is exposed to the stimulus materials, A's reproduction is presented to B, B's reproduction is presented to C, and so on. The method is designed to demonstrate the cumulative effects of social and cultural factors on remembering. Bartlett obtained chains of reproductions for both verbal passages and pictures.

The verbal passages included "The War of the Ghosts" and other tales, as well as stories of strictly local interest to a British audience, e.g., "Fine Batting at Lord's," and "The Art of Lawn Tennis." The cumulative changes were so drastic that the final product usually bore little resemblance to the original. Here are some of the major directions of change identified by Bartlett: (a) There was a strong bias toward making the material concrete. (b) In general, the passages lost their distinctive characteristics and became conventionalized. (c) Abbreviation of the text was the rule. (d) The material was often rationalized so that "an ordinary member of a given social group will accept it without questioning" (p. 175).

In the serial reproduction of pictorial material, changes in the direction of simple and conventional forms are likewise prevalent. However, if simplification is carried too far, representational meaning is restored by a process of elaboration. Such a cycle is illustrated in Figure 3.10, where the original picture of an owl gradually loses its identity but ends up as a reasonably well defined drawing of a cat.

Bartlett's Theory of Memory

The key principle of Bartlett's theory is that remembering does not reflect the reexcitation of fixed traces and is not reproductive in character; rather it is *a constructive process*. The construction is guided by schemata. By a **schema** Bartlett meant "an active organization of past reactions, or of past experiences" (p. 201), which serves as a framework for orderly new responses. Schemata are established at different levels of functioning; they can encompass experiences pertaining to intellectual interests as well as to specific sensory modalities. Yet schemata are not fixed. "They have to be regarded as constituents of living, momentary settings belonging to the organism" (ibid.).

Bartlett's description of the schematic determination of remembering was somewhat obscure. He assumed that a schema is built up in chronological order and includes the past events that one is trying to recall at any given moment. But remembering is not simply retracing the past through a schema. The organism must find a way of "turning round upon its own 'schemata' . . . and rove more or less at will in any order over the events which have built up its present momentary 'schemata' " (pp. 202 f.). This is what Bartlett believed to be the essence of remembering; the organism turns round upon its own schemata and constructs them afresh. Guided by an impression or "attitude" toward the past event, the individual fills in its probable features. Outstanding details that persist are those that were originally valued most highly in relation to the schema operating at the time of perception. A likely outcome of this process is a rationalized and conventionalized construction.

Bartlett's research, if not the details of his schema theory, had a significant and lasting impact on the field. It became a principal point of departure for those who wanted to make research on memory more realistic and "ecologically valid," to study remembering for materials that were representative of the individual's real-life experiences. It is not clear, however, that Bartlett's work was an optimal model for such research. He highlighted the proneness of the memory system to error and distortion at the expense of its capacity to function veridically and accurately. His experimental results almost inevitably fostered support of such an unbalanced view. While he set out to assess memory for normal, real-life experiences, much of the material he used was actually unfamiliar if not puzzling to his subjects, as witness the famous "The War of the Ghosts." Even when the material was familiar and conventional, the amount of study time allowed was usually quite limited. There was no attempt to press for accuracy on the tests of retention. The method of repeated reproduction, which yielded some of his most telling results, by its very nature promoted the perpetuation of errors.

Thus, as Zangwill (1972, p. 128) put it in a restrospective evaluation of Bartlett's work, ". . . both the material . . . and the circumstances in which recall was demanded in his experiments may well have conspired to produce greater inaccuracy than occurs normally." Zangwill cited numerous experimental findings in support of this conclusion. Even in reproductions of "The War of the Ghosts," accuracy increases markedly when subjects were instructed to avoid errors (Gauld & Stephenson, 1967). In the recall of prose passages of varying length, by far the most common errors are omissions rather than inventions (Gomulicki, 1956). When verbatim recall is impossible, the reproduction takes the form of a summary or precis. The implication is that "remembering is better described as an abstractive than constructive process" (Zangwill, 1972, p. 128). Furthermore, just as in the case of Wulf's figures, a reproduction cannot be assumed to reflect faithfully all the information that remains in store. On a test of recognition for short stories, subjects frequently reject the changed versions they had reproduced in favor of the originals (Zangwill, 1939).

All this is not to say that the types of changes and distortions Bartlett described do not occur frequently in daily remembering. They undoubtedly do, but so do accurate recall and recognition. In challenging the generality and validity of the rote-learning paradigm, Bartlett went to the other extreme. He wrote a theory of misremembering rather than of remembering.

CONCLUSION

The stage was set for experimental research on human learning and memory with the publication of Ebbinghaus' treatise. His experimental paradigm was quickly adopted, extended, and refined. Thus, the tradition of research on rote learning was soon firmly established. At the same time, however, our survey shows clearly that Ebbinghaus' paradigm did not dominate or constrain the development of the field in its early years. Not only were many new methods of measurement and types of materials introduced in rapid succession, but the kinds of questions that were asked about memory soon began to move in different directions. Unlike Ebbinghaus, many investigators were unwilling to discard as futile the analysis of memory consciousness (Kuhlmann, 1908). Thus, they proceeded to study the immediate and short-term retention of "simple" as well as "complex" materials (Kennedy, 1898). While they learned little of lasting value about memory consciousness, the experimental procedures they introduced added greatly to the breadth of the field.

Although it is sometimes suggested that memory research in later years remained an extension and elaboration of Ebbinghaus' work, such was clearly not the case. The rote learning of nonsense syllables did become one of the common laboratory tasks, but only one. There was little uniformity with respect to materials, methods of measurement, and experimental manipulations. By contrast, the theoretical situation remained largely static. The language of association theory continued to be widely used; for the most part, experimenters sought to explore the operation of principles of association rather than to test the principles themselves.

Thus, it was still under the auspices of classical association theory that the psychology of verbal learning and memory entered a new period of growth and development in the period between the two World Wars. It was to be an era in which the lingering ties to philosophical associationism and introspectionist psychology were deliberately and definitively severed. In an intellectual climate profoundly influenced by the behaviorist methodological revolution and the functionalist concern with the adaptive significance of learning, the study of associative processses moved steadily in the direction of objective experimental operations and precise quantitative analysis; the identification of the underlying mechanisms of association in specific learning situations became a central focus of inquiry.

In this theoretical climate, research on human learning and memory fanned out in many directions. As we reach the mid-century mark, we are confronted with a voluminous technical literature ranging over a wide variety of topics, a literature rich in empirical information but loose in structure. We can get a good sense of the status of the field at that time by turning to *The Psychology of Human Learning*, the authoritative textbook by McGeoch and Irion, which appeared in 1952. (This is a revision of McGeoch's book published 10 years earlier.) Here are the major topics covered in the book: Intraserial phenomena, distribution of practice and reminiscence, transfer of training, retention and forgetting, the effects of materials and modes of practice and presentation, individual differences. We also find chapters on learning as a function of motive-incentive conditions and on the law of effect; in these sections, the influence of Thorndike is still very much in evidence.

But seeds of profound revision had already been sown, and research in the area was to undergo a rapid transformation during the next few decades. Of course, there has been continuity as well as change. Research in such classical areas as associative learning, transfer, and long-term retention has continued and progressively gained in precision. Old problems, like distribution of practice, are being explored intensively under new experimental arrangements. Still, there is no question that there has been a major conceptual shift—from laws of association and conditioning to principles of information processing, from empirical functions to structural and mathematical models. The pervasive changes in terminology reflect these developments. Investigators today are likely to formulate their experimental questions with reference to the theoretical stages of encoding, storage, and retrieval, rather than to inquire, in the manner of the functionalists, about the conditions of acquisition, retention, and recall. With these changes in orientation, the center of gravity has moved to what Tulving and Madigan (1970) aptly described as the "subculture" of memory, as distinct from that of verbal learning. And within memory, the bulk of experimental effort in recent years has been devoted to the fine-grained analysis of short-term rather than long-term processes.

REFERENCES

Angell, J. R. The province of functional psychology. *Psychological Review*, 1907, *14*, 61–91.

Aristotle. *Basic works*. Translation edited by R. McKeon. New York: Random House, 1941.

Ballard, P. A. Obliviscence and reminiscence. *British Journal of Psychology Monograph Supplements*, 1913, *1*, 1–18.

Barnes, J. M., & Underwood, B. J. "Fate" of first-list associations in transfer theory. *Journal of Experimental Psychology*, 1959, *58*, 97–105.

Bartel, H. Ueber die Abhängigkeit spontaner Reproduktionen von Feldbedingungen. *Psychologische Forschung*, 1937, *22*, 1–25.

Bartlett, F. C. *Remembering: a study in experimental and social psychology*. Cambridge: University Press, 1932.

Bentley, I. M. The memory image and its qualitative fidelity. *American Journal of Psychology*, 1899, *11*, 1–48.

Bigham, J. Memory: studies from Harvard (II). *Psychological Review*, 1894, *1*, 453–461.

Binet, A. *La suggestibilité.* Paris: Schleicher Frères, 1900.

Binet, A. La science du témoignage. *L'Année Psychologique,* 1905, *11,* 128–137.

Binet, A., & Henri, V. La mémoire des mots. *L'Année Psychologique,* 1894, *1,* 1–23. (a)

Binet, A., & Henri, V. La mémoire des phrases. *L'Année Psychologique,* 1894, *1,* 24–59. (b)

Blankenship, A. B. Memory span: a review of the literature. *Psychological Bulletin,* 1938, *35,* 1–25.

Book, W. F. *The psychology of skill.* Missoula: Montana Press, 1908.

Boring, E. G. Review of Robinson's *Association theory to-day. Psychological Bulletin,* 1933, *30,* 451–455.

Boring, E. G. *A history of experimental psychology,* 2nd ed. New York: Appleton-Century-Crofts, 1950.

Brown, A. S. Spontaneous recovery in human learning. *Psychological Bulletin,* 1976, *83,* 321–338.

Bryan, W. L., & Harter, N. Studies in the physiology and psychology of the telegraphic language. *Psychological Review,* 1897, *4,* 27–53.

Bryan, W. L., & Harter, N. Studies on the telegraphic language. The acquisition of a hierarchy of habits. *Psychological Review,* 1899, *6,* 345–375.

Buchwald, A. M. Effects of "right" and "wrong" on subsequent behavior. *Psychological Review,* 1969, *76,* 132–143.

Calkins, M. W. Association. *Psychological Review,* 1894, *1,* 476–483.

Calkins, M. W. Association: An essay analytical and experimental. *Psychological Monographs,* 1896, No. 2.

Calkins, M. W. Short studies in memory and in association from the Wellesley College Psychological Laboratory. *Psychological Review,* 1898, *5,* 451–462.

Cohn, J. Experimentelle Untersuchungen über das Zusammenwirken des akustisch-motorischen und des visuellen Gedaächtnisses. *Zeitschrift für Psychologie,* 1897, *15,* 161–184.

Craik, F. I. M. The fate of primary items in free recall. *Journal of Verbal Learning and Verbal Behavior,* 1970, *9,* 143–148.

Ellis, W. D. (Ed.) *A source book of gestalt psychology.* London: Routledge & Kegan Paul, 1938.

Ebbinghaus, H. *Ueber das Gedächtnis: Untersuchungen zur experimentellen Psychologie.* Leipzig: Duncker & Humblot, 1885. (Translated by H. A. Ruger & C. E. Bussenius as *Memory: A contribution to experimental psychology.* New York: Teachers College, Columbia University, 1913.)

Finkenbinder, E. O. The curve of forgetting. *American Journal of Psychology,* 1913, *24,* 8–32.

Fischer, A. Ueber Reproduzieren und Wiedererkennen bei Gedächtnisversuchen. *Zeitschrift für Psychologie,* 1909, *50,* 62–92.

Foucault, M. Introduction à la psychologie de la perception. Expériences sur l'oubli ou sur l'inhibition régressive. *Revue des Cours et Conférences,* 1913, *21,* 444–454.

Gamble, E. A. McC. A study of memorizing various materials by the reconstruction method. *Psychological Monographs,* 1909, No. 43.

Gates, A. I. Recitation as a factor in memorizing. *Archives of Psychology,* 1917, *6,* No. 40.

Gauld, A., & Stephenson, G. M. Some experiments relating to Bartlett's theory of remembering. *British Journal of Psychology,* 1967, *58,* 39–49.

Gibson, E. J. A systematic application of the concepts of generalization and differentiation to verbal learning. *Psychological Review,* 1940, *47,* 196–229.

Gibson, E. J. Retroactive inhibition as a function of degree of generalization between tasks. *Journal of Experimental Psychology,* 1941, *28,* 93–115.

Gibson, E. J. Intra-list generalization as a factor in verbal learning. *Journal of Experimental Psychology,* 1942, *30,* 185–200.

Goldstein, K. Merkfähigkeit, Gedächtnis und Assoziation. *Zeitschrift für Psychologie,* 1906, *41,* 38–47; 117–144.

Gomulicki, B. R. Recall as an abstractive process. *Acta Psychologica,* 1956, *12,* 77–94.

Guilford, J. P., & Dallenbach, K. M. The determination of memory span by the method of constant stimuli. *American Journal of Psychology*, 1925, *36*, 621–628.

Hamilton, R. J. Retroactive facilitation as a function of degree of generalization between tasks. *Journal of Experimental Psychology*, 1943, *32*, 363–376.

Hanawalt, N. G. Memory trace for figures in recall and recognition. *Archives of Psychology*, 1937, *31*, No. 216.

Hilgard, E. R. *Theories of learning*, 2nd ed. New York: Appleton-Century-Crofts, 1956.

Hovland, C. I. Experimental studies in rote-learning theory. I. Reminiscence following learning by massed and by distributed practice. *Journal of Experimental Psychology*, 1938, *22*, 201–224. (a)

Hovland, C. I. Experimental studies in rote-learning theory. II. Reminiscence with varying speeds of syllable presentation. *Journal or Experimental Psychology*, 1938, *22*, 338–353. (b)

Hull, C. L. The conflicting psychologies of learning—a way out. *Psychological Review*, 1935, *42*, 491–516.

Hull, C. L., Hovland, C. I., Ross, R. T., Hall, M., Perkins, D. T., & Fitch, F. G. *Mathematico-deductive theory of rote-learning: a study in scientific methodology*. New Haven: Yale University Press, 1940.

Jacobs, J. Experiments of "prehension." *Mind*, 1887, *12*, 75–79.

James, W. *The principles of psychology*. New York: Holt, 1890.

Jenkins, J. G., & Dallenbach, K. M. Obliviscence during sleep and waking. *American Journal of Psychology*, 1924, *35*, 605–612.

Jost, A. Die Associationsfertigkeit in ihrer Abhängigkeit von der Verteilung der Wiederholungen. *Zeitschrift für Psychologie*, 1897, *14*, 436–472.

Kennedy, F. On the experimental investigation of memory. *Psychological Review*, 1898, *5*, 477–499.

Kintsch, W. Models for free recall and recognition. In D. A. Norman (Ed.), *Models of human memory*. New York: Academic Press, 1970.

Kirkpatrick, G. A. An experimental study of memory. *Psychological Review*, 1894, *1*, 602–609.

Koffka, K. *Principles of Gestalt Psychology*. New York: Harcourt, Brace, & Co., 1935.

Köhler, W. *Gestalt psychology*. New York: Liveright, 1929.

Köhler, W. *Dynamics in psychology*. New York: Liveright, 1940.

Köhler, W. On the nature of associations. *Proceedings of the American Philosophical Society*, 1944, *84*, 489–502.

Köhler, W. *Gestalt psychology*, revised edition. New York: Liveright, 1947.

Köhler, W., & Von Restorff, H. Analyse von Vorgängen im Spurenfeld. *Psychologische Forschung*, 1935, *21*, 56–112.

Kuhlmann, F. The present status of memory investigation. *Psychological Bulletin*, 1908, *5*, 285–293.

Lepley, W. M. Serial reactions considered as conditioned reactions. *Psychological Monographs*, 1934, *46*, No. 205.

Martin, E. Transfer of verbal paired associates. *Psychological Review*, 1965, *72*, 327–343.

McDougall, R. Recognition and recall. *Journal of Philosophical Psychology and Scientific Methods*, 1904, *1*, 229–233.

McGeoch, G. O. Whole-part problem. *Psychological Bulletin*, 1931, *28*, 713–739.

McGeoch, J. A. Forgetting and the law of disuse. *Psychological Review*, 1932, *39*, 352–370.

McGeoch, J. A. The vertical dimensions of mind. *Psychological Review*, 1936, *43*, 107–129. (a)

McGeoch, J. A. Studies in retroactive inhibition: VII. Retroactive inhibition as a function of length and frequency of presentation of the interpolated lists. *Journal of Experimental Psychology*, 1936, *19*, 674–693. (b)

McGeoch, J. A. *The psychology of human learning*. New York: Longmans, Green, 1942.

McGeoch, J. A. & Irion, A. L. *The psychology of human learning*. New York: Longmans, Green, 1952.

Melton, A. W. Learning. In W. S. Monroe (Ed.), *Encyclopedia of Educational Research*. New York: Macmillan, 1941.

Melton, A. W. Learning. In W. S. Monroe (Ed.), *Encyclopedia of Educational Research*, revised edition. New York: Macmillan, 1950.

Melton, A. W., & Irwin, J. McQ. The influence of degree of interpolated learning on retroactive inhibition and the overt transfer of specific responses. *American Journal of Psychology*, 1940, *53*, 173–203.

Melton, A. W., & von Lackum, W. J. Retroactive and proactive inhibition in retention: evidence for a two-factor theory of retroactive inhibition. *American Journal of Psychology*, 1941, *54*, 157–173.

Meumann, E. *The psychology of learning*. New York: Appleton Company, 1913.

Müller, G. E. Zur Analyse der Gedächtnistätigkeit und des Vorstellungsverlaufes. *Zeitschrift für Psychologie*, Ergänzungsband, 1913, *8*, 1–567.

Müller, G. E., & Pilzecker, A. Experimentelle Beiträge zur Lehre vom Gedächtnis. *Zeitschrift für Psychologie*, Ergänzungsband, 1900, *1*, 1–300.

Müller, G. E. & Schumann, F. Experimentelle Beiträge zur Untersuchung des Gedächtnisses. *Zeitschrift für Psychologie*, 1894, *6*, 81–190.

Münsterberg, H. Die Assoziation successiver Vorstellungen. *Zeitschrift für Psychologie*, 1890, *1*, 99–107.

Münsterberg, H., & Bigham, J. Memory: studies from the Harvard Psychological Laboratory. *Psychological Review*, 1894, *1*, 34–38.

Murray, D. J. Research on human memory in the nineteenth century. *Canadian Journal of Psychology*, 1976, *30*, 201–220.

Myers, G. C. A study in incidental memory. *Archives of Psychology*, 1913, *4*, No. 26.

Netschajeff, A. Die Entwicklung des Gedächtnisses bei Schulkindern. *Zeitschrift für Psychologie*, 1900, *24*, 321–351.

Newman, S. E., & Saltz, E. Isolation effects: Stimulus and response generalization as explanatory concepts. *Journal of Experimental Psychology*, 1958, *55*, 467–472.

Osgood, C. E. Meaningful similarity and interference in learning. *Journal of Experimental Psychology*, 1946, *36*, 277–301.

Osgood, C. E. An investigation into the causes of retroactive inhibition. *Journal of Experimental Psychology*, 1948, *38*, 132–154.

Osgood, C. E. The similarity paradox in human learning: A resolution. *Psychological Review*, 1949, *56*, 132–143.

Perkins, N. L. The value of distributed repetitions in rote-learning. *British Journal of Psychology*, 1914, *7*, 253–261.

Poffenberger, A. T. The influences of improvement in one simple mental process upon other related processes. *Journal of Educational Psychology*, 1915, *6*, 459–474.

Pohlmann, A. *Experimentelle Beiträge zur Lehre vom Gedächtnis*. Berlin: Gerdes & Hödel, 1906.

Poppelreuter, W. Nachweis der Unzweckmässigkeit die gebräuchlichen Assoziationsexperimente mit sinnlosen Silben nach dem Erlernungs- und Treffer- verfahren zur exakten Gewinnung elementarer Reproduktionsgesetze zu verwenden. *Zeitschrift für Psychologie*, 1912, *61*, 1–24.

Pyle, W. H. Concentrated versus distributed practice. *Journal of Educational Psychology*, 1914, *5*, 247–258.

Radossawljewitsch, P. *Das Behalten und Vergessen bei Kindern und Erwachsenen*. Leipzig: Nemnich, 1907.

Ranschburg, P. *Das kranke Gedächtnis*. Leipzig: J. A. Barth, 1911.

Riley, D. A. Memory for form. In L. Postman (Ed.), *Psychology in the making*. New York: Knopf, 1962.

Robinson, E. S. *Association theory to-day*. New York: Century, 1932.

Smith, W. G. A comparison of some mental and physical tests in their application to epileptic and normal subjects. *British Journal of Psychology*, 1905, *1*, 240–260.

Starch, D. Periods of work in learning. *Journal of Educational Psychology*, 1912, *3*, 209–213.

Steffens, L. Experimentelle Beiträge zur Lehre vom oekonomischen Lernen. *Zeitschrift für Psychologie*, 1900, *22*, 241–382; 465.

Stern, W. *Zur Psychologie der Aussage*. Berlin: J. Guttentag, 1902.

Strong, E. K., Jr. The effect of length of series upon recognition memory. *Psychological Review*, 1912, *19*, 447–462.

Strong, E. K., Jr. The effect of time-interval upon recognition memory. *Psychological Review*, 1913, *20*, 339–372.

Thorndike, E. L. *Educational psychology*. New York: Teachers College, 1903.

Thorndike, E. L. *Educational psychology: Vol. II. The psychology of learning*. New York: Teachers College, 1913.

Thorndike, E. L. *Human learning*. New York: Century, 1931.

Thorndike, E. L. *The fundamentals of learning*. New York: Teachers College, Columbia University, 1932.

Thorndike, E. L. *The psychology of wants, interests and attitudes*. New York: Appleton-Century-Crofts, 1935.

Thorndike, E. L. *Man and his works*. Cambridge: Harvard University Press, 1943.

Thorndike, E. L., & Woodworth, R. S. The influence of improvement in one mental function upon the efficiency of other functions. *Psychological Review*, 1901, *8*, 247–261, 384–395, 553–564.

Tulving, E. Theoretical issues in free recall. In T. R. Dixon & D. L. Horton (Eds.), *Verbal behavior and general behavior theory*. Englewood Cliffs, NJ: Prentice-Hall, 1968.

Tulving, E., & Madigan, S. A. Memory and verbal learning. *Annual Review of Psychology*, 1970, *21*, 437–484.

Underwood, B. J. "Spontaneous" recovery of verbal associations. *Journal of Experimental Psychology*, 1948, *38*, 429–439.

Underwood, B. J. Interference and forgetting. *Psychological Review*, 1957, *64*, 49–60.

Underwood, B. J. Ten years of massed practice on distributed practice. *Psychological Review*, 1961, *68*, 229–247.

Volkmann, A. Ueber den Einfluss der Uebung auf das Erkennen räumlicher Distanzen. *Berichte Sächsischer Gesellschaft der Wissenschaften, Mathematisch-Physische Klasse*, 1858, *10*, 38–69.

von Restorff, H. Ueber die Wirkung von Bereichsbildungen im Spurenfeld. *Psychologische Forschung*, 1933, *18*, 229–342.

Wallace, W. P. Review of the historical, empirical, and theoretical status of the Von Restorff phenomenon. *Psychological Bulletin*, 1965, *63*, 410–424.

Ward, L.B. Reminiscence and rote-learning. *Psychological Monographs*, 1937, *49*, No. 220.

Whipple, G. M. An analytic study of the memory image and the process of judgment in the discrimination of changes and tones. *American Journal of Psychology*, 1901, *12*, 409–457.

Whipple, G. M. The observer as reporter: A survey of the "psychology of testimony." *Psychological Bulletin*, 1909, *6*, 153–170.

Whitely, P. L. The dependence of learning and recall upon prior intellectual activities. *Journal of Experimental Psychology*, 1927, *10*, 489–508.

Whitely, P. L., & Blankenship, A. B. The influence of certain conditions prior to learning upon subsequent recall. *Journal of Experimental Psychology*, 1936, *19*, 496–504.

Witasek, S. Ueber Lesen und Rezitieren in ihren Beziehungen zum Gedächtnis. *Zeitschrift für Psychologie*, 1907, *44*, 161–185; 246–282.

Wolfe, H. K. Untersuchungen über das Tongedächtnis. *Philosophiche Studien*, 1886, *3*, 534–571.

Woodworth, R. S. *Experimental psychology*. New York: Holt, 1938.

Wulf, F. Über die Veränderung von Vorstellungen (Gedächtnis und Gestalt). *Psychologische Forschung*, 1922, *1*, 333–373.

Wylie, H. H. An experimental study of transfer to response in the white rat. *Behavior Monographs*, 1919, No. 16.

Young, R. K.   Serial learning. In T. R. Dixon & D. L. Horton (Eds.), *Verbal behavior and general behavior theory*. Englewood Cliffs, NJ: Prentice-Hall, 1968.

Zangwill, O. L.   Some relations between reproducing and recognizing prose material. *British Journal of Psychology*, 1939, *29*, 370–382.

Zangwill, O. L.   *Remembering* revisited. *Quarterly Journal of Experimental Psychology*, 1972, *24*, 123–138.

4 Comparative Psychology And Ethology

Joseph B. Cooper
San Jose State University

What has come to be known in modern scientific circles as "comparative psychology" emerged from man's early interest in infrahuman animals. It has been suggested that historically this interest may have developed through several sequences (Cooper, 1972). As the focus of attention shifted from one interest to the next, the earlier did not disappear, but continued as functional parts of a growing fascination with infrahuman creatures. Various of these sequences may be grouped into three primary phases.

The first was that of the *hunt*. As might be suspected, this phase was closely tied in with religious ceremony (Waters, 1946, 1950). Mesopotamian cave drawings of long-bow-carrying hunters with dogs in pursuit of prey, as well as artifacts of the hunt such as chipped flint arrow heads and carved bones, strongly suggest that the hunting of wild animals for use as food and clothing had reached a relatively high level of sophistication by 7000 to 5000 B.C. (Adams, 1962). It may be supposed that, along with these learned proclivities for the hunt, the hunters had also assimilated much valuable information about the ways of large and otherwise dangerous animals in a constant effort to avoid becoming prey themselves.

The second phase was that of *domestication*. It incorporated part of the first phase, but with the introduction of new techniques and controls designed to provide a relatively constant supply of useful animals. These animals were improved over the generations by selective breeding; improved, that is, from the standpoint of particular human consumers. *Domesticating* is to be distinguished from *taming*. Taming is the process of arranging conditions in such ways that individual animals, either domesticated or non-domesticated, learn not to flee or attack in the presence of their human handlers. It simply represents an instance of

135

socialization to man. Some "wild animals," such as African lions and black bears, can be tamed if the training is started early enough, but this in no way implies that they are domesticated. Domestication involves a designed human instrusion into the genetic and habitat conditions of a segment of the population of a given species. Man's intention has been, of course, to modify the structural and/or behavioral characteristics of a population of a species. This may ordinarily be accomplished only over the span of several generations. Such changes presumably render individual animals more suitable for human use as defined by the group's criteria (Hediger, 1950; Hale, 1962; Boice, 1973).

The specific motivational reasons for the beginnings of the art of domestication will probably never be definitively known. While at first glance we might suspect it to have been economic, there is some evidence to support the thesis that interests in certain species for esthetic and religious reasons predated economic concerns. For instance, Isaac (1962) suggest that ". . . the motive for capturing and maintaining the urus in the captive state was to have available a supply, for sacrificial purposes, of the animal sacred to the lunar mother goddess worshipped over an immense area of the ancient world" (p. 198). Subsequently, cattle were paraded as sacred creatures and used to draw religious vehicles, and in this way were gradually transformed into beasts of burden. Thus, as man began agriculture and reduced his nomadism, it was provident for him to domesticate animals for economic use. Since, as already mentioned, dogs were used in the hunt, it seems evident that some amount of domestication had gone on before what we are referring to here as the phase of domestication. Then, too, we are reminded that any attempt to assign time periods to these so-called phases would be quite inaccurate. In reality each phase represents an emphasis upon human purpose and the techniques man has devised and employed in dealing with infrahuman species.

The third phase is the *scientific*. From the standpoint of history, it is the most recent; and, of course, we know most about it because one of the exacting requirements of the scientific process is that of recording events. By the time Occidental man had prospered sufficiently to provide himself with a modicum of leisure, some men began systematically to speculate about and make empirical inquiry into the nature of the universe. One class of phenomena to which such attention was in time directed was the animal kingdom.

Although the first two phases are still very much a part of the contemporary scene, the third, the scientific, is now an important aspect of the total interest in the infrahumans. The most salient characteristic of science is its dedication to the empirically systematic search for understanding. In the case of the scientific approach to the study of infrahuman species, two general methodologies have been followed. One has been to bring the animals to be studied into conditions of confinement; sometimes these are properly referred to as laboratories. This has been the preference of those who eventually chose to think of themselves as comparative psychologists. The other approach has been to study animals under the conditions of their native habitats; that is, in the field without physical restraints. Those who have followed in this latter methodological tradition are usually referred to as ethologists. Additional comments with reference to this methodological distinction will be provided in the final part of this chapter.

The scientific phase of man's interest in the animal kingdom has not been without its imbalances and misconceptions. The Belgian biologist Raymond Bouillenne has referred to man as the "destroying biotype," and has gone on to say that ". . . man's persistent disruption of natural equilibria poses a constant threat to his means of subsistence . . . man seems reluctant to accept his place in nature" (1962, p. 706). When we consider that most of this depredation has gone on within and in spite of the scientific phase, we are justified in asking: Why has this been so, in view of our almost constant declarations of faith in science as our salvation? Part of the reason lies in the fact that until very recently the scientific study of the infrahumans has very openly used anthropomorphic and anthropocentric orientations. The frame of reference has been not only to think of the lower animals as imperfect human imitations, but to view them as being here on earth to serve man—to be used and destroyed as man sees fit. More and more students of animal behavior are now taking the position that the proper scientific frame of reference is not the economic utility and exploitation of infrahuman species. Rather, it is that of developing an ever increasing understanding of all the infrahuman forms, as well as ourselves, as interacting and contributing to the overall quality of life on our planet.

WESTERN SCIENCE AS A BEGINNING FOR THE STUDY OF INFRAHUMAN BEHAVIOR

Modern western science is the progeny of ancient Greece. It would be beyond the scope of this chapter to attempt to detail a list of the early Greek scholars who brought science into being. However, the person who represents the culmination of these many efforts was Aristotle (384-322 B.C.), a towering intellectual of his time. Among his many achievements, and specific to the present interest, was his founding of biology as systematic science. It is reported that Alexander the Great, who as a youth had been tutored by Aristotle, provided him with as many as a thousand men to collect animal and plant specimens throughout Greece and Asia. These were brought to Athens where Aristotle studied and classified them. Although philosophically he was supportive of a deductive logic, his study and descriptions of the specimens were essentially inductive in nature—an important ingredient of modern science.

His classification of animals was vastly different from our modern system, both in volume and conception. It did not appear in one place; it is scattered throughout his works, and has been set in tabular form by later scholars. The classification cited below is taken with minor modifications from Ley (1968). It is noted that rather than arranging animal forms along a scale of complexity, as is the case with our contemporary classification, Aristotle developed an arrangement that recognized two main categories: animals with blood, and animals without blood.

Aristotle's Classification of Animals

I. Animals with blood
  1. Four-legged that bear their young alive—viviparous mammals
  2. Four-legged that lay eggs—oviparous; most of the reptiles and amphibians
  3. Flying animals—birds
  4. Air and water breathers—whales
  5. Water breathers—fish
II. Animals without blood
  1. Plant—like animals (Aristotle considered these to lie between true plants and true animals)—sea urchins, jelly fish
  2. Cephalopods—octopus and squid (common to the Mediterranean Sea)
  3. Crustaceans (weak-shelled animals)—crayfish, lobsters
  4. Molluscs (hard-shelled animals)—oysters, clams
  5. Insects—flys, spiders

Aristotle's scientific productivity was enormous. Here, however, attention can be given only to his contributions that laid the foundation for what centuries later developed into comparative psychology. The three of his major written works which contain the seminal concepts for the beginnings of a comparative psychology were: *The Parts of Animals, The Movements of Animals,* and *The Generation of Animals.* While many of his specific conclusions about animals were incorrect, it is more to the point that he emphasized a methodology devoted to empirical observation. One of the principal tenets of Aristotle's system was a universal teleology: that every object and event has a purpose. Science, as he conceived it, is committed to discovering the purpose inherent in nature's storehouse of objects and events. An example of this was his explanation of the purpose for the "thorn" (a pointed pile of corneus tissue) hidden beneath the tuft of bushy hairs at the tip of a lion's tail. It was Aristotle's thesis that this "thorn" contains a rage-producing humor; when stressed, the animal whips its tail from side to side thus injecting the humor into its body. He thereby literally lashes himself into a rage with a consequent increase in strength, speed, and bravery. It is interesting in this vein also to note one of Aristotle's truly comparative psychological concepts having to do with temperament. He envisioned each trait of man's temperament to be specifically characteristic of each of the lower animals. For example, there is the brave lion and the sly fox.

As the title of the third of Aristotle's works mentioned above indicates, he was interested in and developed a theory of organic evolution. His theory envisioned each species as developing independently over long periods of time. Then, perhaps borrowing a page from Plato, his former teacher, he proposed that each species continues to improve toward perfection, in a teleological sense, by way of an "internal perfecting principle."

Aristotle's profound concern for matters psychological also is attested to by his keen interest in learning. His great interest in logic led him to look into the origin of ideas. It was his thesis that new ideas are generated out of associations of preexisting ideas. He then described four types of associations which govern the production of ideas: contiguity, similarity, contrast, and succession. This was the basis for the school of thought which came to be known as *associationism,* and provided the epistemological foundation upon which, much later, British Associationism was built. This tradition is of significance to the rise of modern comparative psychology because of its early interest in the learning process. Essentially, Aristotle's epistemology is the basic paradigm upon which stimulus-response types of learning theory have been built—classical conditioning theory, for example. Finally, Aristotle propounded the principle of "pleasure seeking"; that animal organisms move toward pleasurable stimulation. Much later this thesis came to be known as the "law of effect" in learning theory parlance.

EUROPE'S DARK AGES AND THE RENAISSANCE

Not long after Aristotle's death in 322 B.C. Europe retreated into a scientific slumber. Then, as the Christian Chruch accumulated greater and greater power, freedom of inquiry became more and more restricted. The Church hierarchy established itself as the repository of all knowledge and wisdom. Its claim to infallibility rested upon two sources: the Bible, and Aristotle. It may seem curious that Aristotle would have been looked to as an authority through these Dark Ages. In this regard it has been said that the Church used the "worst" of Aristotle; that is, it accepted the conclusions with regard to natural phenomena which he drew on the basis of the deductive process—for example, the purpose for the tail-thorn of the lion. The Church supported the finite and immutable knowledge thesis that Aristotle's pronouncements regarding nature were ex-cathedra; questioning them was heretical, and searching for new knowledge by way of empirical inquiry was sacrilegious.

With the coming of the Renaissance, the shackles of the Dark Ages were broken and science came into greater and greater prominence. This was not accomplished without time and struggle, however.

Reference to two Renaissance persons will illustrate the innovations of most importance to the rise of the biological sciences. One was Francis Bacon, the great English statesman, philosopher and practical-scientist. He rebelled at the medieval prohibition of free inquiry and gave great publicity to his thesis that *knowledge is power.* He contended that we need to examine natural phenomena empirically in order to bring nature under human control. Thus, he was a complete champion of inductive logic. It will be recalled that Aristotle had perforce used induction as part of his program of doing science, but it was deduction which dominated his thinking. It was only when induction came to have equal status with deduction, and both came to be used appropriately in balance, that modern science came into its own.

Another prominent person was René Descartes, the Seventeenth century French mathematician, philosopher, and scientist. His intellectual quest was to discover the existence of an absolute principle. In order to have knowledge, one must experience ideas, or thoughts; the acquisition of knowledge is an *inductive* process providing *awareness of self as a knowing creature.* This is the absolute he sought. Once this is accomplished, one is ready to operate deductively with sense-provided data. The deductive part is what we now refer to as hypothesis construction or, more elaborately, as building a theory. Of specific psycho-biological interest was his explanation of body movement (Fearing, 1980). On a visit to Versailles, Descartes became fascinated by the mechanics used in the moving statuary. When he was told that the movements were produced by water hydraulic systems, his thinking turned to the development of a theory of body movement in animals. First, he noted inductively that energy (excessive heat, for example) applied to a body part (the hand, for example) is followed by body movement; in this case, withdrawal of the hand from the heat source. The problem then became deductive—to develop a non-teleological theory to explain the mechanics involved. With some modification, he used the hydraulic designs of Versailles as his theoretical model. This became the first formalized reflex-arc hypothesis. His specific hypothesis was elaborated into what may be regarded as a theory, complete with diagrams. In essence, he proposed that an animal orga-nism is an automaton, moving in both simple and elaborate ways as a function of the physical energies (stimuli) with which it comes into contact. The muscles are filled with a volatile fluid which is circulated to the brain by way of the nerves; the nerves being tubes. Upon receiving a message from a sense organ, the brain directs an additional amount of this volatile fluid to the particular muscle respon-sible for the appropriate response. That muscle then becomes highly inflated with the volatile fluid, swelling in width and shortening in length. It is the shortening in length, between the muscle's two attachments, that produces the movement.

This was, for its day, an ingenious theory, but Descartes failed to test it. He did not come back to the inductive process and thereby evaluate its validity. The inductive test (an empirical evaluation) was made a few years later by the Dutch biologist Swammerdam. He demonstrated experimentally that the part of the theory which hypothesized the flow of a volatile fluid into a muscle, thereby increasing its volume, was wrong. He placed a freshly excised frog leg in a glass tube, then filled the tube with water until it covered the muscle. When the attached nerve (which was exposed to the outside through a hole in the tube just above the water line) was stimulated, the muscle contracted but the water level remained the same. Thus, Swammerdam provided empirical evidence (inductive data) showing that a change in muscle volume is not responsible for muscle movement. Obviously, the mechanical details of Descartes' theory were shown to be wrong. To this day, however, the basic design of his reflex-arc theory—afferent events, central control, efferent events—is accepted as valid. Descartes had no inclination to flout Church dogma and was careful to declare that, while the lower animals are mere automata, man has a soul. He proposed that the soul is located in the pineal gland, thus giving credence to his preference for a physical interpretation of the universe. However, since man has a soul, he can, when appropriate, be directed by divine power. Otherwise, man's behavior is also to be understood in terms of mechanics.

DARWINIAN BIOLOGY AND THE BEGINNINGS OF COMPARATIVE PSYCHOLOGY

Following in the wake of Bacon and Descartes were numerous biologists who in a variety of ways laid the groundwork for an eventual comparative psychology. Brief reference will be made to the more important of these figures shortly; first, attention must be given to the giant of modern biology, Charles Darwin (1809-1882).

Although Darwin's scientific interests were broad, he is by far best known for his theory of organic evolution. As a young man much interested in biology and geology, he was signed on as an unpaid naturalist aboard the H.M.S. Beagle for a 5-year, round-the-world cruise. The points of greatest interest for Darwin were the Argentine and the Galápagos Islands. Particularly in the Galápagos he observed and collected many plant and animal specimens. One of the most interesting to Darwin were the finches, since there was such great variation—especially in the structure of their bill—from island to island. Such variation was also impressive in the giant tortoises (Hendrickson, 1965). It has been pointed out that the significance of such striking variability, highly correlated, as it was, to geographic locations, was not immediately apparent to Darwin (Huxley & Kettlewell, 1965). This is quite understandable when it is realized that he was in the Galápagos for only a month. It was not long after his return from the expedition, however, that he began to record his germinating new ideas "on transmutation of species" and revealed himself to be an evolutionist. Michael Ghiselin has evaluated Darwin's role in the history of science in the following way: "Darwin may be considered the Newton of biology; it was he who showed how all the phenomena of life can be related to one comprehensive theory . . . Equally we might recognize him as the Galileo of psychology" (1973, p. 968).

Darwin's Theory of Evolution

Darwin's theory of organic evolution was described in his book, *On The Origin of Species,* published in 1859. That book, which he referred to as "my abstract"

(Stauffer, 1959) of a much longer, detailed manuscript, set forth three basic theses. First, within most species there is considerable *variation*. In effect, this means that a species' chances for survival are relatively great despite drastic environmental changes. There are apt to be some individuals that can thrive and continue successfully to breed in the new environment, even when that environment is lethal to most of the species members. When the first widespread use of DDT came about some years ago, it was confidently predicted that this meant the virtual end of the common house fly; for a short time, this appeared actually to be happening. Then the house-fly population rather quickly grew back to normal. Those who had made the prediction had failed to take into account the probability that a few individuals of that species-population would be DDT resistant or impervious to its effects. These few that prospered went on to reproduce and soon repopulated to the pre-DDT level. One of the many implications of this thesis is that a species is to be thought of not as a number of discreet, identical individuals, but as a multi-individual, diversified "organism." In addition, following such an adaptation to environmental changes, the species is not the same as before; in some respect it is a "new" species.

The second basic thesis is referred to as *struggle for existence*. This principle holds that those individuals of a species that survive, prosper, and reproduce must struggle. The meaning of the term "struggle" as used here connotes being active in such matters as food procurement, avoidance of danger, and occupancy of space in which to live. One of the reasons Darwin was so important to the beginnings of comparative psychology is to be found in this very point—his emphasis upon behavior. He insisted that it is not simply a matter of structural evolution, but that behavior contributes to evolution and is, in fact, itself evolving. Darwin's abiding concern with the importance of behavior is attested to even more explicitly in two of his other books: *The Descent of Man* (1871), and *The Expressions of the Emotions in Man and Animals* (1872).

The third thesis is that of *natural selection*—sometimes also referred to as *survival of the fittest*. The term "natural selection" is frequently used in referring to Darwin's entire theory of organic evolution. In fact, it compresses the interlocking parts of the theory, even though somewhat anthropomorphically, into the notion that "nature selects" for survival those indivduals of a species that display characteristics which permit them to cope successfully with the exigencies of a given environment. In a sense, then, this most comprehensive of the three theses defines the meaning of evolution in terms of outcome: *success in reproduction*.

These theses, describing Darwin's theory of organic evolution, were used to support his contention that species are not immutable; that "new" species emerge from those already established. But, as previously intimated, Darwin's most specific contributions to the inception of comparative psychology are to be found in *The Descent of Man* (1871) and *The Expressions of the Emotions in Man and Animals* (1872). Here he went beyond the basic hypothesis that man descended from earlier man-like creatures, and proceeded to the more particulate hypothesis that animals—from the simplest to and including man, the most complex—are to be thought of as on a scale of complexity. The animals composing this scale are conceived of as differing from one another quantitatively, not qualitatively. He supported this position by arguing that all animals have similar sensory channels, basic instincts, emotions and mental processes, and that these psychological properties became more and more complex as we ascend the phylogenetic scale. It was his hope that by identifying instances of mental-behavioral continuity along this supposed scale, an eventual understanding of the origins of man's psychological life could be provided.

Evaluations of Darwin's Theory

It is well known to most that Darwinian theory generated great controversy, particularly by way of the Orthodox Church, since it challenged the dogma of immutability. Fortunately, many respected scientists stood up in his defense, and in time his theory came to be accepted as the very foundation for the framework of modern biology. Despite the scientific and philosophical success of Darwinian theory, two qualifications must be mentioned before leaving this aspect of the history of comparative psychology. First, this theory, as described by Darwin, is not to be thought of as beyond any question. For one thing, some of his terminology is open to disagreement with reference to interpretation; for instance, there are omissions. The most serious omission is that his lack of information about genetics prevented him from accounting for the underlying mechanisms responsible for evolution. It was not until 1900 that the work of Gregor Mendel was "rediscovered" and the "new genetics" got under way (Beadle, 1967). By integrating this genetic information within the natural selection frame of reference, a new "synthetic theory" of evolution—that is, a collection and dynamically organized synthesis of all known biological facts—now makes these facts interpretable and increasingly understandable (Simpson, 1958).

Second, Darwinian biology is still under condemnation in some quarters. Note, for historical example, the notorious "monkey trial" of 1925 in which a Tennessee court found a biology high school teacher guilty of teaching Darwinian theory in defiance of a State anti-evolution law. While that law was repealed in 1967, both bodies of that State's legislature, by overwhelming majorities, enacted a new law in 1973 which stipulated that whenever Darwinian theory is presented in any biology textbook equal space must be given to a competing "theory"—such as, for example, that found in the book of Genesis. A Federal court recently ruled that "scientific creationism," as the foremost competing "theory" is now popularly called, is not in fact a scientific theory at all, but rather a religion. For this reason, they ruled that "scientific creationism" need not be taught as an alternative theory. Kentucky is considering an appeal against that decision. Agitation for equal space and/or allocation for competing "theories" has occurred in several other states, especially in California (Wade, 1973).

Darwin's Influence on the Beginnings of Comparative Psychology

Darwin's influence on the scientific beginnings of psychology was most directly channeled through comparative psychology. Specifically, his convincing argument concerning the evolution of behavior with its mental manifestations gave new impetus to the analysis of psychological phenomena. It must be recognized, however, that the roots of modern psychology were not in England alone. On the continent, especially in Germany, precise laboratory studies were by this time under way. These studies, however, were essentially patterned on a mechanical model, whereas in England the model was much more a biological conception of adaptation to change. In Germany, Wilhelm Wundt founded what is usually recognized as the first psychology laboratory (University of Lipszig, 1879), emphasizing the analysis of mind by introspective techniques. Although a far cry from the Darwinian biology which emerged into comparative psychology, Wundt advocated a comparative approach to the study of "animal psychology" in his *Lectures on Human and Animal Psychology* published in German in 1863. Wundt's work seems to have been influenced little, if at all, by Darwin, but it does indicate that early interest in comparative psychology was not of English origin alone.

It should be pointed out that French science was also very much involved. In an attack upon Darwin's theory of organic evolution, Pierre Flourens, inveighing against naturalistic observation in the tradition of his mentor, Baron Cuvier, literally founded comparative psychology in 1864 by titling a book *Psychologie Comparée*. His emphasis was upon comparing the psychological characteristics of man and the lower animals by way of exact laboratory analysis (Jaynes, 1969).

One of Darwin's most ardent disciples was the British naturalist George J. Romanes. It seems to have been Romanes more than anyone else who attempted to apply evolutionary theory to human and infrahuman mentality (Romanes, 1888). In so doing, he argued for the continuity of mind throughout the animal kingdom. Romanes accepted and illustrated the Darwinian view of phylogenetic continuity, emphasizing quantitative rather than qualitative differences from species to species. However, since the evidence he used to support this position was for the most part anecdotal, thus lacking empirical substance, his contributions to the origins of comparative psychology were essentially in the nature of publicizing a new field of scientific inquiry. His central scientific concern was to support the Darwinian view that the lower animals have the same psychological endowments as those of man. For instance, he gave as evidence for an "imaginative faculty" in infrahumans the story of a collie dog that had been taught, whenever pigs wandered into an adjacent field, to chase them away on command. Later on, even though there was no pigs to be chased, whenever the word "pigs" was uttered the dog invariably began running about wildly chasing what Romanes termed "imaginary pigs." Still later, when the dog was let out doors after the evening meal, he went into the "same drama" (*Mental Evolution in Man*, 1888). It goes without saying that it takes a good measure of human imagination to draw such a conclusion from such an anecdote.

It should not be concluded from these comments about Romanes that he was totally off-base as a scientist. As Margaret Washburn pointed out in evaluating the anecdotal method, "All this is not to deny that much of the testimony to be found in Romanes' 'Animal Intelligence' and Darwin's 'Descent of Man' is the trustworthy report of trained observers; but it is difficult to separate the grain from the chaff . . . [in so far as interpretations are concerned] . . . Romanes, whose adherence to the anecdotal method we have noted, made in 1881, rather as a physiologist than as a psychologist, a number of exact and highly valued experiments on coelenterates and echinoderms . . . He also recorded some rather informal experiments on the keenness of smell in dogs" (1926, pp. 7-9).

Comparative Psychology Comes of Age

Anthropomorphism was implicit in Romanes' search for anecdotal evidence in support of Darwin's quantitative interpretation of behavior evolution. A British psychologist, C. Lloyd Morgan (1894), took sharpest issue with those who advocated anthropomorphic interpretations of infrahuman behavior. His famous book, *Introduction to Comparative Psychology,* has led some people to refer to him as the founder of contemporary comparative psychology (Weld, 1928).

Morgan declared his support of evolutionary theory as follows: "Now, the keynote of modern biology is evolution . . . and we are logically bound to regard psychological evolution as strictly co-ordinate with biological evolution" (pp. 36–37). Beyond this, however, he analyzed the logical and factual value of such anecdotes and their interpretations—as, for example, the story of the pig-chasing dog cited earlier. Basically, he argued that anthropomorphism is at best based upon highly questionable analogical inferences concerning the mental life of lower animals. These are in fact nothing more than *human* experiences of *human* mental operations. In commenting on this situation he said, "Unfortunately many able men who are eminently fitted to make and record exact observations on the habits and activities of animals have not undergone the training necessary to enable them to deal with the psychological aspect of the question. The skilled naturalist or biologist is seldom also skilled in psychological analysis" (1894, p. 52). Morgan brought his thinking with regard to this main issue together in a psychologically tailored statement of the principle of parsimony—today widely known as "Morgan's Canon." It reads: "In no case may we interpret an action as the outcome of the exercise of a higher psychical faculty, if it can be interpreted as the outcome of the exercise of one which stands lower in the psychological scale" (1894, p. 53). Although this interpretative guideline has greatly influenced the shaping of contemporary comparative psychology, and general experimental psychology as well, it has been a point of contention for some psychologists with Gestalt orientations. They have objected on the grounds that it denies the role and efficacy of cognitive processes (Hilgard, 1956) and that, in comparative psychology, where most of all there is need for qualitative descriptions and interpretations, the canon is preemptive (Waters, 1946). Nevertheless, it has remained as a central investigational and interpretational guideline for most comparative psychologists.

Other Early Contributors

Although Morgan remains the best known of those responsible for ushering in contemporary comparative psychology, there were many others in Europe and in the United States, particularly, who made quantum contributions to this new psychobiological enterprise. One such figure was Sir John Lubbock, who as a boy had known the great Charles Darwin. Darwin's influence on the young Lubbock was significant (Pumphrey, 1959), and throughout his long life (1834–1913) he made contributions of comparative psychological substance, many of which were experimental in nature. His book, *Ants, Bees, and Wasps* (1883), for instance, contained accounts of experiments on the sensory systems and "intelligence" of these insects. Particularly significant were his experiments on color perception in bees, preceding by many years the much better-known work of von Frisch. Of him Pumphrey has written : "As a zoologist, he wrote as one of the first to realize that it is what animals do that makes them interesting, and that the whole of classical taxonomy and anatomy and physiology is not an end in itself but an instrument for the understanding of their behavior. He was also the first to appreciate that behavior is only explicable in terms of the information animals receive from the environment" (1959, p. 1090).

A number of other biologists who, like Lubbock, were intensely interested in behavior and thereby contributed to the emerging contemporary comparative psychology should also be mentioned. One of these was Jacques Loeb, a European. The publication which most clearly sets forth his specifically important contributions was published in 1918 under the title *Forced Movements, Tropisms, and Animal Conduct,* (Loeb, 1918) although he had started to publish about 1900. He was probably the most ardent foe of anthropomorphism of his time. For the infrahumans his only concession to a strictly non-mechanistic position was to admit the possibility of "associative memory" in some of the higher forms. In every other way he adhered to the strict Cartesian view that animals are buffeted about in their environments by physical stimuli. His attempt to explain animal behavior was by way of the *tropism* concept, borrowed from botany. This was the thesis that organisms possess particular physical-chemical systems that are activated by particular types of physical energy (in the form of stimuli). An example is "phototropism," light-controlled movements such as a moth's flying toward, literally being propelled toward, a light source (radiant energy). Loeb and the proponents of his position made no concession to the thesis that animal behavior shows spontaneity. Although for the most part he studied relatively simple animal forms, it was his intention to extend this purely mechanistic theory to the higher animals as well. Much controversy was created by Loeb's anti-anthropomorphic, anti-mentalistic position. While it was treated with respect by those students of animal behavior who advocated an empirical, non-anthropomorphic approach, not all of these agreed that it was adequate to interpret the facts.

One of the most articulate opponents of Loeb's tropism theory was the American biologist H. S. Jennings. At the same time he was completely empirical, non-anthropomorphic, and non-anecdotal. He started to publish the findings of his early studies of the behavior of protozoan forms very early in this century (Jennings, 1906). One of his chief interests was in investigating whether or not the behavior of such simple animals as amoeba and paramecia is modified as a function of previous responses. Very clearly, his question was: Is there any indication of learning? In one study of amoebae, for example, a particular small animal had been observed to have twice been engulfed by a larger amoeba. On both occasions it had been able to escape, after which the larger animal no longer pursued the smaller. Jennings thought an understanding of the behavior of even such simple animals cannot be provided solely in terms of the stimuli that are presently operating. That is, past behavior appears to leave an impression that affects future performance. He was able to show that there are instances in which responses are "tried out" by paramecia before the successful completion of an act is accomplished. Jennings referred to such occurrences as "trial and error," arguing that it is much more appropriate as a description of adaptive behavior than is tropism. This orientation was much closer to the heavy emphasis upon learning which was soon to become virtually an all-consuming research area in twentieth century psychology in the United States.

COMPARATIVE PSYCHOLOGY IN THE TWENTIETH CENTURY

From these comments it is apparent that biologists had much to do with the shaping of comparative psychology. However, within the confines of systematic psychology, early twentieth century research and theory took a turn toward quantitative experimentation. At the same time, the broad interests in infrahuman behavior experienced a kind of retrenchment. Experimentation on learning became the central occupation of concern to more and more psychologists who had earlier committed themselves to a broad comparative psychology. Psychologists came more and more to agree that the origins of behavior, whether human or infrahuman, constitute the central psychological issue. In accord with this point of view, many psychologists began to discount the efficacy of instinct theory and to embrace the monumental importance of learning as the mechanism through which new behavior comes into being and by which the appearance of new behavior can be explained.

Analysis of professional literature under the heading of comparative psychology from 1911 to 1965 (Beach, 1950; Cooper, 1972) indicates that while there was a steady increment in the number of articles published during that time, two other rather surprising things were happening. First, the percentage of papers devoted to various aspects of learning steadily increased, whereas those concerning other behavioral phenomena, such as sensory function, reflexes and simple reaction patterns, steadily decreased. Second, the Norway rat became the overwhelming choice as an experimental animal. Since psychology in the United States has tended to be highly anthropocentric, infrahuman animals, rats for the most part, have frequently been used in research intended to increase our understanding of human learning.

The Era of Thorndike

As a graduate student in psychology shortly before the turn of the century, Edward L. Thorndike was encouraged by William James, himself a keen student of animal behavior, to experiment with the learning capacities of lower animals. In time he experimented with fishes, chicks, cats, dogs, and monkeys. With several newly developed experimental tools, such as puzzle boxes and mazes, he set out to demonstrate the invalidity of Darwin's thesis that psychological functions are qualitatively similar throughout the phylogenetic scale. It was Thorndike's hope to be able to show experimentally that there are qualitative differences from species to species throughout this theorized scale. However, the learning curves he discovered for those species he compared not only were essentially the same, but were similar to human learning curves as well. In view of these findings, he was obliged to alter his position and agree with Darwin that intelligence defined by learning facility—varies quantitatively, but not qualitatively, from species to species.

Thorndike's was an associative type theory, nicely described by the title of his doctoral dissertation: *Animal Intelligence: An Experimental Study of the Associative Process*. As has been said, Thorndike brought Aristotle's theory of learning into the experimental laboratory.

Even though Thorndike began as a comparative psychologist, in time his interests shifted to learning at the human level, and eventually he came to be known as an educational psychologist. In essence, whether at infrahuman or human levels, his was a psychology of learning, whereby he attempted mechanically to explain how such adaptive behavior comes into being. He reasoned that neural connections are "stamped in" and "stamped out" in terms of two major "laws": exercise, and effect. In so far as modern learning theories are concerned, Thorndike's ideas, which eventually came to be known as "Trial-and-Error Theory," are a basic point of departure for any and all views of learning that are recognized within the framework of general experimental psychology (Hilgard & Bower, 1966).

OTHER EARLY CONTEMPORARY FIGURES AND THEORIES

Although Thorndike's position in introducing experimental procedures as such into comparative psychology is well established, he did not accomplish it single-handedly. During this century it seems that most psychologists have simply taken comparative psychology for granted, agreeing that it is an interesting area and sometimes necessary in order to test some theory for which it would be dangerous or impossible to use human subjects. However, there have been a relatively few psychologists who have regarded comparative psychology as seriously as did Darwin and Romanes. Of these few, all cannot here be named, nor can their works or the significance of their works be evaluated. The point is that some psychologists consider an *understanding* of the behavior of organisms to be of primary importance. While it is of immediate significance to one engaged in psychotherapy to relieve an anxiety state in a troubled person, it is perhaps more important to discover the reasons for the anxiety in the first place. A comprehensive view and evaluation of the ontogeny of behavior in animal organisms—from amoeba to Homo sapiens—may well help to provide information that will clarify and hopefully solve such immediate problems.

In 1898, L. W. Kline of Clark University published two papers having to do with comparative psychology. One was concerned with methods and the other with subject matter to be dealt with in the undergraduate course. In 1900, in the same laboratory, W. S. Small demonstrated the maze as a reliable learning measurement instrument. Another important figure of this time was Robert M. Yerkes, who made significant contributions both experimentally and theoretically. He is probably best remembered for founding the Yale University Primate Laboratory. Another of the most active and prolific comparative psychologists of that time was Margaret Floy Washburn of Vassar College. She proposed to examine the "mind" of the lower animals; that is, their capacities for conscious experience. She set out to accomplish this by way of her own empirical findings and an examination of the works of others. Her best known publication which embodied this effort, was her classic, *The Animal Mind,* first published in 1908. Although she was unable to provide a satisfactory answer to the question to which she had addressed herself, she did provide an account and theoretical discussion of a virtually definitive list of references on comparative psychology. In the third edition (1926) there were over 1100 entries. Her best remembered contributions were: (a) her work showed that the discovery of "mind" in the infrahumans is a tautological matter, and (b) her exhaustive lists of references had great value for other students of animal behavior.

Of great theoretical-experimental interest to many comparative psychologists during the early twentieth century were the writings of the Russian physiologist Ivan Pavlov. They began to appear in English at about the turn of the century. While his methods and findings were of most direct importance to experimental psychologists specializing in learning, comparative psychologists of the time were certainly interested. It has been suggested that Pavlov's findings and pronouncements actually may have been somewhat inhibiting to some comparative psychologists, since his neurophysiological conceptions rejected the possibility that there might be a problem in generalizing findings from the dog directly to humans. Pavlov claimed to have been influenced in his scientific thinking by the writings of Charles Darwin; however, he seems to have been much more impressed by what he took to be the universality or likeness of physiological function at all levels of the animal kingdom. It is interesting to note that Thorndike had described the same basic conditioning process, referring to it as "associative shifting," and had downgraded it as an inferior form of learning; certainly not to be regarded, as did Pavlov, as the central paradigm to be used in gaining an understanding of the modification of function. There can be no doubt as to the great impact Pavlov's theory and research findings had upon experimentally developed theories of learning in the United States and elsewhere. It can be argued with considerable justification that the accelerated preoccupation with the experimental study of learning, so dramatically stimulated by classical Pavlovian conditioning theory, exerted a debilitating effect upon the development of a genuine and systematic comparative psychology. What is specifically meant by this assertion is that many comparative psychologists shifted from the broad study of behavioral systems of a wide variety of animal species and came more and more to investigate the learning process in the Norway rat.

Another line of animal research which gained much attention beginning about 1915 had to do with localization of function. The two psychologists who did the pioneering work in this area were Shepard I. Franz and Karl S. Lashley. It was their purpose to map the brains of animals as to the locations of centers that might be responsible for particular functions or types of behavior. Their experimental animals were mostly rats, cats and monkeys. Their experimental procedure was to extirpate varying amounts of cortical tissue and measure the amounts of functional change that resulted. Their pioneering findings can be most conveniently summarized in the companion principles of "mass action" and "equipotentiality." The former refers to their conclusion that the entire cerebral cortex is involved in complex problem solving—as, for example, when a monkey learns how to solve an oddity problem. The latter refers to the thesis that any given cortical area is equally as important as any other for such complex cognitive processes. While this research is regarded today as essentially within the neurophysiological domain, it began with comparative psychology and employed methods for the study of behavior that had been developed by comparative psychologists.

One of the most controversial schools of thought in all of modern psychology was "radical behaviorism." Its founder was John B. Watson, who described its formulation as an attempt to objectify psychology and make of it a rigorous, mechanistic, and completely empirical discipline. His pronouncements had a strong appeal for those psychologists who were weary of and rebellious toward the mentalistic trappings of "structuralism," the school of thought which held that psychology is properly the analysis of the adult, normal, human mind. Watson worked to eliminate from the psychological lexicon such subjective work-concepts as "mind," and sought to establish observable and verifiably measurable behavior as the subject matter of scientific psychology. During these early rebellious days of his career he worked within the general area of comparative psychology, being most concerned with sensory control of learning and with the general problem of behavior ontogeny. With reference to the latter, as early as 1907 he conducted field experiments on the development of following behavior in young birds, later called "imprinting" by ethologists. Instead of agreeing with most of his elders that such patterns of behavior as following are inborn instincts, he attempted quite successfully to objectify the matter by identifying independent variables.

Another controversial school of psychological thought that emerged early in the twentieth century was Gestalt theory. It began as an inquiry into the "perception of apparent movement" and expanded into a comprehensive and detailed theory of cognition. The greatest relevance the theory had for comparative psychology came by way of Wolfgang Köhler's (1925) classic book, *The Mentality of Apes*. Probably the most dramatic demonstration of infrahuman *insight* (the Gestalt term for cognitive learning or problem solving) described by Köhler was one in which a naive chimpanzee connected the ends of two bamboo poles, and then immediately reached out through the bars of his cage with the now long pole and drew in a banana. The Gestalt thesis is that the fitting of the poles together for the first time was done by chance; even though it resulted in a pole sufficiently long to reach the banana. This was *not* the insight. Rather, insight was achieved at the moment the perceived banana (out there) and the perceived long pole (in here) were cognitively organized as a solution to the problem of procuring the banana. Within comparative psychology, Gestalt theory and research came as a serious challenge to the stimulus-response, associationistic, behavioristic approach which described learning and problem solving in associationistic terms. Perhaps today we are justified in claiming that the nature of the problem, the learning and manipulative equipment of the organism involved, and such other factors as previous experience and motivation must be brought into the picture before either an associationistic or an insightful interpretation—or some combination of the two—is appropriate.

As we come closer to the present time it becomes increasingly difficult to identify those scientists who have made and are making the major contributions in comparative psychology. This is in part due to the facts that their number is now greatly increased, many contributions are now being made by persons in fields of study other than comparative psychology as such, and the amount and distribution of publication is so enormous that accurate current assimilation is impossible. It needs to be mentioned that the psychologists best known to most students of animal behavior were certainly influenced and taught by those who have gone before, but for various reasons made no ''great names'' for themselves. For these reasons, this section concludes with several ''one liners'' mentioning the names of some relatively recent figures.

One of the most consistent opponents of the view that behavior is controlled by heredity (instinct), and most adamantly in support of the view that all functions—from body movements to food preferences—are solely determined by experience, was the Chinese-American psychologist Zing-yang Kuo. His behavioristic position and long years of empirical research orientation are best described by the title of his early paper, *A Psychology Without Heredity* (Kuo, 1924). Others working from a similar orientation, but from more rigorously systematized experimental programs, are Clark Hull and B. F. Skinner. Over many years of research and writing, both have insisted that modification of function as a result of experience (learning) is the independent variable responsible for the control of behavior. Hull's hypothetical-deductive system, which centers around the establishment of habit by way of classical conditioning principles, is probably best summarized in his book, *A Behavior System* (Hull, 1952). Skinner's basic paradigm is that of operant conditioning, emphasizing, as it does, the importance of behavioral consequences in the control of behavior. His early book, *Behavior of Organisms* (Skinner, 1938), presents the substantive framework of his system, and a later work, *Science and Human Behavior* (Skinner, 1953), puts it to work in the form of a textbook.

Representatives of those who are less known as system builders but who have been in the forefront of systematic comparative psychological research as such since early in this century are the following: T. C. Schneirla, who specialized in the study of learning, orientation and social organization of insects (Schneirla, 1941, 1946, 1952); Henry W. Nissen, best known for his studies of learning and perceptual development in chimpanzees (Nissen, 1954) and his writings on the problems of behavior comparison (Nissen, 1958); W. N. Kellogg, who, along with his wife, began the study of socialization in chimpanzees (Kellogg & Kellogg, 1933) and, among many other things, did pioneering work on sonar navigation by dolphins (Kellogg, 1961); C. Ray Carpenter, who is recognized as a pioneering student of the social organizational behavior of a variety of primate species under both captive and native habitat conditions (Carpenter, 1934, 1963, 1965); and N. R. F. Maier, who gave impetus to early explorations into means for experimenting with such diverse phenomena as cognitive processes and abnormal behavior (Maier, 1929, 1943). Of more recent origin is an exhaustive series of researches, both experimental and observational, by Harry Harlow and his co-workers, centering essentially on the ways in which several infrahuman species "learn to learn"—another approach to the study of cognition. These studies led to comprehensive, long-range investigations into the subtleties of affectional development in primates, the portent of which is revolutionary for the entire area of child rearing at the human level (Harlow, 1962). Finally, the person who probably has had more to do with the shaping of present day trends in comparative psychology than any other is Frank A. Beach. He is best known from a research standpoint for his studies of the hormonal controls of behavior, particularly sexual behavior (Beach, 1948, 1967). His influence upon research directions has come about by way of his insistence that comparative psychology devote itself to the systematic study of behavior based upon the broadest possible range of animal species (Beach, 1950, 1960).

ETHOLOGY

Comparative psychology has not been without competition as a field of inquiry designed for and devoted to the study of animal behavior. This competition has come primarily from ethology. In a glossary prepared to promote objectivity in the study of behavior, William Verplanck refers to an ethologist as "as behaviorist who likes his animals" (Verplanck 1957, p. 14). His meaning was, of course, that ethologists not only do not dissect the animals they observe, they also make special efforts to study sequences of behavior within environmental contexts that are as much like those to which the various species have adapted as can possibly be created or found.

The method that ethologists use lies somewhere between exact experimentation designed to identify contextually significant independent variables *and* observational, naturalistic field studies under native habitat conditions. Under such environmental conditions ethologists often introduce a variety of independent variables in the attempt experimentally to identify the one which best elicits a particular dependent variable. For example, many years ago, in an attempt to identify the color-form configuration that releases food-begging behavior in newly hatched herring gull chicks, Niko Tinbergen (1951) constructed variously colored and patterned cardboard models of adult bills. By presenting these to the chicks and recording the number of pecks they delivered to each, he was able to show that the most effective stimulus-configuration (independent variable) was a bill with a red spot on the lower mandible which contrasted well with the background color of the entire bill.

The Beginnings of Ethology

According to Julian Jaynes (1969), ethology, as a speciality devised for the study of animal behavior, was given its name by Geoffroy-Saint-Hilaire, the younger, in 1859. In early nineteenth-century France there arose a great controversy between two eminent biologists, Baron Cuvier and Geoffroy-Saint-Hilaire, the elder. Cuvier was the champion of species immutability, holding persuasively to a program which recognized only the admissibility of laboratory-derived findings. Hilaire argued for an animal behavior program which emphasized the importance of studying animals under native habitat conditions. It is Jaynes' interpretation that comparative psychology grew out of the Cuvier side of the debate, emphasizing as it did laboratory analysis; and that ethology emerged from the Hilaire side, arguing as it did for naturalistic observation.

The term *ethology* has had a somewhat unstable history. It comes from the Greek word *ethos,* meaning the distinguishing, core, predominant beliefs of a person, institution or organization. It was from this meaning, the essential character of a person, that the word *ethology* came to be used in referring to an actor who depicted human characters in the theatre. In time the Anglicized word came to mean the "building of character" as a result of growing up in a given family or nation. Its biological meaning, however, continued in the French tradition and has come to mean, as previously mentioned, the empirical study of animal behavior under conditions that at least closely resemble the native habitat.

Important Figures in the Development of Modern Ethology

Many biologists and psychologists are working today in what may properly be thought of as ethology. While at least some of these are still doing pioneering work, some few persons should be identified as having given ethology its contemporary form and character.

Eckhard Hess has conveniently identified and commented on those persons who had most to do with the shaping of contemporary ethology (Hess, 1962). It was a University of Chicago zoologist, C. O. Whitman, who in 1898 pronounced the birth of modern ethology by declaring that instincts are to be thought of and studied from the standpoint of orthogenic evolution. Instinctive actions are to be examined and interpreted as inherited parts of an organism that are brought into play in the presence of particular environmental stimulus conditions. Even though instinctive actions show little variability under normal circumstances, at the same time they can adapt to changing environmental conditions. In 1918, Whitman's student, Wallace Craig, took this ethological concept of instinct beyond the purely descriptive level to a level of analysis in which his observations of animal behavior led him to conclude that such consummatory (instinctive) acts occur only under appetitive conditions, and that appetitive conditions are made known to the observer by searching behavior. Such consummatory acts came to be known among ethologists as species-specific patterns, and were regarded as just as much endogenous to the species as any characteristic morphological features.

As a close parallel to the Whitman-Craig position, but developed independently, was the teacher-student theorizing of Oskar Heinroth and Konrad Lorenz. From his observational studies of ducks and geese, Heinroth marshalled evidence in support of the thesis that the phyletic homology concept applies as well to instinctive action patterns as to anatomical characteristics. While Heinroth was largely content simply to describe similarities and differences among various closely related taxonomic groups, it was his student, Lorenz, who most explicitly expanded his basic views, as well as those of the Whitman-Craig tandem. Lorenz more than any other single figure forged ethology into a scientific movement or school of thought. Niko Tinbergen, a Dutch-British biologist closely associated with Lorenz, has been of great importance in promoting contemporary ethological theory and research. Best known for his research and theorizing on such matters as releasers for "innate behavior patterns" and hierarchical orders of appetitive and consummatory behavior patterns, he has given attention recently to the possibility of applying ethological principles to human behavioral problems.

Significant Ethological Concepts

Over the years ethologically oriented research and theory have developed many conceptions—some new, some reformulated—which have added significantly to our understanding of infrahuman behavior. Several of these which are of special interest to comparative psychologists will be mentioned briefly.

Species-specific Behavior.   Species-specific behavior refers to both the sending and responding to messages in ways that are unique within a given species. Some of the clearest examples are to be found in many avian species whose success in reproduction depends upon the production of and accurate response to particular vocalizations. After a male of the species has "staked out" a territory, he then proceeds to defend it by particular behavior displays, some of which may be vocalizations specific to the species. As Nice (1943) has described such interactions in song sparrows, when the females of the species arrive later in the spring, each enters a single male's territory after some amount of male display. The male's displays have had and continue to have a threatening meaning for other males; for the flock of females just arrived, however, they have an approach-invitation meaning. Some ethologists have in the past maintained that such species-specific displays emerge full-blown, without having been practiced. It appears today that no such generalization is warranted; that each species must be studied in its own right in order to determine the extent to which its species-specific displays are dependent upon nature and/or nurture.

Such species-specific displays—localizations, body movements and stances, pigmentation changes, plumage shifts—are, in ethological literature, often referred to as *releasers*. Lorenz (1952) has described the "appeasement ceremony" of the night heron as an instance in which both plumage and head movements "release" appropriate behavior in the nestlings. When the parent returns to the nest, it raises its three thin, white plumes. After this ceremonial act, it steps down into the nest and proceeds with its brooding routines. In an experiment in which a parent's plumes were pasted down so that they could not be raised, the nestling young attacked the parent. The absence of the three raised plumes is a stimulus-signal releaser for attack, while their presence is a releaser for parent acceptance. It is obvious that such species-specific releaser systems have adaptive value.

The variations found within the ethological releaser construct are many, but two short examples will suffice to illustrate. In reviewing studies on releasers, Hess (1962) has called attention to a phenomenon known as *super-optimality of releasers*. A broody herring gull will retrieve eggs that are larger than normal gull eggs if given a choice. This is to say that the larger egg releases retrieving behavior in a situation in which a visual comparison with its own egg is possible. The phenomenon has also been observed in a particular species of butterfly. By using a mechanical model which could simulate the alternation in color the female displays in her wing-fluttering courtship routine, the effectiveness of the display could be increased, as measured by the male's reciprocating courtship responses, by increasing the flutter speed. Thus, again, a superoptimal stimulus was found to be more effective as a releaser than the normal stimulus.

Fixed-action patterns.   Another ethological construct that has received attention is the *fixed-action pattern* (FAP). Fixed-action patterns are regarded as species-specific and defined by four characteristics (Moltz, 1965). First, they are consummatory movement patterns that are highly stereotyped and extremely similar from display to display and individual to individual. Second, they need only to be elicited by outside stimulation; then they continue to completion even though the eliciting stimulus is removed. Third, FAPs are spontaneous in nature; on occasion, they go into action without the normal stimulation. For example, the male stickleback fish may engage in nest-fanning in the absence of the species-typical releaser. Fourth, FAPs are not learned; that is, in the sense of the associationistic paradigm. Ethologists take pains to stress that stereotyped as FAPs are, they are not to be confused with reflexes. The probability of the appearance of a FAP depends in part upon the length of time since it was last performed. One component of the egg-retrieving behavior of a broody grey lag goose is a sagittal (straight back) movement of the bill by which the egg is moved toward her body as she moves backward to her nest. Even if the egg is removed before she reaches the nest, the FAP continues until the nest is reached.

Imprinting.   Ethologists and psychologists have tended to disagree on a definition of imprinting. While ethologists, such as Lorenz, have been adamant on the point that imprinting is quite different from associative learning, psychologists have been less willing to totally foreclose that possibility. In reviewing different attempts at a satisfactory definition, Sluckin (1965) has commented, "There is little that can be said by way of defining imprinting that can not be challenged or queried" (p. 15). Perhaps an operational statement will suffice: The process of imprinting is that by which very young animals develop strong attachments to other animals, foods, and physical environments. Such long-lasting attachments are functions of perceptions of and responses to these particular stimulus configurations. The many biopsychological values of these attachments all center around individual, group, and species survival.

Although the first known truly experimental study of imprinting was reported as recently as 1951, the first scientific writing on the subject appeared in 1873 (Hess, 1962; Gray, 1963). In 1873, Douglas A. Spalding published a paper in which he reported on the following behavior of newly hatched chicks that had been restricted in darkness for varying periods of time from 1 to 4 days. Those chicks that were freed into daylight from 1 to 3 days after hatching followed the first moving object placed before them. Those that were released on the fourth day, however, tended to run from the same moving objects. Some time later, William James called attention to these observations in his discussion of his own "Law of Inhibition of Instinct," commenting that "Mr. Spalding's wonderful article on instinct shall supply as with the facts" (1902, Vol. II, p. 396). He then proceeded to describe Spalding's findings, just mentioned. In introducing his own "Law of Transitoriness," James stated: "Many instincts ripen at a certain age and then fade away . . . [as with the chicks] it is obvious that the instinct to follow and become attached fades out after a few days, and that the instinct of flight then takes its place . . ." (1902, Vol. II, p. 398).

As mentioned earlier, John B. Watson (1908), the founder of "radical behaviorism," studied the behavior of terns on an island off the coast of Florida. His program involved comparing the flight behavior of birds raised normally by their parents with that of those raised under human handling conditions. He believed his findings confirmed the conclusions of Spalding (1873). Of particular historical interest is the observation by Philip Gray that "Watson was the first to use the approach now called ethological for the study of wild birds" (1963, p. 338).

Three basic characteristics of the imprinting process are embedded in the early studies and observations. First, long-lasting attachments of a social nature are normally formed by young animals for the first objects regularly encountered. These ties are usually, of course, but not always, to a parent. Second, somewhat later any or all moving objects, save those to which positive imprinting has been established, may elicit flight or panic. Third, imprinting occurs only during a very early, short span of life—known as the critical period.

The recent experimental and field-controlled approaches to the study of imprinting have absorbed the attention of many scientists. Essentially, these many studies have confirmed the three basic characteristics mentioned just above. A review of this recent work details the intricacies of the imprinting process, emphasizing its variations throughout the animal kingdom, and suggests that imprinting is also a fundamentally important phenomenon at the human level (Hess, 1962; Gray, 1958, 1963a, 1963b).

· SOCIOBIOLOGY

As we have seen, comparative psychology and ethology are both disciplines that attempt to describe and explain behavior in terms of evolutionary processes. This is the common theme that links these disciplines together, despite the fact there are differences in emphasis and methodology. A third endeavor must now be added to this list; the most recent attempt at understanding behavior from an evolutionary perspective has resulted in the creation of a new specialty called *sociobiology*. As Edward O. Wilson (1975) has put it, sociobiology is "the systematic study of the biological basis of all social behavior." Comparative psychology, ethology, and sociobiology differ in many ways, not the least of which is the emphasis placed on the kinds of behavior that are studied: Comparative psychologists study learning, although the stress placed on understanding this process has changed in recent years; ethologists are most concerned with describing and understanding fixed-action patterns; and sociobiologists place the greatest emphasis on understanding social behaviors.

As is widely known, sociobiology "appears" to have been born in 1975 when E. O. Wilson, who has been called the high priest of sociobiology by some of his detractors, published a truly remarkable book titled *Sociobiology: The New Synthesis*. Since the publication of this encyclopedic volume, theoretical and research activity in and around sociobiology has progressed at a remarkable pace. To illustrate the phenomenal growth of this nascent discipline, and remember that we are speaking of a history that dates back 7 or 8 years at most, one can point to the following facts:

1. Where none existed before, there are now two journals devoted to the publication of sociobiological research. These are *Behavioral Ecology and Sociobiology* and *Ethology and Sociobiology*, journals that started publishing articles in 1977 or 1978, respectively.
2. Major universities are advertising for and hiring sociobiologists where other academics are faced with the most depressed job market in decades.
3. Courses in sociobiology—virtually unheard of before 1975—are now common-place offerings in college, curricula, and, even where no courses in sociobiology exist, lectures, and discussion of sociobiology are now

commonly included in courses in disciplines as diverse as biology, psychology, economics, anthropology, and sociology.

4. The number of papers that now reference Hamilton's 1964 paper, *Genetical Evolution of Social Behavior*, a true milestone and "classic" in what is today sociobiology, has grown from a few dozen in 1965 to literally hundreds in 1982.

5. Finally, there are today any number of individuals who when asked what their specialty is will answer, "I am a sociobiologist"; no one so identified themself even 10 years ago.

All this seems very recent, and one may wonder what a discussion of sociobiology is doing in a chapter on the history of comparative psychology. The answer is that the problems that sociobiologists deal with go back at least to Darwin and by extension to Malthus. Specifically, the origins of sociobiology can be traced to two historical questions or problems that have been called evolutionary paradoxes. These are: (1) Individual animals of many species have an enormous reproductive potential which, if realized, would soon over-burden the carrying capacity of the environment. This does not happen. Natural populations maintain a fairly constant size somewhat below the carrying capacity of the environment; given an enormous reproductive potential, individuals of a species must practice reproductive self-restraint. This, in turn, means that individuals must reduce their personal fitness, and that presents us with an evolutionary paradox. (2) Darwin, writing in *On the Origin of Species*, proposed a critical test of his theory: He argued that if even a single instance of a trait in a species could be identified to have the sole purpose of benefiting another species, his theory would be annihilated. And, as was recognized by many biologists, evolutionary theory would have similar difficulties explaining such behaviors among conspecifics. To put this in another way, apparent example of "altruistic" acts in animals of a species present us with another evolutionary paradox.

These seeming paradoxes are the subject matter of Hamilton's 1964 paper, which we have alluded to previously. Specifically, Hamilton attempted to explain the social caste system of certain *Hymenopteran* insects such as bees, wasps, ants, etc., animals in which the worker caste is typically sterile. These workers maintain the hive, defend it, forage for food and so forth, but they do not reproduce. The paradox concerns the evolution of such a social system: How does one explain the evolution of a sterile caste consisting of individuals that altruistically assist the reproduction of con-specifics. The answer, apparently, depends on the genetic makeup of these animals. Worker bees, for example, share three-fourths of their genes with other workers whom they help rear, whereas they would share only one-half of their genes with their daughters if they were to reproduce.

In classical evolutionary theory, the unit of selection is the *individual*, with fitness being defined as the number of offspring an organism leaves to the next generation—individuals who themselves reach reproductive age. This is the reason why parents reproduce at considerable cost to themselves, and why organisms of some species expend considerable energy on the care of young. One's genes are represented in the next generation *only* through offspring. However, if the unit of selection is the *gene,* not the individual, then the survival of relatives with whom one shares genes in common is also important. This was Hamilton's great insight—namely, that offspring are only a special case of relatives in general. To insure genetic representation in the next generation, parents should behave altruistically towards their offspring, but individuals should also behave altruistically towards other relatives, and more altruism is to be expected towards closer relatives than towards more distantly related individuals. This principle, called *kin selection,* gives rise to what has been called the central theorem of sociobiology, *inclusive fitness.* Genetic representation in the next generation depends on the survival of relatives, including those special relatives we call children. Given that the gene is the unit of natural selection, given inclusive fitness, one can now explain altruistic behavior in terms of the following general formulation: Altruistic behavior is to be expected given that

$$k > \frac{1}{r},$$

where *k* is the ratio of recipient's benefit to altruist's cost, and *r* is the coefficient of relationship between altruist and recipient, summed over all recipients.

Given such a formulation, one can now understand the evolution of social caste systems in certain insects, as well as many other behaviors, such as alarm calling in prairie dogs, etc., that had previously been difficult to understand in terms of classical evolutionary explanations. One more theoretical step is necessary to explain altruistic behavior between unrelated individuals. The following explanation, called *reciprocal altruism,* was offered by Trivers (1971): If altruistic behavior between unrelated individuals does indeed occur, only one addition to sociobiological theory is necessary, namely, a sufficient likelihood of reciprocity, making it very easy to change the phrase ''reciprocal altruism'' into plain, ordinary selfishness.

One clarification must be made: Altruism and selfishness, as sociobiologists use these words, are defined strictly in terms of their consequences for the inclusive fitness of two or more individuals. Consciousness or motivational states are irrelevant; all that matters is inclusive fitness, and this is the reason why certain sociobiologists can speak about altruistic viruses without blushing.

To summarize: Sociobiology attempts to explain social behavior, including human social behavior, in terms of inclusive fitness. Selfish acts are seen as having evolved through classical Darwinian selection. Altruistic behaviors between related individuals are explained in terms of kin selection. And, finally, altruistic behaviors that occur between unrelated individuals are explained in terms of reciprocal altruism. Inclusive fitness differs from Darwinian fitness in that it considers the fate of genes rather than of offspring.

Any current discussion of sociobiology would be incomplete without mentioning that sociobiology has many critics, and that a good deal of controversy surrounds the field. These disputes seem to be grounded in both scientific and political concerns. Some of this controversy can be attributed to the following factors: Some sociobiologists give the impression that their discipline is the first to consider evolutionary explanations of behavior. This is certainly not the case; other attempts to explain behavior in evolutionary terms have been very successful. These other attempts include comparative psychology and ethology, discussed in this chapter, and behavioral genetics, discussed in a previous chapter. Some sociobiologists think of kin selection and inclusive fitness as the only constructs of a unified theory that explains all aspects of social behavior. As a consequence, they confidently predict the demise of the other sciences, and it is therefore not too surprising that sociobiology is viewed with considerable suspicion by individuals in other fields. The extension of sociobiological thinking to human social behavior, in the absence of any reliable empirical evidence, is of great concern. Given the nature of the domain of sociobiology, it is natural that theory and research in this field often touch on sensitive areas, and the language used by some sociobiologists to describe certain phenomena—for example, referring to forced copulation as "rape" when describing the behavior of ducks— is found offensive by some individuals.

Nevertheless, sociobiology has resulted in new and exciting ways of thinking about social behavior, and it has generated an enormous amount of research.

COMPARATIVE PSYCHOLOGY, ETHOLOGY, AND SOCIOBIOLOGY IN QUEST OF UNDERSTANDING

Comparative psychology, ethology, and sociobiology are distinct disciplines, each with its own history, but all have the common purpose of describing and understanding behavior. Individual scientists in these fields all study the similarities and differences in the behavior of organisms of different species. These similarities and differences are often explained in terms of evolutionary processes; that is, explanations and understanding are often sought in terms of the fitness value of a given behavior, given the ecology in which the animals live. Nevertheless, there are differences among these fields in terms of both methodology and theoretical orientation. Comparative psychologists tend to emphasize learning, ethologists concentrate on studying simpler, unlearned behaviors, and sociobiologists tend to study reproductive behaviors and other social interactions between animals of the same or different species.

Not long ago Niko Tinbergen, the famed European ethologist, responded to an interviewer's question regarding possible fundamental differences between ethology and comparative psychology. This was his comment: "Because American psychologists overemphasized learning, which is a form of interaction with the environment, we overemphasized nonlearned things. But we both simplified it. We could both have learned from experimental embryology that the only thing that is given genetically is the genome . . . to say that any characteristic of a full-grown animal is innate is an oversimplification" (1974, p. 70). Similar observations might be pertinent in describing the differences between comparative psychology and sociobiology and between ethology and sociobiology. There seems little doubt that in the not too distant future the three disciplines will fuse, perhaps imperceptibly, into a unified attempt to understand the complexities of animal behavior from an evolutionary perspective.

REFERENCES

Adams, R. M. Agriculture and early life in southwestern Iran. *Science*, 1962, *136*, 109–122.

Beach, F. A. *Hormones and Behavior*. New York: Hoeber, 1948.

Beach, F. A. The snark was a boojum. *American Psychologist*, 1950, *5*, 115–124.

Beach, F. A. Experimental investigations of species-specific behavior. *American Psychologist*, 1960, *15*, 1–18.

Beach, F. A. Experimental studies of mating behavior in males of various species. *Science*, 1967, *157*, 1951.

Beadle, G. W. Mendelism, 1965. In R. A. Brink & E. D. Styles (Eds.), *Heritage from Mendel*. Madison: University Wisconsin Press, 1967.

Boice, R. Domestication. *Psychological Bulletin*, 1973, *80*, 215–230.

Bouillenne, R. Man, the destroying byotype. *Science*, 1962, *132*, 706–712.

Carpenter, C. R. A field study of the behavior and social relations of the howling monkeys (Alouatta palliata). *Comparative Psychological Monographs*, 1934, *10*, 1–168.

Carpenter, C. R. Societies of monkeys and apes. In C. H. Southwick (Ed.), *Primate Social Behavior*. New York: Van Nostrand Reinhold, 1963.

Carpenter, C. R. The howlers of Barro Colorado Island. In I. Devore (Ed.), *Primate Behavior*. New York: Holt, Rinehart and Winston, 1965.

Cooper, J. B. *Comparative Psychology*. New York: Ronald, 1972.

Craig, W. Appetites and aversions as constituents of instincts. *Biological Bulletin*, 1918, *34*, 91–107.

Fearing, F. *Reflex Action*, Baltimore: Williams and Wilkins, 1930.

Ghiselin, M. T. Darwin and evolutionary psychology. *Science*, 1973, *179*, 964–968.

Gray, P. H. Theory and evidence of imprinting in human infants. *J. Psychology*, 1958, *46*, 155–166.

Gray, P. H. A checklist of papers since 1951 dealing with imprinting in birds. *Psychological Record*, 1963, *13*, 445–454. (a)

Gray, P. H. The descriptive study of imprinting in birds from 1873 to 1953. *Journal of General Psychology*, 1963, *68*, 333–346. (b)

Hale, E. B. Domestication and the evolution of behavior. In E. S. E. Hafez (Ed.), *The Behavior of Domestic Animals*. Baltimore: Williams and Wilkins, 1962, 21–53.

Hall, E. Ethology's warning. *Psychology Today*, 1974, *7(10)*, 65–80.

Hamilton, W. D. The genetical theory of social behavior: I and II. *Journal of Theoretical Biology*, 1964, *7*, 1–52.

Harlow, H. F. Development of affection in primates. In E. L. Bliss (Ed.), *Roots of Behavior*. New York: Harper, 1962.

Hediger, H. *Wild Animals in Captivity*. London: Butterworth, 1950.

Heinroth, O. Beitrage zur Biologie, namentblich Ethologie und Psychologie der Anatiden. *Verh. 5th Int. Orinth, Kongr.*, 1910, 589–702.

Hendrickson, J. R. Reptiles of the Galápagos. *Pacific Discovery*, 1965, *18*, 28–36.

Hess, E. H. Ethology: An approach toward the complete analysis of behavior. In *New Directions in Psychology*. R. Brown, E. Galanter, E. H. Hess, and G. Mandler, (Eds.). New York: Holt, Rinehart and Winston, 1962, 157–266.

Hilgard, E. R. *Theories of Learning*. New York: Appleton, 1956.

Hilgard, E. R., & Bower, G. H. *Theories of Learning*. New York: Appleton, 1966.

Hull, C. L. *A Behavior System*. New Haven: Yale University Press, 1952.

Huxley, J. S., & Kittlewell, H. B. D. *Charles Darwin And His World*. New York: Viking Press, 1965.

Isaac, E. On the domestication of cattle. *Science*, 1962, *137*, 195–204.

James, W. *The Principles of Psychology*, Vol. II. New York: Holt, Rinehart and Winston, 1902.

James, W. T. Conditioned responses in the opossum. *Journal Genetic Psychology*, 1958, *93*, 179–183.

Jaynes, J. The historical origins of "ethology" and "comparative psychology." *Animal Behaviour*, 1969, *17*, 601–606.

Jennings, H. S. *Behavior of Lower Organisms*. New York: Columbia University Press, 1906.

Kellogg, W. N. *Porpoises and Sonar*. Chicago: University of Chicago Press, 1961.

Kellogg, W. N., & Kellogg, L. A. *The Ape and The Child*. New York: McGraw-Hill, 1933.

Köhler, W. *The Mentality of Apes*. New York: Harcourt, Brace, 1925.

Kuo, Z. Y. A psychology without heredity. *Psychological Review*, 1924, *31*, 427–451.

Ley, W. *Dawn of Zoology*, Englewood Cliffs, NJ: Prentice-Hall, 1968.

Loeb, J. *Forced Movements, Tropisms, and Animal Conduct*. Philadelphia: Lippincott, 1918.

Lorenz, K. *King Solomon's Ring*. London: Methuen, 1952.

Lubbock, J. *Ants, Bees, and Wasps*. London: Kegan, Paul, and Trench, 1882.

Maier, N. R. F. Reasoning in white rats. *Comparative Psychological Monographs*, 1929, *6 (3)*, 1–93.

Maier, N. R, F. Delayed reactions and memory in rats. *Journal Genetic Psychology*, 1929, *36*, 538–550.

Maier, N. R. F. Studies of abnormal behavior in the rat. XIV, Strain differences in the inheritance of susceptibility to convulsions. *Journal Comparative Psychology*, 1943, *35*, 327–333.

Moltz, H. Contemporary instinct theory and the fixed action pattern. *Psychological Review*, 1965, *72*, 27–47.

Morgan, C. L. *Introduction To Comparative Psychology*. New York: Scribner's, 1894.

Nissen, H. W. The nature of the drive as innate determinant of behavioral organization. In the Nebraska Symposium On Motivation, II, (Ed. by M. R. Jones). *Current Theory And Research In Motivation*. Lincoln, Nebr: Uni. Nebr. Press, 1954, 281–321.

Nissen, H. W. Axes of behavioral comparison. In A. Roe & G. G. Simpson (Eds.), *Behavior And Evolution*. New Haven: Yale University Press, 1958.

Nice, M. M. *Studies In The Life History Of The Song Sparrow*, II. New York, Proceedings of the Linnean Society, 1943, *6*, 1–329.

Pumphrey, R. J. The forgotten man: Sir John Lubbock. *Science*, 1959, *129*, 1087–1092.

Romanes, G. J. *Mental Evolution In Man*, New York: Appleton, 1888.

Schneirla, T. C. Social organization in insects, as related to individual function. *Psychological Review*, 1941, *48*, 465–486.

Schneirla, T. C. Problems in the biopsychology of social organization. *Journal of Abnormal and Social Psychology*, 1946, *41*, 385–402.

Schneirla, T. C. A consideration of some conceptional trends in comparative psychology. *Psychological Bulletin*, 1952, *49*, 559–597.

Simpson, G. G. The study of evolution: Methods and present status of theory. In A. Roe & G. G. Simpson (Eds.), *Behavior And Evolution*. New Haven: Yale Uni. Press, 1958.

Slukin, W. *Imprinting And Early Experience*. Chicago: Aldine, 1965.

Spalding, D. A. Instinct, with original observations on young animals. *Macmillan's Magazine*, 1873, *27*, 282–293.

Stauffer, R. C. "On the Origin of Species": An unpublished version. *Science*, 1959, *130*, 1449–1452.

Tinbergen, H. W. *Learning And Instinct In Animals*. Cambridge: Harvard University Press, 1956.

Trivers, R. L. The evolution of reciprocal altruism. *Quarterly Review of Biology*, 1971, *46*, 35–57.

Verplanck, W. S. A glossary of some terms used in the objective science of behavior. *Psychological Review* (Supplement), 1957, *64*, 1–42.

Wade, N. Evolution: Tennessee picks a new flight with Darwin. *Science*, 1973, *182*, 696.

Washburn, M. F. *The Animal Mind*. New York: Macmillan, 1908, 1926.

Waters, R. H. The nature of comparative psychology. In R. H. Waters, D. A. Rethlingshafer, & W. E. Caldwell (Eds.), *Principles Of Comparative Psychology*. New York: McGraw-Hill, 1960.

Watson, J. B. The behavior of noddy and sooty terns. Papers Marine Biol. Lab. Totrugas, *Carnegie Institute of Washington*, 1908, *2*, 187–255.

Watson, J. B. *Psychology From The Standpoint of A Behaviorist*. Philadelphia: Lippincott, 1919.

Watson, J. B. *Behaviorism*. New York: Norton, 1924.

Weld, H. P. *Psychology As Science; Its Problems and Points of View*. New York: Henry Holt and Co., 1928.

Whitman, C. O. Animal Behavior: *Biological Lectures*. Wood's Hole, MA: Marine Biology Laboratory, 1898.

Wilson, E. C. Sociobiology, The New Synthesis. Cambridge: Harvard University Press, 1975.

5 Sensory Processes: Vision

Lorrin A. Riggs
Brown University

Sight is universally regarded as the most highly developed of all human senses. Hence it is not surprising to find that the question, "How do we see?," has been faced, and variously answered, since earliest times. Psychologists have a special interest in the question, because the visual input plays such a dominant role in our experience and behavior. Such expressions as "seeing eye to eye" with a person, "seeing the point" of a joke or an argument, and discovering that someone is not very "bright" attest to the fact that the language of *vision* often enters into our everyday speech and thinking.

This chapter will begin with an overview of the ideas, both true and false, that the earlier writers expressed about vision. After describing the beginnings of a scientific approach to the subject in the seventeenth and eighteenth centuries, we go on to the major achievements of physiological optics in the nineteenth century. Finally, we break through into the marvelous technical and conceptual advances that our own twentieth century has brought.

EARLIEST PERIOD

Pre-scientific speculation about vision raised many of the important questions, but provided few good answers (see Lindberg, 1976; MacAdam, 1970; Polyak, 1957).

The Greeks

The Greek philosophers gave much thought to vision. They all considered that the sense of sight was one of the main avanues by which objects in the material world could affect the mind or soul. They also realized that the eye is the organ of sight, and they tried to figure out how the eye works. But they never thought of doing experiments to find this out; the classical tradition was to proceed by reasoning from common observations to speculative conclusions. Nor did they subject these conclusions to any sort of rigorous test. As a result, we find that many false explanations of vision were developed, and there was no way to decide which of many conflicting accounts of the visual process were true.

Plato (427–347 B.C.), for example, adopted and extended an "emanation hypothesis" that had been put forth by Pythagoras in 532 B.C. The basic idea was that the eye had the power to shoot out a stream of rays in the direction of the object of regard. These rays have no effect in total darkness. When light is present, however, the rays coalesce with the light in such a way as to form a single homogeneous probe, reaching out from the eye to the object. This emanation idea stressed the importance of "active seeing," a concept that we shall encounter several times more in the course of this chapter. It is as if the eye could be used to point a weightless wand at the object of regard, and to move the wand around like the beam of a flashlight to probe the details of the object. This is an attractive model from a purely subjective point of view. The subject controls not only the direction of regard, but also the very rays that he shoots out and plays over the surface of the physical world.

Aristotle (384–322 B.C.), however, rejected the emanation theory. He realized the preposterous amount of power that would be required if rays coming out of the tiny pupil of the eye were required to reach the moon or the stars in order for them to become visible to the subject. He also developed the important concept that light must travel through a transparent medium, such as the air, in order to reach the eye. He even observed that the eye itself contained a watery, transparent substance, and he realized that seeing could only occur when the light passed through it to the back of the eyeball. His idea of the final stage in the process was that the eyeballs were in communication with vital fluids that served to conduct the visual signals to the soul or intellect.

While Aristotle rejected the emanation hypothesis, he had no more appreciation of the nature of light than did any other man in ancient times. He presumed that a transparent medium such as the air could undergo an instantaneous change of state when acted upon by colors. He had not the slightest idea that the eye could be involved in the formation of an optical image. Thus, the shapes and sizes of objects, as well as their color, had somehow to be transmitted directly to the intellect by the impression that they made upon the vital fluids.

Other Greeks saw the need for explaining how the soul or intellect could perceive the details of an object. The "atomists," for example, assumed that all visible bodies gave off thin copies of themselves that were somehow small and ethereal enough to enter the eye and impress themselves upon the soul. A more subjective point of view was that of the Stoics. They started with the notion of a "seat of consciousness" that played the active role of dispatching a vital fluid to the eye. The fluid then excited the air adjacent to the eye; and the air, so stressed, made contact with external objects whenever they were sufficiently supplied with light from the sun. A sort of continuous flow of the vital fluid kept the seat of consciousness aware of the objects so contacted.

Such were some of the speculations—one might almost call them superstitions—indulged in by the great philosophers of the Classical period. In addition, mention should be made of the fact that Euclid (about 300 B.C.) first derived a geometry of vision based on the rectilinear propagation of light. He conceived of the eye as occupying a position at the vertex of a cone of rays that emanate from the pupil and interact with the light. Much later, Claudius Ptolemy (127–148 A.D.) accepted the idea of the cone emanating from the eye and placed its vertex more precisely at the center of curvature of the cornea. Still later, Galen (about 175 A.D.) attributed photoreception to the lens of the eye. Earlier Greeks had overlooked that structure, and had more generally localized interactions of visual rays with the eye at some indefinite region within the fluid center of the eyeball.

The Muslims

Because the Dark Ages put a stop to progress in Europe, we jump now to the awakening of Muslim culture during the period from the ninth to eleventh centuries A.D. Muslims in Baghdad and other Near Eastern centers had begun to study the early Greek and Roman texts, and they were turning out new texts of their own. Al-Kindi, for example (see Lindberg, 1976), wrote a book on optics in the early ninth century and advanced his own arguments for accepting the old theory that visual rays emanate from the eye. He was ahead of the Greeks on one thing, though: He realized that vision must involve some sort of point-for-point representation at the eye of the objects in the world. This led him, unfortunately, to the assumption of a pictorial representation of visual forms at the cornea. He probably got that idea from the observation that if you look carefully at someone's cornea, you can see in it a miniature reflected image of the luminous objects in front of the eye.

Several other Muslims shared these views. However, the greatest scholar of them all, the one called Alhazen or Al Hathem (about 965–1039), had many ideas of his own. Alhazen was the first to integrate physics, physiology and mathematics into a comprehensive theory that led to a firm rejection of the idea that the eye could generate its own visual rays. He cited several lines of evidence that the rays must come to the eye from the objects themselves. First, there was the fact that light and color issue in all directions from every point of a luminous object. Second, the eye can undergo painful injury by an excessively strong source such as the sun. Still another point is that a strong source can cause a persistent afterimage. These were convincing arguments in favor of an intromission theory. Thus, the emanation theory became unnecessary; but is there any direct proof that the eye does not send out rays? Alhazen saw such a proof in the fact that, at night, the rays from the eye would have to fill the entire universe in order for stars to be seen. Because such a drain on the eye would soon destroy it, the idea of visual rays emanating from the eye must be not only useless but false. Yet, like all his predecessors, Alhazen failed to recognize the image-forming function of the optical structures. This failure is all the more surprising in view of the fact that the gross anatomy of the eyeball was described with increasing accuracy in the writings of Hippocrates, Herophilos, Galen, and Alhazen himself.

The Renaissance

Optical and visual science seems to have lagged behind in the exciting technical developments of the fourteenth, fifteenth, and sixteenth centuries (see Polyak, 1957). Lenses and mirrors, which had been known for several centuries, were now refined. Spectacles had been developed by Italian glassmakers, first for the correction of presbyopia and then for myopia and other refractive states, but the corrections were achieved without realizing what was being corrected. Perhaps even more remarkable is the fact that a form of *camera obscura* was known to Aristotle, and more elaborate models were accurately described by Alhazen, Bacon, and da Vinci. In the sixteenth century the Venetians introduced a convex lens to replace the simple aperture of the *camera obscura* design. This really made the instrument into a box camera, lacking only the shutter and film to take pictures. As such, it was the optical equivalent of the eye—but still no one had the insight to realize this.

Leonardo da Vinci (1452–1519) came very close. He realized that the eye must somehow form an image out of the rays that it receives from an object. But he had no understanding of the part played by the retina, and to him it was inconceivable that an object could form an upside-down image in the eye. Instead, he proposed several elaborate schemes for the rays to be doubly refracted within the eyeball and somehow funneled right side up into a channel at the center of the optic nerve. In this way he presumed that tiny representations of the objects could be conducted inward to impress themselves upon the hollow ventricles of the brain. There they could commingle with similar representations brought in by other nerves for the senses of touch, taste, hearing, and smell in such a way that all objects could be fully perceived. This is a prime example of what might be called the "wastebasket theory" of brain function. In other words, the brain gets small, unprocessed samples thrown into it from the outside world, and somehow uses these scraps to reconstruct a subjective model of that world for us to contemplate.

THE SEVENTEENTH AND EIGHTEENTH CENTURIES

As we examine the later history of vision, we find a slowly developing realization that the brain is not a "little man" (homunculus) that has to organize all the incoming scraps of information from the sense organs. In fact, the eye and the visual pathways selectively transduce and process those aspects of the visual stimulus that are likely to be of greatest significance for adaptive behavior.

The Retinal Image

It is interesting to speculate that anyone acquainted with the facts about optics, as summarized by Alhazen in about the year 1000 A.D., could have deduced that an inverted image of the outside world is formed on the retina at the back of the eye. Yet this seemingly obvious and fundamental conclusion was not drawn until 600 years later. Johannes Kepler (1571–1630) succeeded where others had failed, in large part because he was able to question—and then to cast aside—several classical notions that stood in the way (see Lindberg, 1976). First was the traditional view that an object's size and form were directly perceived by virtue of the fact that small copies or rays from the object fell directly on a sensitive region of the eyeball. Platter (1536–1614) had realized from the gross anatomy of the eye (Vesalius, 1543) that the crystalline lens of the eye was not part of the sensory structures. He concluded that the lens acts only to magnify the region of the retina over which the rays from an object will fall, but he failed to take the additional step of realizing that the retina would then bear an optical image of the external object. Of the lens he wrote, " . . . placed before the nerve and the pupil, it collects the species passing into the eye as rays and, spreading them over the whole of the retiform nerve, presents them enlarged in the manner of an interior looking glass, so that the nerve can more easily perceive them" (Platter, cited in Lindberg, 1976, p. 176).

A second fallacy that Kepler had to overcome was an idea of the perspectivists, culminating in the work of Della Porta. This was the notion that a clear impression of an external object can only be mediated by the bundle of rays passing through the center of the pupil. The more oblique rays entering through the margin of the pupil were thought to follow a different path that would tend to blur the image—a defect that would not be very serious, since these oblique rays are weakened by being diverted into a more indirect path.

A third concept, and the one that gave Kepler the most trouble, was the firmly established notion that the eye must necessarily receive a right-side-up impression of the outside world. Kepler dealt easily with the other traditional stumbling-blocks, because they disappeared at once when rays were correctly traced as they entered the cornea, traversed the optic media, and were all focused to form a sharp image at the back of the eye (see Fig. 5 1). Lindberg, a historian of optics, speaks thus of Kepler's achievement: "But if Kepler could not satisfactorily solve the problem posed by inversion and reversal of the image, he could escape it by excluding it from optics—that is, by distinguishing between the optical and the nonoptical aspects of vision in such a way as to place this problem in the latter category. Optics, he therefore argues, ceases with the formation of the picture on the retina, and what happens after that is somebody else's busi-

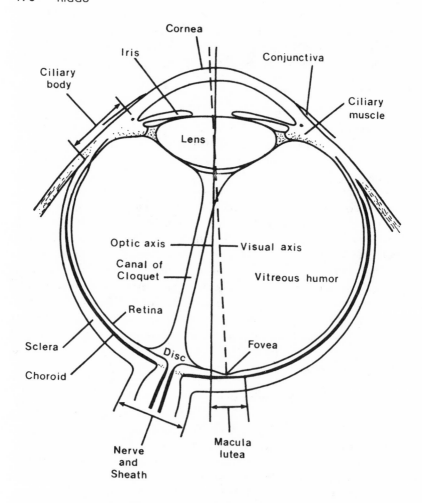

FIG. 5.1. A diagram of the human eye. From "Introduction to Sensa-tion/Perception" by D. H. McBurney and V. B. Collings, Englewood Cliffs, NJ, Prentice-Hall, 1977. Copyright 1977 by Prentice-Hall. Reprinted by permission.

ness" (Lindberg, 1976, p. 203). Lindberg then supplies a quotation from Kepler himself that shows him as still a medievalist:

> I say that vision occurs when the image of the whole hemisphere of the world that is before the eye . . . is fixed on the reddish white concave surface of the retina. How the image or picture is composed by the visual spirits that reside in the retina and the [optic] nerve, and whether it is made to appear before the soul or the tribunal of the visual faculty by a spirit within the hollows of the brain . . . . all this I leave to be disputed by the physicists. (Kepler, cited in Lindberg, 1976, p. 203)

Thus Kepler was fully aware that his optical achievements, although representing a real breakthrough toward the understanding of vision, were only a first step. Even his explanation of the nature of the retinal image was not immediately accepted (see Boring, 1942; Polyak, 1957). Soon, however, Scheiner (1579–1650) gave it a convincing proof by cutting away the opaque coats in back of an animal eye and showing that a reversed and inverted image was indeed formed on the exposed retina whenever an illuminated object was placed in front of the eye. Scheiner also made convincing diagrams in which the optical properties of the eye were compared with those of a simple system of lenses and with the *camera obscura.*

After this objective observation by Scheiner, supporting evidence of another kind was contributed by Mariotte (1668). By carefully fixating on a spot in front of one eye, he was able to cause the disappearance of a test spot lying at a particular location in the temporal field. He was then able to show that the test spot had been imaged directly on the optic disk, which is the place on the retina from which the optic nerve leaves the eyeball. This was indeed an isolated "blind spot," since test objects could be seen all around it. Mariotte correctly concluded that this is proof of the point-for-point "reception of rays which form a picture of objects at the back of the eye." Unfortunately he also drew the erroneous conclusion that the choroid, rather than the retina, is the sensitive membrane. That error is perhaps excusable, because microscopic evidence was not available in his day to show the distribution of the rod and cone receptors, and hence to reveal their absence in the region of the optic disk.

Binocular Fusion

René Descartes (1596–1650) made a significant beginning in the attempt to trace the visual message from the eyes to the brain. He advanced the hypothesis that there is a point-for-point projection of each retinal image on the surface of the brain. Furthermore, he raised the question of how we experience a single, fused visual scene when we look at it with two different eyes. He answered his own questions as well as he could by the use of diagrams that revealed the still-primitive state of the anatomy that had recently been worked out by Vesalius and others of his day. One such diagram shows the optic nerve from each eye going back to the optic chiasm, but maintaining a complete separation as it diverges again to a cerebral ventricle on the same side of the brain (see Fig. 5.2). Corresponding points on the two ventricles are then shown to send nerves to a single point on the pineal body at the center of the brain. Descartes was much impressed by the pineal organ because it was the only unitary structure he could find in a brain that was otherwise completely separated into two hemispheres. He thought, therefore, that the pineal body must be the "seat of the soul" where a single perception could be formed of any external object. Finally, there was an additional set of nerves to take the visual impressions to other brain centers for

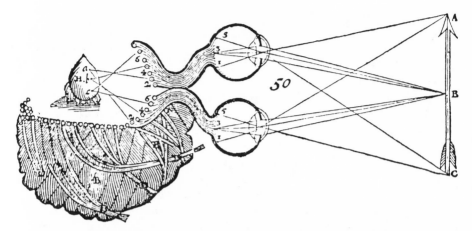

FIG. 5.2. Descartes' diagram of the projection of visual information to the brain. Note that corresponding points from the two eyes are represented as combining their input to the pineal organ (H). From Descartes, R. Traité de l'Homme, 1664.

storage in the memory. All this was thought to be accomplished by "animal spirits" that travelled through tiny pores between the fibers of the optic nerve pathways and carried the messages to brain centers and the pineal gland.

Throughout the remainder of the seventeenth and eighteenth centuries there were many attempts, only partially successful, to improve on Descartes' models for visual transmission and for binocular fusion. Reference to the pineal organ was dropped, and the concept of "animal spirits" gradually began to fade away. Willis (1621–1675), for example, described the optic nerves not as hollow tubes but as bundles of fibers. Neither he nor Briggs (about 1685), however, understood the fact that fibers of the optic tract extended to the superior colliculi and to the striate cortex. Briggs joined Galen (about 129–201), Vesalius (1514–1564), Descartes, and many others in the belief that no exchange of fibers took place in the chiasm. Some others maintained that within the chiasm there is a complete crossing of fibers (as indeed there is in some animals) from each eye to the opposite side of the brain. Still other writers began to view the chiasm as a place where messages from one eye could combine with those from the other.

Sir Isaac Newton (1642–1727) had the insight to realize that a partial crossing of the optic nerve could take place in the chiasm such that fibers originating from the left half of each retina would travel to the *left* hemisphere, and those from the right half to the *right* hemisphere (see Fig. 5.3). This hypothesis turned out to be the correct one, as eventually proven by clinical cases of partial loss of vision. A brain tumor in the *right* hemisphere, for example, was shown to produce a loss of vision ("hemianopia") for objects appearing to the left of the point of fixation. This is explained by the fact that such objects are imaged on the *right* half of the

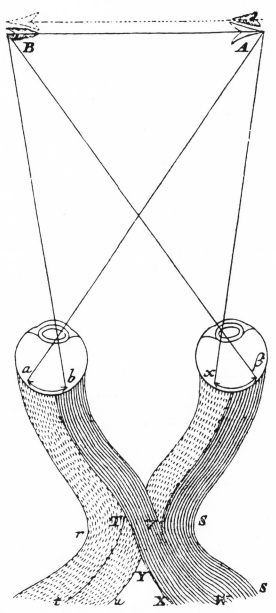

FIG. 5.3.   Partial crossing of optic nerve fibers in the optic chiasm as first recognized by Newton. From J. Taylor, Mechanismus des menschlichen Auges, 1750.

retina of each eye, and are therefore represented only on the defective (right) side of the brain.

Despite the above, there was scarcely any recognition of the importance of the cerebral cortex until far into the nineteenth century. The reason may lie in the fact that the eyes and the optic tracts were more readily accessible, and of more obviously specialized function, than were the hemispheres of the brain. It is also true that microscopes of sufficiently high quality and magnifying power were not used very much for observation of the brain or the retina until well into the nineteenth century (see Polyak, 1957).

Color Vision

The seventeenth and eighteenth centuries also failed to produce much new knowledge about color vision. However, a few men of genius in those times did deduce, mainly from astute observation of common experiences, some of the fundamental principles.

Mariotte, for example, anticipated by 150 years the "Law of Specific Nerve Energies" that is commonly attributed to Müller, Bell, and Magendie. To quote from Weale (1957), Mariotte (1620–1684) wrote:

> It is difficult not to confuse that which derives from the objects from that which derives from our senses . . . push a finger against the corner of your eyes during the night, and on the opposite side you will see appear a luminous circle. If one strikes a wall with one's head violently, one sees flashes of lightning and lights; if one closes one's eyes having looked at the sun one sees for some time thereafter a type of light the brightness of which gradually diminishes, and changes successively into less lively colours, such as red, green, blue and violet. From which it follows that light, heat, and the majority of other sensory effects do not belong to their objects; but that these phenomena are determined by modification of our senses, whatever the cause of such modifications may be. This being so, one clearly sees that it is not easy to talk of Colours. (Mariotte, cited in Weale, 1957, p. 650).

Mariotte did have something to say about colors, too, after observing the spectrum formed by passing white light through a prism. It seemed to him that there were three primary colors: red, yellow, and blue. Green was there, too, but he was not using a pure spectrum and he thought that green could be accounted for as the result of overlapping in the yellow and blue portions of the screen on which his poorly focused rays were seen.

In short, Mariotte has some claim to be the originator of the trichromatic theory of color. The three categories referred to the light, however, and not to the visual receptors as in the later theories of Young and Helmholtz. Leonardo da Vinci in 1519 had considered that there were four primaries, and Newton in 1666 spoke of seven or more colors that are "original and inherent" properties of light that has been refracted by a prism. Newton did appreciate the point that Mariotte had stressed a few years earlier: The rays themselves are not colored, but rather they have the power to set up a sensation of color in an observer. Yet Newton's genius was used more intensively to deduce some of the physical laws pertaining to light, rather than to visual phenomena (see Boring, 1942; MacAdam, 1970; Polyak, 1957).

The contrast between Mariotte and Newton nowhere appears more clearly than in the conclusions that each drew after forming a spectrum with rays of white light refracted by a prism. As we have seen, Mariotte's major interest was in the appearance of colors. He realized that the whole range of colors could be described quite well as a blending of three principal colors: a trichromatic theory. Newton, on the other hand, was mainly concerned with the light rays themselves, and he realized that the spectrum represented a continuum in which seven or more colors could be recognized. The continuum was of major interest to Newton because it demonstrated that all visible light could be analyzed in terms of the angle of its refraction by the prism. He also showed that the color of an object depended on the relative amounts of reflection from its surface of the various spectral components. Most important of all was his finding that all the components could be recombined to produce white.

The stature of Newton as a scientist is no more beautifully illustrated than in his *Opticks* written in 1704. He proceeds by stating theorems and giving proofs of each that are mostly not the results of common observation or speculation, but of crucial experiments performed in his rooms at Trinity College, Cambridge. In the course of his color experiments he demonstrated additive and subtractive mixtures, flicker fusion, desaturation, and selective reflection. Although he did not have a periodic wave concept of light, he did fancy at one time that there was an analogy between the sequence of the seven spectral colors and the musical scale of seven full tones. He made a "color circle" diagram to express the relationships among the colors, but he did not relate it to a trichromatic system. He therefore failed to grasp the fact that complementary colors should lie opposite one another on the diagram, and he did not believe that a white could be produced by the mixture of two complementary colors. He was also in error in thinking that dispersion was the same for all types of glass prism.

It is particularly significant that up to this time in history, no one had made such a sharp distinction between light and vision. From the time of Newton onward, physicists began to study light for its own sake. In the remainder of this chapter we shall continue to survey the history of vision without going into such major developments in the physics of light as the corpuscular theory of Newton, the wave theory of Huygens, the electromagnetic theory of Maxwell, or the twentieth century theories of wave mechanics. Nor can we include the invention of devices such as the telescope, microscope, spectrometer, camera and a host of light sources, light detectors, and optical devices for measurement and control that have greatly aided the progress of vision research.

Near the close of the eighteenth century, Joseph Priestley (1777) gave an account of a case of a color vision defect that we would now call protanopia. This, surprisingly enough, was apparently the first historical record that has yet been found of color blindness. Walls (1956) has noted that Priestley's article stimulated a number of other observers to notice color vision defects; among them was the distinguished physicist, John Dalton, whose description of his own perceptions (Dalton, 1798) shows that he was probably a deuteranope. Walls also called attention to the works of Palmer (1777), whose trichromatic theory of color vision clearly went beyong Marriotte's concept of three types of light. It antedated that of Thomas Young (1801) and explained color blindness thus, as edited by MacAdam (1970):

> It is quite evident that the retina must be composed of three kinds of fibers, or membranes, each analogous to one of the three primary rays and susceptible of being stimulated only by it. Equal sensibility of these three classes constitutes true vision; any deficiency of sensibility as well as excessive sensibility of any class constitutes false vision. There are persons who, although they can see clearly, cannot distinguish colors . . . because each kind of fiber is stimulated by all of the three rays. (Palmer, as edited by MacAdam, p. 48).

As Walls points out, this is an explanation of color blindness as a condition in which the differential color selectivity of the receptors does not develop normally. This is the hypothesis commonly thought not to have originated until a hundred years later, in the writings of Aitken, Leber, and Fick; for details see Graham (1965).

Palmer also experimented with a spectrum. He concluded, as had Mariotte, that only three spectral colors are fundamental, and that green results from a mixture of yellow and blue. Palmer also described an experiment in which he mixed little particles of blue, red, and yellow pencil materials in the correct proportions so that when viewed at a distance they matched a gray sample. This experiment provided added support for his theory that there are only three fundamental kinds of color.

In summary, the seventeenth and eighteenth centuries involved a gradual breakdown of the classical dependence on tradition and authority in the field of vision and color. The beginnings of scientific scepticism and experimentation produced, in some few original thinkers, ideas that were to be exploited more elegantly in the nineteenth and twentieth centuries.

THE NINETEENTH CENTURY

The study of vision, like all other branches of knowledge, made enormous progress in the nineteenth century. In attempting to review it, we could follow certain lines of thought as they evolved through the work of one researcher after another. For instance, we could show that the earlier concerns of Mariotte and Palmer about sensory quality led to an expanded tradition of visual phenomenalism in the nineteenth century writings of Goethe (1749–1832), Purkinje (1787–1869), Müller (1801–1858), and Hering (1834–1918). Another intellectual line could perhaps be drawn from the earlier works of Kepler and Newton through the nineteenth century empirical and experimental tradition of Young (1773–1829), Helmholtz (1821–1894), Maxwell (1831–1879), and von Kries (1853–1928). But these lines of intellectual descent are by no means pure, and would leave out such new fields as visual histology, neurophysiology, and photochemistry. So let us try instead to look at some of the highlights in the nineteenth century subject areas of color vision, the neurophysiology of vision, brain centers for vision, and physiological optics.

Color Vision

Thomas Young (1801, 1802) wrote only a few pages about color vision, but his reasoning was clear. He carried out pioneering experiments on optical interference, experiments which convinced him that light was a form of wave motion. He therefore concluded that, in general, a visual stimulus includes waves of all possible lengths throughout the spectrum. So how does the eye distinguish colors? What he wrote was,

> Now, as it is almost impossible to conceive each sensitive point of the retina to contain an infinite number of particles, each capable of vibrating in perfect unison with every possible undulation, it becomes necessary to suppose the number limited; for instance to the three principal colours, red, yellow and blue, of which the undulations are related to magnitude nearly as the numbers 8, 7 and 6; and that each of the particles is capable of being put in motion less or more forcibly by undulations differing less or more from a perfect unison; for instance, the undulations of green light being nearly in the ratio of 6½, will affect equally the particles in unison with yellow and blue, and produce the same effect as light composed of those two species; and each sensitive filament of the nerve may consist of three portions, one for each principal colour. (Young, 1802, p. 20).

Trichromatic Theory.   These statements are the essence of what we now know as the Young-Helmholtz trichromatic theory of color vision. Young's unique contribution was to reconcile the idea of three types of sensory unit, having overlapping sensitivities to wavelength, with the physical fact of a continuous range of wavelengths of light. He later changed the three color designations to red, green, and violet. As we have seen, the idea that there are three basic colors was not new; Mariotte (1717) and Palmer (1777) had advocated it, and even Lomonosov (1757) had expounded a rather fanciful chemical model of it (see Weale, 1957). But Young's was clearly a physiological model; his theory was not that there are three types of light rays, but three types of physiologically sensitive material in the eye. This version of trichromacy was not accepted at first, in part because the wave theory of light had not yet received much support. Even Helmholtz (1852) at first rejected Young's theory. It was not until after Maxwell's adoption of it (1855) and after some further experiments of his own that Helmholtz (1860) finally gave it his approval and developed it more fully in his *Handbook of Physiological Optics* (see Hurvich & Jameson, 1949). Helmholtz greatly strengthened the theory by his experiments on additive and subtractive mixtures of color. But the direct measurements of three types of cone pigment had to await the refinement of techniques that were not available until the 1960s. Rather than continue the misleading label of "Young-Helmholtz" theory, it would seem best from now on simply to call it the "trichromatic theory" of color vision. By 1860 Helmholtz was able to give a thorough account of the trichromatic theory, together with evidence by Grassman (1853) and Maxwell (1952, 1857) on the mixture of colors (see MacAdam, 1970).

The trichromatic theory, in the simple form given by Young, was initially thought to have problems. First, there was the mistaken notion that the theory rested on the assumption that three particular wavelengths could be found that were uniquely capable of arousing the three basic "particles" in the retina. On this assumption, it should be true that additive mixtures of the three wavelengths could always be adjusted to match any color in the spectrum or in extra-spectral space. Experiments soon revealed, however, that no three wavelengths could accomplish this. Instead of simply adding the three primary wavelengths together, it was found to be necessary to add one of the primaries to the unknown color and match this mixture to an additive mixture of the other two primaries. This manipulation can be thought of as the mathematical equivalent of giving one of the primaries a negative sign and giving the other two positive signs. But if the theory is supposed to represent the stimulation of color receptors, how can one of the stimuli have a negative effect?

Another unfulfilled prediction concerns one of the four "laws" of color mixture stated by Grassman (1854), namely that the total intensity of a mixture is the sum of the intensities of the lights mixed. The development of effective devices for the mixing of colors showed this statement to be quite inaccurate. Helmholtz (1866) developed an optical system for selecting spectrally pure lights and combining them on a screen. Maxwell (1856) developed the now familiar color wheel for the high-speed fusion of three primary colors on interlocking sector disks. No three primaries were ever found to be completely satisfactory for producing mixtures that would be equivalent in brightness to the sum of the brightness values of the three components (see Boring, 1942).

Opponent-Color Theory. Hering, in 1872, vigorously opposed the trichromatic theory and proposed an opponent-color theory to account for the phenomenal appearance of colors. Like da Vinci and Goethe, Hering adopted a four-color theory, on the grounds that the average observer recognizes four pure and simple hues: red, yellow, green and blue. He went on to point out that red and green oppose one another; for example, if you stare at green for awhile, you get a red afterimage as the light is turned off. Likewise, yellow and blue are opponent colors. Another example is found in the appearance of mixtures of color; here, the cancellation of one opponent color by the other is a familiar fact: No one ever speaks of a reddish green or a yellowish blue. Instead, when yellow and blue are added together the hues cancel, and the result is perceived as an achromatic gray.

Hering developed a theory to account for these phenomena. He assumed that there was a red-green visual substance in the retina and that it could respond in either of two directions (see Fig. 5.4). An "assimilative" response occurred when green light hit the retina; a "dissimilative" response occurred with red light; and no response occurred in this particular substance with an equal mixture of the two. Similarly, a second visual substance responded assimilatively to blue and dissimilatively to yellow, and a third visual substance responded with assimilation to black and dissimilation to white. Some writers have thought that Hering meant this substance to be a visual pigment in a cone receptor. Hurvich and Jameson (1964) have attacked this view, however, and maintain that Hering was

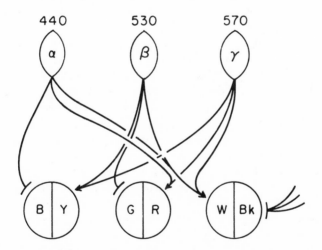

FIG. 5.4.   Schema for the opponent-process neural mechanisms. The three types of cone receptor, α, β and γ, have peak sensitivities for lights of 440, 530, and 570 nm, respectively. Lines show the connections from these cones to the three opponent-process mechanisms, blue-yellow, green-blue and white-black. One type of connection is excitatory and the other is inhibitory; which is which is arbitrary. From "Opponent Processes as a Model of Neural Organization" by L. M. Hurvich and D. Jameson, *American Psychologist,* 1974, *29,* 88–102. Copyright 1974 by the American Psychological Association. Reprinted by permission.

speaking more generally of a neural element, not necessarily in the eye but within the visual tract.

Hering put forward this theory as an example of a fundamental principle in physiology, namely that of an equilibrium state. He also found that principle to apply to the temperature sense, where warm or cold is felt by the body only as a departure from a physiological neutral point (see Boring, 1942; Hurvich & Jameson, 1964). The neutral point itself could be raised or lowered by prolonged exposure, as when tepid water is felt as cold after one steps out of a hot bath. Similarly, the eye adjusts to wearing yellow sun glasses, and removing them makes white objects look blue.

Hering criticized Helmholtz for treating color contrast as a product of experience or as an unconscious inference made by the mind. For Hering, contrast was built into the nervous system and did not need to be learned or deduced.

Hering's ideas quickly met with opposition, not only because of their polemical tone, but also because they seemed to contradict established facts. Particularly incredible was the idea that a physiological substance could respond in two opposite ways to stimuli, depending on their quality. Physical scientists scoffed at that idea, because they were used to seeing a single continuum of large responses to strong stimuli running down to progressively smaller responses as stimulation was reduced to an absolute threshold. A more specific objection was to Hering's claim that red and green lights cancel one another. Had not Newton found that spectral yellow light could be matched by a mixture of spectral red light plus green, and had not Helmholtz found this to be true even in the case of binocular mixture? Still another objection was that protanopia (one form of color blindness) involves a loss of sensitivity to red light without a corresponding loss of sensitivity to green. How could that be true, if red and green responses are simply two opposite reactions within the same visual substance? One more inconsistency was that white and black did not cancel each other as did the opposite colors. Instead, the result of mixing white with black is not zero but a gray that is intermediate between the two.

Let us defer the answers to some of these questions until the end of this chapter, because they depend on facts and viewpoints only recently developed. We shall conclude this section by describing the one serious attempt that was made within the nineteenth century to resolve the apparent conflict between the views of Helmholtz and Hering (see Boring, 1942).

Zone Theory. Donders, in 1881, put forth what has come to be known as a "stage" or "zone" theory of color vision. His idea was that the trichromatic theory might well hold for the retinal receptors, whereas opponent processes might take place in the brain. Thus, yellow could be signalled in the brain as a simple and fundamental color whenever the red and green retinal units were nearly equally stimulated.

Another sort of stage theory was proposed by G. E. Müller in 1896. Müller specifically proclaimed that psychic events all have correlates in brain activity. He spoke of "cortical gray" as being a sort of resting state in the brain, and he pointed out that in the dark we experience gray, rather than black or nothing at all, when the receptors are unstimulated and the Hering opponent mechanisms are all at rest. This idea anticipates the discovery by neurophysiologists that the brain exhibits spontaneous activity in the absence of stimulation.

In 1892, Christine Ladd-Franklin added a new twist to the stage theory. This was the notion that color vision evolved by stages out of a more primitive achromatic vision. She suggested that primitive animals have a black-white system, and that a more advanced stage in the evolutionary process provided a differentiation of white into blue and yellow. The final stage (so far!) is the breakdown of yellow into red and green.

All these nineteenth century theories of color vision excited much controversy and stimulated a good deal of experimentation. We shall return to them at the end of our survey of twentieth century knowledge of the color domain.

Neurophysiology of Vision

Neurophysiologists made enormous progress during the latter half of the nineteenth century. Until that time the process of photoreception and the neural processing that occurs within the retina were but poorly understood. In fact, it was not until the end of the nineteenth century that neurophysiologists began to build up an understanding of brain function. Polyak (1957) has given a thorough account of these developments, a brief summary of which is given below.

Retinal Neurophysiology. The gross anatomy of the eye was well known, but retinal histology was still in a primitive state in the early nineteenth century. Purkinje (1787–1869) was a keen observer of subjective phenomena that might help him to infer the functioning of retinal structures. He rediscovered, for example, the finding of Mariotte that the sensory structures can be excited to elicit sensations of light when the eyeball is turned to one side and a finger is pushed against the back of the eye. The resulting "phosphenes" were "seen" on the opposite side of the visual field, in agreement with the fact that the retina is normally stimulated by a reversed optical image of the field. He also described (Purkinje, 1825) the "blue-arc" phenomenon. This is best seen with monocular vision in a darkened room. If you fixate with the right eye, for example, on a point just to the right of a small patch of red light, you will notice a blue arc of light running around and above the fovea, and another blue arc below it, with the arcs seeming to stream out from the upper and lower ends of the red patch to the region of the blind spot. Purkinje made use of these arcs to deduce the paths of optic nerve fibers as they run along the vitreal surface of the retina and exit from the eyeball in the region of the blind spot. The explanation of this phenomenon (see Brindley, 1970) is probably that it is due to an electrical leakage from the nerve fibers that are strongly excited by the patch of red light. The leaked current somehow excites the blue-response retinal cells wherever they are sufficiently close to the active nerve fibers.

Still another phenomenon is the "Purkinje tree." This is the apparent trunks, branches and twigs that result from light entering the eye through a pinhole and casting shadows of the retinal blood vessels on the photoreceptors lying beneath them. The "Purkinje shift" is the fact that a spectrum seen in strong daylight looks brightest in the greenish-yellow range of wavelengths, whereas the brightest part of a weaker spectrum seen at night is found to have shifted about 50 nm toward the bluish-green region. Purkinje also noted the relatively poor discrimination of red and green colors as seen with the periphery of the retina, where yellow and blue could still be clearly differentiated. All these observations were put to good use, first by Purkinje himself and later by others, to verify hypotheses about retinal function.

Heinrich Müller (1820–64) was another pioneer student of retinal function. In 1854 he gave the first convincing proof that the visual photoreceptors lie at the back of the retina, next to the choroid layer. Even with the relatively crude microscopic viewing that was available at that time, Müller had been able to measure fairly accurately the thickness of the retina and the positions of the retinal blood vessels in human eyes available at autopsy. He had also been the first to notice a reddish color in the outer segments of the rod-shaped cells, and he guessed that these might be photoreceptors. To find out, he used Purkinje's technique of placing a small pinhole immediately in front of his own eye. Moving the pinhole from side to side of the pupil caused a displacement in the tree-like shadow pattern of the blood vessels. By measuring the extent of the displacement resulting from a given lateral movement of the pinhole, he could calculate the distance through the retina from the blood vessels to the receptors. The result was to show that the receptors must lie within the layer of the retina where microscopy had revealed the rods and cones. Only then was it possible to refute the old idea that the receptors must lie at the front of the retina, where light could stimulate them directly without the seemingly improbable necessity to travel first through the many nuclear and plexiform layers of the retina.

A particularly bizarre nineteenth-century theory (see Polyak, 1957) was the "catoptric hypothesis" of Bidder (1839). He had observed the true position of the retinal rods at the back of the eye, but he thought that they served mainly to reflect light back to the optic nerve fibers, which he believed to be the real photoreceptive structures at the front of the retina.

Polyak (1957) pointed out that, although optical microscopes had been available since Leeuwenhoek (1632–1723) and Malpighi (1628–94), their usefulness was very limited for examining nervous tissue, which is nearly transparent in ordinary light. Early types of histological stain, such as chromic acids and salts,

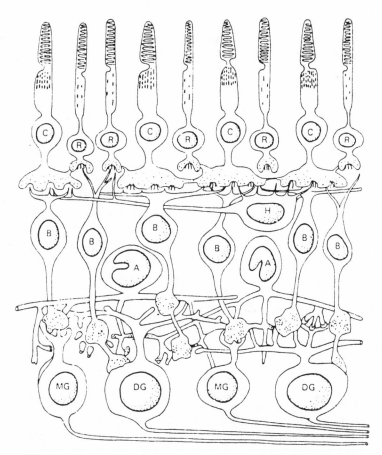

FIG. 5.5.   Diagram of retinal cells: C, cone; R, rod; B, bipolar; H, horizontal; A, amacrine; G, ganglion cells of various types. From "Organization of the Primate Retina" by J. W. Dowling and B. B. Boycott, *Proceedings of the Royal Society (London)*, 1966, *166B*, 80–111. Copyright 1966 by The Royal Society. Reprinted by permission.

were introduced between 1840 and 1860; they permitted a greatly improved viewing of the nerve cells and fibers of the retina, but left unsolved the true function of the plexiform layers. Then in 1873 a microscopic revolution occurred when Golgi introduced his famous silver stain; and in 1886 Ehrlich started using methylene blue to reveal retinal structures. These techniques revealed minute details of individual cells and their synaptic interconnections. Immediately it became apparent that the "cell theory" of Schwann (1838) and Schleiden (1838) was beautifully borne out in the retina. Separate and distinct bipolar cells and ganglion cells of various forms were identified and classified (see Fig. 5.5). At the same time, more and more evidence piled up for the "duplicity theory" of

Schultze (1825–74) that there were two types of photoreceptor—those that functioned under night-time conditions of low illumination (rods), and those that required higher light levels (cones). By the end of the century, Cajal (1852–1934) had contributed some of his magnificent drawings of retinal histology, showing the individual forms of retinal cells in a variety of animal species. The duplicity tbeory became firmly established with the evidence that nocturnal animals have rod receptors, diurnal ones have mainly cones, and many species, including man, have the best features of both.

Photochemistry of the Retina. Parallel to the progress in the histology of the retina was the development of retinal photochemistry (see Brindley, 1970; Dartnall, 1972). Thomas Young had supported the view that was common until the later nineteenth century, namely that waves of light somehow stimulate the optic nerve fibers by a physical process of sympathetic vibration. Before the end of the nineteenth century, the photochemical effects of light were formalized in the Grotthus-Draper Law (that only the radiation absorbed by a substance produces a photochemical effect) and the Bunsen-Roscoe Law (that the photochemical effect depends on the product of the intensity and duration of exposure). Boll (1876) described "visual purple" (now called rhodopsin) as a photochemical pigment in the retina of the frog; a year later, he verified that this pigment came from the rod receptors, as Heinrich Müller had first noted. Kühne (1878) extracted retinal rhodopsin with a solution of bile salts so that the bleaching effects of light and the chemical properties could be studied in vitro. Ayres and Kühne (1882) showed that bleached rhodopsin is regenerated in the retina, and that this process has a time course roughly parallel to that of dark adaptation. König (1894) measured the spectral absorption curve of rhodopsin and showed that it was closely related to the human scotopic luminosity function. Finally, Abelsdorff (1897) had the idea of measuring spectral absorption by the living retina, an idea that is basic to the current use of human retinal densitometry. The photochemical basis for rod (night) vision thus was well established by the end of the nineteenth century, but little was known of the pigments involved in cone (daytime) vision.

Retinal Electrophysiology. As early as 1819 Purkinje had observed that visual "phosphenes" could be produced by passing an electric current through the eye. In 1848 DuBois-Reymond noted that the eye itself is electrically polarized; the cornea behaves like the positive pole of a dry cell, and the back of the eyeball acts as the negative pole. Holmgren (1865) measured an increase in this voltage in response to a flash of light. Kühne and Steiner (1880) carefully removed the retina from the rest of a frog eye and found that it was the retina that generated the electrical response; the remainder of the eyeball was incapable of responding to a flash of light. For this reason, the response had come to be known as the electro-retinogram (ERG). However, no further progress in electrical recording was possible until the development of twentieth-century devices such as fast-acting galvanometers, amplifiers, and instruments for making permanent records (see Granit, 1947).

Brain Centers for Vision

In contrast to the rapid development of the anatomy and physiology of the eye was the relatively slow progress of research on the brain. Polyak (1957) observed:

> It is a remarkable fact that . . . until approximately the middle of the nineteenth century, only sporadic attempts were made to investigate the minute structure of the great cerebral hemispheres and to determine their probable function. This was especially true of the cerebral cortex and its connections with the rest of the nervous system. It almost seems as if there had been a tacit agreement among the scientists not to intrude into the sacred precinct of human anatomy—the repository of the soul, the seat of the reasoning mind. (p. 117)

There was little agreement in the early nineteenth century among the few who dared to speculate about brain function. Gall (1758–1828) presumed that particular psychic functions were represented by particular areas of the brain. His doctrine of phrenology assumed further that individual differences in the size of these centers were so great as to cause detectable protuberances on the corresponding locations on the skull. Fluorens (1794–1867) held the opposite view that the cerebral cortex was a functionally homogeneous mass. He did, however, clearly recognize the functional distinctness of the various motor and sensory connections with the cortex, and he was the first to appreciate the fact that vision has input into the cortex.

Meanwhile, various forms of experimental and clinical evidence began to appear. Baillarger (1840) found structural variations within the cortex, including six identifiable layers from the outer to the inner surface. Fritsch and Hitzig (1870) found a point-for-point representation in the motor cortex of the anesthetized dog such that electrical stimulation of each point would elicit the response of a given muscle group. Munk (1839–1912) also used the dog to demonstrate an accurate representation of retinal hemi-fields on the contralateral hemisphere in the occipital region. Graefe (1828–70) observed unilateral brain defects in patients showing hemianopia; and Hun, in 1887, mapped the visual fields of certain patients to demonstrate cases in which a particular quadrant of the field was rendered blind by a correspondingly located brain lesion.

By the end of the nineteenth century, Flechsig (1896) had shown the progressive myelination of nerve fibers in the human visual system before and after birth. Early myelination took place in the particular "projection centers" for smell, taste, somesthesis, vision, and hearing. The corresponding "association areas" developed more slowly.

Thus, the old "omnivalence" doctrine that the cerebral hemispheres were only for higher "psychic" functions began to give way to the more mechanistic view of functional specialization and localization as we know it today (see Polyak, 1957, p. 145).

Physiological Optics

Helmholtz's *Handbook of Physiological Optics* appeared in three volumes in the years from 1856 to 1866. This monumental encyclopedia, in the best tradition of German scientific handbooks, attempted to cover all aspects of the subject and to include all relevant literature. So great was its impact that even today the third edition, twice published in English translation (Helmholtz, 1962), is frequently consulted by visual scientists. Helmholtz defined "physiological optics" as "the science of the visual perceptions by the sense of sight." He has been called "the last universal scientist"; a physicist, physiologist, and psychologist. Indeed, the three volumes of his handbook were concerned with (I) the path of light in the eye, (II) the nervous mechanism of vision, and (III) the interpretation of visual sensations.

Our coverage of physiological optics in the nineteenth century must necessarily be brief, calling attention to a few of the main ideas explored in Helmholtz's handbook and pointing to a few contributions of other visual scientists. We exclude topics covered in the Perception chapter (Chap. 7, this volume) even though Helmholtz included them in his coverage of physiological optics. We arbitrarily group the remaining areas of physiological optics under the three headings of eye movements, dioptrics of the eye, and visual psychophysics. The historical treatments by Boring (1942, 1950) and Polyak (1957) may be consulted for details.

Eye Movements.   In the nineteenth century there was a clear recognition of the importance of eye movements. Johannes Müller (1826) wrote a monograph on them, and further descriptions were given by Donders, Listing, Wundt, Helmholtz, Hering, and many others. In the absence of objective measurements of eye position and rotation, most of the studies were based on the assumption that, "When the head is clamped . . . the globe of the eye assumes a perfectly definite orientation . . . for each direction . . . of fixation" (Donders' Law, 1847), and, "Any movement of the eye . . . is equivalent to an angular displacement of the globe around an axis passing through the center of rotation of the eye" (Listing's Law, 1854). In other words, it is assumed that the eye movements are under perfect visual control such that the foveal center of the retina is always lined up with the center of rotation and with the point of fixation. If this is granted, one may then proceed to a geometrical description of visual space in which any given point of fixation is characterized as the intersection of two lines,

POINT OF FIXATION

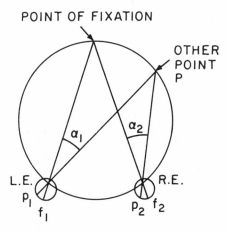

FIG. 5.6.   The Vieth-Müller horopter: the locus of points determined when the included angles α_1 and α_2 from the two eyes (L.E. and R.E.) are equal. Corresponding points on the retina are p_1 and p_2 when the eyes fixate at a point that is imaged at f_1 and f_2. From ''Binocular Vision'' by K. N. Ogle, Philadelphia, Saunders, 1950. Copyright 1950 by Saunders. Reprinted by permission.

namely those proceeding from the fovea and center of rotation of the left and right eyes, respectively.

Given the above geometrical construction for a particular point of fixation, it was shown by Vieth (1818) and J. Müller (1826) that all other points stimulating geometrically corresponding points on the two retinas lie on a horizontal circle drawn through the point of fixation and the optical (nodal) points of ray intersection within the two eyeballs. This Vieth-Müller circle (see Fig. 5.6) is a ''horopter'' defined as the geometric locus of points in external space that should stimulate corresponding points on the two retinas. This later history of the horopter concept, as developed by Helmholtz, Hering, Hillebrand, Tschermak, Ogle, and others, has brought out the following: Corresponding geometrical points on the two retinas do not necessarily correspond with points seen as single in binocular viewing. In fact, the single-vision horopter is never truly a circle. It is concave only for near viewing; it becomes nearly linear at a middle distance, and convex at greater distances. The exact form of the empirical horopter is, in fact, dependent on stimulus parameters such as color and intensity, as well as on individual differences from one subject to another.

Despite the failings of a strictly Euclidean geometry of space, it gradually became clear that the positions of the two eyes must be controlled with extraordinary precision in order that a fixated point in space shall be imaged on corresponding points of the two retinas. Donders, Helmholtz, Hering, and Wundt all made use of an afterimage method to verify this: A bright point that is fixated binocularly for a few moments will generate a dark afterimage in the central fovea of each eye such that, wherever the eyes are subsequently moved, the afterimage seems to coincide in position and stereoscopic depth with the newly fixated point. Hering (1879, transl. 1942) was particularly impressed with the accuracy and spontaneity of this control. He formulated a law of "central unitary innervation for coordinated eye movements" and viewed the whole system as exemplifying his nativist ideas of behavioral development. For him, the "corresponding points" on the two retinas represent innate neural connections with a common point in the brain, and this is the basis for stereoscopic disparity and the horopter. Helmholtz (1856, transl. 1962) espoused a more empirical approach in which the cues for visual depth are learned through childhood experience that associates kinaesthetic and tactual sensations with the sensory and motor activities of the visual system. Helmholtz also emphasized that no purely retinal interpretation of visual space can be successful. He pointed out, for example, the fact that visual objects seem to *stay still* even when you examine them by moving your eyes voluntarily from one point to another. These eye movements, of course, cause the images of the objects to move correspondingly across the retina. However, if you close one eye and push lightly on the lid of the open eye to make it move passively, then the world *does* seem to move through a corresponding distance. This demonstrates a tie-in between the message sent out by the brain to command the eye to move and the sensory message from the retina that a visual movement has occurred. If these two messages correspond perfectly, the subject makes the "unconscious inference" that the *eye* has moved and not the objects out in space. In other words, a person uses his "sense of effort" in moving the eyes to correct for, or disregard, the corresponding amount of retinal displacement.

In summary, the importance and precision of eye movements were first clearly recognized during the nineteenth century, and many theoretical problems about them were raised and partially answered by ingenious subjective observation. It remained for twentieth century advances in technique to make accurate records of eye movements and to probe the neural mechanisms for their initiation and control.

The Dioptrics of the Eye.   The nineteenth century brought many advances in the knowledge of the eyeball as an optical instrument. We have already noted that Kepler, in the early seventeenth century, made the basic discovery that an inverted image was formed by the rays from an object as they were focused by the cornea and lens. We have also noted Mariotte's discovery in 1668 of the blind spot, and the increasingly accurate knowledge of the eye contributed by Descartes (1637), Platter (1583), and Scheiner (1619). However, the *dioptrics* of the eye—the accurate measurement and correction of image formation on the retina—was mainly a nineteenth century development (see Polyak, 1957). The profession of optometry (testing and correction of optical defects; the United

States equivalent of the British term, "ophthalmic optics") became well established as the dioptric principles became known.

Thomas Young, in 1801, first clearly demonstrated that the human eye can accomodate for distance by changing the shape of the crystalline lens. Until that time, various erroneous explanations had been offered, including a change in the overall shape of the eye, a change of corneal curvature, and a simple assumption that the eye was incapable of any accommodation. It was Purkinje who, in 1823, discovered that he could see multiple reflections of a candle flame when he looked into a person's eye. The brightest reflection came from the front surface of the cornea; this is now called the "first Purkinje image." Dimmer ones came from the posterior surface of the cornea (second image), the anterior surface of the lens (third), and the posterior surface of the lens (fourth). Helmholtz (1856) refined the observation of these images so as to measure their size. He found that only the fourth image changed in size during accommodation, and that the size change was just sufficient to account for the increase in curvature of the posterior lens surface that is required to provide clear vision for near objects. In later studies, Wundt (1861) showed the importance of accommodation as a cue for judging the distance of near objects, and Donders (1864) measured the progressive loss of accommodation that must be attributed to failure of elasticity of the lens as a function of age. "Presbyopia" refers to the nearly total loss of accommodation in old age.

Helmholtz and Donders also gave systematic accounts of other dioptric deficiencies: The myopic eyeball is one in which the distance from cornea to retina is too large; near objects are thus seen clearly, but far ones are imaged in front of the receptors. Hyperopia is the opposite condition, in which the cornea-to-retina distance is too short and near objects are hard to see. Finally, astigmatism is an asymmetry of focus for lines seen in various orientations. This condition, identified in 1801 by Young, is mainly caused by a cornea that has a slightly cylindrical curvature in addition to its principal spherical shape. Appropriate testing procedures and corrective lenses were well advanced by the close of the nineteenth century.

Ophthalmology, as a separate branch of medicine, is often said to have been founded by Albrecht von Graefe. It was he who first demonstrated in 1856 the value of a careful study of a patient's visual "fields." He had the patient look directly at a fixation point, and then presented visual test objects at various distances and directions from that point. He showed that various clinical conditions could be diagnosed by the characteristic loss of vision resulting from them. Macular degeneration was an impairment of retinal function in and around the center of fixation. Tunnel vision was the opposite condition of normal central vision with impaired peripheral vision. Hemianopia was a loss of the right or left half of the visual field. Scotomata were isolated regions of impaired vision. The arc perimeter, introduced by R. Förster in 1867, greatly enhanced the ability of the examiner to place a test light at any desired distance and direction from the fixation point, thus facilitating the exploration and mapping of visual field defects. Diagnosis was immeasurably aided by Helmholtz' invention of the ophthalmoscope in 1851. This device gives the ophthalmologist a clear view of the *fundus,* or back of the eye, and thus reveals the condition of the blood vessels, optic disk, and other principal structures associated with the retina. Binocular depth perception and stereoscopic acuity could be measured by the use of the mirror stereoscope introduced by Wheatstone in 1838, or by the more compact refracting stereoscopes made by Brewster in 1849 and Holmes in 1861.

Visual Psychophysics. The nineteenth century was a period of increasing emphasis on quantification and measurement in all the sciences. Thus, when Fechner (1801–1887) first systematized the field of psychophysics, visual scientists were quick to seize upon this means of relating the intensities of sensory experience to the strengths of stimuli that produced them. Seemingly in imitation of their colleagues in the physical sciences, physiologists and psychologists engaged in a wide range of parametric studies of visual sensitivity. Absolute sensitivity was defined as the reciprocal of the threshold (minimum detectable) energy of the stimulating light; differential sensitivity was defined as the minimum perceptible change in the light. These thresholds were determined by one of the three basic procedures (methods of limits, average error, and constant stimuli) described by Fechner in his *Elemente der Psychophysik* in 1860 (see Boring, 1942).

Strangely enough, no physical device was available to measure the energy of light until 1881, when Langley produced a bolometer capable of this task. Langley himself later made the first determination of the absolute energy threshold of the eye, but neither he nor any subsequent investigator set up really suitable conditions for this determination until the experiments of Hecht and his colleagues in 1942. However, König in 1891 attempted to measure the relative brightnesses of spectral colors at various absolute intensities, and von Kries in 1894 used these determinations to give a quantitative account of the "duplicity theory" whose broad outlines had been proposed by Schultze (1886). By the close of the nineteenth century, this theory had been well developed. Human vision was shown to be duplex: Night (scotopic) vision was mediated by the rhodopsin-bearing rods, with a maximum spectral sensitivity at about 505 nm, while daytime (photopic) vision was mediated by pigments not yet identified in the cone receptors and showed maximum sensitivity at about 555 nm.

Other generalizations also became established at this time on the basis of threshold determinations (see Boring, 1942; Graham, 1965). Bloch (1885), for example, showed that the Bunsen-Roscoe Law of photochemistry is applicable to measurements of the psychophysical threshold for all short flashes of light. That is, the intensity (I) and duration (t) of a barely detectable stimulus flash are reciprocally related. Thus, Bloch's Law can be written as $I \cdot t = K$, where t is small, I is the minimum detectable intensity of light, and k is a constant. Similarly, Riccó (1877) established the reciprocity of area (A) and intensty (I) of a uniformly illuminated patch of light at threshold. Riccó's Law states that $A \cdot I = k$ for all small values of A, where I is again the minimum detectable light intensity and k a constant.

Bloch's and Riccó's laws apply most widely to scotopic conditions (full dark adaptation and peripheral stimulation). Here, the limiting durations and diameters of field may reach 0.1 sec and 2°, respectively. Under photopic conditions (light adaptation and foveal stimulation), the limiting values of t and A are much lower.

Another form of psychophysical threshold is the critical frequency of fusion (cff). Successive flashes of light are seen as flickering if the flash rate is below the cff. At higher rates, however, the light appears steady. Talbot (1834) and Plateau (1835) made brightness matches between a physically constant light and a light flashing at a rate well above the cff. The results led them to the Talbot-Plateau Law: The brightnesses appear equal when the fused flashes have the same time-averaged luminance as the steady light. For example, if the light and dark intervals in the fused beam are of equal duration, the flash luminance must be exactly twice as high as that of the steady light in order to match it in birghtness. This finding is, of course, consistent with Bloch's Law.

Ferry (1892) and Porter (1902) determined the cff as a function of luminance (L). The resulting Ferry-Porter Law may be written as,

$$\text{cff} = a + b \log L,$$

where a and b are constants. As could be expected, this generalization holds over separate ranges, with different values for a and b, for photopic and scotopic conditions.

Various other visual phenomena were discovered during the nineteenth century. Maxwell (1856) described the effect of looking at a field that is alternately illuminated with yellow and blue lights of high brightnesses. During the blue phase, a small dark spot is seen at the center of the fovea, with a larger dark ring surrounding it. This phenomenon, known as Maxwell's spot, probably results from differential absorption of the blue light by the *macula lutea*, a pigment that overlies the central region of the retina.

Haidinger (1844) described a pale yellow figure that can be seen with polarized light. This figure, known as Haidinger's brushes, can easily be seen when a bright field is viewed through a slowly rotating disk of polarizing film. The resulting figure looks like a bow tie centered on the point. It rotates in accordance with the plane of polarization. Its extent is similar to that of the Maxwell spot; hence it may result from differential absorption of polarized light by the macular pigment.

Benham (1894) produced illusory colors by rotation of a complex light-dark pattern illuminated by steady white light. The "Benham top" colors, like earlier

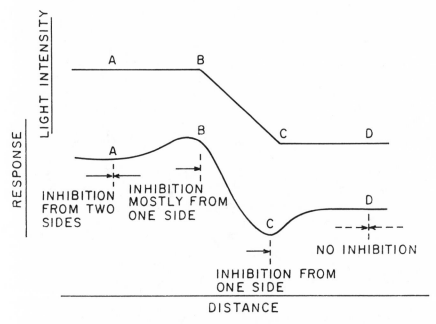

FIG. 5.7.   Prediction of the appearance of the Mach-band pattern from the facts of lateral inhibition in the scheme of Ratliff (1965). From "Introduction to Sensation/Perception" by D. H. McBurney and V. B. Collings, Englewood Cliffs, NJ, Prentice-Hall, 1977. Copyright 1977 by Prentice-Hall. Reprinted by permission.

ones described by Prévost (1826) and others (see Wade, 1976), can be attributed, at least in part, to afterimages that appear during the dark phase of the white-dark cycle. The afterimages from different color receptor mechanisms are supposed to have differing latent times, so that particular colors appear when the dark intervals are most favorable.

Another temporal effect, described by Brewster (1834) and Brücke (1864), is that flashes of light appear particularly bright when delivered at a rate of about 5 to 15 flashes per second. This is presumably related to the phenomenon described by Broca and Sulzer (1902). The Broca-Sulzer phenomenon is that a short flash of light appears to grow brighter if its duration is increased, and appears brightest if it has an intermediate duration, usually about 100 msec. Longer flashes, surprisingly, appear somewhat less bright. In all these cases of brightness enhancement there is presumably a complex interplay of on- and off-effects within the various components of the retinal network.

Brightness enhancement in the spatial domain was noted by Ernst Mach (1886). The *Mach bands* he observed were illusory border effects that occur at the edges of a pattern in which there is a steady change from dark to light (see Fig. 5.7). At one edge, a bright band is seen where the gradually increasing luminance gives way to a uniform region in which the luminance is no longer increasing. Conversely, a dark band is seen at the other edge where the luminance stops decreasing and stays at a steady level. No real increment or decrement of luminance is present, but the bands arise in the regions where there is an abrupt change in the slope of the spatial luminance distribution. Mach's interpretation of the effect, confirmed by much recent evidence (see Ratliff, 1965), is that bright and dark bands appear at the points of minimum and maximum spatial inhibitory interactions from one region of the retina to another.

In summary, the nineteenth century brought visual science to the point where nearly all the presently recognized phenomena had been described, many of them measured, and some of them well understood. This came about because of progress in the underlying scientific fields of physical optics, photo-chemistry, neuroanatomy, neurophysiology, and experimental psychology.

THE TWENTIETH CENTURY

As we approach our own period, we find an enormous acceleration in all areas of scientific research. The early part of the twentieth century saw a modest increase in the establishment of new institutes, departments, laboratories, and societies for vision research. The two World Wars drew heavily on scientists for the solution of military problems related to vision, and government support for vision research has continued to expand in both the applied and basic sectors. There are certainly more vision research people living today than the total of all those living in the past, and the published literature of the last 30 years probably includes more pages devoted to vision than the accumulated total from all previous generations.

Several questions arise at this point. First, has all this activity resulted in significant new discoveries and understanding, or has it merely filled in the details of a grand picture that had really assumed its final form by the time of Helmholtz, Hering, Maxwell, and Mach? Second, is it possible during a period of such hectic activity to evaluate, or even to summarize, the most significant discoveries? Or should this chapter come to a close at this point and leave to some future author the evaluation of our own progress in the field? Finally, even if our first two questions are answered with optimism, is there any way in which the vast number of accomplishments of the twentieth century can be summarized in the few pages that remain in this chapter?

Maintaining the optimistic view, I will attempt to outline the recent progress in vision research. It will be my thesis that most of this progress is the direct result of technical advances in all fields of science as they have been applied to vision. It seems to me that the new techniques have permitted us to go beyond the previous stages of subjective observation of visual phenomena. We are now studying the visual mechanisms themselves. For this reason, the remainder of this chapter will survey the highlights of discovery in the processing of visual information throughout the pathways from the receptors to the brain. Fortunately, the facts about vision have been gathered together in numerous books, handbooks, and chapters, to which the reader may turn for detailed explanations and for proper attribution to individual authors. In this chapter we can only sketch out the most novel of the ideas and discoveries.

Receptor Function

Selig Hecht (1892–1947) made a systematic attempt to account for the quantitative and qualitative characteristics of visual experience on the basis of receptor photochemistry. His main thesis was that psychophysically determined luminance and color thresholds could be accounted for by the extent to which light bleaches the receptor pigments of the rods and cones. Opposing these photochemical processes are reactions that proceed independently of light to restore the bleached pigments. The state of equilibrium between these processes was assumed to account for the level of adaptation, flicker fusion, brightness and color discrimination, and visual acuity. So ingeniously did Hecht proceed to fit the experimental data with his relatively simple theory that for many years before and after World War II this was accepted as the principal theoretical account of the visual process. Ironically, even though in nearly every case the processes that Hecht assumed to explain visual function have turned out to be wrong, or at best to be grossly oversimplified, his equations (Hecht, 1934) still provide a close approximation to many of the data.

A separate achievement of Hecht and his colleagues (Hecht, Shlaer, & Pirenne, 1942) has turned out to be of major significance. They set up conditions for optimal stimulation of the fully dark-adapted human eye, and measured the smallest amount of light necessary for detection of a flash. The outcome was that only about 5 to 14 individual quanta absorbed by the receptors constitute the absolute threshold of light. Furthermore, the test patch stimulated a region of the peripheral retina in which only about 500 rod receptors are present. It was further shown, by statistical (Poisson) analysis, that (1) a single quantum of light is sufficient to trigger the response of a single rod receptor, (2) the number of rods so triggered is 5 to 8 at threshold, and (3) the variability of responding to a stimulus flash at threshold is due to the physical uncertainty in the number of quanta per flash, rather than to neural or behavioral variability of responding. In the main, these conclusions are still supported by modern evidence (chapters by Barlow, Baumgardt, and Nachmias in Jameson & Hurvich, 1972).

The electron microscope became available after World War II, and Sjöstrand in 1948 began an extensive series of studies in which it was used to reveal the untrastructure of retinal cells. Each rod outer segment was shown to be stacked with hundreds of thin sacs or disks oriented crosswise of the rod. Later studies by Sjöstrand and others have revealed many further facts about the outer segments:

The lamellar structure is found in cones as well as in rods. The photosensitive pigment molecules are oriented crosswise of the disks. An "early receptor potential" (Brown & Murakami, 1964) is a graded response to light that is developed only if the molecular orientation remains intact (Cone, 1963; Goldstein & Berson, 1969). Hence, it is presumed that the lamellar structure functions as a battery of cells for the transduction of light into electrical signals (see Fuortes, 1972).

But what is the photochemical process itself? The volume edited by Dartnall (1972) is an authoritative account. Wald (1935) bleached rhodopsin extracted from the retinas of cattle and obtained a pale yellow carotenoid substance that he called retinene and that Morton and Goodwin (1944) showed to be aldehyde of Vitamin A. The presumption was that rhodopsin is a combination of retinene (now called retinal) with a protein named opsin. Furthermore, Hubbard and Wald (1952) found that a particular molecular configuration, namely the 11-cis form of retinal, was required for the rhodopsin to be sensitive to light. Thus, a critical feature of the photochemical response is a configurational change; the effect of light is to change the molecule from the 11-cis to the all-trans configuration.

The above is an over-simplified statement of the action of light on the photosensitive pigment. It omits the many additional stages in the process identified by Wald and his group and by Lythgoe, Dartnall, and many others. Nor does it elucidate the responses of cone pigments, which have turned out to be much more difficult to extract from the receptors. The books by Brindley (1970) and Rodieck (1973) provide summaries of this information, as well as much of what is to follow in this section on receptor function.

As early as 1939 Granit and Svaetichin introduced microelectrode recording for the isolation of responses from single visual cells. These early electrodes, however, were of relatively large tip diameter. They were useful only for making extracellular contact with large ganglion cells of the retina. Many years of electrode refinement, together with the design of low-noise amplifiers, were needed before it became possible, in the late 1960s, to penetrate and record from single cone receptors. Of particular interest is a 1967 study of Tomita, in which hundreds of single cones of the carp were successfully penetrated. Of these, 142 gave sufficiently reliable responses so that spectral response curves could be obtained. They grouped themselves into three types, showing peak sensitivities at 462, 529, and 611 nm, respectively. This is specific evidence for a trichromatic system of color vision at the cone receptor level.

Further evidence for three classes of cone receptor is provided by techniques of microspectrophotometry. Marks, Dobelle, and MacNichol (1964) and Brown and Wald (1964) accomplished the delicate task of measuring the absorption of light by individual cone cells from enucleated human and monkey eyes. Although there is some disparity of results from the very few cones that were successfully isolated, and there are difficulties of interpretation (see Liebman's account in Dartnall, 1972), the implication is that three classes exist, with peak sensitivies at about 440, 540, and 570 nm, respectively. Peaks of about 540 and 570 nm were obtained by Rushton and his colleagues in living-eye experiments on human subjects for hypothetical pigments called chlorolabe and erythrolabe, respectively.

Rushton's technique (see his account in Dartnall, 1972) was to shine mono-chromatic test lights into the subject's fovea and to measure the proportion of this light that is reflected back out of the eye to a sensitive phototube. This was done before and after flooding the fovea with light intense enough to bleach the pigments in the cone receptors. Thus, it was possible to compute a "difference spectrum," i.e., to state the specific amount of bleaching that had taken place in the pigments at each wavelength. From this it was possible to derive the spectral absorption curve of the pigments.

The normal human fovea presumably contains cone receptors of the three types, each with one of the pigments mentioned above, but Rushton's method of reflection densitometry has technical limitations such that it cannot be used with wavelengths below 500 nm. Thus, the short-wave pigment ("cyanolabe" in Rushton's terminology) has no effect on the measurements. A further simplifica-tion in some of Rushton's experiments was to use colorblind subjects. A pro-tanope, for example, lacks the long-wave pigment ("erythrolabe") and hence should yield a spectral sensitivity function characteristic of the only foveal pig-ment that he possesses with absorption above 500 nm. In accord with this prediction, the reflection densitometry results show peak sensitivity for this pigment (called "chlorolabe" by Rushton) at about 540 nm. Similarly, a deu-teranope was found to have an erythrolabe peak at about 570 nm. In each case, the shape of the difference spectrum was independent of the wavelength of the light used to obtain it. This attests to the fact that only a single pigment is effective in each case.

When used with normal trichromats, the method of reflection densitometry shows that the shape of the difference spectrum does depend on the wavelength of the bleaching light. In a way, that supports the idea that normal subjects have cone receptors with erythrolabe as well as those with chlorolabe in their foveal regions. Furthermore, the time course of recovery from the bleach is consistent with dark-adaptation curves obtained psychophysically on the same subjects.

From the above evidence, supplemented by a major part of the psycho-physical experiments contributed by many authors, it has become likely that Young's original trichromatic theory holds in its simplest form: Normal tri-chromats have three types of cone receptor, each with a single pigment that has its own spectral sensitivity curve. Dichromats, as was suggested without proof by Helmholtz (1866) and König and Dieterici (1893), lack one of the pigments; there is a presumption, but no proof, that dichromats have the same number of cones as do normals, but that these are of only two types rather than three. Using the classification of von Kries (1902) and the terminology of Rushton (1972), we conclude that protanopes (color-blind persons of the first kind) lack erythrolabe (red-sensitive pigment). Similarly, deuteranopes lack chlorolabe, and tritanopes (a rare condition, not so well documented) presumably lack cyanolabe. The above conclusions represent that rare and gratifying stage in the history of science wherein earlier and more complicated explanations can now be abandoned. For example, Leber (1873) and Fick (1879) had proposed that deuteranopes might have the normal three pigments, but that there was a neural defect such that the signals from the two corresponding types of cone receptor were not differentiated in the normal fashion by the retina. Others had supposed that color discrimination might depend not on pigments, but on physical differences in the ultrastructure of the cone outer segments. In favor of that view is the fact that these segments, because of their small diameter in relation to the wavelength of light, must have some of the properties of tuned dielectric antennas or waveguides (Toraldo di Francia, 1949). Enoch (1961) has shown that different-sized cone receptors transmit different colors preferentially, even after their pigments have been bleached. Brindley and Rushton (1959), however, found that monochromatic lights reaching the receptors by scatter from the side of the eyeball appeared to have the same hues as if stimulating the cones from the normal pupillary aperture. This evidence would seem to reinforce the conclusion that

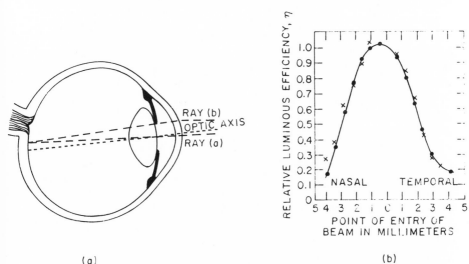

(a) (b)

FIG. 5.8. (a) Diagram of the eye to show the directions of rays hitting a cone receptor from the center (a) and the edge (b) of the pupil. (b) Graph showing the relative efficiency of rays entering the eye at various distances from the center of the pupil. From "The Luminous Efficiency of Rays Entering the Eye Pupil at Different Points" by W. S. Stiles and B. H. Crawford, Proceedings of the Royal Society (London), 1933, *112B*, 428–450. Copyright 1933 by the Royal Society. Reprinted by permission.

pigments are the primary basis for wavelength differentiation (see LeGrand, 1971; Wyszecki & Stiles, 1967; Boynton, 1979).

This is not to say that directional effects are unimportant with regard to stimulating the cones. Stiles and Crawford (1933) indeed made one of the few truly original psychophysical discoveries of this century when they found that light is much more effective when entering the cone receptors straight on than when striking them obliquely (see Fig. 5.8). This is due to an optical funneling ("light-trapping") that takes place within the tapered region of the cone. Although the Stiles-Crawford effect is less obvious in the rods than in cones, it may substantially improve the chances that photons entering the eye from the center of the pupil will be absorbed by the pigments in the outer segments of both types of receptor. By the same token, acuity may be improved because optical aberrations are least evident for light entering the eye through the center of the pupil, the light that is most effective by virtue of the Stiles-Crawford effect.

Function of the Retinal Horizontal Cells and Bipolars

In the last 25 years it has become clear (see Rodieck, 1973) that the bipolars, horizontal cells, amacrines, and ganglion cells are no mere conductors of signals from the receptors to the optic nerve. The electron microscope has revealed, for example, that no one-to-one relationship is ever found, even in the primate fovea, from a single cone to a single bipolar to a single ganglion cell. Instead, there are numerous specialized junctions between each receptor cell and processes from horizontal cells and bipolars. Similarly, bipolars interact with amacrines and ganglion cells through other forms of synaptic and non-synaptic contact. Only the ganglion cells generate true "spikes" or nerve impulses; these are required because it is the axons of the ganglion cells that make up the fibers of the optic nerve. These fibers, about 500,000 in number, are so long and so slender that only true nerve impulses are capable of transmission all the way from the eye to the brain.

Like the receptors themselves, the bipolars, horizontal cells and amacrines exhibit graded, electrotonic potentials rather than nerve impulses. These graded potentials are the electrical signs of chemical processes involving changes of ionic balance due to the release of transmitter molecules. It is probable, for example, that a transmitter substance is released by cones in the dark. The action of light is to diminish this process rather than to increase it, and there is some indication that the same is true for the bipolars. Thus, light may cause hyperpolarization and a consequent reduction of noise in both cones and bipolar cells.

The Electroretinogram. This new understanding of chemical and electrotonic processes within the retina throws a new light on much older visual research (see Granit, 1947). The electroretinogram (ERG), for example, is a response potential wave first observed by Holmgren in 1865. Analyses by Granit

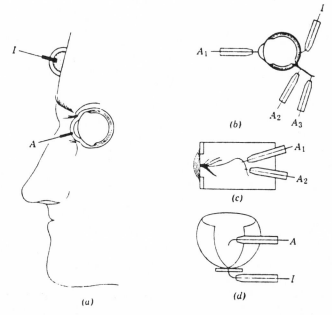

FIG. 5.9. Placement of large-sized electrodes for recording responses of the eye.
In each drawing *A* is an active electrode and *I* is an indifferent electrode. (*a*)
Electrodes in position for recording the human action potential by the use of a
contact lens; (*b*) connections with an excised eye for measuring the resting or
action potential; (*c*) top view of arrangement for recording impulses from a single
fiber dissected out from the optic nerve of *Limulus;* (*d*) side view of arrangement
for recording impulses from a fiber dissected out from a vertebrate retina. From
Riggs, 1956, in C. H. Graham (Ed.), 1965.

(1933), Adrian (1945) and many others showed that it arose from cells of the
retina that include the receptors and bipolars but not the ganglion cells. Microelectrode studies such as those of Tomita (1963) and Brown and Wiesel (1961)
have revealed more specifically the sites in which the various components of the
ERG waves are developed. Granit (1933) has elucidated the various inhibitory
and excitatory processes that make up the ERG, and Adrian (1945) has distinguished the photopic and scotopic components as they appear in the ERG of
primates. When stimulated by light, so many of the retinal cells are activated
simultaneously that the result is a mass response potential wave that traverses the
entire eyeball and can be recorded externally (see Fig. 5.9). In 1941 Riggs
developed a contact-lens electrode that can be used without damage to the eye,
and since that time many ERG laboratories have been established for research
and clinical diagnosis of diseases of the retina. The ERG thus serves, for the eye,
a medical function analogous to that of the EEG for the brain or the EKG for the
heart.

Adaptation.   In addition to its clinical value, the ERG has turned out to be a significant indicator of normal visual function. Recent ERG studies by Dowling and his colleagues, for example, have clarified a particularly vexing problem with regard to light and dark adaptation. We have seen that rhodopsin is the photosensitive pigment of the rod receptors, and that its bleaching by light and regeneration in the dark were assumed by Hecht and earlier investigators to account for light and dark adaptation in the scotopic visual system. More recently, however, evidence has accumulated that a neural component must be present, in addition to the photoreceptor component of visual adaptation. The recent ERG experiments have made this clear (chapters by Tomita and Gouras in Fuortes, 1972).

In the retina of a fish, for example, Dowling and Ripps (1970, 1971, 1972, 1976, 1977) have used the *b*-wave of the ERG as an index of the sensitivity to test stimuli in complete dark adaptation. It is known that this response arises in the bipolar layer of the retina. They then flooded the eye with light that was too dim to produce any detectable bleaching of the rhodopsin in the receptors. Nevertheless, they found that the ERG amplitude was greatly diminished, and that test flashes of higher intensity had to be used to achieve an equivalent size of *b*-wave. However, when they recorded the responses of earlier retinal elements (the receptors and horizontal cells) they found no loss of sensitivity resulting from the adapting light. They were thus forced to the conclusion that some change had occurred in the neural retina to make the eye less sensitive in the presence of an adapting field that was too weak to produce any measurable effects on the receptors themselves.

Innumerable earlier experiments had pointed, albeit less directly, to a neural component of adaptation (see Brindley, 1970; Rodieck, 1973). Granit, (1947) in the frog, Johnson and Riggs (1951) in the human, and Dowling and Wald (1960) and Weinstein, (1967) in the rat eye had all shown significant ERG diminution with a level of light adaptation that was insufficient to produce significant bleaching of the rhodopsin in the rods. Crawford (1947) and Baker (1953) had observed initial increases in human sensitivity in the first few seconds of adaptation that were too rapid to be accounted for by recovery of rhodopsin. Lythgoe (1940), Wald (1954), and Rushton, (1955) found unsatisfactory agreement between the psychophysical threshold data on adaptation and the kinetics of rhodopsin. Lipetz (1961) in the frog and Rushton (1963) in the human eye used light-adapting fields that consisted of alternate bright and dark bars. The resulting elevation of threshold was found to be nearly the same for points within the lighted areas of the retina as for points within the dark-bar areas. Rushton invoked a "neural pool" hypothesis to account for these results. He assumed that, when the adapting light has gone off, each rhodopsin molecule that has absorbed a quantum of light continues to send a signal (called "dark light" or "background noise") to some neural location that pools these signals over a considerable area. Rushton (1965 Ferrier Lecture) pointed out that the sensitivity of a fully dark-adapted human eye is significantly depressed by the action of an adapting field that is so weak that only 10% of the rods absorb a quantum of light over a 2-second period of time. At the present time, it seems likely that these hypothetical processes may in fact represent the release of neurotransmitter substances that affect the ionic balance within cells such as the bipolars, the activity of which is electrotonic in nature.

We may summarize the modern view of visual adaptation as follows: The eye is able to respond effectively to the lightest and darkest portions of the visual field, which differ in brightness typically by 2 to 3 logarithmic units. This dynamic range holds true for scotopic vision by dim artificial light as well as for vision in bright sunlight. Thus, the 2 to 3 log unit dynamic range must be capable of functioning at any level over a total range of more than 10 log units in the absolute amount of light entering the eye. The situation is analogous to that of a radio receiver: With automatic gain control, the sound output is held to within a relatively restricted constant range despite huge variations in the signals it receives from radiotransmitters at all different distances. In the case of the eye, a large percentage of the dynamic range is provided by the neural adaptation mechanisms recently discovered. But the much greater (and slower) adjustment required in going from moonlight to sunlight can only be achieved through combining the neural adaptation with the bleaching and restoration of the pigments in the receptor cells (see Brindley, 1970; Rodieck, 1973).

Wavelength Discrimination.   One other function that has been extensively studied in retinal neurons is wavelength discrimination (see Fuortes, 1972; Rodieck, 1973). Microelectrode studies have shown, for example, that the horizontal cells of the fish retina receive input from large numbers of cone receptors. Svaetichin (1956) first recorded the slow waves that are now known as S-potentials. He thought that they were generated by cone receptors, but later studies by Tomita (1957), MacNichol and Svaetichin (1958), and Kaneko (1970) showed that they were from the horizontal cells of the retina. A striking feature of many S-potentials is the fact that their size and polarity vary with the wavelength of the stimulating light. This shows that color-opponent responses are occurring at a very early stage of retinal processing in the fish. Naka and Rushton (1966) have found, however, that these wavelength-dependent responses are shifted along the spectrum as the intensity level is changed. Thus, there are difficulties in concluding that color-opponent S-potentials can be the basis for a Hering-type theory of color vision in which the primary hues due to wavelength are affected very little by intensity of light. Furthermore, technical limitations have so far precluded the recording of responses from single receptors, horizontal cells or bipolars in the primate retina. We therefore have no direct evidence of any color-opponent responding prior to the level of the ganglion cells in monkey or man. Even in the fish there are some S-potentials that always exhibit hyperpolarization when light of any wavelength is turned on (Svaetichin, 1956). We can be sure that horizontal and bipolar cells in all species serve to integrate in some way the signals they receive from large numbers of receptors; single horizontal cells extend over considerable distances, and there is evidence of interconnections among horizontal cells that extend their effectiveness over still greater retinal distances (Kaneko, 1970).

Retinal Ganglion Cells

The function of the ganglion cells is to initiate the nerve impulses that are conducted from the eye to the brain (see Brindley, 1970; Fuortes, 1972; Rodieck, 1973). This conduction is along the ganglion cell axons, i.e., the individual fibers that make up the optic nerve. The first records of optic nerve impulses were made by Adrian and Matthews (1927), using newly developed techniques of amplification and recording. This study, on the optic nerve of the eel, established the discrete nature of the impulse spikes and showed that they responded with higher frequency and lower latency as the area or intensity of the stimulus light was increased.

In 1932, Hartline and Graham dissected out single optic nerve fibers in *Limulus,* the horseshoe crab, and showed that the frequency of nerve impulses over a considerable range was proportional to the logarithm of the stimulus intensity. In 1938, Hartline accomplished the extremely difficult task of dissecting and recording from individual ganglion cell fibers in the retina of the frog. He found that, unlike *Limulus,* the frog had several types of fiber. Some responded as the stimulus light went on, some as it went off, and some at both on and off. In the course of these studies, Hartline also introduced the concept of the *receptive field* of a fiber, defining it as the retinal region within which a small test spot of light was capable of eliciting nerve impulses. In 1939, Granit and Svaetichin began the use of microelectrodes to record the activity of single ganglion cells in the retina. Granit (1947) has summarized the results of many experiments of this kind with a variety of vertebrate preparations and with a wide range of stimulus wavelengths and intensities.

Kuffler (1953) used a significantly improved method of microelectrode recording. To contact the ganglion cells he did not first remove the cornea and lens as had the earlier investigators. Instead, he kept the animal intact except for inserting a hypodermic needle through the side of the eyeball and pushing a fine electrode tip through it until it met the inner retinal surface. This technique preserved the eye's own optics and permitted an accurate focusing of the stimulus light onto the portion of retina that was in contact with the electrode. With these superior arrangements, experiments on the anesthetized cat revealed a new principle. In a light-adapted state, the receptive field of a ganglion cell displayed a center-surround antagonism. Thus, a given ganglion cell might respond vigorously when a tiny spot of light was turned on at the center of its receptive field. The same cell, however, gave no response to a light turned on at the edge of the field, but gave a vigorous response when that light was turned off. Other ganglion cells had the opposite characteristics. They responded to a light going on at the edge of the field and to a light going off at the center. Simultaneous presentation of light spots to center and surround elicited very little response; clearly, the two evoked opposite effects and inhibited one another. It thus became clear that cat ganglion cells are stimulated most strongly by edges and other spatial patterns containing light and dark areas that are adjacent to one another. Large, uniform fields are relatively ineffective.

The experiments of Hartline, Granit, and Kuffler led to many subsequent studies of ganglion cell function. Barlow and others noted that the same ganglion cell could be activated by rod-initiated signals at scotopic levels, and by cone-initiated ones at photopic levels. Furthermore, it became clear that optic nerve impulses continue to be produced even when no light is present. In fact, this low-level, spontaneous activity characterizes the whole central nervous system of higher animals and has led to much speculation about its significance for the organism. Does it provide for continuity in the conscious life of the organism such that its disappearance would result in unconsciousness? Does it represent a delicately balanced background level against which small increments or decrements of stimulation can be judged? Does it arise from the release of neurotransmitters by the receptors and other retinal structures? These questions have not yet been given satisfactory answers; they are obviously of great significance at all levels of the visual system and may eventually be tied in with questions of visual aftereffects and perceptual learning.

In 1966, Enroth-Cugell and Robson discovered that cat ganglion cells could be divided into two groups they called X-cells and Y-cells. The distinction has been confirmed and made more explicit by many subsequent investigators. It now appears that X-cells give more linear and tonic or sustained responses, whereas Y-cells give non-linear, phasic or transient responses. Furthermore, X-cells predominate in the central retina, have smaller receptive fields, and send their axons mainly to the lateral geniculate nucleus (LGN). In contrast, the Y-cells are larger, have more extensive receptive fields, and have axons that send branches to the superior colliculus (SC) as well as to the LGN. In addition, Y-cells exhibit the "periphery effect" described by McIlwain (1964), whereas X-cells are not much influenced by it (Cleland, Dubin, & Levick, 1971). This effect is a marked change in impulse rate for a ganglion cell caused by a large visual stimulus lying far outside the region usually considered to be the receptive field of the ganglion cell.

Of particular interest are ganglion cell responses recorded from the monkey retina, since there is good evidence that the human visual system is very similar. Gouras (1968, 1969) has distinguished tonic and phasic responding of monkey ganglion cells, and Hubel and Wiesel (1977) have found wide variation in receptive field sizes. However, the monkey retina has a true fovea in which very small receptive field sizes are found.

The monkey ganglion cells are richly differentiated with regard to the effects of wavelength. Gouras (1968) has reported, for example, ganglion cell activity of a phasic type that shows center-surround differentiation of red and green within the receptive field. A second type of cell shows tonic responses. It is relatively more common near the fovea, and has a central excitatory region that responds to blue, green, or red light. Its surround region is inhibitory when stimulated by a color different from that at the center.

In conclusion, the signals from the receptor cells have undergone an encoding within the retinal neurons such that the brain receives both transient and sustained information about spatial patterns of bright-dark edges, temporal patterns of on-off or moving stimulation, and chromatic patterns of spatially and temporally contrasting colors. Nearly all of the discoveries about information processing within the retina have taken place since Hecht (1934) and Polyak (1941) took the view that the main function of the retinal neurons was to convey to the brain a faithful representation of the effects of light upon the rods and cones (see Brindley, 1970; Rodieck, 1973).

Central Processing

It was not until the twentieth century that many of the anatomical features of the visual brain were identified. Polyak (1957) summarizes the achievements in the first half of this century, while Brindley (1970) and many chapters in Jung (1973) may be consulted for recent developments. Minkowski in 1920 noted that a large percentage of the fibers in the optic tract, after the partial decussation that occurred within the optic chiasm, proceeded to the lateral geniculate nucleus (LGN) on the corresponding side of the brain. In the monkey LGN he identified six separate layers, each of them with a topological representation of the hemi-retina on the corresponding side of the eyes. Three layers are supplied from uncrossed fibers from one eye and three from crossed fibers from the other. Synapsing with these fibers within the LGN are geniculostriate fibers that terminate within a middle layer (IVC) of the primary visual projection area of the occipital cortex (area 17 in the terminology of Brodmann, 1909) on the same side. There again is a topological representation of the visual half-field, and in this cortical map both eyes are represented. Much information on the anatomical arrangements came from clinical studies of brain injuries during World War I (Holmes, 1918) and later (Teuber, 1960). Finer details are now becoming known chiefly through electrical recording from single primate cells in the visual cortex.

Less is presently known about the smaller percentage of optic tract fibers that do not terminate in the LGN. Some fibers divide into two branches, one going to the LGN and the other to some other structure. Of the latter, some go to the superior colliculus and others to the pre-tectal region. The non-geniculate pathways take part in the control of the pupil and the external eye muscles. It is the LGN portion of the optic tract, however, that is mainly responsible for vision.

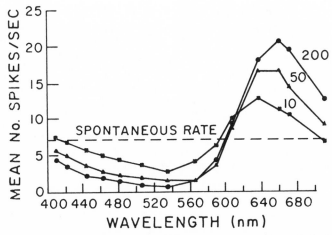

FIG. 5.10.   Average response rates of red(+)-green(−) opponent cells in the lateral geniculate body of the monkey, showing results of three different intensities of monochromatic light (200, 50 and 10 arbitrary units) at the wavelengths shown on the abscissa. "Spontaneous rate" is about seven nerve impulses per second in the absence of stimulation. From "Analysis of Response Patterns of LGN Cells" by R. L. DeValois, I. Abramov, and G. H. Jacobs, *Journal of the Opitcal Society of America*, 1966, *56*, 966–977. Copyright 1966 by The Optical Society of America. Reprinted by permission.

Well-defined regions of blindness may result from localized injury to the geniculostriate pathways.

The Lateral Geniculate Nucleus (LGN).   DeValois (in Jung, 1973) and his colleagues have made extensive studies of cells in the LGN of macaque monkeys, starting about 1958. A majority of the cells in Minkowski's layers 3, 4, 5, and 6 were found to be of the spectrally opponent type. Two types of red-green cell were found: those responding to red light with an increment and green with a decrement over the spontaneous rate of firing (see Fig. 5.10), and those having the opposite characteristics. Similarly, there are two types of blue-yellow opponent cells. In addition, a smaller number of black-white opponent cells were found, again coming in two types: those showing an increment and those showing a decrement of firing rate in response to light, whether white or of any other color.

In general, the LGN cells of all layers exhibit a spatially opponent organization. A small spot of light causes an increment or a decrement of firing rate (and a black spot *vice versa*) depending on whether it is presented at the center or in the surround area of the receptive field. Thus, the behavior of these cells is like that of Kuffler's (1953) cat ganglion cells. In fact, there is reason to suppose that very similar results would have been obtained by DeValois if he had recorded from cells of the retina rather than those of the LGN. In both cases, the center-surround receptive fields were roughly circular and their sizes varied within wide limits.

Further experiments by DeValois (1965), Wiesel and Hubel (1966) and Abramov (1968) have made use of selective adaptation by monochromatic lights to depress the responses of particular types of cone receptor. This has permitted them to deduce the spectral sensitivity functions of remaining types as they respond singly to monochromatic test lights. This is essentially the technique earlier employed by Stiles (see Boynton, 1979) in an extensive series of psychophysical experiments. The outcome of all these experiments is to reaffirm the spectral sensitivity functions of three fundamental receptor types having maxima in the neighborhood of 570, 540, and 440 nm, respectively.

In spite of extensive recent research on the physiology and histology of the LGN, no clear picture has emerged of its functional significance. On present evidence, the cortical areas for vision might be as well served if they received signals directly from the eyes through the fibers of the optic tract. Some day, perhaps soon, we may expect to find out how the LGN may modify those signals. Brindley (1970) has evaluated the evidence that there are corticogeniculate fibers, and that presynaptic inhibition may occur within the LGN as a consequence of signals from the cortex and from the mesencephalic reticular formation. He also raises the possibility of other functions for the LGN: selective facilitation or inhibition of signals from the eyes to the cortex on the basis of previous visual responses, saccadic eye movements, or signals from other sensory modalities.

The Function of the Visual Cortex.   We have seen that the sensory mechanisms of the retina began to be explored in the 1920s, that gross ERG recording preceded the work with microelectrodes, and that enormous progress in understanding retinal function has taken place since about 1953. The same statements apply to the sensory mechanisms of the visual cortex, except that progress here has taken place even more recently (see Brindley, 1970; Jung, 1973). It was in 1929 that Berger reported spontaneous electroencephalogram (EEG) activity originating in the human brain and recorded through scalp electrodes. Adrian and Matthews (1934) confirmed the existence and rate (about 10 waves per second) of the Berger rhythm. They also explored its relation to visual stimulation: The spontaneous activity tended to appear most clearly with eyes closed, or in uniform fields or in darkness. They also found they could generate response potential waves in the brain by stimulating the eyes with intermittent large fields of light at from 8 to 25 flashes per second. In the 1930s and 1940s many investigators took up the recording of this activity with gross electrodes on the surface of the brain in experimental animals or with scalp electrodes in human subjects. The clinical significance of the work soon became evident, and visually evoked cortical potentials (VECP) were found useful for the diagnosis of brain lesions and sensory deficits in animals and in patients incapable of verbal communication. Pattern-specific and wavelength-specific sensitivities came into the range of clinical diagnosis after the VECP (as well as the ERG) could be recorded in the microvolt range with response-averaging computers (Calvet, 1956; Siebert, 1959; Clynes, 1962) and the employment of stimulus alternation procedures (Riggs, Johnson, & Schick, 1964; Cobb, Ettlinger, & Morton, 1967; Regan, 1968).

Surface electrodes were placed on the monkey cortex by Talbot and Marshall (1941) and records were made of the response to a small spot of light on a screen in front of the eyes. This technique yielded a surface map, with the estimate that each millimeter distance along the cortical surface represents a visual angle of about 2 minutes (i.e., a retinal distance of about .01 mm) for the central foveal projection. Field representation becomes more and more gross and imprecise as the stimulus is moved into the peripheral parts of the visual field. This distribution has been extensively worked out by Daniel and Whitteridge (1961).

Several investigators, including Foerster (1929), Penfield and Foerster (1930) and Penfield and Jasper (1954), have reported electrical stimulation of points on the exposed cortex of conscious human patients. This could only be done during brief intervals of a brain operation, and the patient was under stress. However, there was a consistent report of points, lines, clouds of light, and occasionally more complex visual forms as the brain surface was probed in areas 17, 18, and 19. Non-visual areas gave other sensations, motor areas caused muscles to twitch, and temporal area probes evoked memories of familiar sounds.

In a daring attempt to help blind people, Brindley and Lewin (1968) and several later investigators have implanted arrays of electrodes under the skull, in direct contact with the surface of the visual projection area. Electronic circuits are connected by a cable to the electrodes so that the brain can be given patterns of electric pulses. The results have been successful only to the extent that the patient "sees" spots and patterns of light. Nothing like object perception seems to occur, no matter how well the pulse patterns are made to simulate real pictures (Brindley, in Jung 1973). Perhaps the difficulty lies in the fact that all the normal processing that takes place in the retina and in some of the deeper layers of the cortex has been bypassed with these procedures. The normal input to the cortex is not by way of the outer surface but through layer IV: The geniculocortical fibers, as we have seen above, are carrying highly specialized information about brightness and color contrast rather than intensity or wavelength.

In 1958, Hubel and Wiesel published the first of a long series of articles on the functions of single cortical cells of the visual areas. A recent summarizing article (Hubel & Wiesel, 1977) has presented the main features of this ongoing research as it applies specifically to area 17, the primary visual projection area of the macaque. The experiments combine four basic methods for finding out how the brain works:

1. The microelectrodes are used not simply to contact the surface, but to penetrate through the gray matter at all different depths and angles of incidence.
2. The visual stimulus is not merely spots of light turned on and off in various parts of the field; lines and rectangles of various sizes, shapes and slants are moved over a uniform light or dark background.
3. Experimental animals (cats, monkeys) are suitably chosen for experiments on binocularity, color vision and other characteristics shared with human subjects.
4. Animals at various ages, with controlled amounts of visual experience, are used to elucidate the developmental aspects of vision.

The first major discovery made by Hubel and Wiesel was that a majority of cortical cells have receptive fields that are elongated rather than circular in shape. The logical presumption from this is that such a cell receives input from a linear

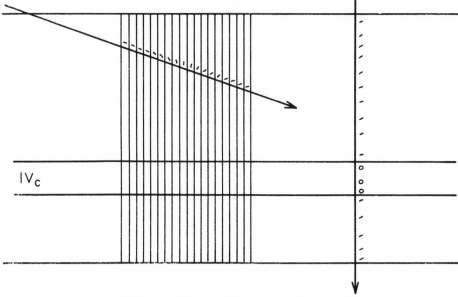

FIG. 5.11.   Diagram to illustrate orientation columns in monkey striate cortex. Two penetrations are illustrated—one vertical, the other oblique. In the vertical penetration, orientation is clearly defined and constant, from cell to cell, in layers above and below IVc. In layer IVc, the cells have fields with circular symmetry, and there is no orientation preference. In the oblique penetration, there is a systematic variation in orientation, clockwise or counterclockwise, in steps of about 10° or less, that occur roughly every 50 μm. From "Functional Architecture of Macaque Monkey Visual Cortex" by D. H. Hubel and T. N. Wiesel, *Proceedings of the Royal Society (London)*, 1977, *198B*, 1–59. Copyright 1977 by The Royal Society. Reprinted by permission.

array of geniculate cells, each of which has itself only a center-surround organization of responding. The result is that a line or edge can stimulate such a cortical cell most effectively if its slant or orientation, as well as its specific location, agrees with those of the linear array (see Fig. 5.11). Cells of this type were labelled "simple cells" by Hubel and Wiesel.

"Complex cells" presumably are those that receive input from an array of simple cells having a similar preferential orientation. Complex cells are also sharply tuned for orientation, but the receptive field of each is much larger than that of a simple cell.

"Hypercomplex cells" also have large receptive fields and selectivity for orientation, but they have other characteristics as well. Some of them respond vigorously to short lines, but less vigorously or not at all to longer ones. Others favor lines that are curved or bent rather than straight.

Selectivity for orientation is but one of the major characteristics of cortical cells. Another major feature is eye dominance. The majority of cells are "binocular." They can be activated by an appropriate stimulus delivered to either eye, and as a rule they are most strongly responsive to stimuli that are similar in location and orientation and presented to both eyes simultaneously. But some cells are "monocular," excitable only through the left eye or the right but not both. However, Bishop reports that nearly all such "monocular" cells are subject to inhibition when the other eye is stimulated. It is thus clear that nearly every cortical cell is "binocular" in the sense that its responses are governed by the patterns of stimulation to both left and right eyes. Furthermore, recent experiments by many investigators (Barlow, 1967; Nikara, 1968; Hubel & Wiesel, 1970; Poggio & Fischer, 1977) have shown that cortical cells in areas 17 and 18 are often selective for stereoscopic disparity. Such a cell gives a preferential response to a stimulus that is at a certain location in depth (far or near) with respect to the fixation point.

Hubel and Wiesel (1977) have built up a "functional architecture" of the primary visual cortex on the basis of their microelectrode studies. The cortex is organized into layers and columns. Each layer of cells is at a particular depth with respect to the cortical surface; the input to the cortex, namely the termination of optic tract fibers coming into the cortex from the lateral geniculate body, is in layer IV. The columns are at right angles to the layers. Within a given column, all the cortical cells tend to have the same preferential sensitivity to orientation as the various layers are traversed by a microelectrode driven straight down through the various layers. If the microelectrode enters the cortex at a slight angle away from vertical, it traverses one column after another, each column having a slightly different orientation selectivity from its neighbor. It turns out that all the various orientations are laid out progressively in this way, and that the entire range of orientations is represented by cells lying within a "hypercolumn," which is composed of all the columns that are clustered within about one square millimeter running through all the layers of the cortex.

In a somewhat similar fashion, Hubel and Wiesel describe ocular dominance columns. Again, cells that are contacted by an electrode that is driven straight down through the various layers tend to have similar characteristics, this time a preferential responding to stimulation of one of the two eyes. For example, when such an electrode encounters (in layer IVC) an incoming neuron from the lateral geniculate body, the neuron can only be excited through one of the eyes. Typically, however, the cells lying above or below it in other layers of the same column are capable of being driven binocularly; yet most of the cells within that column respond more vigorously when driven by the eye that activates the neuron entering the column at level IVC. It turns out that columns that are strongly responsive to the left eye are roughly 0.5 mm distant from the nearest columns that are strongly responsive to the right. Thus, it is clear that, "... contained in each small block of cortex, roughly 1 mm × 1 mm, is the machinery needed to subserve both eyes in all orientations" (Hubel et al., 1978).

It is particularly significant that, "... recordings from newborn monkey cortex are in fact very similar to those obtained in the adult" (Wiesel & Hubel, 1974). "Cells in layers outside IVC occur in simple, complex and hypercomplex types, with orientation and directional specificity that appear to be about as well developed as in the adult" (Hubel & Wiesel, 1977). In other words, no visual experience is necessary for the development of these particular kinds of cortical specialization. However, studies of visual deprivation show that the lack of visual experience during early infancy can produce marked deficits. For example, sewing shut the eyelids of one eye at the time of birth has the effect that cells of the striate cortex that normally subserve vision in that eye are taken over, during the next few weeks, by the other eye. A profound functional loss has occurred during that critical period for vision in the deprived eye, and the brain deficit is not recovered after this period even if the eye itself is allowed to resume normal function by removing the lid sutures. Strangely enough, sewing both eyes shut has much less effect on the visual system (Wiesel & Hubel, 1965). This fact serves to emphasize the point that there is a competition between the two eyes during the first few weeks after the monkey's birth. If one eye is visually deprived, the other comes to take over most of the cells of the striate cortex.

The experiments on primates may help to explain the permanent losses of pattern vision that are characteristic of amblyopia in human subjects. Amblyopia is a condition that arises in early childhood when a "lazy" eye falls into disuse because of poor alignment or other defect that interferes with normal binocular function. Modern practice is to identify the condition as early as possible and to correct the underlying malfunction, at the same time forcing the child to use the amblyopic eye by special exercises and sometimes by wearing a temporary eye patch over the normal eye. This may force the "lazy" eye to function normally and develop its full complement of connections to the individual cells of the cortex.

The extraordinarily revealing studies by Hubel and Wiesel are concentrated mainly on the striate, or primary region designated as Area 17 in the Brodmann terminology. Fewer of their experiments have probed areas 18 and 19. Other workers have since probed the same regions or have made some attempt at microelectrode exploration of areas having input from other senses in addition to vision. An inferotemporal region has been found by Gross (in Jung, 1973), for example, to include cells that are best activated by complex patterns. The exploration of the brain in this way has scarcely begun, however. Obviously there must be centers or systems concerned with the integration of vision with eye movements, the recognition of perceived objects, the integration of vision with other senses, and the long- and short-term memory for objects seen in the past. Are these functions accomplished in serial order, starting with the eyes and proceeding through the LGN and areas 17, 18, and 19? Or is there parallel processing of particular aspects such as color, motion or form in separate regions that later "report" to a master control station as yet unidentified? It is fair to conclude at this point that even the visual system of the brain, where many exciting discoveries have already been made, is like the Universe as described by Peter De Vries (*Let Me Count the Ways,* 1965). It is ". . . like a safe to which there is a combination. But the combination is locked up in the safe."

Before concluding this brief coverage of twentieth century progress in vision, we must turn our attention to three systematic developments of great promise for future exploration. All three are derived from recent developments in the field of engineering.

Ratio of Signal to Noise.   The first and second of these developments arise from information theory, an outcome of communications engineering related to telephone and radio transmission. The first principle is that information is normally communicated in the form of a meaningful "signal" that must be detected against a background of "noise." In visual psychophysics, for example, a very dim light is reported as "seen" if it produces a significant change in the ongoing spontaneous activity, or "noise," of the visual system. Thus, the old idea of a "threshold" is rejected as too simplistic. There is no "absolute threshold" in the sense that a fixed amount of light is needed to initiate an afferent nerve impulse. Instead, in terms of information theory, there is an increasing probability that the subject will say, "I see it," as the amplitude of the neural response due to the stimulus grows in comparison with the ongoing neural activity due to "noise" alone. In modern psychophysics, then, we may determine the percentage of "yes" judgments that accompany the stimulus (these are called "hits") and also the percentage due to "noise" alone (known as "false alarms"). Psychophysical functions can then be used to find what are known as ROC (receiver operating characteristic) curves for the visual system. Modern psychophysical texts (Green & Swets, 1966; Engen, 1971) may be consulted for details of procedure.

Two principal advantages may be mentioned here: First, the ROC curves permit a more valid measurement of visual sensitivity than does the traditional "threshold" because a "forced choice" procedure can be used that cancels out the observer's bias toward any particular outcome of the experiment. Second, ROC curves cover a relatively wide range of visual performance, and comparisons are meaningful from one subject to another and from one experimental condition to another. Incidentally, the same kind of ROC analysis can be used to analyze other kinds of visual response. Examples are the electroretinogram or visually evoked cortical potentials in which some stimulus trials contain the visual signal plus "noise" and others "noise" alone. In these cases one can plot the results in terms of rising amplitude of response as the signal-to-noise ratio is increased.

Information Channels. A second concept that has been taken from information theory is that of "channels." A given channel, for example, may be tuned to respond selectively to information that falls within its own range, or "band width." Thus, we may speak of channels in the visual system that are tuned for wavelength, line orientation, binocular disparity, etc. A particularly intriguing new concept is that of channels for "spatial frequency." That term is used to specify the coarseness or fineness of elements in a visual scene. A grating pattern, for example, consists of alternating bright and dark lines, and each "cycle" consists of one bright and one dark line (see Fig. 5.12). The fineness, or "spatial frequency," of such a pattern is then specified as the number of cycles per degree of visual angle that it subtends at the eye. Another important dimension of the pattern is its contrast, or "modulation." This is defined as the ratio of the difference between the luminance of the bright bars and the average luminance of the pattern, to the average luminance itself. It turns out that the visual system is very sensitive to contrast over a moderate range of spatial frequencies; modulations well under 1% can be detected. At higher or lower spatial frequencies, however, the visual performance falls off, as shown by what is called a contrast sensitivity function. Furthermore, the use of sinusoidally modulated grating patterns makes it possible to analyze any visual scene in terms of the distribution of spatial frequencies of which it is composed. The engineering technique of Fourier analysis then becomes applicable for handling the experiments and their results over the whole range of spatial frequencies.

Of particular interest is new evidence (Campbell & Robson, 1968; Braddick, in Held, Leibowitz, & Teuber, 1978) that the visual system contains channels that are selectively tuned for spatial frequency. Prolonged staring at a grating having one particular spatial frequency, for example, results in diminished contrast sensitivity for that particular spatial frequency, but not for others that differ substantially from it. This is interpreted to mean that the corresponding visual channels have become "fatigued," or rendered less sensitive, while the remaining channels are unaffected during the prolonged exposure. Other evidence

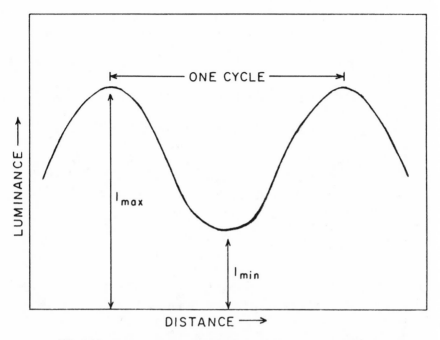

FIG. 5.12. Diagram showing the distribution of light in a sinusoidal grating. One cycle represents a complete course of luminance change from a given point on the grating to a corresponding point. The number of cycles that subtend one degree of visual angle is the *spatial frequency* of the grating. The *contrast* of the grating is defined as $(I_{max} - I_{min})/(I_{max} + I_{min})$, where I_{max} and I_{min} are the maximum and minimum values of luminance. From "Contrast and Spatial Frequency" by F. W. Campbell and L. Maffei, *Scientific American*, 1974, *231*, 106–114. Copyright 1974 by Scientific American, Inc. Reprinted by permission.

comes from single-unit studies of cats and monkeys. These have shown that individual "simple" cortical cells are more or less narrowly tuned for spatial frequency so that the whole effect is one of analyzing the visual scene in terms of its spatial-frequency components. It has long been known that the auditory system is capable of selective responding in the temporal frequency domain; now we see that a somewhat analogous function is present for spatial frequency analysis by the visual system.

Particularly intriguing evidence for "channels"comes out of a discovery made in 1965 by Celeste McCollough, namely that there is an interaction between line orientation and color in the perception of patterns. Specifically, the "McCollough Effect" is the gradual appearance of colors in an achromatic grating test pattern. The procedure may be illustrated by staring alternately at a red vertical line grating and a green horizontal line grating. After a few minutes of doing this, a gray test grating will appear pinkish in a region containing horizontal lines and greenish in a region containing vertical ones. Thus, it seems that the prolonged staring at colored patterns has depressed the sensitivities of the particular channels mediating line orientation and color. The effect may last for hours or even days; it is a sort of perceptual learning that must take place in the brain rather than the eyes (Stromeyer, in Held et al., 1978).

Control of Eye Movements. A third application of engineering principles has opened up new possibilities for the study of eye movements in relation to vision. Some of the gross outline had become clear during the nineteenth century: The two eyes are normally well coordinated in their movements of pursuit, saccades and vergence, with the net result that the objects of chief interest are kept within the foveal field of each eye. It has only been within the latter half of the twentieth century, however, that more analytical studies have been possible. First, small, involuntary motions of the eye were found to be present at all times, even during attempted steady fixation (Ratliff & Riggs, 1950; Ditchburn & Ginsborg, 1953). Second, the significance of these movements for the maintenance of vision was evaluated by the use of techniques for stabilization of the retinal image (Riggs & Ratliff, 1952; Ditchburn & Ginsborg, 1952; Riggs et al., 1953; see Ditchburn, 1973; Carpenter, 1977). In the "stabilized image" experiments, the visual test objects are viewed through a mirror system that counteracts the normal movements of the eye. Thus, the test objects are imaged on the retina in the same way as if the eye were rigidly clamped and prevented from moving. The astonishing result is that the test objects fade out and eventually disappear. We therefore conclude that eye movements are so essential for normal vision that we would all go blind if they ceased to exist. Third, techniques were developed for the recording of single cell responses in the cortex of alert, unanesthetized monkeys during eye movement experiments (Wurtz, in Monty & Senders, 1976). Finally, the engineering techniques of feedback control and analysis have been brought to bear on the problem of how the eyes are used to optimize sensorimotor coordination in such complex visual tasks as pursuit, inspection and recognition (Robinson, in Monty & Senders, 1976).

Attention has recently been redirected toward some of the old problems of the relation of eye movements to vision. For example, current thinking has it that there is a "feed-forward" or "corollary" signal (Sperry, 1950) that accompanies the "command signal" directing the eyes to move. This corollary signal is apparently used to modify the visual signals from the retina to the brain so that the brain interprets the retinal image movement not as a movement of the visual world but as a movement of the eyes in relation to a steady visual world. There is evidence that some such corollary discharge does take place, but so far it has not been possible to obtain neurophysiological records that indicate the pathways for suppression of the relevant movement signals from the two eyes.

Another function of the "command signal" for a saccadic eye movement appears to be the partial suppression of vision during the subsequent saccade. The most careful experiments (Volkmann, in Monty & Senders, 1976) have revealed an approximately three-fold loss of visual sensitivity for test flashes delivered immediately before, during or after a voluntary saccadic eye movement.

We may conclude from all these studies that vision and eye movements are extraordinarily well coordinated in a fashion that is subject to engineering control systems analysis. Eye movements function to maximize the benefits of foveal vision for both moving and stationary objects. But there are also built into the machinery for eye movements the means for disregarding the operation of the machinery itself: The "command" signals for making an eye movement are accompanied by saccadic suppression and a perceptual disregard for directional changes due to the eye movements themselves.

CONCLUSION

We conclude this chapter with a brief overview of the progress it has surveyed. From earliest times it was realized that the visual system must somehow bring us a very detailed knowledge of objects in the environment. Thus, mystical concepts such as the emanation of rays from the eyes or the entry of "eidola" into the mind were put forward. With the advent of scientific analysis, however, it became possible to resolve some of the mystery by explaining the optics of image formation, the neurophysiology of the visual pathways, the selective responding of the brain to particular features, and the operation of eye movement control systems. But much of the mystery still remains. We do not yet know much about the systems for visual recognition or remembering, and we are just beginning to appreciate the ways in which vision can be coordinated with other sensory modalities. The brain is estimated to contain at least 10^{10} individual cells, only a minute fraction of which have been analyzed even by single-unit methods of recording. It remains for future research to attempt the seemingly endless task of obtaining the single-unit records from animals and going on from there to a comprehensive account of how human vision can take place.

REFERENCES

Abelsdorff (1897) see Dartnall, 1972.
Abramov (1968) see Boynton, 1979.
Adrian (1945) see Riggs, 1965.
Adrian & Matthews (1927) see Riggs, 1965.
Armington, J. C. *The electroretinogram.* New York: Academic Press, 1974.
Armington, J. D., Krauskopf, J., & Wooten, B. (Eds.). *Visual psychophysics and Physiology.* New York: Academic Press, 1978.
Ayres & Kühne (1882) see Dartnall, 1972.
Baillarger (1840) see Polyak, 1957.

Baker (1953) see Graham, 1965.
Barlow (1967) see Jung, 1973.
Barlow, H. B., & Fatt, P. (Eds.). *Vertebrate photoreceptors.* London: Academic Press, 1977.
Benham (1894) see Brindley, 1970.
Bidder (1839) see Polyak, 1957.
Bloch (1885) see Graham, 1965.
Boll (1876) see Dartnall, 1972.
Boring, E. G. *Sensation and perception in the history of experimental psychology.* New York: Appleton, 1942.
Boring, E. G. *A history of experimental psychology.* (2nd ed.). New York: Appleton, 1950.
Boynton, R. M. *Human color vision.* New York: Holt, Rinehart, and Winston, 1979.
Brazier, M. A. B. *Electrical activity of the nervous system* (4th ed.). Baltimore: Williams and Wilkins, 1977.
Brewster (1834) see Graham, 1965.
Brindley, G. S. *Physiology of the retina and the visual pathway* (2nd ed.). London: Edward Arnold, 1970.
Brindley & Rushton, (1959) see Brindley, 1970.
Broca & Sulzer (1902) see Graham, 1965.
Brown & Wiesel (1961) see Riggs, 1965.
Brücke (1864) see Graham, 1965).
Campbell & Robson (1968) see Held et al., 1978.
Carpenter, R. H. S. *Movements of the eyes.* London: Pion, 1977.
Cleland, Dubin, & Levick (1971) see Rodieck, 1973.
Cobb, Ettlinger, & Morton (1967) see Regan, 1972.
Cornsweet, T. N. *Visual Perception.* New York: Academic Press, 1970.
Cornsweet, T. N., & Crane, H. D. Accurate two-dimensional eye tracker using first and fourth Purkinje images. *J. Opt. Soc. Amer.,* 1973, *63,* 921–928.
Crawford (1947) see Graham, 1965.
Daniel & Whitteridge (1961) see Jung, 1973.
Dartnall, J. J. A. (Ed.). *Photochemistry of vision.* Part 1, Vol. VII of *Handbook of sensory physiology.* New York: Springer-Verlag, 1972.
Descartes (1637) see Polyak, 1957.
DeValois (1965) see Boynton, 1979.
DeVries, P. *Let me count the ways.* Boston: Little, Brown, 1965.
Ditchburn, R. W. *Eye movements and visual perception.* Oxford: Clarendon Press, 1973.
Donders (1864) see Ogle, 1950.
Dowling & Ripps (1970, 1971, 1972, 1976, 1977) see Pöppel et al., 1977.
Dowling & Wald (1960) see Pöppel et al., 1977.
Engen, T. Psychophysics: I. Discrimination and detection. In J. W. Kling & L. A. Riggs (Eds.), *Experimental psychology.* New York: Holt, Rinehart and Winston, 1971.
Enoch (1961) see LeGrand, 1971.
Ferry (1892) see Graham, 1965.
Fick (1879) see Boynton, 1979.
Flechsig (1896) see Polyak, 1957.
Fraisse, P. The evolution of experimental psychology. In P. Fraisse & J. Piaget (Eds.), *Experimental psychology: Its scope and method.* Vol. 1. *History and method.* New York: Basic Books, 1968.
Fritsch & Hitzig (1870) see Polyak, 1957.
Fuortes, M. G. F. (Ed.). *Physiology of photoreceptor organs.* Part 2. Vol. VII of *Handbook of sensory physiology.* New York: Springer-Verlag, 1972.
Gouras (1968, 1969) see Rodieck, 1973.
Graham, C. H. (Ed.). *Vision and visual perception.* New York: Wiley, 1965.

Granit, R. (1933) see Riggs, 1965.
Granit, R. *Sensory mechanisms of the retina*. New York: Oxford University Press, 1947.
Grassman (1853, 1854) see MacAdam, 1970.
Green, D. M., & Swets, J. A. *Signal detection theory and psychophysics*. New York: Wiley, 1966.
Haidinger (1844) see Brindley, 1970.
Hecht, S. Vision: II. The nature of the photoreceptor process. In C. Murchison (Ed.). *A handbook of general experimental psychology*. Worcester, MA: Clark University Press, 1934.
Hecht, S., Shlaer, S., & Pirenne, M. H. (1942). See Pirenne, M. H. *Vision and the eye*. London: Chapman and Hall, 1948.
Held, R., Leibowitz, H. W., & Teuber, H.-L. (Eds.). *Perception*. Vol. VIII of *Handbook of sensory physiology*. New York: Springer-Verlag, 1978.
Helmholtz (1866) see MacAdam, 1970.
Helmholtz, H. von. *Treatise on physiological optics*. Trans. from 3rd German edition (1909–1911) by J. P. C. Southall. Rochester, NY: Optical Society of America, 1924–25. Also, New York: Dover, 1962.
Hering, E. *Outlines of a theory of the light sense*. (Translated and edited by L. M. Hurvich & D. Jameson.) Cambridge, MA: Harvard University Press, 1964.
Hering, E. *Spatial sense and movements of the eye*. English translation by C. A. Radde of the 1879 original in German. Baltimore: American Academy of Optometry, 1942.
Holmgren (1865) see Riggs, 1965.
Hubel & Wiesel (1970) see Jung, 1973.
Hubel, D. H., & Wiesel, T. N. Functional architecture of macaque monkey visual cortex. *Proc. Roy. Soc. Lond. B., 1977, 198*, 1–59.
Hubel, D. H., Wiesel, T. N., & Stryker, M. P. Anatomical demonstration of orientation columns in Macaque monkey. *J. Comp. Neurol., 1978, 177*, 361–379.
Hurvich, L. M., & Jameson, D. Helmholtz and the three-color theory: An historical note. *American Journal of Psychology, 1949, 62*, 111–114.
Hurvich & Jameson (1964) see Hering, 1964.
Jameson, D., & Hurvich, L. M. (Eds.). *Visual psychophysics*. Part 4, Vol. III of *Handbook of sensory physiology*. New York: Springer-Verlag, 1972.
Johnson & Riggs (1951) see Riggs, 1965.
Julesz, B. *Foundation of cyclopen perception*. Chicago: University of Chicago Press, 1971.
Jung, R. (Ed.). *Central processing of visual information*. Part 3A and 3B, Vol. VII of *Handbook of sensory physiology*. New York: Springer-Verlag, 1973.
Kaneko (1970) see Rodieck, 1973.
König (1894) see Dartnall, 1972.
Kuffler (1953) see Riggs, 1965.
Kuffler, S. W., & Nicholls, J. G. *From neuron to brain*. Sunderland, MA: Sinauer Associates, 1976.
Kühne (1878) see Dartnall, 1972.
Kühne & Steiner (1880) see Riggs, 1965.
Leber (1873) see Boynton, 1979.
LeGrand, Y. *Light, colour and vision*. (2nd ed.). Somerset, NJ: Halsted Press, 1971.
LeGrand, Y. History of research on seeing. In E. C. Carterette & M. P. Friedman (Eds.). *Handbook of perception*, Vol. V. *Seeing*. New York: Academic Press, 1975.
Lindberg, D. C. *Theories of vision from Al-Kindi to Kepler*. Chicago: University of Chicago Press, 1976.
Lipetz (1961) see Rushton, 1965.
Lomonosov (1757) see Weale, 1957.
Lythgoe (1940) see Rushton, 1965.
MacAdam, D. L. (Ed.). *Sources of color science*. Cambridge, MA: MIT Press, 1970.
MacNichol & Svaetichin (1958) see Rodieck, 1973.

Mariotte (1717) see Weale, 1957.

Maxwell, J. C. Theory of the perception of colours. *Transactions of the Royal Scottish Society of Arts*, 1856, *4*, 394–400.

Maxwell (1952, 1957) see MacAdam, 1970.

McIlwain (1964) see Rodieck, 1973.

Monty, R. A., & Senders, J. W. (Eds.). *Eye movements and psychological processes*. Hillsdale, NJ: Erlbaum, 1976.

Müller, G. E. Zur Psychophysik der Gesichtsempfindungen. *Zeits. für Psychol. und Physiol. der Sinnesorgane*. 1896, *10*, 1–82; 321–413.

Müller, J. (1826) see Graham, 1965.

Naka & Rushton (1966) see Rodieck, 1973.

Nikara (1968) see Jung, 1963.

Ogle, K. N. *Binocular Vision*. Philadelphia: Saunders, 1950.

Palmer, G. *Theory of colours and vision*. London: Leacroft, 1777.

Plateau (1835) see Graham, 1965.

Platter (1583) see Lindberg, 1976.

Poggio, G. F., & Fischer, B. Binocular interaction and depth sensitivity in striate and prestriate cortex of behaving Rhesus monkey. *Journal of Neurophysiology*, 1977, *40*, 1392–1405.

Polyak, S. *The retina*. Chicago: University of Chicago Press, 1941.

Polyak, S. L. *The vertebrate visual system*. (H. L. Klüver, Ed.) Chicago: University of Chicago Press, 1957.

Pöppel, E., Held, R., & Dowling, J. E. Neuronal mechanisms in visual perception. *Neurosciences Research Program Bulletin*, 1977, *15*, 313–553.

Porter (1902) see Graham, 1965.

Prévost (1826) see Wade, 1976.

Purkinje, J. E. *Beobachtungen und Versuche zur Physiologie der Sinne*. Berlin: Reimer, 1825.

Ratliff, F. *Mach bands: Quantitative studies on neural networks in the retina*. San Francisco: Holden-Day, 1965.

Regan, D. *Evoked potentials in psychology, sensory physiology and clinical medicine*. New York: Wiley, 1972.

Riccó (1877) see Graham, 1965.

Riggs, L. A. Electrical responses in vision. In C. H. Graham (Ed.). *Vision and visual Perception*. New York: Wiley, 1965.

Riggs, L. A. Vision. In J. W. Kling & L. A. Riggs (Eds.), *Experimental psychology*. New York: Holt, Rinehart and Winston, 1971.

Riggs, Johnson, & Schick (1964) see Riggs, 1971.

Rodieck, R. W. *The vertebrate retina*. San Francisco: Freeman, 1973.

Rodieck, R. W. Visual pathways. In *Annual Review of Neuroscience*. Vol. 2. Palo Alto, CA: Annual Review, Inc., 1979.

Rushton, W. A. H. The Ferrier Lecture: Visual adaptation. *Proceedings of the Royal Society (London)*, 1965, *162B*, 20–46.

Rushton (1955, 1963) see Rushton, 1965.

Rushton (1972) see Boynton, 1979.

Rushton, W. A. H., & Henry, G. H. Bleaching and regeneration of cone pigments in man. *Vision Research*, 1968, *8*, 617–631.

Scheiner (1619) see Lindberg, 1976.

Schleiden (1838) see Polyak, 1957.

Schultze (1886) see Polyak, 1957.

Schwann (1838) see Polyak, 1957.

Stiles, W. S., & Crawford, B. H. The luminous efficiency of rays entering the pupil at different points. *Proceedings of the Royal Society (London)*, 1933, *122B*, 428–450.

Svaetichin (1956) see Riggs, 1965.

Talbot (1834) see Graham, 1965.

Tomita (1963) see Riggs, 1965.

Toraldo di Francia (1949) see Brindley, 1970.

Van Essen, D. C. Visual areas of the mammalian cerebral cortex. In *Annual Reviews of Neuroscience*. Vol. 2. Palo Alto, CA: Annual Reviews, 1979.

Vieth (1818) see Ogle, 1950.

Volkmann, F. C., Riggs, L. A., & Moore, R. K. Eyeblinks and visual suppression. *Science*, 1980, *207*, 900–902.

von Kries (1902) see Graham, 1965.

Wade, N. A note on the discovery of subjective colors. *Vision Research*, 1976, *17*, 671–672.

Wald (1954) see Graham, 1965.

Walls, G. L. *The vertebrate eye*. Bloomfield Hills, MI: Cranbrook Institute of Science, 1942.

Walls, G. The G. Palmer Story. *Journal of the History of Medicine and Allied Sciences*, 1956, *11*, 66–96.

Weale, R. A. Trichromatic ideas in the seventeenth and eighteenth centuries. *Nature*, 1957, *179*, 648–651.

Weinstein (1967) see Pöppel et al., 1977.

Wiesel & Hubel (1965) see Jung, 1973.

Wiesel & Hubel (1966) see Boynton, 1979.

Wiesel & Hubel (1974) see Hubel & Wiesel, 1977.

Wundt (1861) see Ogle, 1950.

Wyszecki, G., & Stiles, W. S. *Color science*. New York: Wiley, 1967.

Young, T. On the theory of light and colours. Bakerian Lecture, 1801; *Philosophical Transactions of the Royal Society of London*, 1802, *92*, 20–71.

6 Taste And Olfaction

L. M. Bartoshuk, W. S. Cain, C. Pfaffmann
John B. Pierce Foundation Laboratory, Yale University and The Rockefeller University

The chemical senses, taste and olfaction, although clearly two anatomically distinct sensory systems, are so intimately involved in daily experience that they are often confused with one another. The *taste* of food, as we use the term in everyday life, is really a composite of olfactory and gustatory experiences. The olfactory receptors in the nose are activated by the aroma of corned beef and cabbage, but the taste buds in the tongue are activated by the saltiness of the meat. Lemons have a distinctive odor that can be detected without their being taken into the mouth, but sourness is added to the lemon odor when lemon is consumed. Salt, acid, caffeine, and sugar stimulate taste, whereas pepper and other sharp spices stimulate pain and other trigeminal receptors. These are just a few examples of the many ways in which food produces a multisensory experience. It is not surprising that such propinquity and mutual functioning of the two senses is apparent in the history of writings on taste and smell.

The Greek philosophers used *taste* to refer to the sensations produced by putting substances into the mouth, much as *taste* is used now in everyday life. *Olfaction* was reserved for the sensations produced by sniffing. This lumping of true taste with the olfactory sensations aroused when volatiles from a substance in the mouth rise through the back of the oral cavity and stimulate the olfactory sense generated confusion that was not resolved completely until the nineteenth century.

Chemosensory matters of interest to the Greeks included the location of the sense organs, the nature of the stimuli, fundamental qualities, and hedonic properties such as pleasantness. For instance, in about 500 B.C., Alcmaeon "located" the olfactory receptors inside the brain. Almost two centuries later, Aristotle displaced the receptors to where they belonged, the epithelium of the

221

nasal cavities. Such a progression from the incorrect to the correct seems natural. Another five centuries later, however, the physician Galen (ca. 180 A.D.), whose strong influence lingered for more than a thousand years, managed to place the receptors back in the brain, specifically in the ventricles. As we shall see, it took scientists another 1600 years before the receptors for olfactory stimuli were properly described.

Aristotle and his student, Theophrastus, an expert on foods, botanicals, and perfumes, found themselves stumped regarding the stimulus for smell. They disagreed with philosophers of the atomist school, who saw all matter as composed of atoms. Theophrastus convinced himself that physical emanations could not possibly cause odor because some plants that withered quickly evoked little odor in the process, whereas others that withered slowly evoked potent odor for long periods of time. Such a clever observation had little impact on atomism, a theory that pre-dated Aristotle but, between periods of unpopularity, surged again and again.

One surge, notable for the chemical senses, occurred in the first century B.C. and stimulated the long, didactic poem *De Rerum Natura* (ca. 55 B.C.) by Lucretius. It said, in part, ". . . so that you may easily see that the things which are able to affect the senses pleasantly, consist of smooth and round elements; while all those on the other hand which are found to be bitter and harsh, are held in connexion by particles that are more hooked and for this reason are wont to tear open passages into our senses . . .". Though atomism surged again in the seventeenth century, it could still not explain Theophrastus' observation of the poor correlation between odor intensity and the loss of matter from aromatic plants. It is interesting that during the seventeenth century both Isaac Newton and the great physician, Albrecht von Haller, also made the perplexing observation that substances can give a potent aroma for many years with no discernible loss of weight. Newton used a few grains of musk, a natural secretion of the musk ox, to perfume his office for decades. A satisfactory explanation awaited the nineteenth century observation that olfactory sensitivity varies non-uniformly across odorants. Depending on their physicochemical properties (e.g., solubility, molecular size, functional group, polarity), some substances can trigger smell at concentrations more than a million times lower than other substances. Some plants do give off only infinitesimal amounts of vapor, but the odoriferous molecules of the vapor possess particularly efficacious physicochemical properties. Newton's small amount of musk, with its low rate of evaporation but efficacious properties, could have continued to perfume his office for well over a million years.

Aristotle offered an alternative to the atomist doctrine. He believed that water in itself is tasteless but that it takes on the quality of *sapidity* (the ability to be tasted) by washing sapid substances through it, and he noted that the richest variety of these substances is in the vegetable kingdon (*De Sensu*). Since air can also wash out these sapid properties and air also contains moisture, what is taste in water becomes odor in air and water. Thus, there must be a correspondence between the taste and olfactory sensations that are excited by the same quality of sapidity (*Parva Naturalia*).

The interpretation of Aristotle's views is complicated by a translation problem.[1] He used one word to designate the object that provokes a sensation and another word to designate the sensation. In an effort to make this distinction, translators sometimes use ''flavor'' to refer to the stimuli that produce the sensation of taste. In modern usage, however, ''flavor'' refers to the composite sensation of taste and smell, so a sentence such as, ''The quality of flavours is more distinct to us than that of smells'' (Hammond, 1902), seems puzzling. The translation in modern usage would be something like, ''The sensations evoked by taste stimuli are more distinct than those evoked by olfactory stimuli.''

Aristotle proposed tbe following as basic taste qualities: sweet, bitter, sour, salty, astringent, pungent, and harsh. Six of these seven qualities were also proposed for olfaction because, as described above, Aristotle believed that at least some of the stimuli for the two were identical.

The pleasure associated with taste and smell was also noted by these early scholars. When asked if a person could ever experience pleasure with antecedent or subsequent pain, Socrates, in Plato's *Republic,* appealed to odors: ''For these [the pleasures of smell] with no antecedent pain suddenly attain an indescribable intensity, and their cessation leaves no pain after them.'' Aristotle argued that the function of the pleasures aroused by taste were nutritive; that is, taste directs the choice of foods and beverages such that pleasant tasting substances are consumed while unpleasant ones are rejected. Both Aristotle and Plato recognized that some odors appeal because they arise from objects necessary to physiological well being. Regarding the odor of food and drink, Aristotle remarked: ''Their pleasantness and unpleasantness belong to them contingently . . . These smells are pleasant when we are hungry, but when we are sated and not requiring to eat, they are not pleasant . . .'' (Ross, 1906). Such a view has recently formed part of a general theory of alliesthesia (Cabanac, 1971).

TASTE

Despite some confusion between taste and smell, the study of the two senses began to diverge even in the ancient world.

Roman and Arabic Science

Aristotle (384–322 B.C.) had a greater influence on the development of science than did any other Greek philosopher. Aristotle was the tutor of Alexander the Great, who founded the City of Alexandria in 323 B.C. This vital, cosmopolitan city housed the greatest library of the era (ultimately destroyed in about 47 B.C.).

---

[1] We thank Dr. Victor Bers of the Classics Department of Yale University for clarifying this issue.

Alexandria was eventually absorbed into the Roman Empire as Rome became the center of progress. Galen (A.D. 180–200), who studied in Alexandria as a young man and later moved to Rome to become the personal physician of the emperor Marcus Aurelius, represents the pinnacle of medicine in this era. His extraordinary influence dominated Western medicine until the Renaissance, more than a thousand years later. Galen noted that the abnormal appearance of the tongue as well as certain taste disorders could be symptoms of pathology (Siegel, 1970). He added little to taste perception per se, citing the same seven taste qualities given by Aristotle, but his work on the identification of taste nerves was remarkable. Galen believed that two nerves mediated taste sensations. One of these corresponds to what is now known as the lingual nerve (a branch of the trigeminal or Vth cranial nerve), and the other was a combination of three nerves now known as the glossopharyngeal (IXth), vagus (Xth) and accessory (XIth) nerves. The lingual and accessory nerves do not mediate taste, but the glossopharyngeal and vagus nerves do.

With the fall of the Roman Empire, the center of science shifted to Arabic scholars who translated the works of the Greeks and Romans and added original observations of their own. By the seventh century, many earlier works on philosophy, medicine and alchemy were available in Arabic (Partington, 1937). By the tenth century, Arabic science was flourishing. Avicenna (980–1037), a great Muslim physician and philosopher, represents a high point of this era. Avicenna listed five tastes: sweet, salty, sour, bitter, and *insipid* (Gruner, 1930). Avicenna seemed to use insipid much as a zero in the set of taste qualities. Avicenna, like Aristotle, believed that pure water is tasteless. Although the purity of water available to Aristotle is unkown, Avicenna's *The Canon of Medicine* mentioned the distilling of water as a technique of purifying it (Gruner, 1930).

Early chemistry revolved around activities such as extraction of metals, and the production of pottery, glass, and dyes that were important to the existing cultures. Greek treatises on chemistry (the term probably derives from an Egyptian word) were known in the first century A.D. These works give diagrams of apparatus as well as practical information including information on distillation. Gold was a very valuable metal in these early times as it is now. The chemistry of the era was concerned with transmuting other substances into gold. As science declined in the West and rose in Muslim lands, this interest in transmutation increased. The term, ''alchemy,'' as we now refer to the discipline that searched for the secrets of transmutation, resulted from the Arabic definite article *al* and the Greek *chēmeia* (chemistry) (Partington, 1948).

The Renaissance: Science Flowers Again in the West

By the thirteenth century, the center of scientific enquiry was moving back to the West. In 1542, Jean Fernel, a French physician and philosopher, published *The*

Natural Part of Medicine, the first Western work on human physiology since Galen. Sherrington, a great physiologist and also an expert on Fernel, credits Fernel with the first use of the term *physiology.* The taste qualities listed by Fernel (1581) are the same as those listed by Aristotle and Galen with the addition of "insipid," which Fernel says "is probably not a flavor but the absence of flavor" (p. 137). The addition of "insipid" probably originated from Arabic sources since Fernel, like many in this era, was an Arabic scholar. Around the same time, Laurance Gryll (1566) published what may have been the first work solely on the sense of taste *Two Books of Taste, Sweet and Bitter.*

Although alchemy never succeeded in its primary aim, a great deal of practical chemistry was known by the seventeenth century. For example, Partington (1948) credits Tachenius (1666) for the definition of a salt, "all salts are composed of two parts, of acid and alkali," and Boyle (1675) for the observation that acids can be recognized by their sour tastes.

During the eighteenth century, knowledge about taste accumulated slowly. In about 1752, Johann G. Sulzer produced a taste sensation by inserting his tongue into the notch formed by touching together a piece of zinc and a piece of copper. Volta (1745–1827) independently performed this same experiment in his investigations of the "animal electricity" discovered by Galvani. Volta went even further and showed that if he joined two different metal strips and placed the end of one on his tongue and the end of the other near his eye, he tasted an unpleasant taste and saw a light (Dibner, 1964). Ultimately, he was also able to evoke sensations of touch and hearing with his "metallic electricity."

The conclusion that the tongue was the sole organ of taste was dramatically challenged by observations on people with no tongues. In *A Physical Essay on the Senses,* Le Cat (1750) describes the cases of two children—one born without a tongue, the other who lost his tongue through gangrene from smallpox—who were able to taste. Haller (1786) concluded that taste resides in three kinds of papillae on the tongue rather than generally on the tongue surface (although he seems to have selected the filiform papillae, now known to be devoid of taste, as the primary taste organs).

Just as a variety of diseases were attributed to unpleasant odors and pleasant odors were used to protect the healthy from disease in this era (Cain, 1978), the pleasantness of the tastes and smells of food was believed to offer a guide to a healthful diet. For example, Haller (1786) writes:

> Nature designed the difference of tastes to be felt by the tongue, that we might know and distinguish such foods as are salutary: for in general, there is not any one kind of aliment healthy that is of a disagreeable taste; nor are there any ill tasted matters that are fit for our nourishment. For it must be observed, that we here take no notice of excess, by which the most healthy food may be prejudicial. In this manner nature has invited us to take necessary food, as well by the pain called *hunger,* as by the pleasure arising from the sense of taste. (pp. 264–265)

On the other hand, once disease was present, the medicines believed to cure it could have remarkably noxious tastes and smells. This is not surprising given that so many compounds in nature are bitter. Many of these are poisonous to humans; in fact, this has led to speculation that the unpleasantness evoked by bitter may be a survival mechanism. Yet in proper amounts a poison can be beneficial, a fact known very early in the history of medicine. We can override the unpleasantness of the taste in order to get the benefits of the remedy.

Nineteenth Century

Physiology. Taste buds are now known to be collections of receptor cells (clustered much like the segments of an orange) buried in the tissue of the taste

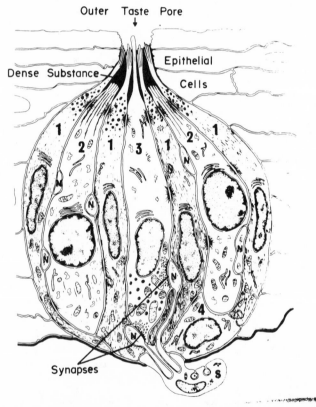

FIG. 6.1.   Longitudinal section of a taste bud from a rabbit foliate papilla. The type 3 cells have been tentatively identified as taste cells. Nerve fibers synapsing with the taste cells are labeled "N." The type 4 cells are believed to be the source of replacement cells in the taste bud. Type 1 cells may be supportive in nature. The type 2 cells do not show synapses but do have extensive contact with neurons and may play a role in the generation of neural signals. A schwann cell (S) surrounds the nerve fibers. Modified from Murray (1973).

papillae that are visible on the tongue. Loven (1867) and Schwalbe (1867) independently discovered these structures in mammals. Retzius (1892) showed that the taste buds did not connect directly with nerve fibers; rather, they terminated nearby and (we now know) formed synapes (see Fig. 6.1). At this time the cranial nerves innervating taste buds were known to be the chorda tympani (VIIth), the glossopharyngeal (IXth) and the vagus (Xth), with the role of the trigeminal (Vth) still controversial.

In 1838, Johannes Müller proposed his doctrine of **specific nerve energies.** According to this view, each sense has its own special nerves capable of giving rise only to the sensations appropriate to that sense. The extension of this doctrine to individual qualities thus proposes that each taste quality must have separate nerve fibers (Natanson, 1844). This very important physiological concept had great influence on the emerging domain of experimental psychology.

Experimental Psychology.   The earlier lists of taste qualities all contain the confusion between taste and other modalities that was present in Aristotle's writings. Horn (1825) finally put much of that confusion to rest by asserting that only sweet, sour, salty, bitter, and alkaline were true taste qualities. He even dispatched the "insipid" quality by stating: "It would never occur to anyone to want to give a color name to something invisible" (p. 76). Later, alkaline was dropped from the list when it seemed to be a composite taste-touch sensation (Öhrwall, 1891). The four basic tastes, *sweet, sour, salty* and *bitter,* dominated nineteenth century taste research, but a major debate arose over their relation to one another.

Helmholtz, who had studied with Müller, proposed a psychological distinction between modality and quality based on the presence of a continuum. He argued that when two sensations were so different that there were no transitions and they could not be viewed as more or less similar, then they belonged to different sensory modalities. He gave "blue," "sweet," "warm," and "high pitched" as examples of sensations from different modalities. On the other hand, when a transition existed (e.g., orange between red and yellow) and some sensations could be described as more similar than others (e.g., red and orange are more similar than red and blue), then the sensations represented different qualities within a single modality.

The application of these ideas to taste produced a battle between the two men who dominated taste research in this era: Friedrich Kiesow and Hjalmar Öhrwall. Both men were academic grandsons of Helmholtz. Kiesow got his Ph.D. with Wilhelm Wundt, who had worked as a physiology laboratory assistant in Helmholtz's department at Heidelberg. Öhrwall studied with Frithiof Holmgren, whose early training was in medicine in Sweden, but who later became an eminent physiologist after visits to the famous laboratories of his day, including that of Helmholtz. Both Kiesow and Öhrwall accepted the four basic tastes. Öhrwall argued that the lack of transitions among them meant that they must be considered separate modalities. Kiesow rejected this view and instead attempted to demonstrate analogies between taste qualities and colors.

Öhrwall published only two major papers in taste, but they were very important ones. The first, in 1891, was "Untersuchungen über den Geschmackssinn" (*Investigations on the Taste Sense*). This paper contains the first systematic attempt to study the sensitivities of individual taste papillae. Öhrwall found that although some responded with only one quality, many were sensitive to stimuli that elicited more than one. This paper also reviews earlier work relevant to the modality-quality issue and puts forth Öhrwall's view that there are four taste modalities—salt, sour, bitter, and sweet.

Kiesow earned his Ph.D in 1891. The results of his studies were published in 1894 and 1896 in *Philosophische Studien*, a journal founded by Wundt in 1881. Kiesow replicated Öhrwall's experiment on single papillae, with some technical improvements but essentially the same results. Another of Wundt's students (Hänig, 1901) showed that sensitivity to the four tastes was differentially distributed across the tongue (see Fig. 6.2), and Kiesow and his students showed that the different qualities disappeared successively in a certain order and not at the same time after the application of topical anesthetics (Kiesow, 1894a; Fontana, 1902; Ponzo, 1909). It was also found that chewing certain plant substances—leaves from *Gymnema sylvestre*, in particular—eliminated sweetness but did not affect saltiness or sourness. Bitter was reduced to some extent. The berries from *Synsepalum dulcificum* (formerly called *Bumelia dulcificum* and

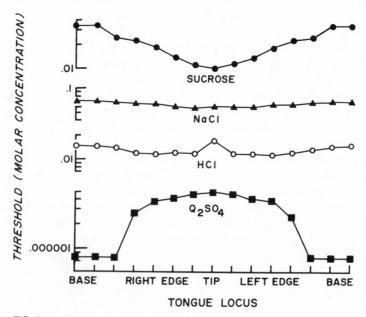

FIG. 6.2. Thresholds on various tongue loci for sucrose, NaCl, HCl, and quinine sulfate (Q_2SO_4). Note that the actual differences in threshold were quite small.

commonly called miracle fruit) modified some taste qualities while leaving others unaffected (Shore, 1892; Kiesow, 1894b; Skramlik, 1926).

Other phenomena, those of taste contrast and mixtures, were the source of more controversy and debate. If established, it would counter Öhrwall's extreme position that the different taste qualities were just different modalities. In his experiments on contrast, Kiesow tested salt, hydrochloric acid, sucrose, and quinine. He studied both simultaneous and successive contrast. For *simultaneous contrast*, he applied one taste stimulus to one edge of the tongue and a second taste stimulus simultaneously to the other edge of the tongue. For *successive contrast*, he first applied one taste stimulus to the tongue tip and subsequently applied the second stimulus to the same area. The taste of the second stimulus was intensified for some, but not all, pairs of taste qualities in both the simultaneous and successive designs. However, contrast was best when the second stimulus was relatively weak.

When Kiesow mixed different tastes, he found that substances in the mixture could be identified, but were less intense than when unmixed. When he mixed weak sucrose and salt, the resulting solution lost both qualities and took on a new, *flat* taste that Kiesow found hard to describe. He felt that his loss of taste quality was analogous to the loss of color that results from the mixing of opponent colors.

Öhrwall responded in 1901 with a paper highly critical of Kiesow: "Die Modalitäts—und Qualitätsbergriffe in der Sinnesphysiologie und deren Bedeutung" (*The Concepts of Modality and Quality in Sensory Physiology and their Significance*). Öhrwall renewed his insistence that the four tastes are separate modalities; furthermore, perhaps more interesting to us today, he made some insightful comments about Kiesow's experiments. He pointed out that Kiesow's analogies with color vision were faulty. Color contrast was an impressive phenomenon; taste contrast was not. Some of Kiesow's subjects did not report contrast at all, and the increase in intensity in the second substance often was not in the correct quality. The experimental resolution of whether or not taste contrast exists was not to come for more than 70 years. Modern work by McBurney, Bartoshuk, and others does not support the existence of either simultaneous or successive contrast in taste. Similarly, the loss of color that results when two opponent colors are mixed is impressive, whereas, in taste mixtures, Kiesow found a loss of quality in only one case—the mixture of weak salt and weak sucrose. Öhrwall doubted that even his phenomenon was truly analogous to color mixing.

Despite Öhrwall's sage remarks, Kiesow's views prevailed. Part of this influence was probably due to Wundt's central position as a teacher of experimental psychology. Kiesow began his studies with Wundt in 1891 and remained in Leipzig until he began a department of experimental psychology in Mosso's institute in Turin, Italy, in about 1889 (Kiesow, 1930). Wundt had many American students who later wrote influential textbooks or whose students did so. Kiesow's views are usually reflected, it not explicitly cited, in these texts.

A discussion of nineteenth century taste psychology would not be complete without mention of Fechner. In 1860 Gustav Fechner published *Elemente der Psychophysik*. Fechner meant his "psychophysics" to solve the problem of measuring the magnitude of sensation. Because be believed that such measurements could not be made directly, he developed an indirect approach: the measurement of sensitivity. The logic relating sensitivity to the perceived intensity of stimuli was as follows. First, the **absolute threshold** was to be measured. This was the amount of stimulus necessary just to produce a sensation. Second, the increment in the stimulus necessary to produce a **just noticeable difference** (j.n.d.) in sensation was to be measured. Theoretically, one could keep on measuring j.n.d.s across the whole stimulus range. The perceived intensity of any particular stimulus would then be expressed as the number of j.n.d.s between threshold and that stimulus. In practice, simplifying assumptions were made that decreased the amount of experimental work.

Chemistry. Identification of the stimuli that produce the sour and salty taste qualities depended upon the development of physical chemistry. Arrhenius' (1887) theory of electrolytic dissociation provided the necessary insight into the nature of solutions and was followed by three important papers written independently but containing some similar conclusions about the tastes of electrolytes. Kahlenberg (1898) and Richards (1898) both attributed sourness to the H^+ ion, but they noted that the concentration of H^+ alone did not predict the perceived intensity of the sourness because organic acids were more sour than inorganic acids at the same H^+ concentration. Höber and Kiesow (1898) and Kahlenberg both concluded that the salty taste is produced by anions, particularly Cl^- ions. They arrived at this conclusion by comparing the salty tastes of sodium salts. For example, Kahlenberg found a concentration of NaCl that was just slightly salty, while a sodium acetate solution containing the same concentration of Na^+ (i.e., an equimolar solution) was not salty at all. Although the attribution of the salty taste quality to Cl^- ions still finds its way into some textbooks, it is challenged by modern work.

Sweetness and bitterness were also considered in relation to the periodic table of elements. Many salts were known to be bitter. For example, anions heavier than chloride (i.e., bromide and iodide) and alkali cations heavier than sodium (i.e., potassium, rubidium, and cesium) were known to be bitter. In addition, certain salts were sweet. Sternberg (1898) singled out the elements lead, beryllium, bismuth, carbon, nitrogen, and oxygen as likely stimuli for sweetness. However, real progress with sweetness and bitterness had to await the development of organic chemistry. Even knowledge of the structure of sugars (e.g., Emil Fischer discovered the configuration of D-glucose in 1891) did not provide an explanation of why some sugars are sweet and some are not, nor did it explain the sweetness of a variety of other organic compounds (e.g., amino acids, saccharin).

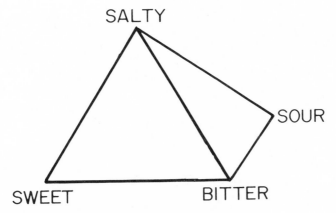

FIG. 6.3.   The taste tetrahedron.

Twentieth Century

Hans Henning (1927) formalized the status of the four basic tastes by suggesting that taste be represented by a *tetrahedron* (see Fig. 6.3). The four basic tastes were placed at the corners. Substances with two tastes (e.g., KC1, which is bitter-salty) were represented on the edges, and substances with three tastes were represented on the faces. Henning believed that the tetrahedron was hollow because no compounds produced all four taste qualities. Because he thought that mixtures of simple stimuli could not duplicate the tastes of compounds with complex tastes, he believed that the tetrahedron did not represent mixture tastes. However, Skramlik (1926) showed that the tastes of a variety of salts with complex tastes could be duplicated by mixtures of the four basic tastes. This observation led to the more common interpretation of the tetrahedron as representing all tastes whether produced by mixtures or substances with complex tastes.

In 1930, Helmut Hahn began a series of studies on **adaptation** of the taste sense in an effort to approach the question of the primacy of the basic tastes in a new way. Hahn studied taste adaptation by measuring the effects of adaptation on taste thresholds. The threshold, measured by the method of constant stimuli, rose with adaptation time. With complete adaptation (i.e., loss of taste of the adapting solution), it reached a value just above the adapting concentration (Hahn, 1949). This was one of the most important observations in the psychophysics of taste because it mapped quantitatively for the first time the time course and shape of taste adaptation (see Fig. 6.4). The accuracy and precision of these measurements resulted from Hahn's use of a "Geschmackslupe," a glass flow chamber with its aperture resting upon the tongue surface, thus insuring that a constant area was stimulated and that all saliva was excluded by an initial rinse.

Next, Hahn investigated cross-adaptation among substances with similar qualities. He found that adapting for 2 minutes to an acid elevated the threshold

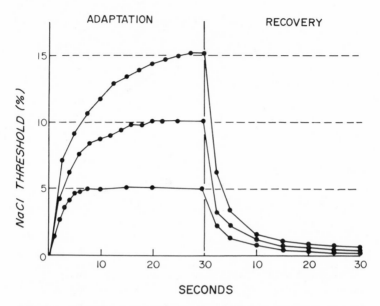

FIG. 6.4.   Adaptation and recovery functions for NaCl as measured with taste thresholds. As the NaCl was flowed across the tongue through the ''Geschmack-sluppe,'' the threshold rose until it reached a point just above the concentration of the adapting solution. When water replaced NaCl (recovery), the thresbold returned to its preadaptation value. Modified from Hahn (1934).

for all other acids tested. However, for sweet, bitter, and alkaline stimuli, adapting to one substance did not always elevate the threshold for other substances of the same quality. In the case of salts, the result was even more extreme. There was no cross-adaptation among the 24 salts tested. The failure of salts to cross-adapt is perhaps Hahn's most famous observation. The simplest interpretation of cross-adaptation is that it provides information as to which substances affect the same receptor sites. If the tongue is adapted to Substance A, the threshold for A is elevated. If Substance B is then tested and its threshold is also elevated, A and B are said to stimulate the same receptor sites. By this logic, Hahn's data required 24 separate receptor site types for the tastes of salts. It is not surprising that his results led to considerable consternation among taste investigators. Sweet, bitter, sour, and salty had won general acceptance as true taste primaries. Hahn's work seemed to show that only one of these tastes could be coded by a unique receptor mechanism. The other three seemed to possess more than one, salt being the extreme case. However, Hahn himself rejected this view. After a decade (1930–1940) of research during which, by his own count, he had measured nearly 15,000 thresholds for 108 taste substances on 43 subjects (each threshold requiring at least 30 minutes), Hahn decided to approach the problem in a new way.

These new studies were terminated by World War II and were not published until 1948. Hahn devised a new procedure which he felt would answer the question that adaptation could not: Are there unique receptor mechanisms for sweet, salty, sour, bitter, and alkaline? Hahn determined thresholds for several substances, then added half-threshold concentrations of pairs of substances with similar and dissimilar qualities. When the qualities were similar, the mixtures (containing two solutes either of which alone would be at half-threshold concentration) produced a threshold sensation. When the qualities were not similar, the mixture did not produce a threshold sensation. The only exception occurred with the alkaline stimuli. Some of these added to produce a sensation, but others did not. Strangely enough, Hahn still concluded that alkaline should be considered a basic taste quality. While Kiesow stressed the interactions between taste qualities, Hahn, like Öhrwall, argued that the qualities were essentially independent.

After Hahn, taste psychophysics became almost exclusively an American discipline. The research, although diminished in volume, was certainly not diminished in quality. Excellent studies were published by Americans who traced their intellectual lineage to the German experimental psychologists (e.g., Brown, 1914; Dallenbach & Dallenbach, 1943). In addition, the sensory evaluation of food became an important specialty within a field of food technology, and two groups, one within the food technology department of the University of California and the other within the Quartermaster Corps of the U.S. Army (now the Behavioral Science Division of the U.S. Army Natick Laboratories), made contributions that added considerably to our knowledge about taste, particularly taste mixtures (see Amerine, Pangborn, & Roessler, 1965, for a survey of these data). However, the point of view left by Kiesow was not seriously challenged in the early postwar era.

The New Psychophysics.   In the 1950s, S. S. Stevens and his colleagues at Harvard developed new psychophysical methods radically different from the indirect methods of Fechner. The basic disagreement between Fechner and Stevens concerned the j.n.d. Stevens noted that the j.n.d.s could not all be psychologically equal because the j.n.d. scale did not make proper predictions concerning perceived intensity. For example, if the perceived intensity of sound A were 5 j.n.d. units while that of B were 10 j.n.d. units, then B should sound twice as intense as A. In fact, this kind of prediction failed. Stevens concluded that j.n.d.s are not all equal, and he dropped the indirect measurement of sensory magnitude in favor of direct methods that produced scales with ratio properties (i.e., a stimulus with a scale value of 10 would be perceived to be twice as intense as a stimulus with a scale value of 5).

The significance of Lemberger's (1908) early effort on this issue was not appreciated at the time. She determined the successive j.n.d. stops for sweetness for two different substances, sucrose and saccharin, so that stimulus concentrations falling at equal j.n.d. steps above threshold could be specified. Such concentrations were not equally sweet when compared directly. At higher concentrations, saccharin was relatively less sweet than sucrose of equal j.n.d. value. The fact that two different chemicals were used to elicit sweetness probably obscured the basic psychophysical origin of this effect.

The earliest **ratio scales** for taste were produced by Lewis (1948) using fractionation (Harper & Stevens, 1948). Essentially, this method consisted of determining how much concentration would have to be decreased in order to halve the perceived intensity of a particular taste stimulus. Once Lewis had determined these values for a series of concentrations, he could plot perceived intensity as a function of stimulus concentration. He produced ratio scales for NaCl, sucrose, quinine sulfate, and tartaric acid.

Beebe-Center and Waddell (1948) then linked the scales Lewis had constructed by finding concentrations of sucrose, quinine sulfate, and tartaric acid that had perceived intensities matching the perceived intensity of a standard sucrose concentration. They called these ratio scales "gust scales" (after the Latin *gustus*, meaning taste).

These scales are only of historic interest now because fractionation was succeeded by a much more efficient direct method: **magnitude estimation.** With this method, subjects simply assign numbers proportional to the perceived intensities of the stimuli. This method was first used with taste in 1953. Beebe-Center and a group of students at Harvard, including J. C. Stevens, who was later to play an important role in the development of the new direct methods, used magnitude estimation to scale sweetness. In 1960, J. C. Stevens, then an instructor of psychology at Harvard, used magnitude estimation to scale sucrose, dextrose, and saccharin. This appears to be the first time magnitude estimation was used to generate matches. These data were not published at the time but were later included in a summary article by S. S. Stevens (1969).

Donald McBurney, a student of Pfaffmann at Brown, published the first studies using magnitude estimation in taste (McBurney, 1966). McBurney and his students ultimately studied *cross-adaptation* and *adaptation* within each of the four basic tastes. The results showed that Hahn was correct in rejecting the apparent implications of his own cross-adaptation studies. Hahn, after 10 years and 15,000 thresholds, had found little cross-adaptation. With the new psychophysics, McBurney's research required only a fraction of the effort previously necessary and showed that, with some exceptions for bitter and sweet, cross-adaptation was virtually complete within each taste quality. In addition, cross-adaptation occurred only slightly, if at all, across the four taste qualities. Hahn's conclusions about the independence of sweet, sour, bitter, and salty were vindicated, even though his cross-adaptation experiments were flawed. Hahn's failure may have resulted from his use of detection thresholds to measure cross-adaptation. Most salts have complex tastes; that is, they taste salty but have other taste qualities as well. Only the common taste qualities between two salts would be expected to cross-adapt. For example, KCl is bitter as well as salty. Adaptation to NaCl will cross-adapt the saltiness of KCl but not the bitterness, so a subject can still detect the bitter taste.

The new psychophysics also permitted the resolution of the confusion surrounding insipid and water tastes. Insipid was originally intended to represent true tastelessness (Fernel, 1581). Öhrwall (1891) later identified insipid with the flat taste of distilled water. We now know that the taste sensation produced by distilled water is actually a response to the removal of saliva from the tongue (Bartoshuk, McBurney, & Pfaffmann, 1964). Many substances, for reasons not well understood, can induce a taste in water. That is, when the substances are rinsed from the tongue with water, a taste sensation results.

Although the new psychophysics has led to reemphasis of the four basic tastes, there is an important difference between this contemporary attitude and that of the nineteenth century. Current research is oriented toward determining the properties of sweet, bitter, sour and salty rather than looking for proof that these are exhaustive categories.

Structure-function relations.   Advances in chemistry as well as new insights about taste function have clarified the nature of taste stimuli. Hydrogen ions were recognized as the source of sourness very early, and that fact has never been seriously challenged. Beidler's (1953) early electrophysiological work led him to conclude that the cation is the actual stimulus in a salt, while the anion plays an inhibitory role. Sodium salts with a variety of anions produced neural responses of about the same size, whereas chloride salts with a variety of cations produced neural responses of variable size. The earlier workers made an assumption put well by Richards (1898): ". . . most properties of solutions are additive, and we cannot well conceive of a minus taste . . ." Thus, the logic of these early studies did not take into account the possibility of inhibition. The earlier work can be reinterpreted in the light of Beidler's logic. NaCl can be seen as the saltiest salt because Cl^- is the least inhibitory anion, not because Cl^- is the source of saltiness.

A general theory of sweetness depended on developments in structural chemistry. Shallenberger and his colleagues described a triangular configuration that a molecule must possess in order to taste sweet. The three corners of this configuration presumably bind to taste receptors. This insight came from determining the actual shape of sweet molecules in solution. Many molecules can theoretically twist into more than one shape, and the overall shape affects the triangular part of the molecule that produces the sweet taste.

The determination of the structure of bitter compounds has not led to the identification of a unitary chemical structure associated with bitterness. Rather, a variety of chemical characteristics have been associated with bitter taste. These include the N-C = S grouping found in many compounds including phenylthiocarbamide (PTC). The PTC taste-blindness phenomenon was discovered by Fox, a chemist working at DuPont, when he noted that the compound tasted bitter to some individuals but was tasteless to others (Fox, 1931). Family studies have found that individuals who cannot taste this and other compounds containing the N-C = S group carry two recessive genes, while those who can taste it carry either two dominant genes (are homozygous for tasting) or one dominant and one recessive gene (are heterozygous for tasting). The sensitivity to PTC is not directly related to sensitivity to chemically unrelated compounds; for example, both tasters and non-tasters can be very sensitive to quinine.

Sensory electrophysiology. Despite the differences between Kiesow, on the one hand, and Hahn and Öhrwall, on the other, all three men were profoundly influenced by Müller's doctrine of specific nerve energies and its extensions, and assumed that the individual qualities were mediated by specific taste nerve fibers. The advances in electrophysiological techniques in Adrian's laboratory at Cambridge University were to have an enormous impact on that view.

The chorda tympani, glossopharyngeal, and vagus nerves had been correctly identified as mediating taste, but the role of the trigeminal nerve remained controversial. In human patients, removal of the gasserian ganglion (which contains the cell bodies of the nerve fibers in the trigeminal nerve) was believed to disrupt taste (Krause, 1895). However, Harvey Cushing (1903) found that these losses recovered with time. He concluded that the trigeminal nerve did not mediate taste and that the losses in taste function reported earlier resulted because the real taste pathways passed near the extirpated ganglion and so were temporarily affected by the surgical trauma.

The chorda tympani, which innervates the front of the tongue, came into its own in the 1940s. Pfaffmann, working in Adrian's laboratory, recorded electrical impulses from single fibers in the cat chorda tympani. He found three types of fibers: those responding to acid only, those responding to acid and salt, and those responding to acid and quinine (Pfaffmann, 1941). None responded to sugar, a sensitivity now known to be lacking in cats. The four basic tastes were not found to be mediated by specific fibers; thus, the neural code for taste quality had to depend on activity in more than one neuron. This was the origin of the **cross-fiber patterning theory** of taste quality.

Beidler, whose academic lineage also traces back to Adrian, and colleagues visiting his laboratory from Japan found that even the taste receptor cells, clusters of which form the taste buds, were not specific to substances of a single quality (Kimura & Beidler, 1961). Pfaffmann and Beidler each founded laboratories for researching the chemical senses—Pfaffmann at Brown University in 1940, Beidler at Florida State University in 1950. Between these dates, in 1946, Yngve Zotterman, who had also worked with Adrian, developed his sensory physiology laboratory, which included study of the chemical senses, in Stockholm at the Royal Veterinary School. He and his coworkers described the sugar sensitive fibers in dog and their suppression by gymnemic acid. With Diamant, an otological surgeon, he was able to record human chorda tympani response to taste, including the specific suppressive action of gymnemic acid only on the sugar response. Melvin Cohen, Susumo Hagiwara, and Zotterman (1955) essentially confirmed and extended the results of Pfaffmann's experiments with the cat chorda tympani, but added an additional fiber type, the *water fiber*. This fiber responded to water, acid and quinine, but not to salt. He had observed a response of the frog's taste fibers to pure water in 1949. The discovery of water fibers added a new twist to the old issue of the number of basic tastes; Zotterman and his colleagues, after studying several species (Zotterman, 1961), came to believe that some species (e.g., cat, pig, monkey) had water fibers while others (e.g., man and rat) did not. According to more modern work, this apparent species difference is clearly dependent upon adaptation of the receptors.

In the post World War II years, several new chemical senses laboratories were founded in Japan. Among these were Masayasu Sato's laboratory established in 1954 at theKumamoto University of Medicine, and Yojira Kawamura's laboratory, which dates from 1959, at the Osaka University Dental School (Kato, 1965).

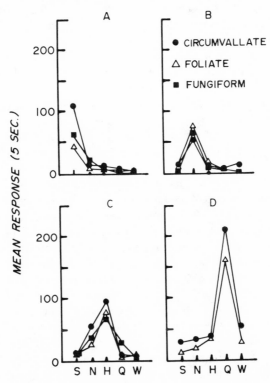

FIG. 6.5. Examples of taste fiber types in the rat. Stimuli were placed on the fungiform, foliate, or circumvallate papillae. Stimuli were sucrose (S), NaCl (N), HCl, quinine (Q), and water (W). Modified from Nowlis and Frank (1977).

As single taste fiber recordings from these laboratories and the laboratories of Pfaffmann and Beidler accumulated, the distinctions among fiber types began to blur. Robert Erickson (1963), a student of Pfaffmann, extended the patterning idea. He suggested that the code for quality might be the profile of responses across a population of single taste neurons of varying sensitivities. More recent studies on more species with larger samples of single units now indicate that although taste units may respond to a range of chemicals, four groups of fibers can be identified according to their "best" stimuli as "sucrose-best," "NaCl-best," "HCl-best" and "quinine-best" (see Fig. 6.5). The sugar-best and quinine-best classes appear to be more specific, i.e., with less overlap in their responsiveness to other chemicals, than are those reactive to electolytes, but investigations of the details of such specificity and its chemical basis continue to be an active area of current research and some controversy.

Animal Behavior. Electrophysiological recordings shifted attention from human psychophysics to comparative studies across many species. From the beginning, these physiological studies went hand in hand with behavioral studies. The earliest of these were the two-bottle preference studies (Richter, 1939) in which an animal simply was provided with two bottles from which to drink over a relatively long time (usually 24–48 hours). One bottle contained water; the other, a taste solution. Consumption of more of one than the other implied the ability to taste the difference, and the choice that was made reflected the hedonic value of the solution (preferred or rejected). The rat, for example, prefers sugars and sodium chloride and rejects acid and quinine solutions. Most dramatic was the great increase in preference for solutions of sodium chloride in rats that had been adrenalectomized. Removal of the adrenal gland leads to excessive excretion of sodium chloride so that death ensues if salt intake is not increased. The laboratory rat's increased salt preference is sufficient to maintain it in good health. This was but one of a number of Richter's (1942) classic and important studies of self-selection behavior toward solutions of minerals, sugars, vitamins, and other nutrients showing that taste played an important part in guiding an organism's ingestive behavior in keeping with the demands of homeostasis.

The deceptively simple two-bottle preference procedure turned out to be very complex. In addition to its greater intake of suprathreshold concentrations, the salt-needy organism sbows a preference for weaker salt solutions than does the normal animal. Originally interpreted as evidence for increased taste sensitivity, direct electrophysiological recording showed that the receptor threshold was not changed (Pfaffmann & Bare, 1950), a finding confirmed in recent studies with the additional observation that the neural response to the stronger concentrations of salt was reduced, a receptor change which would tend to make the stronger salts less noxious and more tolerable for the salt-needy organism.

The distinction between sensory *versus* hedonic properties of taste, i.e., quality and intensity as distinct from pleasantness and unpleasantness, is an important one. Engel (1928) showed that pleasantness of taste could be measured for human subjects and that it varied with both quality and intensity—sweet mostly increasing in pleasantness with concentration, and bitterness increasing in unpleasantness. Taste hedonics, however, was a neglected subject from about 1930 to 1960, a victim of the behaviorist taboo against subjectivity. Working mostly with animals, Young (1959) and Pfaffmann (1960) led a counter trend, and it is now becoming apparent that their correlation of acceptance with pleasantness and aversion with unpleasantness has a neural basis (Pfaffmann, Norgren & Grill, 1977). Cabanac (1971) has documented how sensory pleasure serves as a sign of biological usefulness, whereas displeasure serves as a warning sign, and he has shown that these hedonic processes are sensitive to changes in internal bodily state. The psychophysics of human hedonics has now become an active domain of applied and basic research. Attributing hedonic processes to animals is further validated by observations of oro-facial expressions of pleasure or disgust in preverbal human neonates (Steiner, 1973) and in animals. The latter studies also reflect a recent interest in the question of animal awareness.

Preferences are not entirely unlearned. Dramatic examples of the modification of preference by past experiences are provided by research on *conditioned taste aversion* pp. 31, 61, this volume). For instance, a rat may be given a stimulus to taste and then made sick with drugs or radiation. When the rat recovers, it will avoid the substance tasted just before the illness, as well as other substances with similar tastes. This latter effect has been utilized as a method for classifying how animals perceive different taste stimuli. Which substances taste similar to one another and to what extent is indicated by the degree to which the aversion *generalizes*. In general, the similarities of taste function across mammals are impressive, but species differences, where they exist, can be determined and specified. This bodes well for the use of these animal models in the study of human taste experience. The comparative study of taste has developed into an enormously productive discipline largely because of the care and ingenuity with which electrophysiological and behavioral techniques have been integrated. In 1903, Sherrington wrote to Cushing concerning the latter's work clarifying the role of the trigeminal nerve in taste (Cushing, 1902–1905). In that letter Sherrington discussed his earlier attempts to study taste in animals: "It is pushing animal physiology beyond its legitimate capability to try such observations: but I did not feel that so strongly then as now. Sensation can only be adequately judged of as between man and man." Fortunately, Sherrington was too pessimistic.

OLFACTION

The history of thought on olfaction comprises a strange mixture of the rational and the mystical. Philosophers of ancient Greece pondered and debated, in characteristically rational manner, various issues that would challenge scientists more than two thousand years later. In the interim, however, the mystical predominated. What is the primary reason for the early slippage from the rational to the irrational? Hygiene. The Greeks practiced it, but subsequent Western cultures did not. Hygiene, odors, and medical practice have historically borne an intimate interconnection.

The sophistication of a society determines its medical practices. Sophisticated civilizations rely primarily on prevention of disease through hygiene and hygienic therapy. Unsophisticated societies rely primarily on faith healing, but often with heavy assistance from "drugs." Hippocrates declared war on magicoreligious medical practice in ancient Greece. He sought a fully scientific medicine, with hygiene at its core, and managed to attain a partly rational one. He possessed a limited arsenal of somewhat dubious drugs, but used them cautiously. Subsequently, drugs saw more promiscuous use. Both drugs and faith healing often survive the same invalid test: A sick person touches a magic charm or takes a drug and gets better, hence the charm or the drug gets credit for the cure.

In many cultures, disease, particularly contagious disease, was commonly thought to arise from "bad" air. How could a person discern bad air from good air? By smell. Foul smelling air possessed a property (miasma) that caused disease. When hygiene lapsed and streets literally became open sewers, the perceived importance of bad air became amplified and the use of so-called drugs increased markedly. The drugs of medieval Europe were mainly spices. Europeans actually sought these cherished substances (which served as the major basis of commerce with the East and led to the discovery of America) as medicine rather than as condiments.

How could a doctor decide which "medicine" to prescribe in any particular case? The capricious and unsystematic nature of medical practice made the choice idiosyncratic. Nevertheless, if a disease seemed to have arisen from a bad odor, then it seemed reasonable to replace the bad odor with a "better" one. Burning sulfur served as one strategy. Even Hippocrates advocated this measure during epidemics. Use of such an acrid odor had special appeal to those who suspected the role of evil spirits in disease. American Indians, for instance, drove out such spirits with acrid smoke from evergreens. Use of pleasant odors, without accompanying "lustration by fire," served as another, more popular strategy.

Use of aromatic herbs to ward off disease reached its zenith during outbreaks of the plague. Unaware that fleas from rats generally transmitted the disease, persons commonly stuffed their ears and nostrils with sweet smelling thyme, rue and pennyroyal. As Haggard (1929) explained:

The physicians of those days protected themselves against the disease by means of suits of leather with leather gauntlets and masks with glass coverings for the eyes and a long snout filled with fumigants for the nose . . . . They lit fires on which were burned aromatic substances to purify the air; and for the same purpose sprinkled perfumed water in the rooms and on their clothing. Eau de Cologne is a survival of one of these plague waters or essences. (p. 210)

Figure 6.6 depicts a seventeenth century Roman physician dressed in his protective suit.

FIG. 6.6 Gehart Altzenbach's "The Plague Doctor." The engraving depicts and the text describes (in three languages) the costume worn by physicians during the Plague of 1656 which claimed about half a million lives in Italy. From the Clements C. Fry Collection, Yale Medical Library. Reprinted with permission.

The Enlightenment: Slow Return to the Rational

Olfaction shed its mysterious aura slowly, well after the Renaissance. Philosophers of the seventeenth and eighteenth centuries lent some help through treatises on how human beings acquire knowledge and a sense of self. The soul figured prominently at first, but gave ground, inch by inch, to a more mechanical conception of mind. If the physical universe operates through laws of mechanics, then, reasoned some philosophers, so should thoughts, images, desires, feelings, and volition. Such a bold conjecture left the philosophers hungry for physiological data on the workings of the brain. Hobbes' (1651) notion that mental events originated from motion in the brain evolved, over the course of a century, to Hartley's (1749) notion that the events originated from vibrations in nerves. Such rudimentary mechanical concepts admittedly failed to offer insight into the physiological basis of ideas. Frustrating though the lack of physiological data was, the mechanical conception of mind still flourished through analyses of the "mechanics" of thought processes themselves. A strategy for such analyses involved consideration of the newborn infant, without speech and without experience. What properties would suffice to permit this infant to grow into a reasonable, reflective being with a complete repertoire of human mental activities and feelings? Would the mere capacity for sense impressions suffice?

For Hartley and his disciples, the British associationists, capacity for sense impressions did suffice. Though not of the British school, Condillac (1754) offered the most extreme form of the "sensationalist" position. He studied psychological mechanics through the hypothetical experiences of a statue, rather than an infant. The statue possessed five senses, unlocked one by one, and ultimately a sixth talent, movement. The statue sought pleasure from its sensory experiences and sought to block out pain. In order to convince others that all mental life could originate merely from an elaborate sequence of sense impressions. Condillac endowed the statue first with the least cognitive of all the senses, olfaction. He then proceeded to "show" that reason, reflection, emotion and all other psychological functions could arise from mere consciousness of odors, without appeal to such superfluous characteristics as innate ideas or autonomous faculties.

Despite Condillac's attention, olfaction, unlike vision, reaped few specific benefits from the insights of the philosophers. Nevertheless, the rational conception of olfaction finally began to supplant the mysterious. Furthermore, the burgeoning industrial revolution forced confrontation with possible links between odors and disease. Factories exposed workers and neighbors to many noxious vapors. Though clearly toxic in some instances, many disagreeable vapors had no evident deleterious effects. In commenting on the paper, "Report of the Physical and Mathematical Class of the Institute Upon the Question, Are Those Manufactures Which Emit a Disagreeable Smell Prejudicial to Health?," the editors of the *Edinburgh Medical and Surgical Journal* (1806) remarked: "A disagreeable smell is by no means a certain criterion of an unwholesome atmosphere. And, on the other hand, the air is often pestilential, when, to our senses, it seems uncontaminated . . .'' The editors still suspected that putrid smelling air held danger, and this long-held attitude may never actually die.

Nineteenth Century

Laboratory science, though hardly new, came of age in the nineteenth century. Even in the Middle Ages, chemists (then known as alchemists) toiled in laboratories using smell as their keenest analytical tool. In a continuation of this tradition, Boyle, well known for his experiments on gases, wrote a treatise on sources of odor, *Experiments and Observations about the Mechanical Production of Odours* (1675). In it, he noted the phenomenon, still unexplained, that odor quality may change with the concentration of an odoriferous material.

Birth of Quantitative Chemistry. It was not until the beginning of the nineteenth century that quantitative chemistry appeared. In quick succession Lavoisier (father of modern chemistry, who overturned the phlogiston theory and enuncitated a new view of the elements), Dalton (quantitative atomic theory), Berzelius (determination of atomic weights), Guy-Lussac (law of the combination of gases by volume), and Avogadro (hypothesis that all gases, at a given temperature, contain the same number of particles) built a foundation; by the middle of the century, chemistry had already become a bustling, experimental science. This spurred some to dabble in quantitative olfactory research and to measure odor thresholds. By 1868, Alexander Bain, in *The Senses and the Intellect*, could list threshold concentrations for six odorants. It had already become clear that the nose could register remarkably small amounts of odorants (less than one part per billion of air), but that sensitivity varied markedly among these substances. Although some studies of threshold came from the chemistry laboratory, such as the laboratory of the great chemist, Emil Fischer, others came from a new type of laboratory devoted to physiology.

The Liberation of Physiology. Like chemistry laboratories, medical laboratories had existed long before the nineteenth century, but the practical demands of medicine had not previously liberated scientists to study physiology for its own sake. Among the early physiologists of the nineteenth century, E. H. Weber, known subsequently for Weber's law, had a direct interest in smell. For instance, he flushed eau de Cologne into his nose and thereby convinced himself that persons cannot smell liquids. This observation sparked controversy since others obtained the opposite result. More heated controversy, however, surrounded the issue of which nerve carried olfactory information.

By the latter half of the seventeenth century, it had become abundantly clear that the nasal cavities did not provide physical access, through tiny pores, directly to the brain. Physicians had ceased to view nasal mucus as cerebro-spinal fluid that had escaped through these imaginary pores. Though the first cranial nerve was known as the olfactory nerve, some researchers, even toward the middle of the nineteenth century, thought this a misnomer. Two prominent physiologists of the era, Francois Magendie and Claude Bernard, denied the olfactory function of the nerve and argued that the fifth cranial nerve, the trigeminal, subserved olfaction. Schiff, in biting criticisms of Magendie's sloppy (and characteristically cruel) experiments on olfaction in dogs and of both Magendie and Bernard's careless observations on patients with anosmia, reasserted the olfactory function of the first nerve. The trigeminal nerve thereafter assumed its proper role as one that mediates, through free endings in the nasal epithelium, the sensations of pungency, stinging, warmth, and cold that arise from many inhaled vapors (e.g., ammonia). Almost simultaneous with the resolution of this controversy, anatomists began to discover the nature of the cells in the olfactory epithelium.

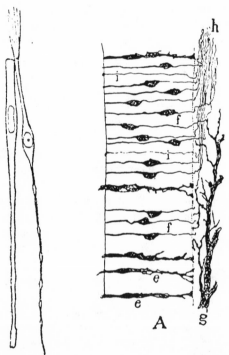

FIG. 6.7. Left: Isolated olfactory receptor neuron (ciliated cell) and sustentacular (supporting) cell first depicted by Shultze in the mid-nineteenth century. From Parker (1922). Right: Schematic cross-section through olfactory epithelium (A) of a full-term rat fetus: e, epithelial (sustentacular cells; f, bipolar olfactory receptor cells; c, free nerve ending; h, olfactory nerve fibers; g, trigeminal nerve fibers. From Ramón y Cajal (1893).

In 1855, Eckhard described two types of cells in the most superficial stratum and thought that one or the other might represent cell bodies of olfactory nerve fibers (Parker, 1922). Ecker uncovered a third type, basal cells, that lay under the others. Subsequent histologists, first through the use of the transitory stain, methylene blue (an organic dye), and then through the use of more permanent Golgi (metal salt) preparations, confirmed the three-fold composition of olfactory epithelium: receptor cells (bipolar neurons that contained the cell bodies of olfactory nerve fibers), ordinary epithelial or supporting cells, and basal cells. The olfactory cells distinguished themselves visually by their shape and by cilia on their distal ends. Schultze had suspected in 1862 that these ciliated cells were the receptor cells but could not prove it. Others did. Figure 6.7 depicts the two types of cells he discovered. For most vertebrates, between 5 and 50 million receptors, with a larger number of supporting cells, occupy the patch of olfactory epithelium in each nasal cavity.

By the end of the nineteenth century, anatomists had also learned that the axons of olfactory receptors coursed into basket-like structures, termed

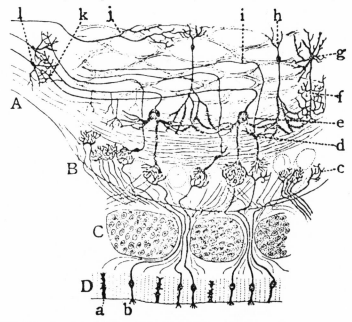

FIG. 6.8.   Ramón y Cajal's (1893) schema of the olfactory apparatus of mammals: A, olfactory lobe; B, olfactory bulb; C, cartilage of the cribiform plate (ethmoid bone); D, nasal mucosa; a, supporting cell; b, olfactory receptor cell and axon; c, arborization of an olfactory fiber in the vicinity of a glomerulus (see dotted circles); d, tufted cell; e, mitral cell; f, an ending in the molecular layer; g, large stellate cell; h, granule cell; i, axon of tufted cell forming part of the olfactory tract; j, arborizations of cells of central origin. A modern scheme would show many of the same details.

glomeruli, in the olfactory bulbs. Here, these first-order axons formed synapses with mitral cells (see Fig. 6.8). Axons of these second-order mitral cells then formed a large part of the olfactory tract. Beginning with the next synapse, the picture became increasingly more complicated. Some fibers in the olfactory tract projected to the pyriform cortex, but others seemed to project to a large portion of the hippocampal region, fornix, peduncle of the corpus callosum, and other nearby structures. No other sensory system seemed to manifest such complex central circuitry. Indeed, the anatomist Broca concluded that the whole limbic region was involved in olfaction. However, he also felt that the region must serve some other function, then unknown. It does. It controls virtually all autonomic (e.g., visceral, emotive, appetitive) functions. Here we find an anatomical substratum for the affective impact of odors.

Experimental Psychology: The New Science. Developments regarding structure rapidly outpaced those regarding function. Almost a half-century after the creation of the first true physiology laboratories, yet another kind of laboratory, that of experimental psychology, sprouted. The word *experimental* deserves emphasis, for there already existed psychologists of a nonexperimental, philosophical sort. When Wilhelm Wundt opened the first laboratory of experimental psychology at Leipzig in 1879, he asserted his discipline's equal status with traditional psychology and with physiology. As Murphy (1929) put it: "For what is experimental psychology if not an embodiment of the notion of a fundamental unity between psychology and physiology . . ." Unfortunately, the chemical senses fared poorly in the hands of these new scientists. Indeed, in 1892, the eminent William James stated in his textbook, *Psychology,* that "almost nothing of psychological interest in known concerning them."

Those few psychologists who paid attention to olfaction at all looked at issues that fell far outside the matter of sensory reception. Some saw the modality primarily as a means of access to cognitive processes and to affect. For instance, Francis Galton (1894) asked whether a person (specifically, himself) could perform mental arithmetic through the use of real or imaginary smells, just as he could through the use of imaginary figures (e.g., visual images of numbers) or sounds (e.g., images of spoken numbers). He taught himself to associate two whiffs of peppermint with one of camphor, three of peppermint with one of carbolic acid, etc., and he managed to calculate simple sums with this system. Taste served similarly well. Galton thereby convinced himself that any sense modality could serve as a channel to sophisticated cognitive operations. This may sound suspiciously similar to the associationism of Hartley and Condillac. As Woodworth (1948) noted, regarding psychologists at the turn of the century: "In theory they stood for an analytical psychology patterned after chemistry, with elementary sensations, images, and feelings, and with complex thoughts and emotions composed of these elements; but in practice they often disregarded this scheme. In theory they were mostly associationists, but not dogmatically so; the high noon of associationism was already past."

Unfortunately, fascination with the analysis of complex psychological events continued to divert attention away from the actual workings of olfaction well after the turn of the century. For instance, Bolger and Titchener and Heywood and Vorschide sought unsuccessfully to confirm, through experiments on the associative power of smells, that odors can evoke vivid memories of the past, complete with visual and auditory images and emotions. The emotional and affective impact of odorants made them popular for the study of the dimensions of affect and affective elements even into the 1920s (Beebe-Center, 1932).

Experimental psychologists of the nineteenth century could claim partial ownership of Gustav Fechner's discipline of psychophysics, the study of quantitative relations between stimulus and sensation. The scientists exercised their proprietary interest in olfactory psychophysics almost exclusively through the work of Eleanor McC. Gamble (1898), whose extensive doctoral dissertation implied that intensity discrimination in olfaction fell well below that in other modalities. Fortunately, physiology also held proprietary stake in olfactory psychophysics, and Hendrik Zwaardemaker, who later described himself as a "physiologist with psychological aspirations," exercised it avidly.

Zwaardemaker, a physician by training, took up olfactory research in the 1880s. Disgruntled with the usual difficulties of stimulus control in olfaction, he constructed a device (an *olfactometer*) that, though imperfect, permitted rapid accumulation of psychophysical data. The device in its most elementary form consisted of two tubes—one of relatively small diameter, and one of diameter just sufficient to fit over the small diameter, but longer, tube. The inner tube was made of glass and the outer was made either of odorous material (e.g., rubber, aromatic wood) or of porous material impregnated with odorant. In a manner similar to the opening of a telescope, Zwaardemaker could slip the outer tube completely over the inner tube or could allow the outer tube to extend beyond the edge of the inner tube. A stream of air that passed through the tubes would pick up more or less odorant depending on the area of the outer tube that the experimenter wished to expose in this telescoping operation. When the outer tube was made of india rubber, a linear extension of .7 cm gave rise to a just detectable, i.e., threshold, odor. Zwaardemaker dubbed the extension just necessary to reach the threshold, whatever the odorant, an *olfactie*. Twice this extension (e.g,, 1.4 cm for india rubber) equalled 2 olfacties, and so on.

Armed with this simple device and unit of measurement, Zwaardemaker went on to explore mixtures, masking, and various facets of adaptation. He found, for instance, that a binary mixture of odorants smells weaker than the sum of the unmixed components, and coined the term *odor compensation* to describe the phenomenon. Some pairs, in certain proportions, seemed almost to neutralize each other and to leave only a vague, desaturated smell. This could hold true even when one component entered one nostril (and hence stimulated the receptors on only one side of the septum) and the other component entered the contralateral nostril. Using a similar strategy (i.e., independent stimulation of the two receptor patches), Zwaardemaker found that olfactory adaptation must occur in part in the central nervous system. A stimulus presented to one nostril would cause short-term loss of sensitivity on both the ipsilateral and contralateral sides. Zwaardemaker summarized his various psychophysical studies, his thoughts on the results of other investigators, and many useful observations on the physics and chemistry of odorants and olfaction in a book, *Der Physiologie des Geruchs*, published in 1895. Thirty years later, he published another impartant treatise *L'Odorat* (1925); an update of the first. Because his tenure, beginning in 1897, as professor of physiology at Utrecht led him to other experimental pursuits (e.g., psychoacoustics, physiological chemistry), Zwaardemaker could not provide the wealth of new material in the second treatise that he had in the first. By 1925, however, others had followed his lead and had begun to investigate or speculate on odor perception. These "neophytes" concentrated primarily on questions of odor quality (theories of odor quality, the psychological organization of quality).

THE MODERN ERA AND THEORIES OF OLFACTION

So-called theories of olfaction have come and gone frequently since the late nineteenth century. Most have arisen from only meager, if any, experimental work and have usually merely made suggestions about which chemical or physical properties of molecules might correlate best with odor quality or trigger transduction. It may seem reasonable that the first theories of this "chemical" sense should propose chemical interaction between odorant and receptor, but such theories actually came second. The first theories proposed vibrational or radiational rather than chemical action. In 1865, Faraday and Tyndall had noticed that odoriferous substances absorb infrared radiation strongly. The kinetic theory of gases, proposed almost simultaneously with Faraday and Tyndall's observation, implied that the frequencies absorbed depended on the frequencies of intramolecular vibrations. This raised the possibility, propounded first by Ogle in 1870 and echoed by Ramsay in 1882 and Haycraft in 1889, that olfactory receptors may actually register vibrations. The attractiveness of this notion seemed to lie less in empirical observations regarding olfaction than in the possibility that waves, whether mechanical or electromagnetic, might form a proximal stimulus for all sense modalities. (Haycraft included taste in his speculations.)

More refined vibrational theories, grounded in some data, eventually succeeded the early versions, and an elaborate one remains alive even today (Wright, 1977). Not all vibrational theorists fixed attention on the infrared band. In 1919, Heyninx, resurrecting one of Zwaardemaker's discarded theories, focused on the ultraviolet. As in the case of infrared theories, the ultraviolet theory attributed differences in odor quality to differences in absorption spectra and to the presence or absence of certain "osmic" frequencies. Some such theories also left open the possibility that transduction could take place without actual contact between odorant and receptor, just as transduction in vision requires no physical contact between the source of radiation and the photoreceptors.

An absorption spectrum reveals much about the structure of a molecule and can even permit identification of an unknown compound. Since molecules closely related chemically often have closely related spectra, it should hardly be surprising that chemical relatedness in one or another of its various forms would crop up as a possibly more parsimonious correlate of odor quality than were absorption spectra. The term *chemical relatedness* covers a diversity of possible commonalities and many have served in turn as focal points of theories (e.g., reactivity; degree of saturation; oxidizability; presence of particular functional groups, linkages, or nuclei; location of functional groups). Most such theories, like most vibrational theories, had only short lives, Their frailty lay in the generality of their assertions. A single or a few counter-examples can deal a heavy blow to such theories, and few theorists exhibited the flexibility or possessed enough supporting data to absorb the blow. The theory of osmophores proved at least a partial exception.

The observation that a particular functional group (e.g., thiol group), linkage (e.g., ether linkage) or nucleus (e.g., pyridine nucleus) may endow a molecule with a particular odor quality brought the term *osmophore* (sometimes called *odoriphore*) into currency during the first part of the twentieth century. The term originated from the observation of Zwaardemaker and others that, within the class of relatively small molecules (but also some molecules with weights above 100 daltons), amines share a fishy-urinous quality, mercaptans and sulfides share a sulfurous odor, most esters share a fruity quality, etc. The various substances within these chemical classes hardly seem identical perceptually. Therefore, other features also determine aspects of quality. Nevertheless, the common perceptual notes that run through such chemically related series possess enough integrity to enable the chemist to identify the functionality of many "unknowns."

For larger and more complex molecules, the notion of osmophores seemed irrelevant. Substitution of one osmophoric group for another may make little or no difference in quality, and the presence of a particular group may seem to add no characteristic quality. This situation, though it sustained interest in vibrational theories, also spawned a third generation of theories based on stereochemistry (size and shape of molecules). The first modern suggestion to focus on structural features exclusively was made in 1930 by the psychologist, L. Troland, best known for his research in vision. Troland stated:

> . . . We are almost tempted to suppose that the actual chemical substances which are involved enter the nerve fibres and pass bodily to the region of olfactory experience. If we then supposed that the olfactory quality was directly determined

by the structure of such molecules, and the intensity by their concentration, we could dispense with the necessity of special representative means in the nerve impulse. Although such an hypothesis is rather too spectacular to warrant serious support, it accounts for the indefinite variety of olfactory experience, and the highly individual character of the dependencies upon specific chemical constitution. (p. 276)

Troland's somewhat off-hand suggestion regarding structure provided no immediate impetus for research. Roughly two decades later, however, more highly developed stereo-chemical theories began to dominate olfactory theorizing. Even the notion that molecules may enter the olfactory receptors, though reminiscent of the primitive speculations of Lucretius and Galen, came alive subsequently, in attentuated form, in a puncturing-and-penetration theory, a theory with an explicit stereochemical focus (Davies, 1971).

Stereochemistry continues to occupy a prominent position in modern theorizing. In fact, even though a strict relationship between a molecule's shape and size and its odor quality remains elusive, there now seems little reason to doubt stereochemistry's determining role. Functional groups and centers of polarity play a role insofar as they orient a molecule favorably as it contacts the protein receptor site on the cell membrane. But the notion of the osmophoric group will not die easily, for the odors of small molecules still seem determined largely by such groups irrespective of stereochemical properties,

Odor Classification. Theories of odor quality have always faced a major limitation: Their formulators have never quite known what ''facts'' to account for. Theories of color vision have sought primarily, though not exclusively, to explain how an additive mixture of three wavelengths can give rise to a hue indistinguishable from that of almost any other wavelength. The hue produced by such mixing will not appear as an analyzable composite of the starting wavelengths. Similarly, a master perfumer can concoct an odor mixture that will mimic the quality of almost any given product, but the concoction will rarely seem a mere composite of its components. This situation argues for an analogy between odor and color. However, the perfumer hardly starts with only three ingredients, but rather with more than a thousand. Does the perfumer truly need so many?

Perhaps a breakdown of odor qualities by category will reveal the minimum number, if not the actual names, of starting materials necessary to produce all qualities. Aristotle erected a classification scheme, but restricted his interest primarily to food odors. Haller in the seventeenth century, and Lorry in the eighteenth, also proposed schemes, but the only system with enough substance to have endured to the twentieth century came from the compulsive taxonomist, Linnaeus, in 1752. (As Asimov [1964] explained, ''Linnaeus' passion for classification amounted almost to a disease''). The Linnaean scheme contained seven classes: (1) aromatic, (2) fragrant, (3) ambrosial (musky), (4) alliaceous (garlicky), (5) hircine (caprylic or goaty), (6) repulsive, and (7) nauseous.

The Linnaean system survived mainly through the efforts of Zwaardemaker, who expanded and refined it, incorporating qualities proposed earlier by Lorry (ethereal) and Haller (empyreumatic or burnt) and adding various subdivisions:

1. Ethereal
2. Aromatic odors of high potency
   a. camphoraceous
   b. spicy
   c. aniseed
   d. citrous
   e. almond
3. Floral and balsamic
   a. scents of flowers
   b. lilaceous
   c. vanilla
4. Ambrosial (amber-musk)
5. Alliaceous (allyl-cacodylic)
   a. garlicky
   b. cacodylic
   c. bromine
6. Empyreumatic (burnt)
7. Caprylic (hircine)
8. Repulsive
9. Nauseous

Little ever came of Zwaardemaker's scheme, perhaps because the categories seemed to lack clear perceptual integrity. The category "spicy," to take but one example, covers a large amount of perceptual territory in that it may incorporate the disparate spiciness of such products as nutmeg, oregano, and red pepper. "Empyreumatic" may incorporate such dissimilar qualities as the smell of burnt rubber and the smell of burnt toast. More refinement (i,e., more division and subdivisions) may have yielded categories of greater integrity, but such refinement could apparently go on indefinitely.

An odor classification scheme may say as much about the cognitive structure of the classifier as it does about the sensory attributes of odorants. Does a classifier include the term "floral" because there exists a true floral attribute, or is it included because various substances seem similar to one or another of those many odors evoked by flowers. Stated more generally: Does a classifier allow knowledge of the objects that evoke odors to influence the classification scheme? The following example may reveal how cognitive factors can intrude on attempts to classify. A neighbor drops in one morning and notices, quite accurately, the smells of coffee, toast, and fried bacon emanating from your kitchen. Such a sensory analysis would hardly be astonishing. But consider that the smell of coffee arises from the action of many, perhaps more than a hundred, chemical

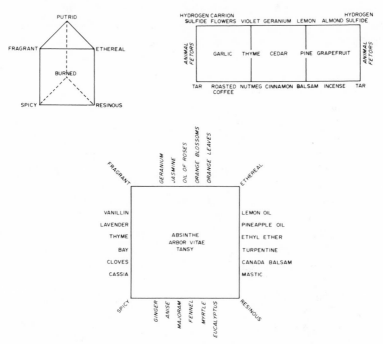

FIG. 6.9.   Various views of Henning's odor prism. Top left: the complete prism (from Woodworth, 1938). Right: the prism unfolded from the putrid-burned edge (from Boring, 1933). Bottom: one face of the prism (from Woodworth, 1938).

constituents. The smells of bacon and toast also arise from many constituents. Yet, from this vast array of airborne constituents, three rather unitary odors (coffee, bacon, toast) emerge. A person who had never smelled coffee, bacon, and toast would obviously find another set of qualities or perhaps a single unitary quality in the same array and could claim equal validity for the observation.

Not surprisingly, Zwaardemaker's system met resistance, particularly from Hans Henning, who used both his own observations and data from experiments to erect another scheme. Henning's scheme represented a clear advance over Zwaardemaker's because it incorporated a quasiquantitative view of odor similarity. As Figure 6.9 shows, Henning actually constructed a model of the psychological space for odors. In theory, this space, a hollow prism, permitted the quality of any odorant to appear as a point on the surface. Similar odors would appear as nearby points; dissimilar odors, as distant points. Henning saw the nodal points of the prism as particularly salient qualities, but would not go so far as to claim that these qualities represented fundamentals for the construction of all other qualities. Nor did he claim that these qualities seemed psychologically purer than others. In fact, he argued that most odorants seemed to have unitary qualities.

Henning's prism stimulated more research than any other single system in olfaction, probably because it made testable predictions. The hollowness of the prism implied that no odorant could resemble three qualities (e.g., fragrant-ethereal-burnt) that failed to lie on the same face. This restriction did not survive experimental tests and by the 1940s the prism held little more than historical interest. Nevertheless, it did serve as a forerunner of more modern multidimensional representations of odor quality, derived from standardized psychophysical procedures and sophisticated means of multivariate analysis.

Henning proffered a theory of the olfactory stimulus along with his prism. He proposed that odor quality depended on three factors: (1) the nucleus of a molecule (e.g., a benzene ring), (2) the atom-groups attached to the nucleus, and (3) the mode or place of attachment. More particularly, he proposed that an ortho-substituted benzene ring gave rise to the quality "fragrant," a para-substituted benzene ring to the quality "spicy," a nitrogen-containing heterocyclic ring to the quality "burnt," and so on. The theory, like most others, had a short life, but its emphasis on structure (i.e., point of attachment of substituent groups) served to bridge the gap between osmophoric and stereochemical theories.

Henning was not the first to notice the importance of structure. In 1892, Passy had pointed out that isomers (molecules that contain the same atoms but arranged differently) may evoke different qualities. An observation such as this all too often became the point of departure for an entire theory. Often the "facts" arose from observations on the qualities of a dozen or so odorants. Under such circumstances, every theorist found another waiting in the wings with his own set of "facts." The inadequacy of Zwaardemaker's classification scheme, and Henning's legitimate refusal to claim that the salient odor qualities constituted fundamentals, offered little solace for those who looked for an easy set of facts from which to spin theories. Perhaps neurophysiology would offer answers that psychology failed to provide.

Olfactory Neurophysiology.   In 1932, E. D. Adrian won a Nobel prize for research on the physiology of neurons. Shortly thereafter, he began to explore the neurophysiology of olfaction. Five other Nobel prize winners also gave attention to smell, though none won the prize for olfactory research! These were Emil Fischer (odor thresholds), William Ramsay (vibrational theory of smell), Santiago Ramón y Cajal (histology of olfactory structures), Linus Pauling (stereochemical correlates of odor), and Georg von Békésy (spatial localization of odors). Aside from Adrian, only the anatomist, Ramón y Cajal, exhibited more than a passing interest.

Adrian elected, for technical reasons, to record afferent neural traffic at the olfactory bulb (second order neurons) and pyriform cortex (third order neurons). Questions of interest were: Would the neurons display a discernible specificity related to the physicochemical properties of the stimuli? Did there exist a limited number of functional types of cells? Did information about quality travel along "labeled lines"? He could answer none of these questions affirmatively, and proposed instead that the nervous system encoded odor quality in terms of complex patterns:

> For a smell to produce a specific pattern of excitation in the olfactory epithelium we need only suppose that the different receptors are not all equally sensitive to different chemical stimuli. Such a differential sensitivity might depend on the intrinsic properties of the receptors, and it might also be due to extrinsic factors such as the amount of mucus in different regions, the rate of diffusion of the active molecules, etc. In this way an endless variety of smells might be distinguished because the process would be comparable not to the discrimination of colors but to that of visual patterns. (Adrian, 1942, p. 472).

The idea that neural patterns might encode quality was hardly new. In fact, J. P. Nafe (1929) had previously criticized Adrian for a naive, labeled-line interpretation of activity in somesthetic neurons and had proffered a pattern theory in its place. Moreover, newly obtained results from single fibers in the chorda tympani nerve of the cat indicated the probable importance of patterns for encoding taste quality (Pfaffmann, 1941). The importance of Adrian's statement actually lay in the analogy between odors and visual (i.e., spatial) patterns and in his recognition that non-neural factors, such as the composition of mucus, could help set up a pattern.

Zwaardemaker had also recognized that non-neural, physical factors might govern the perception of odor quality. His experiments on the severed head of a horse, as well as Paulsen's experiments on the heads of cadavers, led to the conclusion that currents of inhaled odorized air may not reach the patches of olfactory receptors directly but may need to diffuse passively up to the patches. Zwaardemaker reasoned that light, highly volatile odorants would diffuse to the upper portions and heavy, relatively involatile odorants would diffuse only to the lower portions. This led him to propose a mosaic theory of quality coding. Though this diffusion theory never received much attention, Adrian's notion that mucus might participate in the coding process has received considerable attention. The spatial pattern of molecular deposition at the olfactory mucosa can vary substantially from one odorant to another, a factor that may enhance known spatial nonuniformities in the sensitivity of receptors across the mucosal sheet. Hence, the possibility of a spatial code remains strongly in contention (Moulton, 1976).

Neurons in the visual cortex seem rather specifically tuned to certain features of a visual pattern, e.g., a line of a particular orientation, an edge, a "tongue" moving in a particular direction, etc. Vaguely analogous feature detectors may exist in the peripheral portions of the olfactory system. A particular receptor may respond to a wide variety of odorants but may effectively extract information about only one common feature. Some molecules, such as 2-decanone (depicted

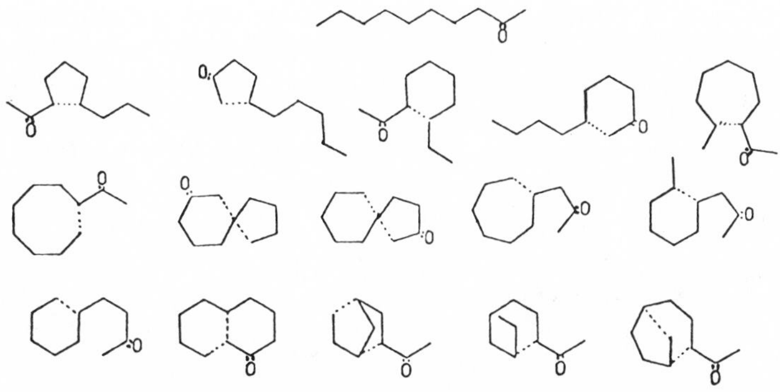

FIG. 6.10.   Some of the many possible configurations and conformations of the molecule 2-decanone. Courtesy A. A. Schleppnik.

in Fig. 6.10), might appeal to many types of receptor sites because of the many conformations it can adopt. A more rigid molecule may appeal to a smaller but still substantial number of receptors, depending on the number of its "extractable" features. The search for pivotal features goes on, particularly with the aid of now-common studies of individual receptor cells. These have never contradicted Adrian's conjecture.

Why did Adrian, who had already received the highest possible recognition, choose to focus on the most poorly understood and most difficult to study of all the sense modalities? Adrian recognized that brain chemistry held the key to brain functioning, and he reasoned that an understanding of external chemoreceptors might provide great insight into the chemical workings of the brain. When asked to offer a keynote for the Third International Symposium on Olfaction and Taste, Adrian (1969) said ". . . We have chosen a subject of real importance to biology, one that may well give some clues for solving the problems of intelligent, conscious behavior." Adrian would have got on well with Condillac.

As we have discussed, it was not until the advances in anatomy and physiology provided a description of taste buds on the one hand and the olfactory receptors on the other that the distinction between taste and smell became accepted and each could be studied in its own right. Another important stage in understanding these senses came with the developments in experimental sensory psychology and physiology particularly led by the German psychophysicists of the nineteenth century. Their main methods relied on sensory report of the human observer under controlled stimulating conditions. The psychophysics of taste and odor sensation laid the groundwork and provided many of the basic observations. Seminal were the works of F. Kiesow, H. Ohrwall, Zwaardemaker, and Henning. Another important development was the increasing understanding of the chemical nature of the stimuli that activated them. In taste, it was not until Arrhenius' theory of electrolytic dissociation in 1887 on the nature of solutions that the various cations and anions could be related to sour and salty taste sensations. Knowledge of the stimuli for other qualities such as sweetness awaited the elucidation of the organic chemistry and structure of sugar and other substances. Advances in olfactory knowledge depended on developments in stereo- and structural chemistry. The study of structure-function relations in both taste and smell is currently a very active but still largely empirical pursuit.

In the classification of the multitude of odors we see an interplay between chemistry, sensory physiology and introspective analysis. Phenomenological order among the variety of olfactory qualities was proposed by Henning's characterization of fragrant, foul, burnt, fruity, spicy, and resinous as salient if not primary odors. He accepted the earlier and more generally agreed upon basic tastes of salty, sour, bitter, and sweet and provided three-dimensional figures to indicate the interrelations of pure and of mixed qualities of both odor and taste. The search for primary or basic sensory attributes reflected the effort generally to reduce perceptions to the basic sensory elements of which they were composed. Such psychological reductionism characterized the atomistic and associationistic orientation of nineteenth century introspective psychology given an experimental context by Wilhelm Wundt. Implicit was the idea that the primary sensations gave clues as to the primary receptors. In the 1920s and 1930s the advent of the new electrophysiological methods developed by physiologists but adopted and adapted by psychologists, made a major impact on the study of sensory processes. Vision, hearing, and somesthesis, first to be attacked, were followed later by the chemical senses (1940s). These methods held the promise of revealing the fundamental primary tastes and odors by a direct method of recording from the sense organ itself in place of inferences by the indirect methods of psychophysics. But at the beginning, the electrophysiological evidence on taste led to increasing complication rather than to simplification, when it was found that the receptors as registered by single afferent nerve recordings were not as specific as classical theory would have it.

The early data on relatively small populations of single nerve elements, emphasized the overlap of reaction spectra or lack of specificity. More recent and extensive data with larger number of units gives a more persuasive picture of the existence of groups or clusters of sensitivity such that taste units may be labelled variously by their "best stimulus" such as sucrose-best, NaC1-best, HC1-best, or quinine-best. Some of these classes have a wider range of responsivity (less specificity), others, like the sugar responsive units, appear to be among the most specific. Clusters of odor specific elements with different chemical sensitivities across the olfactory sensory mucosa have now been differentially mapped. These issues however are still matters of active investigation and debate as more molecular approaches to the study of the mechanism of sensory activation mark the present scene.

The pioneering studies of Curt Richter showing the role of taste in such adaptive behavioral adjustments as the response to sodium deficiency, for example, leading to an enhanced preference or intake of the needed nutrient, has been extended in many directions in subsequent behavioral studies and remains an important and intriguing segment of studying the chemical senses. The dramatically potent and robust one-trial learning observed in the conditioned taste aversion phenomenon is another particularly compelling instance of the chemosensory control of behavior. The role of certain olfactory stimuli, pheromones of natural origin that control many aspects of sexual behavior, reproductive physiology, or social behavior is another current concern. Yet the psychophysics of taste and smell in modern dress, e.g., direct magnitude estimation methods, etc. is still important. Besides clarifying uncertainties in the classical literature it has opened new vistas for further systemization of perceived odor and taste quality, especially when combined with sophisticated statistical methods of cluster, factor analysis, and multi-dimensional scaling.

The affective or hedonic aspect of stimulation by taste and smell that the Greeks and early scholars remarked upon has received more and more attention in recent years not only as an aspect of food acceptance and odor preference but as an innate but modifiable property of these senses. There is also the promise that this feature can help probe the basic affective and motivational systems of behavior and the brain. Much remains to be done to bring knowledge of the chemical senses up to a par with the understanding of such higher senses as vision and hearing. Nonetheless, in some respects the chemical senses are uniquely psychological in import because of their association with affective and/ or hedonic processes and motivated behavior of animal and man, indeed "the pleasures of sensation."

REFERENCES

Adrian, E. D. Foreword. In C. Pfaffmann (Ed.), *Olfaction and taste, III.* New York: Rockefeller University, 1969,

Adrian, E. D. Olfactory reactions in the brain of the hedgehog. *Journal of Physiology,* 1942, *100,* 459–473.

Amerine, M. A., Pangborn, R. M., & Roessler, E. B. *Principles of sensory evaluation of food.* New York: Academic Press, 1965.

Arrenhius, S. On the dissociation of substances in aqueous solution. In *The Foundations of the Theory of Dilute Solutions.* (The Alembric Club, Trans.) Tweeddale Court, Edinburgh: Oliver and Boyd, 1929.

Asimov, I. *Asimov's biographical encyclopedia of science and technology.* Garden City, N.Y.: Doubleday, 1964.

Bain, A. *The senses and the intellect* (3rd ed.). London: Longmans, Green, 1868.

Bartoshuk, L. M., McBurney, D. H., & Pfaffmann, C. Taste of sodium chloride solutions after adaptation to sodium chloride: implications for the "water taste." *Science,* 1964, *143,* 967–968.

Beebe-Center, J. G. *The psychology of pleasantness and unpleasantness.* New York: Van Nostrand, 1932.

Beebe-Center, J. G., & Waddell, D. A general psychological scale of taste. *The Journal of Psychology,* 1948, *26,* 517–524.

Beidler, L. M. Properties of chemoreceptors of tongue of rat. *Journal of Neurophysiology*, 1953, *16*, 595–607.

Boring, E. G. *The physical dimensions of consciousness*. New York: Century, 1933.

Boyle, R. *Experiments, Notes, etc. about the Mechanical Origine or Production of divers particular Qualities: Among which is inserted a discourse of the imperfection of the Chymist's Doctrine of Qualities; together with some reflections upon the Hypothesis of Alcali and Acidum*. London, Printed by E. Flesher, for R. Davis Bookfeller in Oxford, 1675.

Brown, W. The judgment of very weak sensory stimuli. *University of California Publications in Psychology*, 1914, *1*, 199–268.

Cabanac, M. Physiological role of pleasure. *Science*, 1971, *173*, 1103–1107.

Cain, W. S. History of research on smell. In E. C. Carterette & M. P. Friedman (Eds.), *Handbook of Perception*, Vol. VI A. New York: Academic Press, 1978.

Cohen, M. J., Hagawara, S., & Zotterman, Y. The response spectrum of taste fibres in the cat: a single fibre analysis. *Acta Physiologica Scandinavica*, 1955, *33*, 316–332.

Cushing, H. The taste fibers and their independence of the nervus trigeminus. *Johns Hopkins Hospital Bulletin*, 1903, *14*, 71–78.

Cushing, H. Reprints Collected by the Yale Medical Historical Library, 1902–1905, Vol. II.

Dallenbach, J. W., & Dallenbach, K. M. The effects of bitter-adaptation on sensitivity to other taste qualities. *American Journal of Psychology*, 1943, *56*, 21–31.

Davies, J. T. Olfactory theories. In L. M. Beidler (Ed.), *Chemical senses, Part 1, Olfaction, Handbook of sensory physiology* (Vol. 4). Berlin: Springer, 1971.

Dibner, B. *Allesandro Volta and the electric battery*. New York: Franklin Watts, 1964.

Engel, R. Experimentelle Untersuchunger über die Abhängigkeit der Lust and Unlust von der Reizstärke beim Geschmackssinn. *Arch. Ges, Psychol.*, 1928, *64*, 1–36.

Erickson, R. P. Sensory neural patterns and gustation. In Y. Zotterman (Ed.), *Olfaction and taste, I*. New York: Pergamon, 1963.

Fechner, G. T. *Elemente der Psychophysik*. Breitkopf und Härtel: Leipzig, 1860.

Fernel, J. *Therapeutices universalis*. Frankfurt: Andream Wechelum, 1581.

Fontana, A. Ueber die Wirking des Eucain B auf die Geschmacksorgane. *Zeitschrift für Psychologie und physiologie der Sinnesorgane*, 1902, *28*, 253–260.

Fox, A. L. Six in ten "tasteblind" to bitter chemical. *Science News Letter*, 1931, *9*, 249.

Galton, F. Arithmetic by smell. *Psychological Review*, 1894, *1*, 61–62.

Gamble, E, A., McC. The applicability of Weber's law to smell. *American Journal of Psychology*, 1898, *10*, 82–142.

Gruner, O, C. *A treatise on the canon of medicine of Avicenna incorporating a translation of the first book*. London: Luzac, 1930.

Gryllus, L, *De sapore dulci et amaro*. Prague: Georgium Melantrichum ab Auentino, 1566.

Haggard, H. W. *Devils, drugs, and doctors*. New York: Harper, 1929.

Hahn, H. *Beiträge zur Reizphysiologie*. Scherer: Heidelberg, 1949.

Haller, A., von. *First lines of physiology*. New York: Johnson Reprint Corp., 1966. (Originally published, Edinburgh: Charles Elliot, 1786.)

Hammond, W. A. *Aristotle's psychology*. New York: MacMillan, 1902.

Hänig, D. P. Zur Psychophysik des Geschmackssinnes. *Philosophische Studien*, 1901, *17*, 576–623.

Harper, R. S., & Stevens, S. S. A psychological scale of weight and a formula for its derivation. *American Journal of Psychology*, 1948, *61*, 343–351.

Henning, H. *Der Geruch*. Leipzig: Barth, 1916.

Henning, H. Physiologie und Psychologie des Geschmacks. *Ergebinsse der Physiologie*, 1921, *19*, 1–78.

Henning, H. Psychologische Studien am Geschmackssinn. In E. Abderhalden (Ed.), *Handbuch der biologischen Arbeitsmethoden*. Berlin: Urban & Schwarzenberg, 1927.

Höber, R., & Kiesow, F. Ueber den Geschmack von Salzen und Laugen. *Zeitschrift für Physikalische Chemie*, 1898, *27*, 601–616,

Horn, W, *Ueber den Geschmackssinn des Menschen.* Heidelberg: Karl Groos, 1825.

James, W. *Psychology: Briefer course.* New York: Henry Holt, 1892.

Kahlenberg, L. The action of solutions on the sense of taste. *Bulletin of the University of Wisconsin Science Series*, 1898, *2*, 3–31.

Kato, G. (Ed.). *Japanese physiology present and past.* Tokyo: XXIII International Congress of Physiological Sciences, 1965.

Kiesow, F. Ueber die Wirkung des Cocain und der Gymnemasäure auf die Schleimhaut der Zunge und des Mundraums. *Philosophische Studien*, 1894, *9*, 510–527. (a)

Kiesow, F. Beiträge zur physiologischen Psychologie des Geschmackssinnes. *Philosophische Studien*, 1894, *10*, 329–368; 523–561. (b)

Kiesow, F. Beiträge zur physiologischen Psychologie des Geschmackssinnes. *Philosophische Studien*, 1896, *12*, 255–278.

Kiesow, F. Autobiography. In C. Murchison (Ed.), *A history of psychology in autobiography* (Vol. 1), Worcester, Mass.: Clark University Press, 1930.

Kimura, K., & Beidler, L. M. Microelectrode study of taste receptors of rate and hamster. *Journal of Cellular and Comparative Physiology*, 1961, *58*, 131–140.

Krause, F. Die Physiologie des Trigeminics nach Untersuchungen an Menschen bei denen das Ganglion Gasseri entfernt ist. *Münchner medizinische Wochenschrift*, 1895, *42*, 577–581; 602–604; 628–631.

Le Cat, M. *A physical essay on the senses.* London: Printed for R. Griffiths at the Dunciad, in St. Paul's Church-yard, 1750.

Lemberger, F. Psychophysische Untersuchungen über den Geschmack von Zucker und Saccharin. *Arch. ges. Physiol.*, 1908, *123*, 293–319.

Lewis, D. R. Psychological scales of taste. *The Journal of Psychology*, 1948, *26*, 437–446.

Lovén, C. Bidrag till Kännedomen om tungans smakpapiller. *Medicinskt Archiv*, 1867, *3*, 1–14.

McBurney, D. H. Magnitude estimation of the taste of sodium chloride after adaptation to sodium chloride. *Journal of Experimental Psychology*, 1966, *72*, 869–873.

Moulton, D. G. Spatial patterning of response to odors in the peripheral olfactory system. *Physiological Reviews*, 1976, *56*, 578–593.

Murphy, G. *An historical introduction to modern psychology.* New York: Harcourt, Brace, 1929.

Murray, R. G. The ultrastructure of taste buds. In I. Friedmann (Ed.), *The ultra structure of sensory organs.* American Elsevier, New York, 1973.

Nafe, J. P. Quantitative theory of feeling. *Journal of General Psychology*, 1929, *2*, 199–211.

Natanson. Analyse der Funktionen des Nervensystems. In W. Roser & Wunderlich, (Eds.), *Archiv für physiologische Heilkunde.* Stuttgart: Ebner und Seubert, 1844.

Öhrwall, H. Die Modalitäts—und Qualitätsbergriffe in der Sinnesphysiologie und deren Bedeutung. *Skandinavisches Archiv für Physiologie*, 1901, *11*, 245–272.

Öhrwall, H. Untersuchungen über den Geschmackssinn. *Skandinavisches Archiv für Physiologie*, 1891, *2*, 1–69.

Parker, G. H. *Smell, taste, and allied senses in the vertebrates.* Philadelphia: Lippincott, 1922.

Partington, J. R. A short history of chemistry. London: MacMillan and Co., 1951.

Pfaffmann, C. Gustatory afferent impulses. *Journal of Cellular and Comparative Physiology* 1941, *17*, 243–258.

Pfaffmann, C. The pleasures of sensation. *Psychological Review* 1960, *67*, 253–268.

Pfaffmann, C., & Bare, J. K. Gustatory nerve discharges in normal and adrenalectomized rats. *Journal of Comparative and Physiological Psychology* 1950, *43*, 320–324.

Pfaffmann, C., Frank, M., & Norgren, R. Neural mechanisms and behavioral aspects of taste. *Annual Review of Psychology* 1979, *30*, 283–325.

Pfaffmann, C., Norgren, R., & Grill, H. Sensory affect and motivation. *Annals of the New York Academy of Sciences,* 1977, *290,* 18–34.

Ponzo, M. Über die Wirkung des Stovains auf die Organe des Geschmacks, der Hautempfindungen, des Geruchs und des Gehörs, nebst einigen weiteren Beobachtunger über die Wirkung des Kokains, des Alipins und der Karbolsäure im Gebiete der Emfindungen. *Pflügers Archiv,* 1909, *14,* 385–436.

Ramón y Cajal, S. *Nuevo concepto de la histologiia de los centros nerviosos.* Barcelona: Heinrich, 1893.

Retzius, G. Die Nervenendigungen in dem Geschmasksorgan der Säugetiere und Amphibien. *Biologische Untersuchungen,* 1892, *4,* 19–32.

Richards, T. W. The relation of the taste of acids to their degree of dissociation. *American Chemical Journal,* 1898, *20,* 121–126.

Richter, C, P. Salt taste thresholds of normal and adrenalectomized rats. *Endocrinology,* 1939, *24,* 367–371,

Richter, C. P. Self-regulatory functions. *Harvey Lectures,* 1942, *38,* 63–103.

Ross, G. R. T. *Aristotle: De sensu and De memoria.* Cambridge: Cambridge University Press, 1906.

Schwalbe, G. A. Das Epithel der Papillae vallatae. *Archiv für Mikroskopische Anatomie und Entwicklungsmechanik,* 1867, *3,* 504–508.

Shore, L, E. A contribution to our knowledge of taste sensations. *Journal of Physiology,* 1892, *13,* 191–217.

Siegel, R. E. *Galen on sense perception.* New York: S. Karger, 1970.

Skramlik, E. von. *Handbook der Physiologie der Niederen Sinne.* Leipzig: Georg Thieme, 1926.

Steiner, J. E. The gusto-facial response: Observation on normal and anencephalic newborn infants. In Bosmas, J. F. (Ed.), *Fourth symposium on oral sensation and perception,* Washington, Superintendent of Documents, U.S. Government Printing Office, 1973.

Sternberg, W. Beziehungen zevischen dem chemischen Bau der süss und bitter schmeckenden Substanzen und ihrer Eigenschaft to schmecken. *Archiv für Anatomie, physiologie und wissenschaftlich Medizin,* 1898, *65,* 451–483.

Stevens, S. S. Sensory scales of taste intensity. *Perception & Psychophysics,* 1969, *6,* 302–308.

Troland, L. T. *The principles of psychophysiology. Vol, II: Sensation.* New York: Van Nostrand, 1930.

Woodworth, R. S. *Experimental psychology.* New York: Holt, 1938.

Woodworth, R. S. *Contemporary schools of psychology* (rev. ed.), New York: Ronald, 1948.

Wright, R. H. Odor and molecular vibration: Neural coding of olfactory information. *Journal of Theoretical Biology,* 1977, *64,* 473–502.

Young, P. The role of affective process in learning and motivation. *Psychological Review,* 1959, *66,* 104–125.

Zotterman, Y. Studies in the neural mechanism of taste, In W. A. Rosenblith (Ed.), *Sensory Communication.* New York: Wiley & Sons, 1961.

Zwaardemaker, H. *Die Physiologie des Geruchs.* Leipzig: Engelmann, 1895.

Zwaardemaker, H. *L'Odorat.* Paris: Doin, 1925.

7
A History Of Perception

William N. Dember
University of Cincinnati

Marjorie Bagwell
Miami University

Although it is obvious that many psychological processes begin with sensory inputs and perceptual integration, psychological theories differ greatly in the extent to which they attend to perception. On the one hand, radically behavioristic theories take perceptual processes pretty much for granted. Though they are extremely environmentalist in orientation, their environments are reduced to simple physical stimuli; how organisms, whose behaviors are shaped by environmental events (e.g., reinforcement contingencies), process those events is of little, if any, concern. On the other hand, there are psychological theories (e.g., classical Gestalt theory) which focus almost exclusively on perception, and take it for granted that behaviors appropriate to prevailing perceptual states will be forthcoming. In between are those theories which try to be comprehensive and to deal in a balanced manner with the full range of processes that are presumed to underlie the behavior, and experience, of complex organisms. The contemporary scene is, in fact, beginning to be dominated by theoretical approaches characterized by the phrase, "information processing," or by the adjective, "cognitive" (see Dember, 1974).

In the first part of this chapter, we will attend to the very broad interrelated issues, alluded to above, of the status of perception as a scientific concept and of its role in formal psychological systems. Since psychology as a separate discipline and psychological systems have been with us for only about a century, this section will deal mainly with "modern history." In the second part, we will turn to specific substantive topics which are representative of current concerns, though far from an exhaustive list; all have roots in the older disciplines, such as philosophy, physiology, and even astronomy.

PERCEPTION: ITS SCIENTIFIC STATUS AND ROLE IN PSYCHOLOGICAL SYSTEMS

Today, perception is "in." But it was not always so, expecially in American psychology in the first half of the present century. The behaviorist revolution, spearheaded by John B. Watson, was in part a reaction to the subjectivism, and hence the purported non-scientific nature, of earlier psychological systems. The major target of the behaviorist attact was the **Structuralism** of Edward B. Titchener and his disciples. The latter placed heavy emphasis on the investigation of conscious experience, the legitimacy of which Behaviorism called into serious question. To understand Watson's revolt, we need to know what it was in structural psychology that he opposed; and it would be helpful to know something about the origins of Structuralism itself.

The Roots of American Structuralism

The Leipzig Connection.   Titchener was the formulator and chief proponent of the structural approach to psychology in the United States. His research, writing, and teaching were done over a span of 35 years, emanating from Cornell University, where Titchener became Assistant Professor and director of the Psychology Laboratory in 1893 and Professor of Psychology two years later. Titchener came to Cornell a year after receiving the doctorate under Wilhelm Wundt at Leipzig University. Wundt, as almost every introductory psychology text reminds us, founded the first psychology laboratory in 1879. Titchener was British and took his undergraduate training at Oxford, but his two years at Leipzig with Wundt thoroughly imbued him with the German dedication to quantitative, carefully instrumented, experimental research. Titchener took with him to the United States Wundt's passion for precise methodology. It was that legacy, more than Wundt's theoretical orientation, which characterized Titchener's work; indeed, in many ways, Titchener's thinking remained closer to British Associationism than it did to the Germanic tradition with which Wundt was aligned.

British Associationism.   There was a school of thought within British philosophy of the seventeenth through the nineteenth centuries, and extending beyond Britain's borders, known as **Associationism.** The British school was represented by such noted philosophers as Thomas Hobbes (1588–1679), John Locke (1632–1704), George Berkeley (1685–1753), David Hume (1711–1776), David Hartley (1705–1757), Thomas Brown (1778–1820), James Mill (1773–1836), John Stuart Mill (1806–1873), Alexander Bain (1818–1903) and Herbert Spencer (1820–1903). Continental associationists include Etienne de Condillac (1715–1780) in France and Johann Herbart (1776–1841) in Germany. Each of these men had unique interests and made unique contributions, They also shared a common concern—one to which Associationism owed its origin—for the problem of epistemology: How do we come by our knowledge of the world, and how can we determine its validity?

John Locke's *Essay Concerning Human Understanding*, published in 1690, was seminal. Acknowledging that the thinking of the associationist philosophers was not uniform and monolithic, we can nevertheless let Locke speak for the others. A detailed account of their ideas and biographies can be found in E. G. Boring's *A History of Experimental Psychology*.

We must also greatly compress Locke's argument. For present purposes it will suffice to note two basic premises. The first is Locke's assertion that the mind at first is like white paper ("tabula rasa"); that it acquires its contents, or "ideas," through experience. Locke actually refers to two types of ideas: (1) those generated by stimulation of the sense organs, and (2) those arising from the mind's reflecting on its own operations. This insistence on sensory experience as the ultimate base of all knowledge has more to do with Locke's position as an empiricist than it does with his associationist orientation. The latter is manifest in the second premise, that our most complex and abstract ideas are formed from the combination of simple, elementary ideas—the latter, again, originating in sensory experience. How do simple ideas get combined into complex ones? Here Locke turns to Aristotle and assumes that the combining or associating of ideas is brought about simply by virtue of their having occurred together—as we might say now, by their temporal continguity. See pages 6 and 22 for other discussions of Locke.

The Goal and the Method.   The relevance of all this for perception, and for Titchener's structuralism, lies in the notion that complex percepts are composed of simple elements (sensations) joined together through association. It was taken as the major goal of structural psychology to uncover the constituent elements of experience and, conversely, to determine the principles by which simple elements combine to yield complex experiences—a goal which in its most general form Titchener believed psychology shared with the natural sciences. Moreover, the basic method of science—careful, repeatable observation—was in psychology directed inward, whereas it was externalized in the other sciences. The term *introspection* was employed to refer to observations made in the psychological mode; *inspection* referred to those made from the standpoint of the natural sciences.

Behind the distinction between **introspection** and inspection lay Titchener's view that all the sciences start with human experience, "consciousness," as their raw material. However, the natural sciences seek to remove the observer's personal contribution to this experience. As Titchener put it, the material of the natural sciences is experience that is independent of the experiencing person. Psychology, by contrast, leaves the person in; its material is experience that is *dependent* on the experiencing person. The following passage from Titchener's *A*

Text-Book of Psychology reiterates the similarities and differences between psychology and the other sciences, between introspection and inspection, and also suggests some of the special difficulties inherent in making introspective observations:

> It must not be forgotten that, while the method of the physical and the psychological sciences is substantially the same, the subject-matter of these sciences is as different as it can well be. Ultimately, as we have seen, the subject-matter of all the sciences is the world of human experience; but we have also seen that the aspect of experience treated by physics is radically different from the aspect treated by psychology. The likeness of method may tempt us to slip from the one aspect to the other, as when a text-book of physics contains a chapter on vision and the sense of colour, or a text-book of physiology contains paragraphs on delusions of judgment; but this confusion of subject-matter must inevitably lead to confusion of thought. Since all the sciences are concerned with one world of human experience, it is natural that scientific method, to whatever aspect of experience it is applied, should be in principle the same. On the other hand, when we have decided to examine some particular aspect of experience, it is necessary that we hold fast to that aspect, and do not shift our point of view as the enquiry proceeds. Hence it is a great advantage that we have the two terms, introspection and inspection, to denote observation taken from the different standpoints of psychology and of physics. The use of the word introspection is a constant reminder that we are working in psychology, that we are observing the dependent aspect of the world of experience.
>
> Observation, as we said above, implies two things: attention to the phenomena, and record of the phenomena. The attention must be held at the highest possible degree of concentration; the record must be photographically accurate. Observation is, therefore, both difficult and fatiguing; and introspection is, on the whole, more difficult and more fatiguing than inspection. To secure reliable results, we must be strictly impartial and unprejudiced, facing the facts as they come, ready to accept them as they are, not trying to fit them to any preconceived theory; and we must work only when our general disposition is favourable, when we are fresh and in good health, at ease in our surroundings, free from outside worry and anxiety. If these rules are not followed, no amount of experimenting will help us. The observer in the psychological laboratory is placed under the best possible conditions; the room in which he works is fitted up and arranged in such a way that the observation may be repeated, that the process to be observed may stand out clearly upon the background of consciousness, and that the factors in the process may be separately varied. But all this care is of no avail, unless the observer himself comes to the work in an even frame of mind, gives it his full attention, and is able adequately to translate his experience into words. (Titchener, 1911, pp. 24–25)

The end-product of the introspective method was an accumulation of observations which Titchener attempted to organize into an abstract system. The following paragraphs should suffice to give the flavor of that system.

Titchener postulated that there were at most three classes of mental elements: sensations, images, and affections. **Sensations** are the basic elements of perception; **images** are the elements of thought; and **affections** are the elements of emotion. He rejected additional elements, which others proposed, such as conative elements (comprising "will"), believing that all experience could be constituted from his triad—sensations, images, and affections.

Mental elements, though simple (that is, unamenable to further decomposition), can be characterized according to their properties or attributes. Sensations, for example, can be fully characterized according to their values on each of *at least* four attributes: *quality, intensity, clearness,* and *duration.* Some sensations require additional attributes, such as spatial extent (which applies to a color, for example, but not to an odor). Color, indeed, possesses the longest list of attributes, seven in all—including three qualitative attributes (hue, tint, and chroma, in Titchener's terminology), intensity, clearness, duration, and spatial extent.

Sensations differ from affections in two important ways, First, affections totally lack clearness as an attribute. Second, whereas pairs of sensory qualities (red and green hues, for example) which contrast with one another can be experienced at the same time, opposing qualities of affections (pleasantness and unpleasantness, for example, or happiness and sorrow) cannot occur simultaneously; rather than contrast with one another, they are quite antithetical, the one canceling the other. What about "mixed feelings" or, as we say now, "ambivalence"? Can't we, for example, simultaneously experience love and hate? Titchener said "no." We may rapidly alternate between such opposing affections, but they cannot co-exist. "The writer [Titchener] has never found, in his own experience, a definite and unmistakable case of mixed feelings" (Titchener, 1911 p. 236).

One could go on, as Titchener did, but at great risk of eliciting the unpleasant affections which comprise tedium. Perhaps it is for that very reason that Structuralism did not last long. If nothing else, however, it did provide a foil for two emerging theoretical orientations, Behaviorism and Gestalt, both of which had considerable impact on the field of perception. The latter, in fact, represented a reaction against both Structualism and Behaviorism. It makes sense, then, to turn first to Behaviorism and then to Gestalt psychology.

The Behaviorist Revolution

John B. Watson (1878–1958). **Behaviorism** did not emerge full-blown from the brow of John B. Watson. As with any intellectual creation, it had multiple forebears. Watson drew heavily, for example, on the work of Ivan Pavlov (1849–1936) on classical conditioning, and of American "animal psychologists," such as Edward L. Thorndike (1874–1949), Margaret Floy Washburn (1871–1939) and Robert Yerkes (1876–1956). The animal researchers in turn owed a considerable debt to Charles Darwin (1809–1882), whose concept of evolution emphasized the continuity—structual as well as behavioral—among species. With its focus on the adaptive significance of behavior, the Darwinian orientation provided a unifying framework for both animal and human behavioral research. Beyond that, it also suggested a unified methodology; techniques that were developed to investigate animal behavior could be, and this came to mean *should* be, applied also to human subjects. Conversely, what could not be applied to animals should not be used with human beings, In short, introspection— the chief tool of the structuralists—became suspect and, as Watson pursued these suggestions to their logical end, was eventually ruled out as a legitimate scientific procedure.

Watson's graduate training was at the University of Chicago, a center for yet another "school" of psychology known as Functionalism, under the leadership of James Rowland Angell (1869–1949) and John Dewey (1859–1952). In essence, Functionalism, like Structuralism, viewed consciousness as the proper target of psychological investigation, but the major aim of studying consciousness was to determine its function, or adaptive significance, rather than its structure. Functionalism clearly reflected the Darwinian influence. But Watson, trained in the functionalist tradition, came to see it as suffering from the same fundamental flaw that plagued Structuralism: Both assumed the existence and centrality of consciousness, an assumption which Watson came to argue could not be scientifically validated. As a "fictional" entity, consciousness had no place in a scientific psychology and hence ought to be dropped from its vocabulary.

Watson left Chicago in 1904 to take a position as Professor of Psychology at the Johns Hopkins University. It was there that he formulated the tenets of Behaviorism, showing how mentalistic concepts and methods could be replaced by strictly behavioral ones. He argued, for example, that Titchener's "images" were reducible to minute, but in principle observable, movements of the vocal apparatus and "affections" likewise were nothing more than responses of the genitals. He demonstrated how, by using Pavlovian conditioned reflexes and stimulus generalization instead of verbalization, one could get animals to reveal their ability to discriminate among various colors. In short, Titchener's three "mental elements" could be investigated and understood in strictly behavioral terms.

In throwing out the bathwater of consciousness and introspection, Watson, of course, did not mean also to throw out the baby of interesting problems. Nevertheless, it may be that by severely restricting what is considered to be proper methodology, one inadvertently restricts the kinds of investigations that are feasible to carry out—that is, one works on what is convenient methodologically instead of what is intrinsically fascinating.

It was over a brief but highly prolific period, 1913 to 1925, that Watson elaborated and promulgated his ideas. He raised serious doubts about the scientific merits of a psychology which depended for its data on the verbal reports of people's private experiences. Watson asserted that scientific observation must be a public affair and that the essential privacy of the introspective method is inimical to the objectivity demanded of a truly scientific enterprise. That one point, repeated in various formats, set off the behavioristic revolution.

Behaviorism and Perception.   It might seem at first glance that in dismissing introspection as a valid method, Watson was also eliminating perception as a viable field of investigation. In a sense that was true, at least in regard to the way in which adherents to Behaviorism chose to spend their time. In a more profound sense, Behaviorism had a cleansing effect on perceptual research. As already noted, Watson showed how the conditioned reflex could be employed as an indicator response in studying perceptual processes in animals. More generally, Behaviorism cautioned against naively taking people's verbal reports of their experience at face value, treating them as though they were objective descriptions of publicly observable events. An alternative strategy, acceptable to Behaviorism, is to consider verbal reports themselves as observable responses, just like any other behaviors. What those verbal responses might reveal about perception becomes, then, no different a question from asking, for example, what a dog's salivating to a bell implies about the dog's auditory sensitivity. That is, all we have to work with as psychologists are observable stimuli and observable responses. Those constitute our data. How we interpret the data—what they tell us, for example, about perceptual events, which we cannot observe directly—reflects a different issue entirely from the one that Watson was addressing.

In short, Watson considered perception a legitimate topic of scientific inquiry so long as appropriate methods are employed. Furthermore, Behaviorism does not rule out introspection, or any other method, as a *source* of hypotheses. How people come by their ideas is their business. It is only when they turn to *testing* their hypotheses that the behavioristic strictures come into play.

Behaviorism thus helped perceptual research by insisting on the development of sound, objective methodology. The present residue of that contribution can be seen in such notions, and their operationalization, as ''indicator responses'' and ''converging operations.'' It can also be seen in a host of very clever investigations of perceptual processes in animals and human infants, as well as in the standard, adult human observer.

It is clear that by breaking psychologist's dependence on introspection, Watson motivated the creation of perceptual methodologies with great generality of application. Thus, for perceptual research, Behaviorism has been a liberating influence. However, there is another side to the coin. Whatever Watson's intentions, Behaviorism took on more than methodological implications and became a substantive theory. It was Behaviorism as psychological theory to which the Gestaltists raised serious objections. Indeed, from the point of view of Gestalt theory, Behaviorism and Structuralism shared a basic defect; their differences, by comparison, were rather trivial.

Gestalt Psychology

Philosophical Background. The establishment of **Gestalt psychology** as an explicit theoretical doctrine is usually attributed to Max Wertheimer (1880–1943) and his two chief collaborators, Kurt Koffka (1886–1941) and Wolfgang Köhler (1887–1967). Of course, as with other systems, Gestalt theory had multiple intellectual roots—both in those philosophical and psychological orientations against which it reacted, most especially Associationism and Structuralism, and in those from which it drew sustenance. Among the latter Wertheimer himself credited Christian Von Ehrenfels, an Austrian philosopher, who in 1890 published an article on "Gestaltqualitäten" (form qualities). Ehrenfels, in turn, was pursuing an issue raised by the great German scientist, Ernst Mach: Is there anything more in visual forms or in melodies (auditory patterns) besides an aggregation of elements (i.e., lines and angles, or musical notes)? Ehrenfels, as of course did Wertheimer, opted for the separate reality of wholes or patterns over and above their constituent parts. A melody, for example, retains its identity over a wide variety of transformations, such as a change in key. Similarly, rearranging the order of notes in a melody, while preserving the notes themselves as well as the original rhythm, will result in an entirely different melody.

A similar view can be found in the writings of Wilhelm Dilthey, who argued for a fundamental distinction between the natural sciences on the one hand and the biosocial sciences and humanities on the other. The former quite properly seek *explanation* through analysis of complex phenomena into simpler units; the latter gain *understanding* through *description* and *apprehension* of total experiences. To apply the natural sciences method of analysis to the phenomena of mental life is to miss the essential nature of mind. "Mental life does not grow together from parts; it does not build itself up out of elements; it is not a composite, nor a result of cooperating atoms of sensation and feeling: it is primitively and always a comprehensive unity" (Dilthey, as quoted by Hartmann, 1935, p. 15, from his translation of a 1924 reprint of an article originally published in 1894).

Ehrenfels and Dilthey speak, in fact, for a large group of German philosophers writing around the turn of the century. These so-called **phenomenologists,** including Meinong, Husserl, Cornelius, and Avenarius, offered variations on the general theme of the inherent unity of experience and of the necessity of taking experience as it presents itself, rather than approaching it in a preconceived, analytic (and hence artificial) mode.

Though he did not and could not lay claim to having invented the basic Gestalt tenets, Wertheimer accomplished something of greater impact: He turned the philosopher's often obscure message into a clearly articulated, radical movement. His colleagues, Koffka and Köhler, aided greatly in the promulgation of Gestalt psychology, first in Europe and then in the United States in the 1930s and 1940s, where Structuralism and Behaviorism were already vying for domination of the psychological scene (and another European upstart, Psychoanalysis, was breaching the walls of academe).

The Founders. Max Wertheimer had an early and abiding interest in music, and many of the examples of Gestalt phenomena he came to employ were from that domain. He also studied law and did pioneering work on courtroom testimony, including the development of a lie detector test. In 1904 Wertheimer received the Ph.D. in psychology from the University of Wurzburg. In 1910 he began his research on *apparent movement* (the **phi phenomenon**) at the University of Frankfurt, where he was joined by two assistants, Köhler and Koffka. Sensing the Nazi menace, he left Frankfurt in 1933 for a position at the New School for Social Research in New York City, where he continued his research and writing. His classic work on problem-solving, *Productive Thinking,* was published posthumously in 1945.

Wertheimer was preceded to the United States by Koffka, who had become Professor of Psychology at Smith College in 1927. He had already published in 1921 (translated into English in 1924) *The Growth of the Mind,* a developmental text written from the Gestalt perspective. His *Principles of Gestalt Psychology* appeared in 1935; it, perhaps more than any other single work, brought the Gestalt position forcefully to the attention of American psychologists. In that book, which was originally intended as an introduction to Gestalt theory for the general public, Koffka provided an account not only of perceptual phenomena (with which Gestalt theory tends to be identified), but also of such diverse topics as reflexes, the ego, attitude, emotions, will, memory, learning, and society and personality. Koffka's book offered a scholarly, comprehensive coverage of psychology within a unified theoretical framework, an achievement which rivals William James' *Principles of Psychology* (1890) and which subsequently has gone unmatched.

Köhler was the last of the German triumvirate to emigrate to the United States. He had received his Ph.D. in 1909 from Friedrich-Wilhelm University in Berlin, having done his dissertation on hearing. After a brief period with Wertheimer at Frankfurt, he became director of the anthropoid research station of the Prussian Academy of Sciences on Tenerife in the Canary Islands, a post he held from 1913 to 1920. Based on his work there, he published in 1924 *The Mentality of Apes,* in which he documented the use by chimpanzees of insightful problem-solving. Köhler became head of the Psychology Institute and Professor of Philosophy at the University of Berlin in 1921. His *Gestalt Psychology* was published in 1929; it is that book which explicitly lays out the Gestalt case against both Structuralism and Behaviorism or, in Köhler's terms, opposes "dynamics" to "machine theory."

In 1935 Köhler moved to Swarthmore College where he remained for the next 20 years. He took up residence at the Institute for Advanced Study at Princeton in 1956; in 1958 he became Research Professor of Psychology at Dartmouth Col-

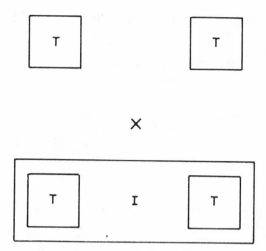

Fig. 7.1. One of the patterns used for investigating figural aftereffects (after Köhler & Wallach, 1944). Subjects fixate the X. After viewing the large rectangle, the inspection figure (I), subjects report that the two bottom squares of the test figure (T) appear closer together than the two upper squares. Results such as this are consistent with Köhler's field-theory conception of the brain.

lege. In that same year he was elected President of the American Psychological Association. Köhler's best known empirical research during his years at Swarthmore was a program of perceptual research, in collaboration with Hans Wallach, on visual figural aftereffects (Köhler & Wallach, 1944), which Köhler believed to reveal the dynamic properties of brain functioning postulated in his version of Gestalt theory (see Fig. 7.1).

Parts and Patterns. A major theme running through Gestalt psychology is that a whole is not simply the sum of its parts. Rather, pattern or form is an inherent property of perception and is not arrived at by the additive combination of elements. Indeed, to the extent that it makes sense to refer to the elements of a pattern, the direction of influence is "from the top down"—the elements acquiring their values from the pattern of which they are parts, not "from the bottom up"—the pattern being assembled from a collection of elements. As Max Wertheimer's son, Michael Wertheimer, has put it: ". . . most wholes are dynamic units in which the nature of the whole determines the nature of the parts; the systemic, integrated gestalt idea is captured . . . in a phrase like, 'the whole is *different from* the sum of its parts' " (Wertheimer, 1978, p. 744).

Recall that the introspective method of the structuralists was aimed at dissecting out or analyzing the constituent elements of complex perceptual patterns. It was assumed that the original patterns were themselves formed by a synthetic process that was the inverse of analysis. Perceptual patterns can be decomposed, and then, unlike Humpty-Dumpty, be put back together again. It is interesting to note that a simply synthesis of wholes from parts, though central to Titchener's structuralism, was not assumed by Wundt. He dealt with the problem of pattern in much of the same way as the Gestaltists, by positing a process of "creative synthesis." To Wundt it was evident that the process of combining sensory elements to form percepts involved more than simply adding the elements together. Something emerged in the total percept that was not in the separate elements themselves, just as water has properties that are not found in hydrogen and oxygen alone.

Structuralism and Behaviorism.   We noted earlier that Structuralism and Behaviorism shared a fundamental defect in the view of the Gestaltists. Köhler points this out with great clarity in his *Gestalt Psychology*. He shows how both systems turn, inappropriately, to associative learning as the explanatory concept for the complex phenomena which happen to be of interest to them. In the case of Structuralism, association-formation is the device which combines separate sensory elements into complex percepts; for Behaviorism, all behavioral sequences represent chains of simpler stimulus-response associations. For Structuralism, the mechanism of association is Locke's and Aristotle's temporal contingency; for Behaviorism, it is Pavlov's conditioned reflex (itself a product of the temporal contiguity of conditioned stimulus and unconditioned reflex). It is their common dependence on associative learning which makes the many differences between Structuralism and Behaviorism trivial by comparison. Köhler does not deny learning, but he does not endow it with the central role it plays in the rival systems; learning is a minor character, at most.

The Origin of Perceptual Organization.   If not in learning, where does perceptual organization originate? Or, as Koffka phrased the question, "Why do things look as they do?" (1935, p. 76). Koffka went on to answer this deceptively simple question, after rejecting a variety of unacceptable alternatives, with the cryptic remark, "because of the field organization to which the proximal stimulus distribution gives rise" (1935, p. 98). What Koffka meant was that perceptual experience relfects patterns of brain activity, which in turn are a product of both the stimulation being fed into the brain (by the "thing" in question and its surrounding context) and the inherent properties of the brain itself (see Fig. 7.2). This may seem an obvious point; what it implied for the Gestaltists, however, was something quite profound. It became their position, especially as championed by Köhler, that the organization evident in perception follows directly from organizing principles governing brain activity and that the brain, being a physical entity, itself is guided in its activity by principles which control all physical systems. In short, the perceptual phenomena of special concern to the Gestalt psychologists (e.g., the *phi phenomenon, constancy, closure, organization* by proximity, similarity, good continuation and so on)

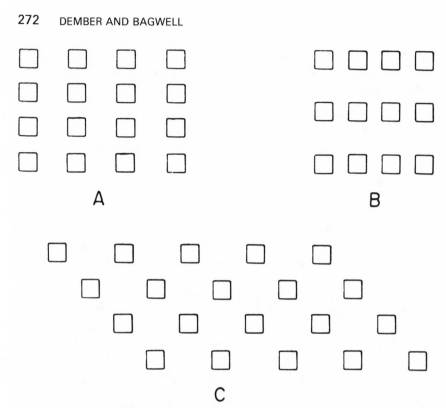

Fig. 7.2. Examples of one of the Gestalt principles of organization: proximity. We see vertical columns in A, horizontal rows in B, and diagonals in C. The organization is not literally "in" the physical stimulation.

were experiential counterparts of corresponding physical phenomena: Perceptual Gestalten were **isomorphic** with physical Gestalten.

The issue of pattern, form and organization, or what have you, thus comes down to this: Perception is the way it is because it shares the properties of the physical system (the brain) which gives rise to it. And the brain, the Gestaltists believed, is not a system which operates according to the principles of Newtonian mechanics, but a system which follows the principles of the (then) more modern version of physics known as "field theory." A brain operating according to field principles quite naturally allows for perceptual "field effects" without the need to postulate ever-changing networks of mechanical linkages (associations) among parts.

The quarrel with associationist theories thus becomes as much a rejection of the physics they implicitly espouse as of their psychology. For example, it is by virtue of thinking that interacting parts require specific connecting links that one comes to assume that perceptual configurations must be held together by "associations." That is, organization poses a problem only if you assume that disorganization is the normative condition. To the Gestaltist, the world—physical and perceptual—comes in organized wholes. The wholes do not need to be manufactured; they are there to start with.

Isomorphism: A Window on the Brain.   The notions of physical Gestalten and of an isomorphic relation between brain processes and perception were offered as alternatives to the neurophysiological assumptions of Structuralism and Behaviorism. They also carry an extra bonus. If percepts take their form from the dynamic, wholistic nature of brain processes, then one can use a knowledge of perception to make inferences about brain processes. That is, if you are primarily interested in how the brain works, but methods for directly investigating brain function are inadequate or incomplete, you have the option of investigating perceptions and thereby studying those brain functions which are not yet accessible to direct observation. So just as Sigmund Freud saw the dream as the "royal road to the unconscious," so did Gestalt psychologists view perception (as well as other psychological processes, such as memory and thinking) as a window on the brain. That is, of course, the position of many contemporary psychologists regardless of their orientation.

Implications for Method.   Research methods tend to be strongly determined by theoretical orientation. In the present instance the Gestaltists' insistence on the primacy of wholes dictated methodology which ruled out the analytic procedure of the Structuralists. Introspection in its most general sense was not proscribed; on the contrary, it was the standard procedure of the perceptual researcher with a Gestaltist leaning. However, the introspective reports to be given were of one's immediate, unanalyzed experience. These were called *phenomenal reports* to emphasize their closeness to the observer's raw experience.

What constitutes a phenomenal report? For a very simple example, consider the phi phenomenon. Two stationary lights are turned on and off sequentially. Observers are asked to report what they see when faced with such a display. Under the proper circumstances, they will say something to the effect that a light (the first one) is moving from one location to another (the locus of the second). Some people may even report seeing movement per se, without reference to a particular light's moving ("pure phi"). To take another simple case, observers might be asked to report on the apparent brightness of a figure. When the figure is located on a very bright background, they will say it is dark; when it is on a dark background, they will call the same figure bright. An example of this phenomenon is shown in Figure 7.3. More complex situations will require more complex reports; for example, observers who are stimulated by a very intense light may be asked to report on the sequence of visual experiences they have after the light is turned off.

Phenomenal reports are still employed in perceptual research. Frequently, however, these reports are used only in the initial stages of research, to obtain preliminary information about some interesting effect or simply to demonstrate

Fig. 7.3. Which circle appears brighter? These two circles are equal in luminance, but the one on the dark background appears brighter, illustrating how the
perception of such simple attributes of stimuli as their brightness is subject to
contextual influences. Neurophysiological accounts of brightness contrast (e.g.,
Cornsweet, 1970) employ the concept of lateral inhibition, invoked by Hartline
and Ratliff (1957) to explain analogous findings in their recordings of the electrical
activity in single ommatidia of the compound eye of the crab, *Limulus,*

that something of interest is happening. To investigate the effect with precision
so that quantitative relations can be determined, phenomenal reports may be
replaced by simple indicator responses—responses which ideally are independent of language. Or, if the indicator responses are linguistic ("yes-no," "left-
right," etc.), the words used are taken not as *descriptive* of the observer's
experience, but as *indicative* of it. It is here that the Behaviorist's emphasis upon
objectivity intersects with the Gestaltist's interest in phenomenology—to the
enrichment of both.

The Contemporary Scene

Where Have All the Systems Gone?   Research on perception has proliferated
over the past half-century; several new journals devoted to perceptual processes
have been started; dozens of texts have been published; laboratories abound,
equipped with highly sophisticated apparatus. Most of this productivity has taken
place outside the framework of the traditional systems. As far as perception is
concerned, the old school ties certainly have been severed. If there are committed Structuralists still pursuing Titchener's goals, they are doing it very quietly.
Gestalt theory has its adherents (many identified with social psychology), but
they no longer have the moral advantage of underdogs. Behaviorism is alive and

well, but strangely enough is living more in the clinic than the laboratory. In any event, its contribution to perception has always been primarily methodological, not substantive.

It is generally agreed that research must be motivated as well as guided by theory. If so, what theoretical force gives impetus to the efforts of contemporary researchers in perception? Perhaps that question can best be answered by future historians of psychology. From the present perspective at least, there seems to be no dominant theory in the sense of the old, comprehensive systems, Rather, there is what we might call a general "approach" and a myriad of "mini-models." The approach only very loosely guides the research, and it certainly is not one which leads its adherents eagerly to seek converts, nor does it give them any special sense of mission. This approach is referred to as "information-processing."

Information Processing. In 1876, Lord Kelvin designed an analog computer for solving complex differential equations. The first operative realization of Kelvin's design was built by Vanevar Bush at the Massachusetts Institute of Technology in 1930. In 1946 the first truly electronic digital computer, dubbed ENIAC (Electronic Numerical Integrator and Computer), was constructed at the University of Pennsylvania. Within a very short time the number, speed, and power of computers vastly expanded. Contemporary computers can process enormous quantities of information at a remarkably fast speed, and they are still being improved.

As computers increased in speed and complexity, they began to be thought of as models of the human processor of information. This is, by the way, surely not the first time that the properties of the created have been attributed to its creator—perhaps not without good reason. After all, it has become commonplace in psychology to interpret people's creations (e.g., paintings, poems, sculpture, musical compositions, dreams, fantasies, and so on) as revealing of their mental states. Perhaps computers tell us something about the mental processes of their designers.

In any event, the high-speed computer did seem to provide a promising general model of human cognitive functioning. In that context, the perceptual system came to be viewed as a set of devices for transforming physical stimulation into information about the external and internal environment. If physical stimulation is the "input," then the resulting information is the human computer's "output." In between are various structures (filters, comparators, memories, feedback loops, and programs) which effect the input-to-output transformation, yielding products that reflect both the values of the input and of the processing structures themselves. This may sound vaguely familiar. It is, essentially, the Gestalt notion of isomorphism written in "machine language."

Because it is crucial that there be devices for receiving the initial input to any information-processing system, human or machine, perception plays a vital role in all information-processing models. Computer analogs of other psychological processes, such as learning and motivation, have a somewhat more tenuous status. (See Haber [1969] for a collection of articles treating perception within the information-processing rubric.)

Computers can be thought of in two ways, as "software" and "hardware." Lord Kelvin's analog computer was pure software; Bush built one that actually worked. Similarly, one can be caught up in the software of perception, without much concern for how the sense organs and attendant neural circuitry are actually constructed and through what mechanisms they perform their functions. The information-processing approach to perception is largely concerned with software. On the contemporary scene, however, there is also a vigorous effort at describing and understanding the perceptual hardware.

Neurophysiological Mechanisms. There are those, then, who are actively engaged in investigating the neurophysiological bases of perception. Rather than try to *infer* how the mechanisms underlying perception might work (as, for example, from phenomenal reports or psychophysical functions), they prefer to go in and look. What these researchers choose to look at varies as a function of their training, skills, access to specialized equipment and so on, as well as of their speculations about where they are likely to find something of interest. Work of this sort goes back to the early anatomists and physiologists, such as Thomas Young, for example, who in 1801 published an account of his discovery of the mechanism controlling accommodation of the lens of the eye. Contemporary investigators come from a wide variety of disciplines, including psychology, and frequently work in multidisciplinary teams.

The most exciting research is now coming from those who record the electrical activity of single neural cells at various way stations in the visual nervous system (e.g., retina, lateral geniculate, cerebral cortex). Of great relevance to many age-old problems in perception is the discovery of neural cells which act as **feature detectors.** That is, such cells are activated only be certain, limited aspects of visual stimulation. Some respond only to the onset of illumination; others only to its termination. Some are activated only by edges; some are activated by lines, some only by moving lines, some by vertical, others by oblique, still others by horizontal lines; some cells respond only to lines moving left-to-right, and others vice versa (see, for example, Hubel & Wiesel, 1968).

Cortical cells also are finely tuned to the spatial frequency of the lines forming grating patterns, responding maximally to a mid-range of frequencies (see Cornsweet, 1970). Sensitivity of the visual system to sign-wave gratings varying in spatial frequency is illustrated in Figure 7.4, Indeed, the most recent speculation is that the visual system performs a spatial frequency (Fourier) analysis of visual stimulation, very much like the auditory system, and that this mode of operation is fundamental to the visual perception of form. In general, a picture is emerging from this recent work of a nervous system which functions in ways dreamed of

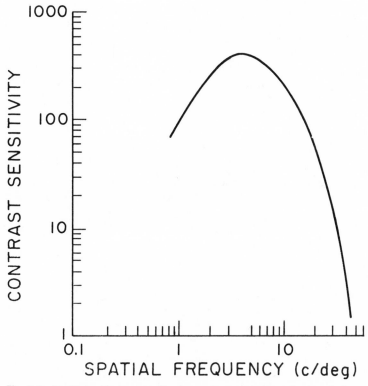

Fig. 7.4 Sensitivity (the inverse of luminance contrast necessary for detection) of the visual system to sign-wave gratings varying in spatial frequency (after Campbell & Robson, 1968). Recent evidence suggests that the visual system performs a Fourier analysis on visual stimulation much like that performed by the auditory system on auditory stimulation. It also seems likely that there are visual "channels" maximally sensitive to delimited ranges of spatial frequency, analogous to (or perhaps underlying) the "feature detectors" discovered by Hubel and Wiesel (1968) and others.

neither by the Structuralists nor by the Gestaltists, Completing that picture is a task for the future. In the meantime, let us take a second look backward.

SOME REPRESENTATIVE TOPICS

In this section we will concentrate on some specific substantive issues that will serve as representatives of the multitude of topics which comprise the enormously broad field of perception, We begin with a very old issue—the **nature-nurture problem.** In the course of discussing that hoary problem (known also by several aliases, such as "nativism-empiricism," "heredity-environment") we will have occasion to allude to many additional topics; it turns out that in trying to bring evidence to bear on that, or any other problem, one eventually has to stop referring to "perception" in general. Thus, the following section is both about the nature-nurture issue and also about the role of experience in the development of specific perceptual functions, such as the constancies, form recognition, and color discrimination. For further discussions of these issues see Chapter 5, this Volume.

The General Issue

In its most general form the nature-nurture issue concerns the origin of the contents and formal properties of mental processes. A specific version of that issue asks the same question about perception. Are the contents and other properties (e.g., speed) of our perceptual processes inherent in our nature (presumably via genetic endowment) or are they at least in part influenced by our life experiences?

The Philosophical Background, Variations on the nature-nurture issue come up repeatedly in the writings of Western philosophers. Plato (app. 427–347 B.C.) articulates the problem, and suggests an answer, in one of his dialogues, *The Meno.* Plato was concerned with the question of how we come by our knowledge, especially of abstract ideas such as justice and beauty. He poses the issue, and gives his answer, in the form of a demonstration, calling on an uneducated slave-boy as his "subject." The burden of the demonstration, conducted by way of a series of cleverly chosen questions (the Socratic method), is to show that in teaching a principle, in this case the Pythagorean theorem, one imparts nothing really new to the learner; rather, the teacher draws out the principle from the learner, in whom it was already latent. In effect, the slave-boy "knows" the Pythagorean theorem. Of course, making that knowledge manifest may require considerable ingenuity.

Skipping over 20 centuries, we come to two major proponents of the poles of the nature-nurture controversy. Gottfried Wilhelm von Leibnitz (1646–1716) built a comprehensive philosophy around the concept of the *monad.* Leibnitz posited the monad as the core constituent of all being, whether physical, mental or spiritual, and endowed it with many properties. Critical here is the notion that the monad is continually developing and that its development proceeds according to its own inner laws, unaffected by external circumstances. Applied to the mental domain, including perception, this notion can be understood as an extreme form of nativism. Its contemporary counterpart in the sphere of personality is the concept of "self-actualization" (see Maslow, 1954).

John Locke, whom we met earlier, reacted vigorously against the point of view expressed by Leibnitz. He argued, as you will recall, that there is nothing in the intellect that was not first in the senses. In the course of explicating his position, Locke (1690) raised the question, posed to him by William Molyneux, of how the world would look to someone who, blind from birth, had the possibility of normal visual functioning restored in adulthood. Would such a newly sighted person be able, for example, to recognize objects visually which were already quite familiar to touch? Molyneux's question was later addressed by Berkeley in the context of the perception of space. In his *An Essay toward a New Theory of Vision,* published in 1709, Berkeley argued that space perception lies properly in the province of the sense of touch and that there is no true conception of space common to vision and touch. Furthermore, there can be no space perception independent of experience. Hence, the newly sighted person would have no perception of space by vision alone.

The nature-nurture issue was played out over the years by philosophers, amateur and professional, whose mode of solution was, essentially, to make assertions backed up by logic and persuasive argument. Most took middle-ground positions. For example, Immanuel Kant (1724–1804), the noted German philosopher, claimed in his *Critique of Pure Reason,* published in 1781, that there must be from the outset certain fundamental concepts, such as those of space, time, and causation: These built-in modes of perceptual and intellectual functioning impose order on what would otherwise be a chaotic world. The order which is evident in perception cannot have emerged solely from chaotic external stimulation. So even prior to experience, there is some order (or "organization," as the Gestaltists would later put it) in the perceptual system. The newly sighted, according to this sort of quasi-nativist position, would thus not be starting entirely as a Lockean *tabula rasa.*

The Scientific Evidence. Philosophical analysis is useful for posing problems and clarifying issues. However, the validity of those statements that claim to assert something about the world of fact must ultimately be assessed by reference to observations about the real world. Thus, the extent to which perception, or any other psychological process, is innately given cannot be determined solely by speculation and argument. The question eventually must be decided on the basis of scientific evidence.

One approach to a scientific attack on the nature-nurture problem involves treating the question raised by Molyneux as more than a rhetorical device—that is, actually assessing the perceptual capabilities of individuals either deprived from birth of normal sensory stimulation or else subjected early in life to atypical stimulation. Since ethical and practical considerations preclude intentionally depriving human infants of normal stimulation, data of that sort must come from taking advantage of "nature's experiments." The prototype of such an investigation was reported in 1932 by a German psychologist, M. von Senden, whose doctoral dissertation at the University of Kiel consisted of a compilation and evaluation of accounts of people born blind because of cataracts of the lens; these people subsequently had the possibility of vision restored by surgical operation.

In their post-operative medical reports lay, potentially, the answer to Molyneux's question. Von Senden's book, originally published in German, has since been translated into English under the title, *Space and Sight* (von Senden, 1960). Unfortunately, clinical records do not always make good sources of scientific data. However, from his reading of von Senden, the noted Canadian psychologist, Donald O. Hebb, felt confident in the assertion that newly sighted adults were quite sensitive to color and were capable of noting the presence of visual figures segregated from their backgrounds—what Hebb (1949) called "primitive unity." Despite the intact nature of those visual functions, these people were severely impaired in their ability to discriminate between visual forms (say a triangle and a square) or to recognize as familiar a recently seen figure.

The following passages from von Senden quote from two of the many case histories which he compiled. These reports clearly confirm Hebb's characterization of the visual abilities and deficits of the newly sighted.

The eye was allowed ten minutes to recover itself; a round piece of card, of a yellow colour, one inch in diameter, was then placed about six inches from it. He said immediately that it was yellow, and, on being asked its shape, said "Let me touch it, and I will tell you." Being told that he must not touch it, after looking for some time, he said it was round. A square blue card, nearly the same size, being put before him, he said it was blue and round. A triangular piece he also called round. The different colours of the objects placed before him he instantly decided on with great correctness, but he had no idea of their form. (von Senden, 1960, p. 107)

I presented her with the cube and the sphere which she had so often had in her hands before, and asked her what they were. She could neither name them correctly, nor in any way describe their form aright; indeed, I remained very doubtful whether she had actually recognized them even as distinct from one another. I could reach no certain decision on this point, since on repeating the experiment several times on different days, and asking her whether the objects presented appeared the same to her, she sometimes said yes and sometimes no. (von Senden, 1960, p. 108)

Hebb also concluded that after a slow, difficult period of "perceptual learning" the initial deficits could be repaired; the handicap was not irreversible, implying that the early deprivation did not result in permanent structural damage to the visual system. Rather, the patients' perceptual development was seriously retarded for lack of adequate opportunity for the learning which is required for the normal adult's smoothly functioning visual system.

Hebb used the von Senden report, along with data from experimental studies on animals—especially those by Austin Riesen (1947) on visually deprived chimpanzees, as support for the notion that perception develops from a primitive, pre-wired base through the establishment of new neural circuits ("cell assemblies'' and ''phase sequences''). Which circuits happen to get established is a function of the developing organism's history of stimulation. An even more extremely empiricist theory was proposed by the economist, Frederick A. Hayek, who tried to show how organization might be imposed on an initially unorganized neural substrate, one with no primitive pre-wired circuits. Unfortunately, Hayek's tour de force, *The Sensory Order,* published in 1952, has not received adequate recognition by psychologists.

Hebb's theory, at least when it was published, provided a plausible, sophisticated alternative to the neural field theory of Gestalt psychology. Perhaps more importantly, it generated an enormously productive and highly creative research effort during the 1950s. In the present context, the most significant line of research consisted of experiments investigating the effects on later performance

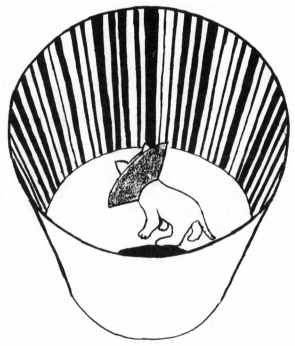

Fig. 7.5. Apparatus used by Blakemore and Cooper (1970) to deprive kittens of a particular visual experience. The visual display consisted of an upright plastic tube with its inner surface covered with high contrast black and white stripes, either horizontal or vertical. The kitten wore a black ruff to hide its body from its eyes. Each kitten stayed in this display for 5 hours a day, from 2 weeks until 5 months of age. The rest of the time they were housed in a completely dark environment. Behavioral testing and electrophysiological evidence revealed that the kittens ''were virtually blind for contours perpendicular to the orientation they had experienced'' (p. 478).

of rearing animals in both impoverished and enriched early environments. This body of research, in general, indicated a very important role for early experience in perceptual, as well as cognitive and emotional, development. The most recent data of this sort reveal a remarkable degree of specificity. For example, cats deprived of early experience with vertically oriented stimuli are found to have reduced numbers of vertical feature detectors in the cerebral cortex and are perceptually impaired as well. For example, they bump into vertically oriented objects such as the legs of tables and chairs as though they failed to notice them, but behave normally otherwise (Blakemore & Cooper, 1970). Figure 7.5 provides an illustration of an apparatus used by these investigators to deprive kittens of a particular visual experience.

Another approach to the scientific investigation of the nature-nurture issue involves examining the perceptual capabilities of very young organisms, including human infants. It is assumed in such studies that if the assessment can be made soon enough after birth, learning will have had little opportunity to make its influence felt.

William James described the perceptual world of the infant as "one giant blooming, buzzing confusion" (James, 1890, Vol. I, p. 488). Is it? How could James know? Finding out about the perceptual experience of another organism—human or animal, mature or immature, articulate or inarticulate—always, as Watson made clear, involves making inferences from the organisms's behavior. It is convenient when experimenter and subject share a language system: The experimenter asks, and the subject tells. Watson, of course, also warned against taking verbal utterances at face value. Human infants cannot talk, but if there is no great magic in language as an indicator of perception, that deficit may not prove to be so important. If not through language, however, how can the infant answer the experimenter's questions?

Many contemporary researchers follow the strategy developed by Robert Fantz (1961) of utilizing infants' natural preferences for some stimuli over others as indicators of discrimination. Thus, if an infant has the opportunity to look at either of two visual patterns and shows a reliable bias toward one, that bias, or preference, tells us that the infant can discriminate between the two. Lack of preference is indicative either of just that, or of an inability to discriminate, or perhaps of insensitive methodology. Preference, however, clearly implies discrimination. So, rather than asking infants what they see, we just have to note where their eyes are gazing. More generally, all we need is some behavior which is reliably different in the presence of different stimuli or which is correlated with changes in a given stimulus. A sample of the results of a pattern discrimination test is presented in Figure 7.6.

Though he exploited the preference technique in a long series of fascinating experiments on form discriminiation and visual acuity, Fantz was not the first to introduce it. Staples (1932), for example, used visual fixation as an indicator of discrimination and found that infants as young as 2 months of age could discrimi-

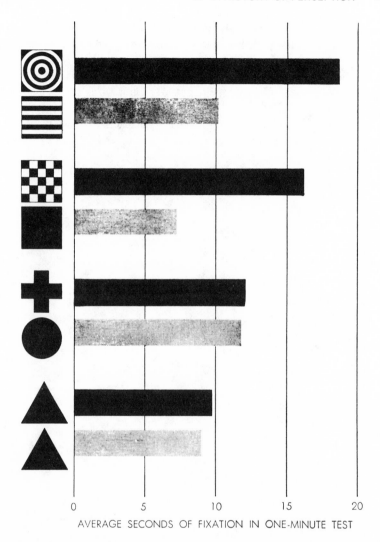

AVERAGE SECONDS OF FIXATION IN ONE-MINUTE TEST

Fig. 7.6. Infants' preference (looking time) for various pairs of visual patterns presented together (after Fantz, 1961). Differences in looking time reveal infants' ability to make form discriminations. Pattern complexity seems to be an important determinant of preference. Results such as these suggest that pattern discrimination is not dependent on a prolonged period of visual experience.

nate between blue, green, yellow, and red on the one hand, and gray on the other. Discrimination among the four hues was evident by 6 months. Chase (1937) supported Staples' conclusions by noting that young infants would visually follow (track) a moving spot of light if the spot differed in hue from its background. Tracking was not elicited if the spot differed from the background only in intensity, suggesting the infants were making discriminations based truly on hue, not on luminosity or brightness differences associated with the different wavelengths of lights.

The preference technique is one of several which have been used to probe the perceptual experience of infants. Peiper (1963) summarizes the results of scores of studies, going as far back as 100 years, that measured reflex responses to sudden, intense stimuli to investigate sensory capacities in neonates. Recent research has relied on components of the "orienting reflex" (a Pavlovian con-

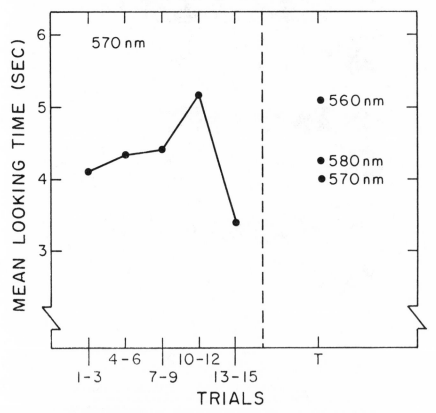

Fig. 7.7. Habituation and dishabituation of visual attention (looking time) in infants as a function of the wavelength of the habituating and dishabituating stimulus (after Bornstein, 1976). On trials 1–15, 3 month-old infants were habituated to a wavelength of 570 nm (greenish-yellow). On the test trials (T), wavelengths of 560 (green) and 580 nm (yellow) were each presented three times. Looking time increased through trial 12 and then abruptly declined (habituation). The test trials showed significant dishabituation to 560 nm but not to 570 or 580 nm. Ability to discriminate between 560 and 570 nm is an exclusive characteristic of trichromats. Thus, these data strongly indicate trichromatic vision in 3-month-old infants.

cept). For example, novel stimuli elicit a temporary decrease in heart rate ("cardiac deceleration"). This reaction has been coupled with an **habituation-dishabituation procedure**—repeatedly presenting a stimulus until the subject becomes indifferent to it and then changing the stimulus in some way. If the infant reacts with cardiac deceleration to the changed stimulus, it obviously has discriminated it from the version of the stimulus to which it had become habituated. Responses such as cardiac deceleration are especially useful for modalities other than vision (hearing, for example) where there is no other obvious behavioral indication (such as visual fixation) of what stimulus the infant is attending to. The habituation-dishabituation procedure can also be used in conjunction with visual fixation as the indicator response. That methodology has been used in follow-up investigations of the work by Staples and Chase (see, for example, Bornstein, 1976), showing quite convincingly that young infants have essentially normal (i.e., adult) color vision (see Fig. 7.7).

Experiments using procedures of the above sort reveal a much greater repertory of perceptual skills in infants than had previously been suspected. That, considered in light of the evidence from deprivation and enrichment studies, seems to pose a paradox. Adequate stimulation appears to be essential for normal perceptual development, and yet many normal, or close to normal, perceptual functions are present in very young infants. One way out of this paradox is to argue that the perceptual system to a large extent is initially well structured. However, experience (learning) does contribute to refinement and elaboration of the system's capabilities; furthermore, perceptual functions may degenerate if not provided with adequate "nurture" in the form of appropriate stimulation. As so often turns out to be the case, it may be that the nativists and empiricists were both in part correct.

Still another way of scientifically investigating the role of experience in perceptual development is to take advantage once again of nature's experiments, this time through looking at the perceptual consequences of growing up in widely divergent cultures and, as a result, in different "environments"—physical, artifactual and linguistic. The classic research was done at the turn of the present century by William H. R. Rivers (1864–1922), a physician-psychologist, who participated in expeditions conducted by a group of anthropologists based in Cambridge, England. Rivers collected data on susceptibility to the Müller-Lyer illusion (see Fig. 7.8) and the vertical-horizontal illusion from Murray Islanders in New Guinea and from a group of Toda herdsmen of southern India. He also had normative data from British adults and children. One conclusion Rivers drew from his data was that his non-western subjects were less susceptible to the Müller-Lyer illusion than his normative groups, but more susceptible to the vertical-horizontal illusion. It is interesting to note that Titchener (1916) was skeptical about the meaning of Rivers' cross-cultural comparisons on grounds that people from different cultures might approach the perceptual task quite differently; hence, any differences might be attitudinal rather than truly perceptual.

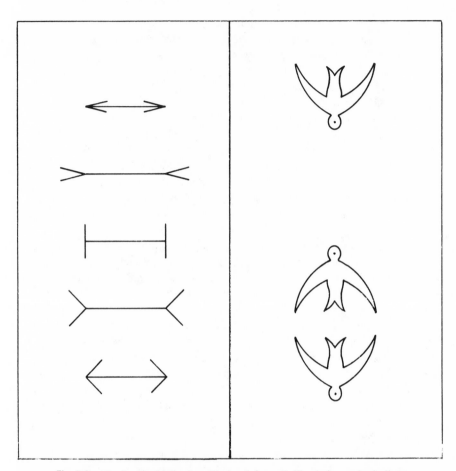

Fig. 7.8.   The familiar Müller-Lyer illusion (left panel), The shafts are physically equal in length, but those with ''arrow-heads'' appear shorter and those with ''tails'' longer. The version of the Müller-Lyer figure in the right panel is taken from Titchener (1911), who borrowed it from Ebbinghaus. See Favreau (1977) for a humorous account (entitled ''Disillusioned'') of how Müller-Lyer is frequently transformed in textbooks into ''Müller-Liar'' by unequal drawing of the shaft lengths, biased in favor of the expected effect. See Titchener (1911, p. 7) for an early instance of Favreau's complaint.

In 1957 Allport and Pettigrew studied susceptibility to the trapezoidal window illusion among urban and rural Zulus. This illusion involves seeing a window-frame oscillate when it really is rotating; the effect is dependent on perceiving the window-frame, which is actually trapezoidal in shape, as rectangular. When conditions are such that the illusory motion (oscillation) is easy to see (viewing with one eye from a distance greater than 10 feet), there were no differences among the rural and urban subjects. However, under difficult conditions, significantly more urban than rural subjects saw the illusory motion. Why should there by any difference? Allport and Pettigrew point to the different environments of the rural and urban Zulus. In particular, the former have much less experience with rectangular architecture, including window-frames, than the latter. Therefore, rural subjects are less likely to translate the ambiguous cues to shape provided under the difficult condition into "rectangular window"; as a result, they are not compelled to see it as oscillating.

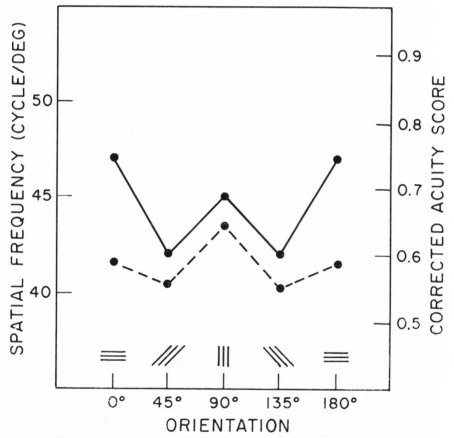

Fig. 7.9.   Visual acuity as a function of test grating orientation for Cree Indians and Euro-Canadians (from Annis & Frost, 1973). The Euro-Canadians (solid line), raised in a visual environment with contours oriented mainly in vertical and horizontal orientations, exhibited relatively poor acuity for obliquely oriented gratings. The Cree (dashed line), raised in an environment rich in contours in all three orientations, did not show significantly different acuity as a function of grating orientation, supporting the hypothesis that early visual experience can influence visual performance of human adults.

In a more recent and comprehensive investigation in this area, Segall, Campbell, and Herskovits (1966) used the phrase "carpentered environment" to characterize the main difference between urban and primitive rural settings. They found differences in susceptibility to illusions which were compatible with the notion that growing up in carpentered environments does predispose people to certain kinds of illusions (those that are probably dependent on perceiving depth in two-dimensional displays). Analogous effects can be found with regard to gross differences in natural environments—for example, those with "broad vistas" versus those that are visually cluttered.

Finally, in another recent study (Annis & Frost, 1973), it was found that Cree Indians, living on the east coast of James Bay in Canada, with little exposure to human artifacts with a rectilinear orientation, did not show the usual increased sensitivity to stimuli which are either horizontally or vertically oriented over those with an oblique orientation (see Fig. 7.9). This tendency is reminiscent of the one mentioned earlier of cats reared in environments devoid of vertically or horizontally oriented stimulation. In general, although the data must be interpreted with great caution because of their essentially correlational nature, the cross-cultural evidence seems consistent with that derived from both clinical and experimental research: One's history of stimulation does influence one's present perceptual performance. It remains to be seen whether it will be possible to draw conclusions less global than that.

Cognition and Affect

The Constancies. As people mature, they develop expectancies about the relations among recurrent events; their motivation and emotional repertories are also elaborated. To what extent do such "higher-order" cognitive and affective functions influence perception?

The so-called **perceptual constancies** provide what many have considered compelling examples of a direct cognitive influence on perception. In the case of *size constancy,* for instance, the perceived size of an object remains remarkably stable despite considerable changes in the size of the retinal image cast by the object with variation in its distance from the observer (the greater the distance, the smaller the retinal image). Constancy also characterizes perceived shape, lightness, hue, and other visual attributes, as well as properties of experience in other modalities, such as the loudness of sounds emanating from an object at varying distance from the hearer.

Herman von Helmholtz (1821–1894), the great German physicist-physiologist-psychologist, attempted to account for the constancies, and related phenomena, by reference to *unconscious inferences* made by the observer. Such inferences, or expectancies, presumably are built up in the course of people's experience with the world—a world in which, for example, objects do remain the same size regardless of where they happen to be in relation to the person who is looking at them. A similar assumption lies at the core of a theory developed by Adelbert Ames, Jr. (1880–1955) and colleagues called **Transactionalism.** In essence, it is argued, our present perceptual experiences are shaped by the countless transactions that we have had with objects and events. It is through these transactions that we come to make assumptions about the world which for the most part support veridical perception. However, if on occasion these assumptions are invalid, they can lead us into substantial perceptual errors. One of the transactionalists' major contributions was the production of a set of demonstrations ("the Ames demonstrations") which dramatically reveal how we can be misled into gross misperceptions by cues which arouse invalid assumptions (see Fig. 7.10). The rotating trapezoidal window-frame used in the cross-cultural research mentioned above was one of the Ames demonstrations: If by virtue of our experience we expect window-frames to be rectangular; if that assumption is bolstered by such cues as shading; and if veridical cues to depth are minimized

Fig. 7.10.   The distorted room, one of the best known of the "Ames demonstrations" (from Ittelson, Proshansky, Rivlin, & Winkel, 1974). According to the transactionalist theory, we respond probabilistically to stimuli which are inherently ambiguous, and we acquire our probabilities through experience (transactions) with the environment. In the present case, we perceive a rectangular room with a level floor (even though it is not physically rectangular and its floor is sloped, with its lowest point at the right rear). Having normalized the room, we must distort the sizes of the people so that one appears grossly taller and larger than the other. Why roomshape should be more stable than people-size is not specified in the theory.

(for example, by monocular viewing), then we can be tricked into seeing the window-frame oscillating instead of rotating.

Interest in the constancies spawned a massive amount of speculation and empirical research. Other key historical figures in this effort are mentioned below, along with a very brief indication of their main contributions. For a comprehensive account, see *Sensation and Perception in the History of Psychology* (pp. 288–299) published in 1942 by Edwin G. Boring (1886–1968) and by now itself an important part of the historical record. For the sake of brevity, we will confine what follows to size constancy.

The starting point of any understanding of size constancy is the concept of the size of the retinal image, a notion that can be traced back to the great Greek geometer, Euclid (3rd century B.C.). But retinal image size cannot be the sole basis for perceived size, which, as Berkeley had noted, depends also on the perceived distance of the object in question, Observations by Gustav Fechner (1801–1887), the founder of psychophysics, and Ewald Hering (1834–1918), best known now for his **opponent-process theory** (p. 178) of color vision, contributed to a second key formulation—**Emmert's Law.** This law, proposed by Emil Emmert (1844–1913), stated the relation between the perceived size of an afterimage and the apparent distance of a surface onto which it is projected. In effect, perceived size is proportional to perceived distance: The farther the apparent distance, the greater the perceived size. Though it deals with afterimages and with variations in their perceived size, Emmert's Law implicitly speaks to the constancy in the perceived size of real objects. Boring (1942) argued that size constancy can be considered a special case of Emmert's Law, or vice versa: Each implies the other. In the one instance, the apparent size of a retinal image of fixed size (the retinal region which generates the afterimage) varies in proportion to the perceived distance between the observer and the apparent source of the retinal image; in the other instance (size constancy), the perceived size of an object casting retinal images of varying size remains fixed so long as the object is perceived as lying at appropriately varying distances from the observer.

Contributions to the empirical investigation of size constancy are too numerous to recount here, Boring (1942) gives special recognition to pioneering experiments published in 1889 by G. Martius and by F. Hillebrand in 1902. Egon Brunswik (1903–1955) and Robert H. Thouless (1894–   ) are also noted for their experimental research in the 1930s, especially for developing mathematical expressions for characterizing the results of size constancy experiments, Boring himself made significant experimental contributions (for example, see Fig. 7.11).

One outcome of the empirical research on size constancy was the conclusion that constancy is not perfect. Given adequate cues to distance, perceived size is indeed relatively constant, but not absolutely so, especially at great distances. Think, for example, of how objects on the ground look from an airplane: cars, buildings, trees—all seem tiny. Even at shorter distances, constancy breaks

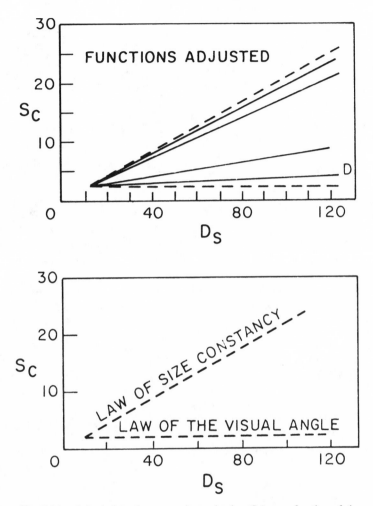

Fig. 7.11. Judged size of a comparison stimulus (Sc) as a function of the distance of the standard stimulus (Ds) under four viewing conditions (after Holway & Boring, 1941). With distance cues virtually eliminated (condition D), the size judgments were determined primarily by the size of the visual angle cast by the standard stimulus, conforming closely to the "Law of Visual Angle." Under the condition richest in distance cues (A), the size judgments were determined primarily by the actual size of the standard stimulus, conforming to the "Law of Size Constancy."

down. Clearly, perceived size is determined by more than the size of the retinal image—a fact, incidentally, which the Gestaltists saw as devastating to any theory that tried to account for perceptual experience by reference to isolated bits of local stimulation impinging on a receptor organ. With regard to the theme of the present section, the constancies strongly suggest some sort of "cognitive" involvement (inferences, expectancies, or what have you) in the perceptual process.

A Brief Diversion: The Moon Illusion. There is one fascinating phenomenon—the moon illusion—which can be thought of as a breakdown in size constancy. The moon, of course, remains fixed in size regardless of its location in the sky, and so does the size of its image on the retina. However, its perceived size varies considerably depending on whether it is seen at the zenith or at the horizon: On the horizon, the moon looks very much larger. Attempts to understand the moon illusion have spanned the centuries; the present brief account is based on a comprehensive review by Ross and Ross (1976),

Ptolemy, who lived during the second century A,D, in Alexandria, is best known for his geocentric theory of the universe. He also offered a very early, if not the earliest, explanation of the moon illusion—actually two explanations, neither of which is tenable. In *The Almagest* he argues that the size of celestial objects is magnified by the atmosphere through refraction by water vapor; since there is more intervening atmosphere for objects at the horizon than at the zenith, the former should look larger. It turns out, however, that if refraction has any effect, it is in the opposite direction. In a second work attributed to Ptolemy, *Optics,* another explanation is proposed, involving the purported effects of the difficulty of looking upwards, which Ptolemy believed would result in a reduction in the apparent size of objects at the zenith. Ptolemy's argument, which is quite ambiguous, is also based on the assumption that "rays" emanate from the eye and strike the object (like radar), rather than *vice versa.*

The idea that the angle of regard from which the moon is viewed may be pertinent, though not for the reason proposed by Ptolemy, was also entertained by Boring. He was, indeed, able to show that the horizon moon lost some of its exaggerated size when viewed with the eyes elevated (Boring, 1943; Holway & Boring, 1940). To achieve this atypical angle of viewing the horizon moon, Boring had his subjects assume unusual postures. Boring's experiments, and the quaint postures they entailed, are captured in the poem below by Helen Bevington. Having heard about "some scientists from Woods Hole" who gazed at the moon with their heads between their legs, she decided to try it herself with her companion, a professor. The experience was then transformed into "Academic Moon," which originally appeared in the *New Yorker* magazine and was later reprinted in Bevington's books, *Nineteen Million Elephants* and *When Found, Make a Verse of.*

ACADEMIC MOON

I have been walking under the sky in the moonlight
With a professor. And am pleased to say
The moon was luminous and high and profitable.
Moonlit was the professor. Clear as day.

He had read, of late, how extraordinary moons are
Upside down. Aloft in the night sky
One drifted upright, in the usual fashion.
But the professor, glad to verify

Hypothesis or truth, when he is able—
Even, it seems, to set the moon askew—
Proposed that we reverse our own perspective.
And, on the whole, it was a lovelier view

Of white circumference—smaller now, he fancied,
A tidier sphere. This last I could not tell
From so oblique an angle. I only remember
Enjoying the occasion very well.

In a letter to the editor of the *New Yorker,* excerpted by Bevington in *When Found . . .* , the noted psychologist M, E. Bitterman offered a bit of scholarly elucidation about the moon illusion and quoted from Boring on how to make the horizon moon shrink:

> When the moon is big upon the horizon, lie down on your back with your head toward the moon, hanging the head over a log or stone or the edge of a table. The moon, huge but a moment before is now quite small, small enough to make you exclaim. Or stoop over and view the horizon moon between your legs.

Subsequent research (e,g., Kaufman & Rock, 1962) confirmed the relevance of eye elevation, but obtained a much smaller absolute effect than had been reported in Boring's experiments, probably because of differences in methods of measurement. The rather small (about 3%) decrease found in the more recent studies in the perceived size of the horizon moon when viewed with eyes elevated obviously cannot account for the full extent of the moon illusion.

A much more plausible explanation of the moon illusion involved the principle of **size-distance invariance:** Of two objects which cast retinal images of equal size, the one judged to be the farther away will be perceived as the larger— Emmert's Law applied to real objects rather than afterimages. The size-distance invariance principle would explain the moon illusion if it could be shown that the horizon moon is judged farther than the zenith moon. An account of this sort was provided by Alhazen (Ibn-al-Haytham, in Arabic), a scientist who lived from approximately 965 to 1040 A.D. Alhazen invoked the size-distance invariance principle and then argued that we tend to see the sky as a flat surface, like a ceiling over our heads; the sky looks flat because we have no cues to its shape, and in the absence of such cues we tend to assign it the shape most familiar to us—in this case, a flat plane. Now, if we do, for whatever reason, see the sky as a flat plane, then it will seem nearer overhead than at the horizon.

Roger Bacon (app. 1214–1294), a British scientist, suggested a different basis for the greater apparent distance of the horizon: He invoked the principle that filled space seems to extend farther than empty space, and noted the considerably greater number of objects intervening between the observer and the horizon moon in comparison with the moon at the zenith. Alhazen's invoking of the size-distance invariance principle and Bacon's reference to filled versus empty space together make for a plausible explanation of the moon illusion. Furthermore, this explanation is supported by recent research (see Kaufman, 1974; Rock & Kaufman, 1962).

The Freudian Influence. Woven throughout the fabric of our discussion of perception thus far are three threads: (1) Perception gets its organization from some sort of associative learning; (2) the patterning evident in perception is the inevitable result of an isomorphic relation between perception and brain processes, which themselves are inherently organized according to general, physical field forces; and (3) particular percepts arise from the interaction between sensory stimulation and cognitive processes, which help vastly to reduce the ambiguity characterizing sensory stimulation (e.g., is this a small nearby object or a large one far away?). A fourth thread must be added, one concerning an hypothesized motivational-emotional (i.e., "affective") influence on perception. The origins of this hypotheses lie most clearly in the psychoanalytic theory of the Viennese physician Sigmund Freud (1865–1939).

Psychoanalytic theory itself has multiple roots, many of them in the philosophical, physiological and psychological works we have already cited, as well as in literature, anthropology, and religion. Some Freudian notions are already familiar to the reader of this book. For example, Freud's reference to unconscious processes is certainly anticipated in Helmholtz's "unconscious inferences," as well as in the earlier thinking of Leibnitz and Herbart. Indeed, Herbart not only alluded to ideas which lay below a threshold of consciousness, but he also endowed ideas with a dynamic property: Ideas tended to be active and self-preservative; if they were not in consciousness, it was because they were being inhibited by other competing ideas. Freud also relied, both in clinical practice and in this theorizing, on a notion of the association of ideas, which, as you know, pervades the history of psychology.

Freud, of course, also made more than his share of original contributions. In the present context the crucial portion of psychoanalytic theory, greatly compressed, may be summarized as follows: Much of mental life is unconscious; unconscious ideas (impulses, memories, fantasies, conflicts, and so on) actively strive for expression; the direct, undisguised expression of unconscious ideas is resisted by various defense mechanisms, repression being chief among them; if they are not allowed direct expression, and hence entry into consciousness, unconscious ideas will find indirect, devious routes of expression, sometimes in the form of psychopathological symptoms and frequently through such safe

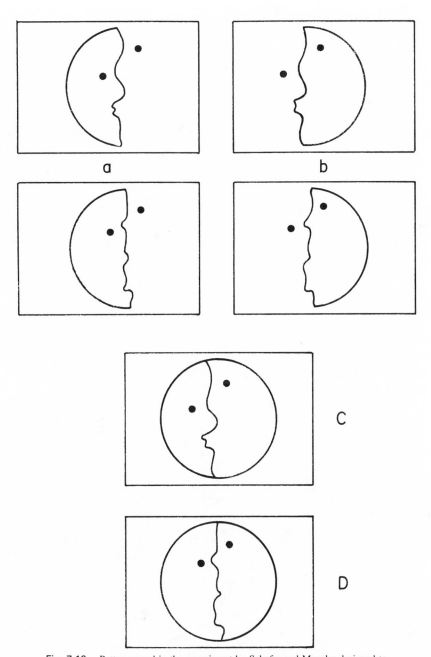

Fig. 7.12.   Patterns used in the experiment by Schafer and Murphy designed to demonstrate how figure-ground organization of ambiguous stimuli can be influenced by rewards and punishments (after Schafer & Murphy, 1943). Subjects received a small monetary reward whenever they saw one profile (e.g., a) and coins were taken away when they saw the alternate profile (e.g., b). Subsequently, when shown the composite (C or D), they tended to call it by the name of the rewarded profile. Whether this effect was truly perceptual, or mediated by an acquired response (naming) bias, is open to question, but follow-up research has generally been supportive of the Schafer and Murphy outcome,

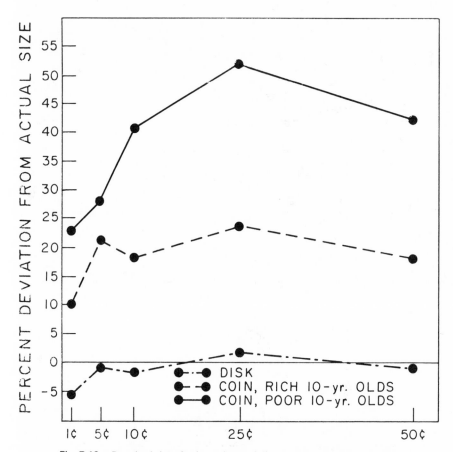

Fig. 7.13. Perceived size of coins and neutral discs (expressed as percent deviation from actual size) as a function of coin denomination and subjects' economic status (after Bruner & Goodman, 1947). In general, coins of higher monetary value were judged larger than coins of lesser value, and the "poor" subjects overestimated the size of coins more than did the "rich" subjects. The subjects were 10-year-old boys. These results were interpreted as showing an effect of motivational variables (need and incentive value) on perception and formed part of the corpus of data which seemed to call for a "New Look in Perception."

outlets as dreams; unconscious influences are also felt in distortions of ordinary mental processes, such as memory and perception, as dramatically exemplified in hypnotically induced and hysterical amnesias and anesthesias. These arguments are convincingly presented in Freud's *The Interpretation of Dreams,* first published in 1899, and in his *The Psychopathology of Everyday Life,* published in 1901. (Both books were, of course, originally published in German; translations, revisions and collections abound; we list in the reference section readily accessible paperback editions published respectively in 1961 and 1965.)

Those who treat Freud's ideas as sources of scientific hypotheses have been intrigued by the challenge of testing their validity. Interesting anecdotes and case histories are not enough, but the task of bringing Freudian hypotheses into the laboratory has proven formidable and frustrating. Systematic efforts at validating Freud's notions in the domain of perception reached their peak in the 1940s and 1950s, under the rubric of *the new look in perception.* This "new look" encompassed a wide variety of issues and procedures and was broader in scope than merely an attempt to test psychoanalytic hypotheses. The general thrust was to demonstrate contributions to perception that originated in the person rather than in the stimulus per se (see, for example, Blake & Ramsey, 1951; Witkin, Lewis, Hertzman, Machover, Meissner, & Wapner, 1954—the latter, interestingly, dedicated to Max Wertheimer). Personal factors included motivational and emotional variables as well as cognitive ones (e.g., expectancies) and, broadly, perceptual styles. Whether the variables under study were necessarily unconscious was not always of concern, and many different experimental paradigms were employed.

One line of research, initiated by Schafer and Murphy (1943), addressed the possibility of influencing figural dominance by differential rewards and punishments (see Fig. 7.12). Another investigated the effects of motivation on people's interpretations of ambiguous stimuli (e.g., Levine, Chein, & Murphy, 1942) and on their judgments of basic attributes (such as size) of visual stimuli (see, for example, Fig. 7.13). Even closer to the Freudian hypothesis were those experiments intended to show that stimuli which were presented at values below the psychophysically defined threshold ("subliminal stimulation") could nevertheless be demonstrated to have behavioral impact.

Perhaps because of their potentially insidious practical application, experiments claiming to demonstrate behavioral effects of subliminal stimulation have received a great deal of public attention—mostly hostile, and with some validity. Vance Packard, in a brief passage in *The Hidden Pursuaders,* published in 1957, was one of the first to warn of the purported use of subliminal messages on movie screens to influence surreptitiously the viewers' purchases of refreshments—and, by implication, the use of subliminal advertising for even more nefarious purposes. Indeed, attempts to influence behavior by subliminally presented stimulation still continue, as indicated in the following clipping from the New York Times (April 23, 1978, Section 4, p. 18):

WORDS AND MUZAK

Shoppers in a large Eastern city are reportedly receiving subliminal moral instruction as they push their carts down the neighborhood supermarket. The messages embedded in the Muzak, so that the conscious mind cannot quite hear them, are along the lines of "I am honest" and "I will not steal." To quote the engineer who takes credit for the experiment: "What the new application does in behavior therapy is provide stimuli on a background music system to set an example in honesty reinforcement and theft deterrence."

We fear we understand what the gentlemen is up to, despite his language, and we don't like it. Even if such subliminal messages worked, and even if supermarket proprietors and engineers are the best guides to moral values, the practice of manipulating people's behavior without their being aware of it has no place outside a mental institution.

Anyway, we have our own message for that engineer—if he can read between the lines.

Is there any experimental evidence for behavioral effects of "subliminal stimulation"? This extensive literature has been reviewed in great detail (e.g, Dixon, 1971). That part of it having to do with the impact of subliminal stimulation on dreams, fantasy, and mood will be the focus of the present discussion, since, as noted, it most closely fits the Freudian paradigm.

A good place to start is with some "N of 1" studies by the French psychologist Alfred Binet (1857–1911), best known now for his role in the development of intelligence tests. In his *Alterations of Personality,* Binet (1892) reported on some investigations using as subjects people suffering from hysterical anesthesia of the skin. Though there was no discernible organic impairment, these people apparently could not feel any tactual sensations when stimulated on certain parts of their bodies.

Classed as hysterical rather than organic, the anesthesia could then be interpreted, consistently with psychoanalytic theory, as serving a defensive function. Thus, tactual stimulation, though having physiological impact, was being kept from awareness by some repressive force. Now, in psychoanalytically oriented thinking, repressed material is not simply erased; rather, it remains active and, though not directly in consciousness, strives for some sort of indirect conscious expression. Hence, it might be that tactual stimulation applied to an area of skin which is hysterically anesthetic, even though not consciously experienced, can nevertheless have an influence on consciousness. For example, Binet would prick the hand of a person who was hysterically anesthetic in that area. The person reported feeling nothing, However, when Binet then delivered the stimulation nine times in rapid succession, the person, upon being asked to think of a number, replied "nine."

In the course of these experiments, Binet noted that his subjects often reported vivid visual images upon tactual stimulation of an anesthetic region. Pursuing that observation, he conducted the following experiment on a young woman suffering from hysterical anesthesia of the skin of the neck. He impressed on her neck a steel disk having on it a drawing in relief. She did not feel the disk, but instead reported seeing "luminous spots of circular shape." When asked to draw what she saw, she produced a picture remarkably like the relief drawing that was on the disk.

Six decades later a similar line of investigation was undertaken by Charles Fisher, an American psychiatrist. Fisher's orientation was Freudian, and his interest was in the psychoanalytic theory of dreaming. In particular, he wanted to test the notion, investigated earlier by Pötzl (1917), that the content of dreams is influenced by the dreamer's experiences of the previous day—experiences which at the time may have been quite trivial and may indeed not even have been noticed. Such trivial fragments of the day's many events are referred to as "day residues."

Fisher's research strategy involved exposing subjects to a very briefly projected visual scene. The subject presumably could not make out any details of what had been presented (just as Binet's subjects could not feel the tactual stimulation on anesthetic portions of their skin). This briefly exposed scene constituted the "day residues" for these subjects, who were asked to report the next day on any dreams they had had the night before. They were also asked to draw whatever scenes they could recall from their dreams. As in Binet's research, the drawings seemed very similar, in structure if not in content, to the scene to which the subjects had been briefly exposed (Fisher, 1954; Fisher & Paul, 1959).

So far so good. But it may be apparent that these experiments are not models of contemporary research design. Efforts have been made to apply more rigorous procedures in research of this sort, both with regard to assuring that the stimulation is truly "subliminal" and to instituting more objective methods for assessing the impact of the stimulation on the behavior being studied. A series of such studies was conducted by George Klein and his colleagues (e.g., Klein, Spence, Holt, & Gourevitch, 1958), with results generally favorable to the basic hypothesis that there can be behaviorally effective subliminal stimulation. From the point of view of careful attention both to methodological rigor and to the spirit of psychoanalytic theory, the most impressive experiment was done as a doctoral dissertation by Cynthia Fox (1959). In that experiment, the subjects, male college students, viewed an outline drawing of a face projected onto a screen. In separate parts of the experiment they performed one of three tasks: (1) check list—they selected 20 adjectives from a larger list which they felt were descriptive of the person whose face appeared on the screen; (2) free description—they described the person in their own words; or (3) free imagery—they were to report any images that came to mind while viewing the drawing on the screen. Unknown to the subjects, additional lines were projected onto the picture of the face which, if visible, would make the face look dysphoric (unhappy) on some trials and euphoric (happy) on others (see Fig. 7.14). These additional lines were, however, not visible to the subjects. The intensity with which they were projected was selected on the basis of careful psychophysical measurement to be well below the detection threshold for *each subject individually*. Furthermore, not only were the subjects unaware of the subliminal lines, but the experimenter also did not know what was being projected on the screen on any trial.

The subjects' responses were analyzed by trained judges, who were blind to the nature of the stimulus associated with a given response and who used an

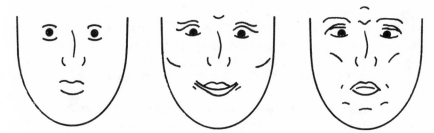

Fig. 7.14.   Line drawings of three faces used to study the effect of subthreshold stimuli on subjects' mood (after Fox, 1959). To the "neutral" face (left), lines could be added which made it appear either "dysphoric" (right) or "euphoric" (center). In the main part of the experiment by Fox (now C. Dember), the affect-inducing lines were projected on a neutral face at an intensity such that for each subject individually the lines were well below the detection threshold. Subjects viewed the face and responded at different times to one of three tasks: (1) select from a list those adjectives which best describe the face; (2) tell what kind of a person is depicted; or (3) report any images that come to mind. Responses to the latter two tasks were found to be systematically related to which lines (euphoric or dysphoric) were subliminally superimposed on the neutral face.

explicit scoring manual. The scoring manual itself was developed on the model of psychoanalytically oriented scoring systems for projective tests, such as the Thematic Apperception Test. For both the free description and free imagery conditions, the data analysis revealed that the presence of the subliminal lines did significantly affect the subjects' responses. It had not been expected that the effect would appear in the check list condition, since that condition was designed to put subjects in an objective, task-oriented frame of mind that contrasted with the more relaxed, internally oriented mood engendered by the other two conditions.

The Fox experiment has been replicated and extended in a follow-up by Allison (1963). Those results, combined with data from related studies, quite convincingly show that stimuli which are undetectable by traditional psycho-physical methods can nevertheless have measurable behavioral consequences under proper testing conditions.

Research of the above sort still generates more skepticism than enthusiasm. The skepticism comes from two sources: (1) those who, continuing to find fault with the experimental designs and procedures employed and with the methods of data analysis and interpretation, view what positive results have been reported as artifacts of poor methodology; and (2) those who point out that even if soundly based, "new look" effects are quantitatively trivial compared with the magnitude of the effects that can be produced in perception simply by manipulating such classical variables as illumination level or the subject's state of dark adaptation. Under the onslaught of both types of criticism, enthusiasm for conducting research on affective influences on perception has been considerably dampened over the past two decades. However, as Freud well knew, powerful, controversial ideas that have been inhibited have a way of coming back with renewed vigor. It will be interesting to see when a "new, new look" will begin to make its appearance on the perceptual scene.

CONCLUSION

In this chapter we have sketched some of the problems which perceptual researchers have explored. Where is the study of perception going? Some might say "in circles"—responding to the frequency with which old issues and phenomena have been rediscovered, and old explanations repackaged in new language or new metaphors. For example, Helmholtz postulated unconscious inferences which help transform sensory events into perceptual experiences. The very same issue is now being addressed by reference to "top down" processing of sensory input, a phrase consistent with the computer metaphor now in vogue in perceptual theory and research. But do we really know any more than Helmholtz did, for example, about brightness or size constancy?

Though it may be the perfect figure in Gestalt psychology, a circle is not the very best figure of speech to employ in assessing the status of perceptual theory. Progress here, as in science generally, is certainly not linear, but there clearly has been and will continue to be progress—empiricial, methodological, and conceptual. More often than not, old problems are resurrected because it has become possible, through new techniques and new ways of thinking about them, to study and understand them in a new light. For example the development of the theory of Signal Detection by Wilson Tanner, John Swets, David Green, and others in the 1950s and 1960s (e.g., Green & Swets, 1966) made it possible, among other things, to re-design and re-evaluate research on the influence of cognitive, motivational, and emotional influences on perception. The application of spatial frequency analysis to visual stimuli has enabled a re-assessment of just what "the stimulus" is and thereby has also raised serious questions about Gestalt psychology's insistence that perceptual organization must emerge from, and hence be revealing of, organizing processes taking place within the brain itself (Graham, 1981). In a similar fashion, and as but one other example, the availability of powerful computers and sophisticated video and audio displays has made it possible to investigate with new precision and in entirely new ways such classical problems as depth perception (Patterson & Fox, 1981), figure-ground segregation (Julesz, 1981) and organization in both visual and auditory perception (Bregman, 1981; Hochberg, 1981; Pomerantz, 1981).

It seems fairly certain that in the next decade the study of perception will benefit enormously from "space-age" technology and that theories of perception will be stated with increasing precision and mathematical formality. At the same time, because of the peculiar nature of their subject matter, perception researchers and theorists will continue to rely, as did their illustrious forebears, on their own experience as a source of problems to study and as a first step in testing the validity of their ideas. This will help assure close contact between the phenomena of interest and the theories developed to explain them.

REFERENCES

Allison, J. Cognitive structure and receptivity to low intensity stimulation. *Journal of Abnormal and Social Psychology,* 1963, 67, 132–138.

Allport, G. W., & Pettigrew, T. F. Cultural influence on the perception of movement: the trapezoidal illusion among Zulus. *Journal of Abnormal and Social Psychology,* 1957, 55, 104–113.

Annis, R. C., & Frost, B. Human visual ecology and orientation anisotropies in acuity. *Science,* 1973, 182, 729–731.

Berkeley, G. *An essay towards a new theory of vision,* Dublin, 1709.

Binet, A. *Les altérations de la personalité.* Paris, Alcan, 1892. Published in English translation by Helen G. Baldwin, as *Alterations of personality.* New York: Appleton, 1896.

Blake, R. R., & Ramsey, G. V. *Perception: An approach to personality.* New York, Ronald, 1951.

Blakemore, C., & Cooper, G. F. Development of the brain depends on visual environment. *Nature,* 1970, 228, 477–478.

Boring, E. G. *A history of experimental psychology.* New York: Appleton-Century-Crofts, 1929 (revised edition, 1950).

Boring, E. G. Size constancy and Emmert's law. *American Journal of Psychology,* 1940, 53, 293–295.

Boring, E. G. *Sensation and perception in the history of psychology.* New York: Appleton-Century-Crofts, 1942.

Boring, E. G. The moon illusion. *American Journal of Physics,* 1943, 11, 55–60.

Bornstein, M. H. Infants are trichromats. *Journal of Experimental Child Psychology,* 1976, 21, 425–445.

Bregman, A. S. Asking the "what for" question in auditory perception. In M. Kubovy & J. R. Pomerantz (Eds.), *Perceptual organization.* Hillsdale, New Jersey: Erlbaum, 1981.

Bruner, J. S., & Goodman, C. C. Value and need as organizing factors in perception. *Journal of Abnormal and Social Psychology,* 1947, 42, 33–44.

Chase, W. P. Colour vision in infants. *Journal of Experimental Psychology,* 1937, 20, 203–222.

Cornsweet, R. N. *Visual perception.* New York: Academic Press, 1970.

Dember, W. N. Motivation and the cognitive revolution. *American Psychologist,* 1974, 29, 161–168.

Dilthey, W. Ideen über eine beschreibende und zergliedernde Psychologie, *Gesammelte Schriften.* Leipzig, 1924, 139–240(reprint of an article published in 1894).

Dixon, N. F. *Subliminal perception: the nature of a controversy.* New York: McGraw-Hill, 1971.

Ehrenfels, C. von Ueber Gestaltqualitäten. *Vierteljahrschrift für wissenschaftliche Philosophie,* 1890.

Fantz, R. The origin of form perception. *Scientific American,* 1961, 204, 66–72.

Fisher, C. Dreams and perception. *Journal of the American Psychoanalytic Association,* 1954, 2, 389–445.

Fisher, C. & Paul, I. H. The effect of subliminal visual stimulation on images and dreams: a validation study. *Journal of the American Psychoanalytic Association,* 1959, 7, 35–83.

Fox, C. Modification of perceptual and associative response by subthreshold stimuli. Doctoral dissertation, Yale University, 1959.

Freud, S. *The interpretation of dreams*. New York: Science Editions, 1961. (Translated and edited by J. Strachey; first published in 1899.)

Freud, S. *The psychopathology of everyday life*. New York: W. W. Norton & Co., 1965. (Translation by A. Tyson; edited by J. Strachey; first published in 1901.)

Graham, N. Psychophysics of spatial frequency channels. In M. Kubovy & J. R. Pomerantz (Eds.), *Perceptual organization:* Hillsdale, New Jersey: Erlbaum, 1981.

Green, D. M., & Swets, J. A. *Signal detection theory and psychophysics*. New York: Wiley, 1966.

Haber, R. N. *Information-processing approaches to visual perception*. New York: Holt, Rinehart and Winston, 1969.

Hartline, H. K., & Ratliff, F. Inhibitory interactions of receptor units in the eye of *Limulus*. *Journal of General Physiology*, 1957, 40, 357–376.

Hartmann, G. W. *Gestalt psychology*. New York: Ronald Press, 1935.

Hayek, F. A. *The sensory order*. Chicago: University of Chicago Press, 1952.

Hebb, D. O. *The organization of behavior*. New York: Wiley, 1949.

Holway, A. F., & Boring, E. G. The moon illusion and the angle of regard. *American Journal of Psychology*, 1940, 53, 509–516.

Hochberg, J. Levels of perceptual organization. In M. Kubovy & J. R. Pomerantz (Eds.), *Perceptual organization*. Hillsdale, New Jersey: Erlbaum, 1981.

Holway, A. H., & Boring, E. G. Determinants of apparent visual size with distance variant. *American Journal of Psychology*, 1941, 54, 21–37.

Hubel, D. H., & Wiesel, T. N. Receptive fields and functional architecture of monkey striate cortex. *Journal of Physiology*, 1968, 195, 215–243.

Ittelson, W. H., Proshansky, H. M., Rivlin, L. G., & Winkel, G. H. *An introduction to environmental psychology*. New York: Holt, Rinehart and Winston, 1974.

James, W. *Principles of psychology*. New York: Holt, 1890.

Julesz, B. Figure and ground perception in briefly presented isodipole textures. In M. Kubovy & J. R. Pomerantz (Eds.), *Perceptual organization*. Hillsdale, New Jersey: Erlbaum, 1981.

Kant, I. *Critique of pure reason*. London: Macmillan, 1881. (Translated by M. Müller; first published in 1781.)

Kaufman, L. *Sight and mind: an introduction to visual perception*. New York: Oxford University Press, 1974.

Kaufman, L., & Rock, I. The moon illusion I. *Science*, 1962, 136, 953–961.

Klein, G. S., Spence, D. P., Holt, R. R., & Gourevitch, S. Cognition without awareness: subliminal influences upon conscious thought. *Journal of Abnormal and Social Psychology*, 1958, 57, 255–266.

Koffka, K. *The growth of the mind*. London: Kegan Paul, 1924.

Koffka, K. *Principles of gestalt psychology*. New York: Harcourt, Brace, 1935.

Köhler, W. *Gestalt psychology*. New York: Liveright, 1947 (first edition, 1929).

Köhler, W., & Wallach, H. Figural after-effects: an investigation of visual processes. *Proceedings of the American Philosophical Society*, 1944, 88, 269–357.

Levine, R., Chein, I., & Murphy, G. The relation of the intensity of a need to the amount of perceptual distortion: A preliminary report. *Journal of Psychology*, 1942, 13, 283–293.

Locke, J. *An essay concerning human understanding*. London, 1690.

Maslow, A. H. *Motivation and personality*. New York: Harper, 1954.

McGinnies, E. Emotionality and perceptual defense. *Psychological Review*, 1949, 56, 244–251.

Packard, V. *The hidden persuaders*. New York: David McKay, 1957.

Patterson, R., & Fox, R. Information processing in global stereoscopic displays. Presented at annual meeting of the Psychonomic Society, Philadelphia, Pa., 1981.

Peiper, A. *Cerebral function in infancy and childhood*. New York: Consultants Bureau, 1963. (Translated by B. Nagler & H. Nagler.)

Pötzl, O. Experimentell erregte Traumbilder in ihren Beziehungen zum indirekten Sehen. *Zeitschrift für dem gesamte Neurologie Psychiatrie,* 1917, 37, 278–349 (English translation published in *Psychological Issues,* 1960, 2, No. 3, 41–120).

Pomerantz, J. R. Perceptual organization in information processing. In M. Kubovy & J. R. Pomerantz (Eds.), *Perceptual organization.* Hillsdale, New Jersey: Erlbaum, 1981.

Riesen, A. H. The development of visual perception in man and chimpanzee. *Science,* 1947, 106, 107–108.

Rivers, W. H. R. Primitive color vision. *Popular Science Monthly,* 1901, 59, 44–58.

Rock, I., & Kaufman, L. The moon illusion. II. *Science,* 1962, 136, 1023–1031.

Ross, H. E., & Ross, G. M. Did Ptolemy understand the moon illusion? *Perception,* 1976, 5, 377–385.

Schafer, R., & Murphy, G. The role of autism in a visual figure-ground relationship. *Journal of Experimental Psychology,* 1943, 32, 335–343.

Segall, M. H., Campbell, D. T., & Herskovits, M. J. *The influence of culture on visual perception.* Indianapolis: Bobbs-Merrill, 1966.

Senden, M. von *Space and sight.* Glencoe, Illinois: The Free Press, 1960 (first published in 1932 as *Raum-und Gestaltauffassung bei Opereirten Blindgeborenen*).

Staples, F. R. The responses of infants to color. *Journal of Experimental Psychology,* 1932, 15, 119–141.

Titchener, E. B. *A text-book of psychology.* New York: Macmillan, 1911.

Titchener, E. B. On ethnological tests of sensation and perception with special reference to tests of color vision and tactile discrimination described in the reports of the Cambridge anthropological expedition to the Torres Straits. *Proceedings of the American Philosophical Society,* 1916, 55, 204–236.

Wertheimer, Max *Productive thinking.* New York: Harper, 1945.

Wertheimer, Michael Humanistic psychology and the humane but tough-minded psychologist. *American Psychologist,* 1978, 33, 739–745.

Witkin, H. A., Lewis, H. B., Hertzman, M., Machover, K., Meissner, P. B., & Wapner, S. *Personality through perception,* New York: Harper & Brothers, 1954.

Young, T. The Bakerian lecture, on the mechanism of the eye. *Philosophical Transactions,* Royal Society of London, 1801, 91, 23–88 plus plates.

8

A History of the Study of the Cortex: Changes in the Concept of the Sensory Pathway

I. T. Diamond
Duke University

INTRODUCTION

Every scientist is a historian in some sense. In order to contribute to an inquiry, it is necessary to understand the work of predecessors. Reports of new results are usually introduced by reviewing earlier studies, and new findings are interpreted in the light of older evidence. This kind of history relies entirely on scientific reports in contrast to biographies, letters, and personal experiences.

The present chapter is a history in the restricted sense of relying chiefly on scientific papers. Thus many important and interesting aspects of the history of science, such as the effects of social, cultural, and technological factors in the development of ideas, are left out. Still I have not tried in principle to avoid making comments about the personal lives of authors, and from time to time I have departed from the analysis of scientific contributions to describe the state of the art at a particular period in time.

I have chosen the cerebral cortex as my topic for several reasons: First, the subject of the cerebral cortex provides a chance to show relations between the various neural sciences and psychology. Second, the transformation of the cortex in vertebrate history is perhaps the most remarkable outcome of evolution; without doubt, the cortex is the basis of those traits that distinguish human beings from other mammals. Finally, the cerebral cortex is the focus of my own research.

I have tried to select a few outstanding pioneers to represent major advances either in concept or in method. Each pioneer has contributed in some way to the *parcellation* of the cortex, by *architectonics*, by *connections*, by *experimental ablation*, or by *electrophysiological* methods. The anatomical division of the

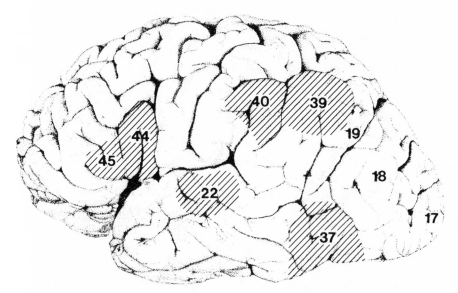

FIG. 8.1.   A lateral view of man's brain showing first that all of it is covered by cortex. The numbers refer to the various subdivisions based on differences in the laminar pattern. The question of whether each subdivision constitutes a functional unit is one of the main problems of this chapter. The region 44–45 in the frontal lobe is Broca's motor speech area. Lesions in this area leave a patient unable to speak. Area 22, according to some neurobiologists, is necessary for auditory association and lesions here lead to an auditory aphasia, a word deficit. Lesions of 37, 39, and 40 lead to deficits in reading. Areas 17, 18, and 19 are visual areas and lesions in these areas result in loss of visual sensation. It is important to underscore that you are looking at the left hemisphere. Why the language functions are localized in the left hemisphere and not the right hemisphere remains a mystery.

cortex is only the starting point to the principal question of the inquiry: What is the functional significance of the subdivisions of the cortex?

One way to try to localize functions in the cortex is to identify a particular set of symptoms in man with the locus of the lesion. The results of such efforts have been maps of different functions such as the one shown in Figure 8.1. That functions such as "writing" or "hearing words" can be localized has fascinated philosophers as well as psychologists and neurologists. Some neurologists such as Kurt Goldstein (1939) have rejected this whole line of inquiry, perhaps because they believed it was carried to an extreme, and instead have argued that truly intellectual functions such as abstract thinking are not localized and that the fundamental symptom of human cortical damage is a general dementia.

It is tempting for historians with a philosophic bent to make this debate the central issue in the study of cortex. Instead I will try to trace the steps that led to the classification of cortical subdivisions into three main classes: sensory areas, motor areas, and association areas. This view was already firmly established by the beginning of this century. It proved to be a marvelously resilient concept, one that has survived one after another assault. The chief question posed in this history is whether or not it continues to be useful in the light of recent evidence.

THE CONCEPT OF A SENSORY PATHWAY

Bell: Sensory and Motor Fibers

In 1811, a remarkable paper was published by Charles Bell that can be taken as the beginning of modern neural science (see Bell, 1811). Bell began his inquiry by dividing the brain into its two most conspicuous parts—the cerebrum and the cerebellum. The cerebrum is smaller in lower mammals and attains its greatest magnitude in humans. On the other hand, the cerebellum is stable throughout the vertebrate scale. From this difference between cerebrum and cerebellum, Bell deduced that the cerebrum, and especially the cerebral cortex, is the basis of higher mental functions, while the cerebellum is the basis of unconscious move- ments of the visceral organs, such as the heart and the blood vessels, as well as the involuntary reflex movements of the skeletal muscles. It is clear from Bell's view of higher and lower functions that he accepted the prevailing philosophy, going back to Descartes, that consciousness is a higher function and a reflection of mind and that motor responses to stimuli need not involve the mind unless they are intentional.

Bell found empirical support for his ideas with experiments in which motion was produced by touching the cerebellum. Most important was the discovery that assured Bell of lasting honor: He noted that the nerves of the body divide into two roots just before they enter the spinal cord. Touching the ventral root with the point of a knife produced motion, while touching the dorsal root did not. Bell leaped to the conclusion that sensory and motor functions were carried by sepa- rate fibers in a peripheral nerve. The Belgium physiologist Magendie made the same discovery independently, and the anatomical and functional distinction between sensory and motor fibers is known as the *Bell-Magendie Law*.

This discovery delighted Bell because it showed that, while the fibers of a peripheral nerve (he called them "strands") look alike, they serve different functions. Bell was then able to argue that the differences between sensory and motor fibers must depend on differences in central connections; that is to say, they not only have different peripheral connections but they also enter different tracts in the spinal cord, and these tracts terminate in different brain centers. Different sensory modalities, Bell recognized, could also be explained by dif- ferences in the central connections of the various nerves that innervate the sense organs. In this way Bell invented a sensory pathway. It is the route from the receptor to the brain *center* that provides a sensation with its special quality—a quality that differs from one modality to another.

Up to the time of Bell, the prevailing view was that differences between, for example, the sensations of pitch and color were provided by differences in the quality of the messages conveyed by the nerves from the receptor. Each receptor, according to this view, was capable of sending a different message corresponding in some unknown way to the stimulus, and these different messages were transmitted to a single common organ. No clue was offered about the ways in which the nerve messages differed. There was only a vague idea that receptors differed in sensitivity—the eye, for example, being much more sensitive than the skin. Touch might be regarded as a very intense light and vision as a very mild touch.

Bell was able to assail this rather crude idea by pointing out that, if it were correct, the slightest touch on the retina would be agonizingly painful. In fact, the retina is insensitive to a knife cut. That receptors in general are insensitive to all stimuli except those of a special sort was supported by his experiments on the tongue. Some spots on the tongue were found to produce a sensation of touch alone or a sensation of taste alone. Bell placed great weight on the principle that receptors are insensitive to all but a special sort of stimulus because it implies that access to the receptor's nerve is limited. When an inappropriate stimulus does gain access to the nerve by virtue of its unusual intensity, as in the case of a blow to the eye, the sensation corresponds to the nerve, not to the stimulus; that is, one "sees stars." This evidence supported Bell's idea that the sensory quality was given by a sensory pathway.

The precise targets of the sensory pathways were unknown, but Bell felt they must go to the cerebrum; whether or not the pathways extended to the surface of the cerebrum, the cerebral cortex, was not clear to Bell. At one point he seems to argue, contrary-wise, that the cortex is a single organ whose intellectual functions are "higher" than modality-specific sensations. At least he believed that the symptoms of cortical damage are "lethargy, stupidity, and a derangement of the mind," and it is significant that this list did not include a loss of vision, hearing, or touch. For the present argument, the chief point is the idea of sensory centers in the cerebrum which set the stage for the discovery of sensory paths to the cortex.

Bell's many contributions can be summarized as follows: He recognized the cerebrum as the hallmark of the human nervous system, and he even distinguished the surface or cortex from the underlying white matter. He viewed the functions of the white matter in the cerebrum to be the same as in peripheral nerves—that is, to convey messages to and from centers. It is only a step, though one that he himself did not take, from this argument to conclude that the white tracts underlying the cortex are conveying impulses from the various centers of the cerebrum to different parts of the cortex. Thus, it can be said that the concept of a sensory pathway ultimately led to the discovery of cortical sensory areas.

Flourens: Ablation Studies in the Bird

Flourens was a pioneer in the use of the ablation method. In his principal experiments originally published in 1824 (see von Bonin trans. 1960) he removed more and more of the cerebrum of birds in successive operations with the result that sensations, vision in particular, were gradually "weakened," as were other mental faculties. Eventually vision was entirely lost, but so were other sensory and intellectual functions. When the entire cerebrum was ablated, the bird just sat still and refused to eat even when food was placed in its mouth. Some responses could be elicited but only under intense stimulation, and then the animal would bump into objects. These symptoms led Flourens to argue that (1) the deficit was *not* a loss of locomotion, (2) it *did* involve vision, and (3) the loss of spontaneous behavior in particular meant that the bird had suffered a loss of "will and judgement."

Since all sensory and intellectual functions were lost gradually in successive lesions, Flourens concluded that the cerebrum acted as a whole and did not contain modality-specific subdivisions. Historians often credit Flourens with the

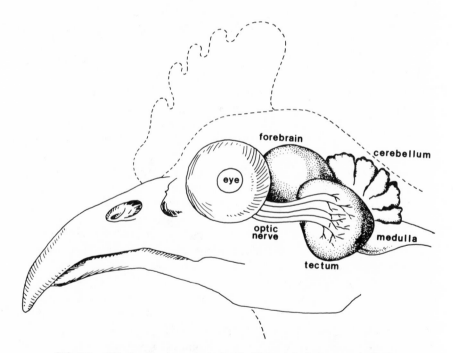

FIG. 8.2. This drawing shows the brain of a bird and the important point is the subdivisions into a number of main parts: the forebrain or cerebrum, the midbrain or tectum, and the hindbrain, which includes the cerebellum and medulla. It should not escape your notice that the eye of a bird is about as big as one of these major subdivisions and that the eye projects to the tectum.

first demonstration that the *cortex* acts as a whole, but the implications of Flourens' experiments for the question of *cortical* localization of function are obscure because the bird *has no cortex* covering the cerebrum! To be sure, be did conduct some experiments with monkeys, but in these the lesions were not restricted to the cortex, aseptic precautions were not taken, and the surgical methods were too crude to form any clear idea of the nature of the lesion let alone the significance of the symptoms.

More significant for the present purpose, it would be wrong to conclude that the evidence reported by Flourens was against localization of function. Quite the contrary, when he removed the tectum in the chicken the animal lost vision entirely but was normal in other ways. No doubt Flourens was able to trace the optic tract from the eye to the tectum of the bird because this tract lies on the surface and can be identified without sectioning and staining the brain and even without hardening the brain (see Fig. 8.2). Since the time of Flourens, it has been established by comparative anatomists that the eye projects to the tectum in all vertebrates from fish to humans. Figure 8.3 shows the similarity of the optic tectum of several vertebrates. In higher mammals the tectum (also called the superior colliculus in mammals) is entirely covered by the growth of the cerebral hemisphere, but the homology of the superior colliculus with the tectum in other vertebrates is apparent.

Flourens held that the other senses were also represented in special centers and that these sensory centers, as well as the tectum, must transmit their sensory messages into the cerebrum, since removal of the cerebrum produces a loss of all sensations. (Incidentally, unilateral removal of the cerebrum produces blindness just in the contralateral eye, so Flourens concluded correctly that the optic tract in the bird is crossed.) The issue for Flourens was whether the various sensory centers project *diffusely* into the cerebrum rather than each having its own sensory area. Because sensations were lost together and gradually, Flourens argued that the projections were diffuse.

Flourens' view of the projections from the tectum to the cerebrum is revealed by his interpretation of the single instance when an ablation of the cerebrum produced an uncomplicated visual loss without a concomitant loss of other modalities. Flourens interpreted this as a sign that the tectum's projection into the cerebrum had been sectioned. He pictured a diffuse *termination* of visual tracts, but he recognized that the tracts must have been localized at some point close to their exit from the tectum. (I cannot resist the temptation to insert here our current view of the visual pathways in the bird. Not too many years ago a major discovery was made by Harvey Karten, then at MIT. The tectum in the bird does indeed project to the thalamus, nucleus rotundus in particular, which in turn projects into the cerebral hemispheres (Karten, 1966). This target of nucleus rotundus was very likely removed by Flourens in his studies of the cerebral hemispheres.)

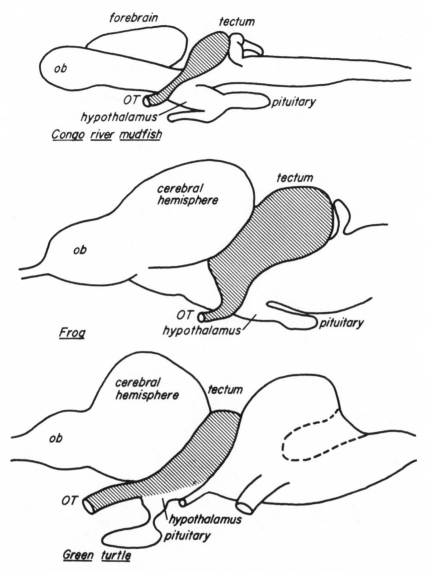

FIG. 8.3.   A lateral view of the brain of three vertebrates: fish, amphibian, and reptile. The chief point is the obvious similarities in the organization such as the location of the olfactory bulb (ob) and the optic tract (OT). The visual pathway is depicted by diagonal shading. Note that the optic tract passes to the tectum in the three groups. These similarities, as well as the locus of the hypothalamus and pituitary, are homologous.

It is easy to see how Bell and Flourens might be opposed as thesis and antithesis on the question of localization of function. Bell emphasized differences in the central connections of different pathways subserving different modalities, while Flourens found no modality-specific area in the cerebrum. In fact, however, there is little basis for concluding that they had any major differences in point of view. Flourens accepted the idea of centers specialized for a given modality and showed that the tectum is the visual center of the bird; he also recognized that there was a further projection from sensory centers, such as the tectum, to the cerebrum. *The issue is whether this projection is diffuse or specific.* Flourens held that it was diffuse. Bell's view on this point is not clear. While I used the term "projection," neither Bell nor Flourens had a clear idea of a neuron or a synapse.

In sum, Flourens was a pioneer in using the ablation method to study the brain. He could be criticized for his crude surgical methods and for jumping to the conclusion that the loss of spontaneous activity means a loss of will, judgement, and intelligence, especially since it is not clear how such traits would be demonstrated in the normal chicken. His chief contribution as measured by the test of history was the proof that the functions of the tectum and the cerebrum are distinct. As is illustrated in Figures 8.2 and 8.3, the tectum and the cerebrum appear to be the main parts of the brain, not only in birds but in all vertebrates.

THE ANATOMICAL BASIS FOR THE CONCEPT OF A SENSORY PATHWAY TO THE CORTEX

The Cell Doctrine: Golgi versus Cajal

While both Flourens and Bell were anatomists in the sense of *starting with structure,* their view of structural subdivisions depended entirely on the gross appearance of fresh brains. Neither had histological methods at his disposal to harden and section brains and to stain them. Both recognized a difference between white matter and gray, and they recognized that white matter in the brain is the counterpart of peripheral nerves. They had little sense of the neuron and its processes, however, let alone any conception of the relation between neurons. Therefore, terms such as connections and terminations and projections could not carry their present meaning. Even 100 years later, when Golgi and Cajal shared the Nobel Prize for their studies of neurons and especially neuronal processes, the axons and dendrites, the question of whether a neuron was a unit and separate entity was at issue. In fact, it was this very issue that was the subject of the lectures given by Golgi (1906) and Cajal (1906) at the time they accepted the prize.

In order to pursue the history of the inquiry into the sensory pathways to the cortex begun by Bell and Flourens, it is necessary to trace, albeit briefly, some of the steps leading to our present-day conception of the terms "neuron," "con-

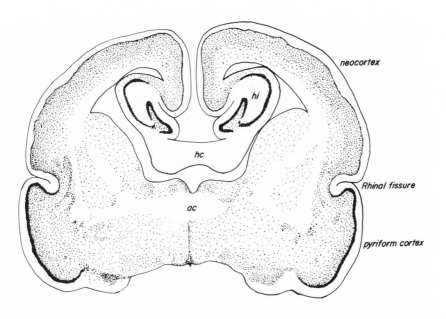

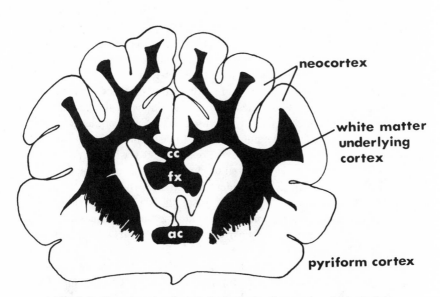

FIG. 8.4.   Frontal section through the forebrain of opossum at the level of the anterior commissure. This drawing depicts cell bodies with dots and fiber tracts devoid of dots. (Abbreviations: ac, anterior commissure; hc, hippocampal commissure; hi, hippocampus.)

FIG. 8.5.   Frontal section through forebrain of cat at the level of the anterior commissure. In this drawing the attempt is to simulate a myelin stain by making the fibers black and the grey matter white. (Abbreviations: ac, anterior commissure; cc, corpus callosum; fx, fornix.)

313

nection," "projection," and "synapse." The last half of the nineteenth century was a period of very great progress in histology. The first step in histological study of the brain was to find a way to harden the tissue. Boiling came first to mind, no doubt because of common experience such as seeing the effects of boiling on the consistency of egg white. Later it was found that the brain would harden if soaked in alcohol or in formalin. With the brain in this congealed state, it became possible to trace large tracts of white matter from center to center by teasing out the tissue with a small instrument. Thus, the optic tract was traced to the lateral geniculate body of the thalamus. Also, the brain could be divided grossly with a knife, such as by cutting the two hemispheres apart. In this way, the commissures that join the two cerebral hemispheres were discovered in a variety of vertebrates and even some very subtle differences between species were detected. For example, Owens reported in 1834 that in marsupials there was no true corpus callosum; rather, this dorsal commissure originated from the hippocampus (see Elliot-Smith, 1910). Figures 8.4 and 8.5 show frontal sections through the anterior commissure in two species of mammals. In both groups there is a second commissure dorsal to the anterior commissure: In the marsupials this dorsal commissure originates from the hippocampus; in the cat the dorsal commissure, or corpus callosum, originates from the neocortex. This difference turned out to be very important in helping Elliot-Smith prove that the hippocampus is older in phylogeny than the neocortex (see section on Evolution). In addition to the commissures, various subcortical parts of the brain, notably the thalamus, were soon identified.

This method of following tracts by gross dissection provided the first demonstration that the optic tract extended into the radiations of the cerebral hemispheres and reached the cortex itself. Working chiefly with primates, including baboons and monkeys, Gratiolet published the first account of a tract from retina to cortex in 1857. He noted that beyond the optic chiasma, where nerves from the two eyes meet, the optic tract appeared to plunge into the lateral geniculate and pulvinar nuclei, both of which can be identified on the surface of the thalamus. A smaller tract then continues to the tectum, or the superior colliculus, as the tectum is called in mammals. From the thalamus the tract continues and radiates in the shape of a fan to reach an extensive area of the occipital and temporal lobes (see Polyak, 1957).

From the perspective of our present-day concept of the visual pathway, the important question is: Does the optic tract terminate in the lateral geniculate and pulvinar nuclei of the thalamus, or does it continue without interruption into the optic radiations? Gratiolet saw no reason to assume that the optic tract terminated in the thalamus. Ten years later, Meynert, working with very thin sections stained with various dyes designed to reveal fibers and cell bodies, argued that the optic tract does indeed terminate in *both* the lateral geniculate and pulvinar bodies (see Polyak, 1957).

The years following Meynert's early work (1867) saw continuing rapid advances in histology. Brains were embedded in materials, such as paraffin, soft enough to cut, but hard enough so that very thin sections could be obtained. This required a large blade that was held in a special device so the stroke through the tissue was smooth and even. The resulting sections were so thin they had to be mounted on glass. Staining methods then proliferated. Some stains showed the soma of the neuron, some the myelin sheath of the axons.

One stain developed by Golgi and called by him the ''black stain'' provided a complete picture of the cell body and its processes, the axon and dendrites. The dendrites, which look like shrubs and bushes of various sizes and shapes, are especially striking (see Fig. 8.6). Ironically, Golgi himself never accepted the

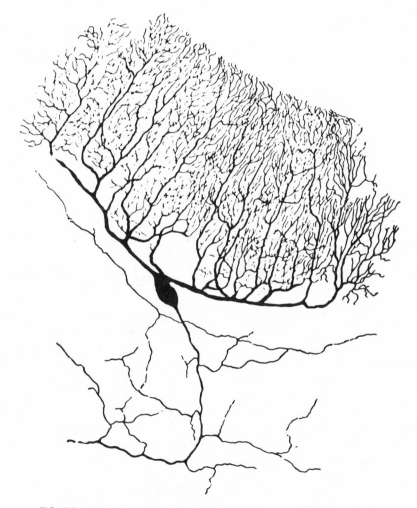

FIG. 8.6. A drawing taken from Golgi's Nobel lecture which illustrates the enormous bushy tree of dendrites. These processes could not be seen either by the myelin stain for axons or the Nissl stain for cell bodies.

idea that the neuron is an embryonic and physiological unit. Instead, he argued that cells are continuous. It was his contemporary, Cajal, who established the *neuron doctrine* as the first principle in the neural sciences.

In his Nobel lecture of December 1906, Cajal put forth the chief tenents of the neuron doctrine:

(a) As nature, in order to assure and amplify the contacts, has created complicated systems of pericellular ramifications (systems which become incomprehensible within the hypothesis of continuity), it must be admitted that the nerve currents are transmitted from one element to the other as a consequence of a sort of induction of influence from a distance.

(b) It must also be supposed that the cell bodies and the dendrites are, in the same way as the axis cylinders, conductive devices, as they represent the intermediary links between afferent nerve fibers and the aforementioned axons. This is what Bethe, Simarro, Donaggio, ourselves, etc. have confirmed quite recently by demonstrating, with the aid of neurofibrillar methods, a perfect structural concordance between the dendrites and the prolongation of the axon cylinder.

(c) The examination of the movement of nervous impulses in the sensory organs such as the retina, the olfactory bulb, the sensory ganglia, and the spinal cord, etc. proves not only that the protoplasmic expansions play a conducting role but even more that nervous movement in these prolongations is *towards* the cell or axon, while it is *away* from the cell in the axons. This formula, called the dynamic polarization of neurons, originated a long time ago by Van Gehuchten and as an induction from numerous morphological facts, is not in contradiction with the new research on the constitution of nerve protoplasm. Indeed we will see that the neurofibrillar framework constitutes a continuous reticulum from the dendrites and the cell body to the axons and its peripheral termination. (p. 221, italics mine)

For our purposes, Cajal's description of a sensory pathway from the receptor to the cortex is his most significant contribution. Figure 8.7, taken from his lecture delivered on the occasion of accepting the Nobel prize, shows how a dorsal root ganglion cell enters the spinal cord and makes contact with internuncial cells which in turn make contact with ventral horn cells. Figure 8.8 shows the steps by which the visual impulses pass through the retina from the rods and cones to the bipolar cells to the ganglion cells. The axons of the ganglion cells in turn project to the tectum, which is shown at the bottom of Figure 8.8. Note chiefly the arborization of the dendritic trees in the superficial part of the tectum, and note that two descending cells are pictured below the layer of dendritic arborization. Finally, Figure 8.9 shows the several pathways to the neocortex. The medial lemniscus is seen projecting to the ventral nucleus which, in turn, projects to the somatic area of the cortex. Cajal also discovered a reciprocal descending pathway from the receptive area of the cortex back down to the ventral nucleus. The pathway to the visual cortex is also depicted, and the dendrites ending in the cortex constitute a band. Below the surface, apical dendrites of deeper pyramidal cells are shown ascending to the surface of the cortex.

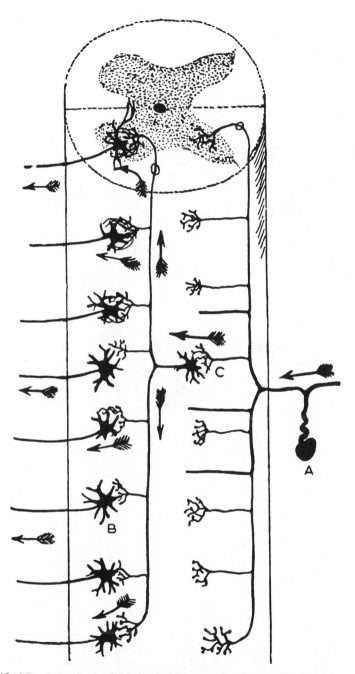

FIG. 8.7. A drawing by Cajal showing the connections between the dendrites and cell bodies, in this case, in the spinal cord. A is a cell body in the dorsal root ganglion. Impulses originate in the periphery (for example, the skin of the hand) and pass toward the spinal cord as indicated by the direction of the arrow. The letter "B" shows a series of ventral horn cells, the axons of which, as shown by the arrows, leave the spinal cord to return to the peripheral muscles. There's an internuncial neuron also shown receiving terminals at the point designated "C."

317

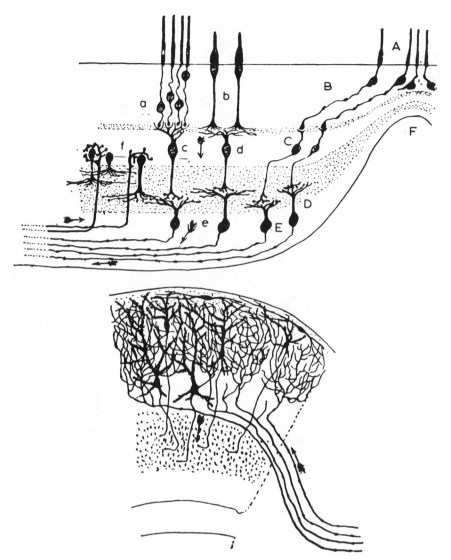

FIG. 8.8. Two drawings of the visual system taken from Cajal's Nobel lecture: On top is a drawing of a section through the retina. The letter A is the receptor layer; B is the outer nuclear layer; a indicates rods; b indicates cones; C is the inner nuclear layer; c and d are bipolar cells; D is the ganglion cell layer; E and e show ganglion cells the axons of which leave the retina as the optic nerve; F stands for fovea. In the lower drawing the optic nerve is shown to continue until it reaches its target in the retina.

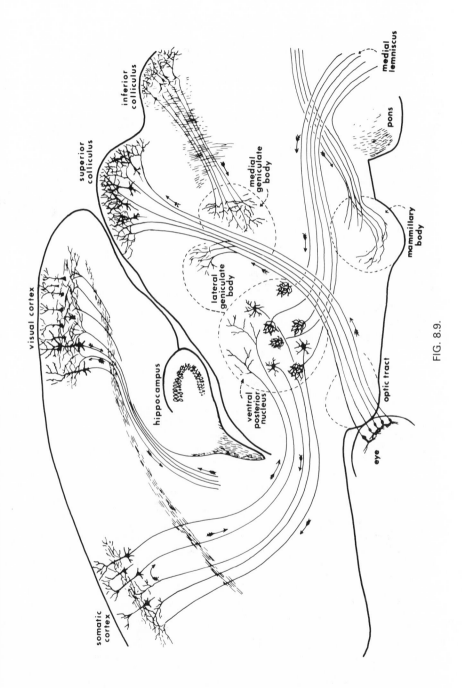

FIG. 8.9.

Experimental Degeneration Methods

Late in the nineteenth century, Marchi discovered that removing an eye led to degeneration of fibers in the optic tract and that these degenerating fibers could be *selectively* stained black against a much lighter background of normal fibers (Polyak, 1957). The degeneration could then be traced in serial sections, and in this way the origin and termination of a tract could be established experimentally. Gross dissection had revealed that the optic tract surrounds and enters the lateral geniculate and that many fibers emerge and can be traced to the cerebral hemispheres. Whether the fibers leaving are the same as the ones entering or whether "new" fibers originate in the cell bodies of the lateral geniculate could not be determined. However, with the new methods of tracing degenerating fibers developed by Marchi, it could be seen that the degeneration ends in the lateral geniculate bodies and that the fibers entering the radiations are normal. In this way, it was experimentally determined that the optic tract *terminates* in the lateral geniculate bodies. Meynert was proved right and Gratiolet wrong. Now many new questions could be addressed: For example, the topography of the projections from the retina to the lateral geniculate could be studied by making small lesions in various parts of the retina.

For several decades the pathways from the ear, eye and spinal cord were traced step by step with the Marchi method. Thus, the dorsal columns of the cord could be traced to nuclei at the base of the medulla and from these nuclei, the gracile and cuneate nuclei, a second tract could be traced to the ventral posterior nucleus in the thalamus. The last link was the projection of the ventral posterior nucleus to the cortex. The auditory pathway was found to have more links or relays than the others, but the final relay was from the thalamus to cortex. The number of links in the visual pathway is deceptive because several relays take place in the retina itself, as is shown in Figure 8.8.

FIG. 8.9. A diagram which is a composite taken from several of Cajal's drawings showing the several sensory pathways in the neocortex. You are looking at the brain from the side. The medulla would be to the right and the rostral extremity of the cortex is to your left. Notice first that the optic tract originates in the eye and passes dorsally and caudally to its target in the superior colliculus. From this path there are collaterals that leave the optic tract to terminate in the lateral geniculate body. The lateral geniculate body, in turn, projects to the striate cortex, and for the sake of clarity you only see the terminal portion of the geniculo-striate pathway. You only see the last portion of the auditory pathway from the inferior colliculus to the medial geniculate body which, in turn, projects to the auditory cortex. The somatosensory pathway is more completely illustrated. The medial lemniscus begins at the spinal cord and passes forward to the ventral posterior nucleus of the thalamus, which, in turn, projects to the somatic cortex. Finally, it is important to note that Cajal noticed that the cortex reciprocated with descending fibers that returned to the thalamus.

A second degeneration method was soon developed that had a very limited use but proved to be of utmost importance when it was applicable. If the eye is removed, not only does the optic tract degenerate, but if the experimental subject survives the operation for a long time (over a year), degeneration is also found in the cell bodies of the lateral geniculate nucleus. This is called trans-neuronal degeneration because it crosses the gap between the axon of one neuron (the ganglion cell of the retina) and the cell body in the lateral geniculate nucleus.

A third method depends on the fact that certain parts of the nervous system exhibit degeneration of cell bodies when the axons are cut: This is called retrograde degeneration, and it is important to note that it does not occur in every part of the nervous system. For example, cutting a peripheral nerve in the arm does not normally produce retrograde degeneration of the ventral horn cell in the spinal cord. On the contrary, the ventral horn cell continues to function and the cut nerve typically regenerates. The method of retrograde degeneration proved to be most useful in the studies of the projections from the thalamus to the cortex, and I shall return to those studies later.

Sherrington and the Synapse

While the experimental degeneration methods showed that tracts plunge into a center and disappear, they could not reveal the actual connection between the axon of one neuron and the dendrite of another. Not until the development of the electron microscope could the structural organization of the synapse be investigated with anatomical methods, even though the idea of a synapse was invented years before. In general, it is probably true that structures are identified first, but there are a few outstanding discoveries in the biological sciences in which a concept was deduced or a function was discovered before a physical basis for the function could be identified. One outstanding example is that Mendel's concept of a gene was derived from breeding experiments long before cytologists had observed the reduction division of chromosomes or had even identified the double or dual nature of chromosomes in the nucleus of cells.

The idea of a synapse was invented by the great English physiologist, Sir Charles Sherrington (1906), who received the Nobel prize for his outstanding contributions to the neurosciences. Before the time of Sherrington, physiologists had devised methods to stimulate at one point along a nerve and to record the electrical signs of neural activity at a different point. In this way, a number of stimulus-response relations that reflect nerve trunk conduction were established. Perhaps the simplest way to picture a method for revealing the properties of nerve trunk conduction is to stimulate a motor nerve and observe the response in the muscle to which the nerve is attached. As a result of such studies, a number of facts about the conduction of nerve impulses had been established before Sherrington's time. For example, it was determined that nerve impulses are conducted in both directions from the point of stimulation; the latency of the response had been measured and could be attributed entirely to the time taken for the impulse to be propagated along the fiber; relations between the intensity of the stimulus and the response had been worked out; the effects of repeating a series of subliminal stimuli had been studied; and a refractory phase had been identified.

Sherrington departed from the earlier workers by undertaking an inquiry into the *integrative* function of the nervous system. By "integration" Sherrington meant that action of the nervous system that attaches an appropriate response to a stimulus. To achieve his goal, he felt it necessary to identify the simplest form or unit of the integrative act, and this he took to be the simple reflex. The simple reflex is revealed in the spinal cord only when the cerebrum and the thalamus are disconnected from the spinal cord. The isolation of the spinal cord leaves only a few links in the chain of events beginning with the excitation of the receptor and ending with the motor act. The receptor activates the sensory neuron whose cell body is in the dorsal root ganglion. This, in turn, excites an internuncial neuron, and the path is completed by the ventral horn cell that innervates the muscle (see Figure 7).

Sherrington began the study of the reflex by distinguishing it from nerve trunk conduction. Some of the differences between the two are as follows: (1) In a reflex, the latency decreases as the intensity of the stimulus increases; (2) a reflex continues to discharge after the stimulus has ceased; (3) in reflex activity, a number of subliminal stimuli, if repeated, can become effective in eliciting a reflex; (4) reflex conduction is one-way; and (5) the refractory stage of a reflex is different from that of a nerve trunk. Sherrington attributed these differences between reflex activity and nerve trunk conduction to the fact that in a reflex there is some "nexus" between one neuron and the next. That connection he defined as the *synapse,* and the organization or integration achieved by the reflex is the result of that synapse. There are, of course, other contributors to the organization of the reflex (such as the receptor, which selects the stimulus in the first place), but that takes us beyond the present purpose.

In conclusion, by the beginning of the twentieth century, the conception of a sensory path approached the view that has lasted for the most part to the present day. This idea of a sensory path is as follows: The receptor serves as a selector, permitting access to its pathway only to certain stimuli. Normally, only light can produce nerve impulses in the optic nerve. The optic nerve "terminates" in the lateral geniculate body in the sense proposed by Cajal. That is, the optic tract neurons synapse on the dendrites of the lateral geniculate neurons. The lateral geniculate neurons, in turn, radiate to the striate cortex where the afferent pathway "ends." I put this in quotation marks because I want the reader to consider what is meant by the idea that the sequence ends. Does it mean the "efferent" or motor path begins?

Similar sensory pathways can be traced for the other modalities. The somatosensory impulses travel up the spinal cord and relay in the medulla, where the medial lemniscus continues the path to the thalamus. A final step is taken by the thalamic projections to the cortex. There is also an auditory area of cortex and a taste area. Finally, there is also an olfactory area, but this sensory pathway differs from the others since the olfactory bulbs lie in front of the cerebrum and therefore there are no olfactory impulses *ascending* the brainstem to reach the thalamus. I will come back to the difference between the olfactory cortex and the neocortex.

CORTICAL ABLATION AS A WAY OF DEFINING SENSORY AREAS OF THE CORTEX: 1870-1900

It is not necessary to wait until the connections of a cortical area are completely known to test the behavioral effects of its ablation. Indeed, the ablation method can be used to help establish connections, as exemplified by the fact that ablation studies were ahead of experimental anatomy in defining sensory areas of the cortex during the last three decades of the nineteenth century. However, the starting point for all of these studies was the concept that the sensory path *did* continue up to the neocortex and that each sensory path had its own special area of neocortex.

To illustrate how cortical ablation studies were used to identify sensory areas of cortex and to summarize the results obtained during this period, I have chosen two experiments, one by Schafer (1888) and the other by Munk (1881). Schafer's paper was the first to report the loss of visual *sensations* in primates after ablation of the occipital pole. The paper by Munk was selected to raise a fundamental question: What is the relation between simple sensory functions and more complex perceptual functions such as the recognition of objects?

Schafer entered the inquiry in the midst of a controversy. Ferrier, who was the first to study the cortex of primates systematically by means of the ablation method, had evidence that removal of the angular gyrus led to blindness in monkeys (see Fig. 8.10 and Ferrier, 1886). Of course, the ablation had to be bilateral to produce blindness in both eyes; unilateral ablation, Ferrier believed, led to blindness of the contralateral eye. Only later was it discovered that half of the visual field of each eye had been affected. On the other hand, Munk localized vision in the occipital lobe. Note that either view was compatible with the conclusions based on gross dissection since Gratiolet had traced the visual radiations from the pulvinar and lateral geniculate nuclei to a wide sector of cortex that extended from the occipital pole to the middle of the parietal and temporal lobes. For our purposes, the area of agreement is more significant than the dispute between Ferrier and Munk. All researchers agreed that the sensory pathways extended to the cortex so that a loss of sensation should result from the appropriate lesion. There was no question that cortical blindness could be produced; only the location of the visual cortex was questionable.

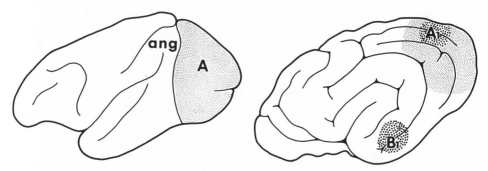

FIG. 8.10. Two diagrams to illustrate the studies of Schafer and Munk. On the left is a drawing of the cerebral cortex of a monkey. The letter A is the visual area the ablation of which, according to Schafer, produced blindness; "ang" stands for the angular gyrus which Ferrier believed to be the site of visual cortex. On the right is a drawing of the lateral view of a dog's cortex. The fine stippled area shows Munk's concept of the visual cortex in the dog. The coarser dots labeled A1 designate Munk's view of the region responsible for visual memory. (B1 can be ignored for the present purpose.)

When Schafer completely removed the angular gyrus in one monkey, the animal showed no appreciable defect either in eye movement or visual perception. This single negative case refuted Ferrier's conclusion. Schafer argued that Ferrier must have undercut fibers to the occipital lobe or destroyed the blood supply to the occipital lobe, for the monkey took no notice of objects on its right side when its occipital lobe was removed. A threatened blow, for example, did not result in any effort to avoid being struck. Schafer recognized that the defect was not total blindness of the right eye as Ferrier had thought but a blindness in the right half of the visual field of each eye as the clinicians had discovered to be the case in man. "Homonymous hemianopsia," the term given to this symptom by the neurological clinic, implies that fibers from each eye decussate (cross), with the result that the left half of each retina projects to one hemisphere while the right half projects to the opposite hemisphere.

A bilateral ablation of the occipital lobe leaving the angular gyrus intact resulted in "a total and persistent blindness. The animal could only find food by groping . . . [and when] brought into a strange place it ran against every obstacle. All other senses appeared to be intact" (Schafer, pp. 368–369).

Further, Schafer was the first to demonstrate experimentally with behavioral methods the topographic projection of the retina on the cortex. With restricted lesions of the occipital lobe, he found blind spots in the upper and lower field corresponding to the locus of the lesion. By producing these selective scotoma, the question of function of the visual cortex seemed to be answered. It only remained for Klüver to confirm some 50 years later that spatial and pattern vision were lost after complete striate ablation, leaving an animal that reacted only to luminous flux.

In the same paper, Schafer reported his efforts to localize hearing in the temporal lobe. Once again he was preceded by Ferrier, who had described a case of total and persistent deafness after a bilateral ablation of the superior temporal gyrus. Schafer was not satisfied. Perhaps the monkey had failed to attend to sound, the test being whether or not the animals responded to various sounds. Schafer removed the superior temporal gyrus in six monkeys; in one case, the whole temporal lobe was removed. None of these animals showed any signs of deafness:

> The animals, even immediately after recovery from the anaesthetic, reacted to slight sounds of an unusual character, such as a smacking of the lips or the rustle of a crumpled newspaper. Some of them were under observation for several months, and there was never any doubt in our minds as to the full possession of their auditory faculties. Nor could the reactions they exhibited to sounds be explained by supposing that they only responded in a reflex manner, for they gave every evidence of understanding the nature of different sounds, such as that caused by turning a door handle or the differences between the footsteps of different people; varying emotions being exhibited according to the anticipations (of food, etc.) which the sounds called forth. (p. 374)

Schafer concluded that the auditory cortex was located in some other part of the cortex. Note that an alternative explanation of his results, and one he does *not* seem to consider, is that the auditory cortex had been removed by ablation of the temporal lobe but that the loss of auditory cortex does not produce deafness.

In the animal with the entire temporal lobe removed, the hippocampus and the medial wall were also ablated. Schafer noted very curious symptoms;

> The condition was marked by loss of intelligence and memory, so that the animals, although they received and responded to impressions from all the senses, appeared to understand very imperfectly the meaning of such impressions. This was not confined to any one sense, and was most evident with visual impressions. For even objects most familiar to the animals were carefully examined, felt, smelt, and tasted, exactly as a monkey will examine an entirely strange object, but much more slowly and deliberately. And once again, after only a few minutes, coming across the same object, exactly the same process of examination would be renewed, as if no recollection of it remained. The disposition also became completely changed; both animals exhibited the utmost greediness, losing all the daintiness which characterises the feeding of monkeys; they also entirely lost their fear of man. (p. 375)

Again, 50 years passed before this curious combination of a lack of fear and the compulsive examination of objects was reproduced and analyzed thoroughly. And once again it was Klüver, working with Bucy, who did the work (see Klüver & Bucy, 1938).

In conclusion, although Schafer did not employ objective behavioral tests that were routinely used in the ablation work of the next century, he must have been a careful observer of animal behavior. Furthermore, he used aseptic precautions in surgery, without which the extent of the lesion is impossible to assess and can hardly be restricted to the intended locus. Finally, he made careful postmortem examinations and sketched the locus of the lesion on a surface view of the cortex.

Munk was also a pioneer in the use of the ablation method, and, like Schafer, his first step was to try to localize the visual cortex, this time in the dog. He found that removal of the caudal part of the suprasylvian and lateral gyri, shown by light stippling in Figure 8.10, led to complete blindness. A unilateral ablation of the same area led to complete blindness in the contralateral eye. (Here I must insert that more refined testing would have revealed that Munk was in error and that whatever the sensory deficit it would be restricted to the hemifield in both eyes, as in the case of the monkey.)

Munk, not content to rest with these results alone, tried to determine the borders of the visual area precisely by resorting to small subtotal lesions that produced field defects. In this way he obtained evidence that the upper half of the retina was represented in the anterior portion of the visual cortex and the lower half of the retina was represented in the posterior portion. Many years later this topography was confirmed by other methods. For the present purpose, the conclusion of greatest interest is that when a subarea (called A1 in Fig. 8.10) was removed, the animal did not appear to recognize any familiar objects. For example, the dog paid no attention to food and ignored a whip that usually produced a withdrawal response. Munk argued that these symptoms were not signs of a sensory loss since the animal avoided obstacles. Instead, he argued that the symptoms were the sign of a "psychic" loss or a memory loss.

The idea of visual memory loss without a *total* sensory loss has historic importance. No one would argue with the proposition that the cortex is involved in higher level functions than simple sensation. When Munk saw his dog unresponsive to familiar objects and yet capable of seeing, he was quick to jump to the conclusion that he had uncovered a pure visual memory loss. The term "psychic" blindness, in contrast to "sensory" blindness, was coined to suggest this higher level loss.

It was natural to regard a recognition of the meaning or significance of objects as the first step beyond sensation of quality, intensity, etc., because that was the prevailing philosophical view. Beginning with Hume, the elements of the mind were regarded as sensory qualities, what Hume called "impressions," and it was thought that these combined to form perception of objects by a process of association and learning. That learning depended on the cortex no one would deny.

It is noteworthy that Munk concluded that the visual cortex mediated *both* sensory and learning functions. A similar conclusion was reached 50 years later by Lashley. The prevailing view for the past 100 years, however, has been that the areas for memory and sensation are separate. The first person to make the separation used neuro-development as the method for subdividing the cortex, as the next section will show.

SENSORY AND ASSOCIATION AREAS DISTINGUISHED: FLECHSIG'S STUDY OF THE DEVELOPMENT OF MYELIN AND CAMPBELL'S STUDIES OF ARCHITECTONICS

Flechsig's Study of the Development of Myelin

It was a neuroembryologist who first provided the basis for an anatomical and spatial separation of sensory and memory functions. Flechsig (1901) classified the various zones of the human cortex into three groups according to the time when the nerve fibers develop myelin. In class I the fibers are conspicuously myelinated at birth. In class III the formation of myelin does not begin until the age of 1 month is reached. Class II consists of zones intermediate in the time of myelin formation. The sensory areas are in class I. The visual cortex, for example, is ranked fourth out of some 40 zones in the order of myelin formation. This temporal sequence is just what would be expected if an infant sees sensory qualities such as color and brightness before these impressions are associated with others to form the perception of objects.

Flechsig also studied the course of fibers which project to the cortex from the internal capsule and came to this far-reaching conclusion: Just the areas in class I are connected by fibers with the centers of the brainstem; the zones in class III only receive fibers from other cortical areas. The cortex was, therefore, divisible into two classes: (1) sensory and motor areas which have connections with the thalamus and brainstem are the first to myelinate, and (2) areas that have connections *only* with other cortical areas. These are the last to develop and were called "association" areas, I suppose, to underscore the fact that their cortical connections were the means by which one cortical area was associated with another.

Architectonics: The Histological Studies of Campbell

With Flechsig's impressive conclusions at the end of the nineteenth century, the story seemed just about complete. One final step was required. By 1900, Campbell in England, and the Vogts and Brodmann in Germany, had already begun their historic inquiry into the laminar organization of cortex (for references to Vogt and Brodmann, see review papers by Sanides, 1970, 1972). It was already known that the cortex was layered and that the layers were different in different zones (see Polyak's 1957 account of the discoveries of Baillarger, whose work was published in the 1840s). This type of analysis (called architectonics) was refined and systematized and reached its peak with the publication of Campbell's monograph on localization of function in 1905. Figure 8.11 shows the difference between the layers in the visual sensory cortex and the adjacent belt of cortex. Next to the exquisite precision with which Campbell could draw architectonic borders, the methods of experimental ablation and the localization of deficits identified in the neurology clinic seemed crude. Campbell criticized the efforts to localize the visual cortex by experimental ablation:

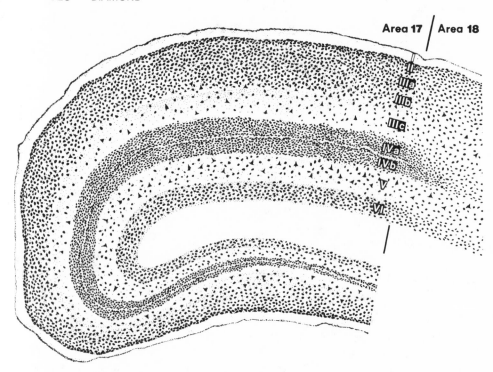

Area 17 / Area 18

FIG. 8.11. Drawing of the visual cortex in the tree shrew, a primitive insectivore with a highly developed visual system. The main purpose of the drawing is to show the layers of the cortex. Note that layer IV is densely populated with small cells and looks much darker than the other layers. Note also the large pyramidal cells in the layers III and V on either side of layer IV. One of the main points of this figure is to show the border between area 17 and area 18. It is this sort of border that led to the architectonic subdivision of neocortex.

Much as we are indebted to experimental methods in helping us to advance our knowledge of the topographical distribution of the cortical visual area, it is fairly obvious that even the most ardent experimenter will refuse to maintain that the means which have been employed hitherto, namely, ablation or destruction of given portions of the brain, can possibly lead to a precise and exact definition of the area. The discrepancies, contradictions, and want of accordance concerning the limits of the area, which appear in the accounts presented by different experimenters, are sufficient proof of the dangerous inaccuracy of ablation methods in determining the mere outside limits of the field; and if, as we have reason for supposing is the case, the cortical visual area be divisible into districts, each having a distinct function to perform, how much more hopeless it is for us to expect to receive much assistance from experiments by ablation in effecting a territorial subdivision of the area! (p. 132)

He concedes in the next paragraph that, "We never shall forget that the labours of these pioneers in an extremely difficult branch of research have served as a

guiding light, leading our knowledge of cortical localization to its present state''
(p. 132).

Campbell was able to identify the visual sensory area in terms of the specific
characteristics of its laminar pattern, all or most of which end abruptly at its
border with the visual "psychic" area. There is little or no chance that a lesion in
man would correspond exactly to these borders, and there is even less likelihood
that an experimental lesion of the extrastriate belt would cause no damage,
vascular and otherwise, to the striate cortex.

Concerning the function of the visual sensory area, Campbell had little reason
to question the prevailing view that total blindness results from bilateral lesions
and that crossed hemianopsia results from unilateral destruction of the visual
cortex. It had not escaped his notice that some visual centers, notably the superi-
or colliculus, remain preserved after ablation of visual sensory cortex. However,
these tectal centers, which may be significant in a lowly frog, could hardly
account for much vision in mammals where the cortex and lateral geniculate
body have assumed the upper hand.

After a criticism of the pathological method as a way of localizing the sensory
area, Campbell concluded that lesions of the calcarine fissure (striate cortex)
produce lasting hemianopsia. His grounds for attributing a "psychic" function
to the extrastriate belt is much shakier. To be sure there was Munk's dog and
countless clinical patients with reading disabilities, spatial disorientation, and the
inability to recognize and interpret objects by sight; but the locus of the lesions
which produce these symptoms in man remained a question. He argued that since
the calcarine area is solely devoted to the reception of primary visual stimuli, the
mere existence of a second area placed in such contiguity suggests the likelihood
that it is concerned with the sorting out and further elaboration of these stimuli.

Campbell was also deeply impressed by Flechsig's embryological results. In
the visual system only the fibers of the lateral geniculate are myelinated at birth,
and these are confined to the visual sensory or calcarine area.

> Needless to say this is in agreement with physiological fact; for in early infancy the
> tracts for the conveyance of visual impulses to the primary cortical centre are
> obviously active, but visuo-psychic processes being in abeyance, there is no de-
> mand for association fibres. (p. 145)

In summary, Campbell begins with the behavioral or psychological distinction between simple sensory processes and some higher level association process. He finds two areas of the occipital lobe: a calcarine or striate area which
receives fibers from the lateral geniculate, the very fibers that myelinate first; and
a belt of cortex adjacent to the striate area which presumably receives no fibers
from the thalamus. It seemed natural to him to assign the simpler functions to the
striate area and the more complex functions to the surrounding belt. We need
only add that integration involving several modalities was assigned to the temporal lobe. While Campbell's efforts were concentrated on the study of man and

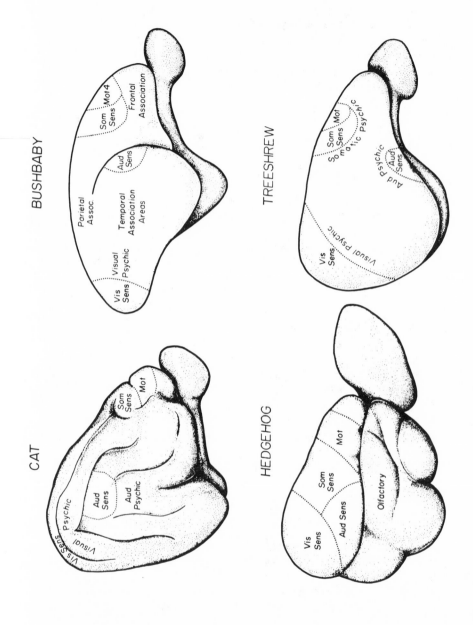

BUSHBABY

Parietal Assoc.

Som Sens Mot

Frontal Association

Aud Sens

Temporal Association Areas

Visual Psychic

Vis Sens

TREESHREW

Som Sens Mot

Somatic Psychic

Aud Psychic

Aud Sens

Visual Psychic

Vis Sens

CAT

Som Sens Mot

Aud Sens

Aud Psychic

Vis Sens

Visual Psychic

HEDGEHOG

Mot

Som Sens

Olfactory

Vis Sens

Aud Sens

higher primates, he devoted one section of his monograph to his comparative findings. I have tried to depict his chief ideas in the diagram shown in Figure 8.12. First, I have selected species that would be most useful in the present context, and, second, I have made some slight modifications more in keeping with present-day evidence. The most notable change is that I reversed the locations, according to Campbell, of the auditory ''psychic'' and auditory sensory areas. The term ''association'' cortex was applied to those areas where several modalities converge as well as to the belt adjacent to each sensory area.

EVOLUTION OF CORTEX

Elliot-Smith's Distinction Between Olfactory Cortex Including Hippocampus and Neocortex

In this section, as in the earlier ones, I will try to convey a sense of the history of the field by describing the contributions of a few pioneers. It is not hard to find the suitable starting point in Elliot-Smith's seminal research.

Elliot-Smith was born in Australia in 1873, and he took advantage of the indigenous marsupials and monotremes to achieve his major contribution—the concept of neocortex. The research he began in Australia shifted to Cambridge, England, and by 1900 his ideas of the origin of the cortex were widely known in Great Britain and throughout the scientific world. Eventually he became Professor and Chairman of Anatomy at University College in London. A symposium in honor of Elliot-Smith was held recently in London on the occasion of the hundredth anniversary of his birth. The reader can get a first-hand view of his life from the first chapter of the proceedings of the symposium, which was written by a former student, Prof. Lord Zuckerman (Zuckerman, 1973).

Elliot-Smith's (1910) inquiry started with a curious and puzzling difference between the brains of the Australian and Eutherian mammals. In placental mammals the cortex of the two hemispheres is connected by a conspicuous fiber tract—the corpus callosum. The Australian mammals do have a commissure in the position of the corpus callosum, but its fibers originate just from cells of the hippocampus. The hippocampal commissure provided Elliot-Smith with the key to understanding the phyletic origin of the hippocampus, and this, in turn, led to the concept of the neocortex. This argument deserves greater scrutiny especially since it has not been given the attention it merits.

FIG. 8.12. Sensory and association cortex in four mammals according to Campbell (1905). Note several points made by these drawings of the lateral surface of the cerebral hemisphere: 1) In lower mammals, such as a hedgehog, there is little association cortex, while in advanced mammals, such as a bushbaby, there is a great deal of association cortex. 2) According to Campbell, a ''modality specific'' psychic area lies adjacent to each sensory area.

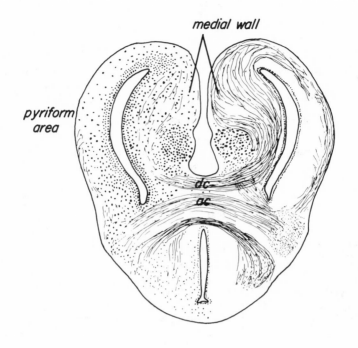

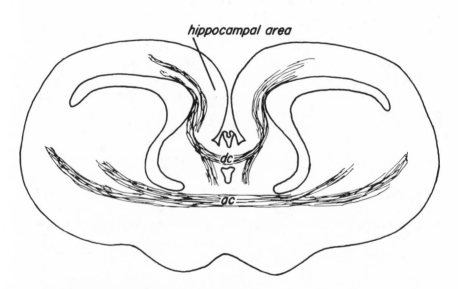

FIG. 8.13–8.16. Comparison of these four figures shows the similarity in different vertebrates of the positions of the dorsal commissure in relation to the anterior commissure; and even more important is the idea that the dorsal commissure originates from the medial wall which in mammals develops into the hippocampus.

FIG. 8.13. Frontal section through the forebrain of the frog at the level of the anterior commissure.

FIG. 8.14. Frontal section through the forebrain of the reptile at the level of the anterior commissure.

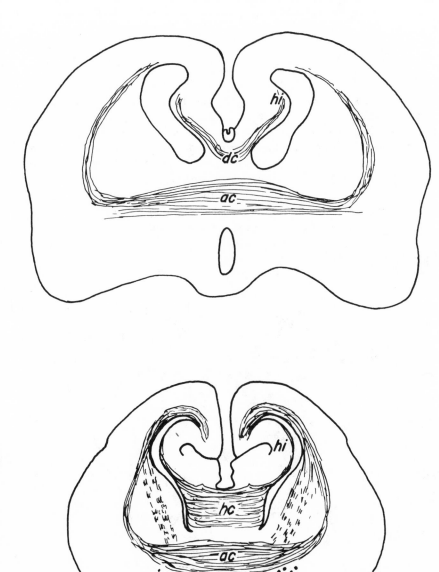

FIG. 8.15.   Frontal section through the forebrain of the fetal monotreme at the level of the anterior commissure.

FIG. 8.16.   Frontal section through the forebrain of the marsupial at the level of the anterior commissure.

First, it is necessary to review the chief conclusions of comparative neurology available to Elliot-Smith. There is no cortex covering the cerebral hemispheres in lower vertebrates. Instead of layers of cells and fibers on the surface, the cerebrum of a salamander, for example, consists of a mix of cells and fibers, mostly of *olfactory* origin. However, as is shown in Figures 8.13 and 8.14, even in these lowly vertebrates, a dorsal commissure (labeled "dc" in Figs. 8.13 and 8.14) connects the medial walls of the two hemispheres. The foetal monotreme provides the missing link: The first part of the argument is its dorsal commissure looks just like that of an amphibian's or reptile's (see Fig. 8.15). The similarity between reptile and foetal monotreme is apparent from a comparison of Figures 8.14 and 8.15, and in both species the dorsal commissure arises from the cortex of the medial wall. The second part of the argument is as follows: when the platypus develops into an adult, the cortex of the medial wall develops into a hippocampus with all of the characteristics that mark this structure (see Fig.

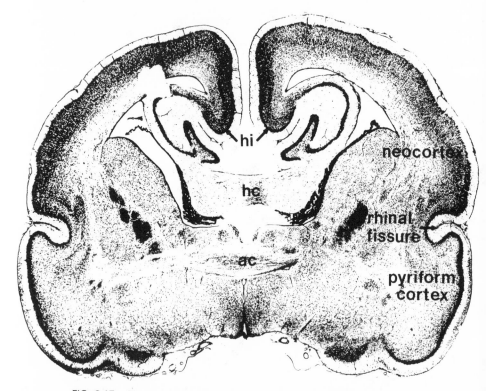

FIG. 8.17. Photomicrograph of a frontal section through the forebrain of the opossum. This section was stained by the Nissl method to reveal cell bodies. Notice the position of the hippocampus (hi), the hippocampal commissure (hc), and the anterior commissure (ac). Also notice that the rhinal fissure divides the neocortex from the pyriform cortex.

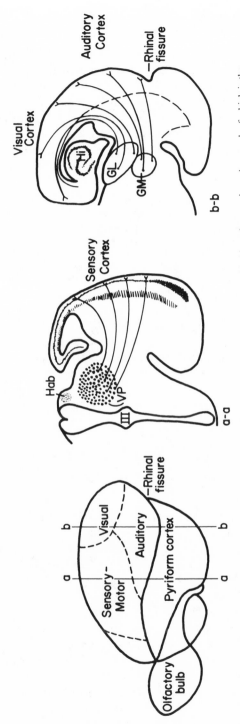

FIG. 8.18. Diagrams from Elliot-Smith (1910) to show how the neocortex in a primitive animal is divided into three main regions each of which is the target of a thalamic nucleus. The middle drawing is a section through the brain of an embryo and illustrates how the thalmic fibers take the shortest route to their target in the cortex. Thus, the position of the auditory or visual cortex is determined by the position of the lateral geniculate (GL) or medial geniculate (GM) nuclei. (Abbreviations: Hab, Habenula; VP, ventral posterior nucleus.)

335

8.16). Elliot-Smith concluded that the hippocampus must therefore be homologous to the medial wall of the early cerebrum, and further, that the hippocampus is phyletically old and should be classified with the rest of the olfactory portions of the cerebrum. The pyriform area, shown in Figures 8.17 and 8.18, was already classed as phyletically old since it receives fibers directly from the olfactory tract. Also, the laminar structure of the pyriform cortex is primitive compared to the dorsal cortex. The dorsal cortex appears to be the special achievement of mammalian evolution, and this concept deserves a special name. Elliot-Smith called the dorsal cortex the neo-cortex.

It is natural to ask, "What are the connections of the neocortex and how do they differ from the connections of the olfactory cortex?" Elliot-Smith showed that the neocortex was the target of the three main nonolfactory pathways after each path had made an obligatory relay in the thalamus. Figure 8.18 is taken from one of his most important papers to show the relation between the relay nuclei in the thalamus and their cortical targets. The neocortex is thus identified with the thalamus and with the visual, auditory, and somatic sensory pathways that relay in the thalamus.

The distinction between the neocortex and the olfactory cortex has significance for understanding the further development of the cortex in higher mammals and primates in particular. The olfactory cortex remains stable while the neocortex increases enormously in higher primates. Further, it is not the sensory areas of the neocortex, but the association areas intercalated between sensory areas that expand the most in higher primates and this idea will become clear in the following sections.

Herrick's View of the Functions of the Olfactory Cortex and the Expansion of the Neocortex in Higher Primates

The origin of the neocortex in mammals set the stage for the most remarkable transformation in all of evolutionary history—the expansion of neocortex in higher primates. Figure 8.19 is a diagram showing the relation between neocortex, pyriform cortex or area, and hippocampus or hippocampal area in four vertebrates: (1) an amphibian, (2) a reptile, (3) a lower mammal such as the hedgehog, and (4) man. Why does the neocortex show an amazing enlargement and differentiation in mammals? This question was addressed by another pioneer in the field of comparative neurology, C. Judson Herrick, who was on the faculty of the University of Chicago from 1900 to 1940. His brother, also a comparative neurologist, founded in 1891 the *Journal of Comparative Neurology*, which remains the leading American journal in the field.

Herrick (1933) thought that the answer to his question must lie in the relationship between the functions of the olfactory cortex, i.e., hippocampus plus pyriform cortex, and the functions of the neocortex. The sense of smell as an

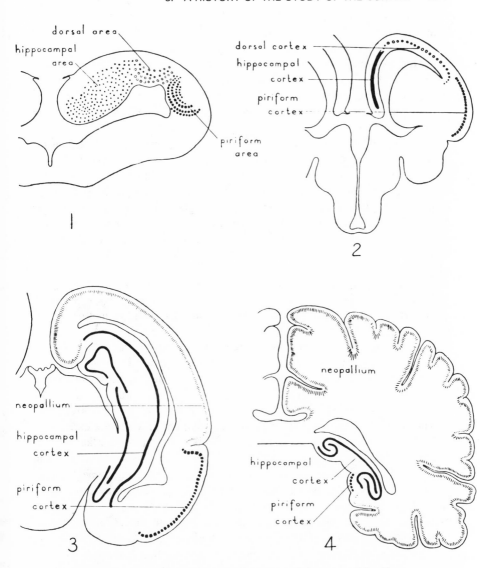

FIG. 8.19.   Diagrams showing approximately the relative extent of the olfactory
and non-olfactory pallial fields as seen in cross-sections of various vertebrate
brains. 1) *Necturus,* with entire pallial field olfactory; 2) the box-tortoise, *Cistudo,*
with differentiated cortex, all of which is under olfactory influence; 3) the
opossum, *Didelphis,* with olfactory cortex (hippocampus and piriform) more extensive than non-olfactory cortex (neopallium); 4) human, with enlargement of
neopallium and reduction of olfactory cortex.

exteroceptor is most important in those vital activities of feeding and mating, and provides vertebrates in general with warnings about the presence of enemies. However, the source of an odor cannot be located except by tracking intensity in the course of locomotion. In contrast, a visual or auditory stimulus instantly provides the exact locus of a distant source. Thus, for the important purpose of localization, the sense of smell must always operate in conjunction with other senses.

This functional difference between olfaction and vision is reflected in the neural organization of the two systems. In the visual pathway the precise spatial organization at any one center is projected topographically to each successive center with the result that a map of the receptor surface is projected upon the visual cortex. The olfactory pathway seems organized according to different principles. The projections are diffuse, and each center for synaptic transmission is designed to maximize the opportunity for amplifying or intensifying the message.

> These arrangements suggest that the olfactory excitations serve chiefly as activators of complex sensorimotor systems whose pattern of performance is determined primarily by other senses with sharper localization. (Herrick, 1933, p. 10)

To put this abstract concept into concrete terms, consider that a fish has the visuomotor apparatus either to follow or to avoid another fish; the choice of sensory motor mechanism depends upon whether the object is a desirable source of food or a potential predator; and it is the olfactory apparatus that makes the choice. In behavioral terms, the olfactory apparatus serves as the motivation.

The argument thus far leads to the conclusion that in lower vertebrates the olfactory cerebrum activates the visuomotor reflexes in the tectum and the auditory or somatic reflexes residing in other centers of the brainstem. Now we can analyze the original issue of cortical evolution, by dividing it into two questions: (1) Why does the olfactory cerebrum expand and differentiate from the reptile stage to the stage of early mammals, where it reaches the peak of its development? (2) After the olfactory brain has culminated in the differentiation of hippocampus and pyriform area, why does the olfactory cortex remain stable and the neocortex expand? The clue to the answer of the first question is that the cortex originated only when the nonolfactory systems began to penetrate the olfactory system. The cortex thus provided new opportunities for the interaction of motivational and cognitive neural mechanisms and permitted the olfactory centers to outgrow their exclusive connection with external olfactory cues. In other words, the capacity of olfactory cortex to activate the sensory mechanisms represented in the early neocortex is no longer tied to external olfactory cues. Perhaps internal visceral cues become more significant; probably the internal state of an organism as reflected by the hormonal system, for example, becomes more significant. This freedom from smell is shown by the fact that the hippocampus is not reduced to a vestigial organ in those mammalian lines that cannot smell at all—for example, in whales and dolphins.

The second question can be answered in this way: Once the neocortex was established, the stage was set for development along two separate lines: (1) An increase in the precision of the system—for example, an increased precision in the topographic representation of the retina; and (2) in a later stage of development, the evolution of a new kind of cortex, the association areas, which provided a basis for advancement in memory, learning and insight.

In summary, Herrick showed that the evolution of the cortex turns on the relationship between olfactory and nonolfactory fibers. He relied on the discoveries of Elliot-Smith in order to classify the hippocampus as "olfactory." Herrick argued that the functions of the olfactory cortex are not limited to the sense of smell alone but include appetite and motivation. The juxtaposition of appetitive and cognitive functions led first to the development of olfactory or old cortex and second to the development of neocortex.

LeGros Clark's Study of Evolution of Thalamus and Hypothalamus

The close anatomical connection between the *neo*cortex and the thalamus suggested that the evolution of the thalamus should parallel the evolution of the neocortex. The close relation functionally between olfactory cortex and visceral activities suggested an anatomical connection between olfactory cortex and hypothalamus. Both leads were pursued by Sir Wilfred LeGros Clark (1932a), who undertook a comparative study of both thalamus and hypothalamus. LeGros Clark was Professor and Chairman of the Department of Anatomy at Oxford University and was a friend and colleague of Elliot-Smith. LeGros Clark showed that there is no thalamus proper in the earliest vertebrates. Instead, the diencephalon, as shown in Figure 8.20, consists mainly of two divisions: a dorsal division, or epithalamus; and a ventral division, or hypothalamus. The hypothalamus lies in close connection with the pituitary. As vertebrates evolved, the thalamus proper differentiated and developed in the region between the epithalamus and hypothalamus, presumably as a result of increasing penetration of visual, auditory and somatic fibers. Eventually, a separate center for each sensory pathway differentiated: the medial geniculate body for the auditory pathway, the lateral geniculate body for the visual pathway, and the ventral posterior nucleus for the somatic pathway (see Fig. 8.21).

While the dorsal diencephalon, specifically the thalamus, is connected to the neocortex, the ventral diencephalon, specifically the hypothalamus, is connected to the old olfactory cortex. This connection between the olfactory cortex and the hypothalamus led to doubts that the function of the olfactory cortex and the hippocampus, in particular, was simply olfactory and supported Herrick's views. In order to understand the significance of this connection, it is necessary to

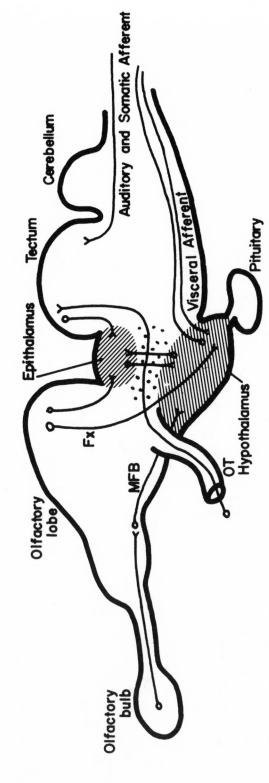

FIG. 8.20. Diagram of the lateral view of a generalized lower vertebrate showing the connections of the diencephalon. The diencephalon is shown by shading; the ventral part is the hypothalamus and the dorsal part is the epithalamus. Note first that the hypothalamus receives visceral afferents from the body and has reciprocal descending projections. The hypothalamus also receives two main fiber tracts from the telencephalon. One is the fornix (Fx) which originates in the medial wall or hippocampal area, and the second is the medial-forebrain bundle (MFB). Notice the reciprocal connections between hypothalamus and eipthalamus.

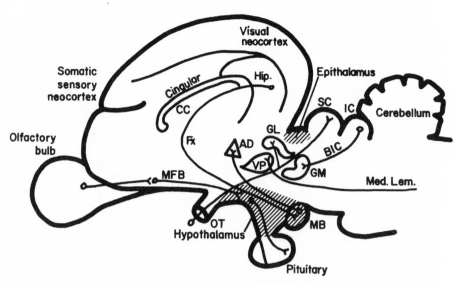

FIG. 8.21.   Diagram to show the connections of the diencephalon in an advanced mammal such as the cat. The chief point is the similarities and differences between the lower vertebrate and the mammal. The hypothalamus and epithalamus (again shown shaded with diagonal lines) continue to have the same connections with the forebrain. For example, note the fornix (Fx) projecting from the hippocampus (Hip) to the mammillary bodies (MB) of the hypothalamus. The chief difference is the differentiation of a number of nuclei between the epithalamus and hypothalamus. These nuclei constitute the dorsal thalamus. (Abbreviations: AD, anterior dorsal nucleus; BIC, brachium of the inferior colliculus; CC, corpus callosum; GL, lateral geniculate body; GM, medial geniculate body; IC, inferior colliculus; MFB, midforebrain bundle; OT, optic tract; SC, superior colliculus; VP, ventral posterior nucleus.)

understand the significance of the other connections of the hypothalamus. In the hypothalamus there terminate fibers that carry sensory impulses from the viscera such as the blood vessels, heart, stomach, intestines, etc. Further, the close relationship between the hypothalamus and pituitary suggests that together they provide a mechanism for regulating and controlling the entire endocrine system including the rhythm of sexual life and appetite.

The hypothalamus may be regarded as a part of the diencephalon which, by its nervous connections and through the direct liaison which it established with the hormonic regulatory system via the pituitary, mediates the integration of visceral impulses and plays an essential part in the control of the internal milieu of the organism. . . . Thus, it stands in direct contrast to the functional implications of the dorsal part of the diencephalon. While the latter is the recipient of impulses on the basis of which the organism may develop an awareness of its *external* milieu and adapts its overt behaviour accordingly, the former is the recipient of impulses on the basis of which the organism may develop an awareness of its *internal* organic activities and through which sensory experiences are endowed with an affective tone. (LeGros Clark, 1932a, pp. 413–414)

Thus, the diencephalon seems to be divisible into two functional parts, perception of the viscera and perception of the outside world. The former may be considered the basis of emotion; the latter, the basis of cognition. This distinction will be considered in the next section. It comes as no surprise that, with the evolution of the higher mammals, the dorsal division (the thalamus, in particular) expands greatly, corresponding to the expansion of the neocortex.

To be more specific and more detailed about connections of the hypothalamus, I have redrawn and simplified some of LeGros Clark's charts to show that the hypothalamus receives two tracts from the olfactory areas of the cerebrum. One pathway, the medial forebrain bundle, labeled MFB in Figures 8.20 and 8.21, passes from the ventral and lateral olfactory centers of the cerebrum to the hypothalamus. The second pathway, called the fornix (see Fig. 8.20 and 8.21), is the major efferent tract of the hippocampus. In addition to these two tracts, the hypothalamus is shown to receive sensory messages from the viscera. More recent studies using ablation or electrical stimulation have shown that the hypothalamus contains centers for hunger, thirst, sex, and emotions (see Hess, 1957).

Of course it is the efferent pathways of the hypothalamus that give it the power to act upon and modify the autonomic nervous system (the motor component of the visceral system). For the present purpose, one efferent path, noted by LeGros Clark, is of special interest because it does not appear to be a motor pathway. That pathway is the projection to the anterior nuclei of the thalamus. Since the thalamus projects to the cortex, this path gives the hypothalamus an opportunity to influence the cortex in much the same way that the eye can influence the cortex.

We might well ask in what part of the cortex does the anterior nucleus project. That question was also answered by LeGros Clark (1932a). Using the method of retrograde degeneration, he showed that the anterior nuclei project to the cingulate cortex which lies in the medial wall above the corpus callosum (see Fig. 8.21, LeGros Clark & Boggon, 1933). In conclusion, LeGros Clark showed that there was a visceral path that can be regarded as a sensory tract in the same way that the visual path is sensory. The visceral pathway projects to the hypothalamus which, in turn, projects to the anterior nuclei, and these nuclei constitute the final link to the cingulate cortex.

Emotion Viewed as Another Sensory Pathway

The purpose of this section is to relate the anatomy of the hypothalamus and hippocampus to theories of emotion. In the nineteenth century, long before

LeGros Clark's anatomical studies, William James (1890) tried to explain emotion as a sensory path just as seeing is explained by the visual pathway to cortex. James argued that the feeling of emotion was only the sensation of the viscera, and to persuade the reader he pictured the following sequence of events: (1) A lion escapes from his cage; (2) this dangerous situation is perceived by an observer; (3) the reflex response to the stimulus evokes a contraction of the visceral muscles, a change in the beating of the heart, and all of the changes concomitant with the flow of adrenalin; (4) sensory receptors that are present in visceral organs are excited by the activity, and impulses are conveyed back to the cortex; and (5) the sensation of fear corresponds to the point in time that the impulses reach the cortex. The last event in the sequence is just like the sensation of red resulting from the excitation of the visual cortex.

James did not say what part of the cortex received emotional impulses, but the knowledge of the pathways gained by LeGros Clark provided an answer to this question. Visceral afferents reach the hypothalamus, which, in turn, projects to the anterior nuclei of the thalamus, and the anterior nuclei relay the message to the cingulate cortex on the medial wall above the corpus callosum.

The role of the cingulate cortex in emotion was carried one further step in 1937 by a Cornell anatomist, James Papez. Papez (1937) started out by showing the dual nature of emotion: It is a way of acting or behaving and a way of feeling. The former can be called emotional expression; the latter, emotional experience. A number of experiments led Papez to regard the hypothalamus as the basis for emotional expression. Bard had shown that an animal without a cortex showed an excessive rage reaction as long as the hypothalamus was preserved (Bard & Mountcastle, 1948). Not only was the rage more intense, but it was also more readily elicited and, in fact, could be provoked by an otherwise innocuous and harmless stimulus. Since the rage was inappropriate, it was called the "sham rage." Sham rage is abolished by destruction of the hypothalamus which is the sort of evidence that led Papez to conclude that the hypothalamus is the basis for emotional *expression*. Additional evidence that the hypothalamus is the substrate for emotional expression comes from electrical stimulation of the hypothalamus in awake cats. For the conscious feeling of emotion, Papez felt a "higher" center, specifically the cortex, was required. The notion that consciousness is a higher level of organization than expression goes back at least as far as Bell, and is one of the dominant themes in the history of neuropsychology. The pathways discovered by LeGros Clark provided Papez with the cortical area he required, the cingulate cortex. Papez pointed out that the cingulate cortex could be viewed as the basis for emotional feeling without necessarily subscribing to the "peripheral" theory of James. Since the cingulate cortex receives input from the hypothalamus and since that activity can be initiated by some central path, it follows that the cingulate cortex is not entirely dependent on sensory impulses originating in visceral receptors. Sensory areas of the neocortex, such as the visual area, also have access to the cingulate cortex by way of cortico-cortical fibers. In this way a cognitive event, such as perceiving that the lion had escaped, could be conveyed to the cingulate cortex where the coldly cognitive perception might gain affective quality. The cingulate cortex is known to project to the hippocampus, and the major efferent projection of the hippocampus, the fornix, terminates in the hypothalamus. The hypothalamus, in turn, can activate the autonomic and endocrine systems to produce the emotional expression. At the same time, the hypothalamus projects to the anterior nuclei and the circuit or neural circle is completed by the projection from the anterior nuclei back to the cingulate. Thus, Papez's circuit not only shows how thought or perception can produce emotion, but also shows how the bodily expression of emotion and the intrinsic activity of the hypothalamus can achieve conscious feeling. Here he takes advantage of LeGros Clark's description of the pathways from the viscera to the hypothalamus and from the hypothalamus to the cortex.

It is appropriate to ask where the cingulate gyrus fits into the subdivision of cortex into olfactory cortex and neocortex or nonolfactory cortex. As often happens in our efforts to divide the world into classes, there are instances that defy the classification system and fall right at the border. The laminar organization of the cingulate cortex is intermediate between pyriform cortex and neocortex. It is therefore not easy to judge whether the cingulate cortex is neocortex or old cortex, and it has been called a transitional area.

ABLATION STUDIES FROM 1929–1942: LASHLEY AND KLÜVER

With the advent of the histological methods for staining cells and fibers and for staining degenerating fibers, the ablation method was overshadowed by architectonic parcellation and by the investigation of connections. The ablation method made a comeback with Lashley's use of objective tests in the 1920s and 1930s. A second pioneer, Heinrich Klüver, had a special genius for being able to reveal the sensory and intellectual abilities of animals before and after surgery. Lashley's and Klüver's careers overlapped at the University of Chicago for a period of years. Klüver remained at the University of Chicago until his retirement, while Lashley developed a center for the study of primate behavior in Florida under the auspices of Harvard University.

Lashley's Studies of the Cortex and Intelligence

This section is devoted to Lashley's ablation studies of the cortex in the rat. Lashley was a pioneer in combining the method of ablation with objective tests of learning and sensory discrimination. Earlier researchers such as Munk observed the behavior of the experimental animal in more or less ordinary, everyday situations which were often a matter of accident. The dog did not seem to recognize the whip so it appeared to have suffered a memory loss, or the dog avoided obstacles so it did not suffer a sensory loss.

To trace the history of the objective tests of learning and sensory discrimination we have to go back to the 1870s when Munk, Schafer, and Ferrier were studying the visual cortex in the monkey. During that period an American psychologist at Columbia University, Thorndike (1911) initiated a study of the evolution of intelligence. He argued that the ability of different species could be compared and contrasted if all could be given the same test. It was necessary then to invent a test that was more or less independent of species-specific behaviors, and yet reflected the ability of the animal to take advantage of experience in adapting to the environment. Such a test was the puzzle box. A cat or a monkey was locked up in a cage that could be opened by pressing a lever or two levers in succession. The first time an animal was placed in the box, pressing the lever was a matter of chance; after several sessions, the animal would learn to go directly to the lever, release the latch and escape the cage. The reward for this effort might simply be food placed outside the cage. A score for learning is easy to obtain; just record the time it takes in each successive day to escape. Thus, the test has the important virtue of yielding an objective score. Thorndike hoped that there would be marked species differences in the learning ability of a monkey, with a great amount of cortex, as compared to that of a rat, for example, with very little cortex.

Lashley (1929) was impressed with the promise that Thorndike's tests held for the study of animal intelligence. Instead of just comparing species, however, he felt that the question of whether intelligence and learning ability were localized in the association areas of the neocortex could be answered more directly by experimental ablation. He was aware of the fact that the available clinical evidence did not point to a clear answer to the question of the localization of intelligence in man. Most neurologists conceded that deficits in language were associated with particular areas of the association cortex (Nielsen & Fitzgibbon, 1936). Some neurologists believed that there was a single unitary intellectual ability, such as the power to abstract or the power of attention and that this unitary ability was the function of the entire cortex (Goldstein, 1939). Their evidence was that dementia was related to the amount of cortical damage and not the locus. Other neurologists held that the frontal lobe had special significance.

Part of the problem was simply a confusion about the meaning of intelligence. For example, does intelligence include memory and, if so, what contribution should memory make to the total score in comparison with verbal or numerical ability? The major contribution to the solution to the question of the nature of intelligence was made in 1927 by the British psychologist, Charles Spearman. Spearman (1927) proved that it was not necessary to decide in advance whether measures of memory or of various cognitive abilities provide a better test for intelligence. When a hodgepodge of different tests, including tests for memory, spatial ability, numerical ability and language facility, was given to a population, the results always showed a positive correlation between the tests. A positive correlation of course means that, for the most part, individuals scoring higher on one test also score higher on a second test and a third test and so on. Spearman argued that general intelligence could be defined as whatever it is that is common to a hodgepodge of tests that correlate with each other, e.g., whatever it is that makes an individual who scores high on language also score high on mathematics.

Lashley saw the implications of Spearman's ideas for the study of animal intelligence. What was necessary was a battery of tests of the sort invented by Thorndike: tests of maze leaning, visual pattern discrimination tests, tests for learning to escape from a latch box—in short, tests that could be given to animals yet seem to bear some kinship to those used in the studies of the abilities of man. When a battery of such tests was given to a population of normal rats, Lashley found no correlation between the tests. Either normal rats do not differ in intelligence or the tests were not sensitive to individual differences. However, after lesions of the neocortex, a strikingly positive correlation was found. Now the chief question of the inquiry could be addressed: Was the degree of the deficit a function of the locus of the cortical lesion or the size of the lesion irrespective of the locus? Lashley found that the severity of the deficit was correlated with the extent of the lesion irrespective of the locus.

Perhaps this correlation was spurious and did not reflect a common function of cortex. For example, a big lesion is more likely than a small lesion to destroy a number of sensory areas in which case the deficit might simply reflect the sum of several separate sensory deficits. A rat might be able to learn a maze without visual cues, but would be handicapped if *both* visual and kinesthetic cues were eliminated. To test this idea Lashley blinded some rats by removing the eyes and then made lesions of the visual cortex. He argued that if a learning deficit could be produced by ablation of the visual cortex in a blinded animal, the deficit could not be attributed to a sensory loss. The results showed that learning deficits did result from visual cortex lesions in peripherally blinded animals. Lashley therefore concluded that the deficit was a general dementia and not a combination of sensory deficits in various modalities. In summary, Lashley believed that his experiments showed the equipotentiality of all architectonic subdivisions, both sensory and association. This does not mean that he believed that sensory and association areas were identical. He conceded that sensory areas were specialized to deal with sensory discrimination; but with respect to higher intellectual functions, memory and intelligence, all areas were equal and the cortex functioned as a single mass.

Klüver's Studies of Cortical Blindness and Psychic Blindness

Klüver was not content just to show whether or not an animal was capable of a particular sensory discrimination. He tried to answer the question: What has an animal learned as a result of a particular sort of training? He wondered if training would have an influence on events beyond the specific conditions of the training procedure. For example, if an animal were trained to prefer a circle and avoid a square, would the animal also prefer an ellipse to a square? Would the trained animal reject a triangle or a pentagon?

To answer these questions Klüver (1933) invented a method for testing the equivalence of stimuli. To continue with our example, suppose a monkey is trained to select the circle when paired with a square. The training consists of receiving reward when a placard bearing the correct pattern is pulled in with a string. After the animal has achieved a high level of performance, other pairs of stimuli are intercalated between regular training trials. For example, one test trial may consist of an ellipse and an triangle. The animal receives reward whatever his choice, and its response is recorded.

The application of this method is best illustrated by a study of the visual cortex in the monkey (Klüver, 1942). Training and testing of an animal for the equivalence of stimuli was followed by a large ablation of the occipital lobe which included the striate cortex. After the operation, the animal was tested and retrained if necessary. Here is one of the best examples of the power of Klüver's analysis. Before the ablation of the striate cortex, the monkeys were trained to choose the brightest of two stimuli. In a test of equivalence the animal will select a small, bright light over a larger, dimmer light even when the amounts of energy from the two stimuli are equal. After the ablation the monkey showed some deficit on the brightness habit, but the number of correct responses exceeded chance right from the beginning, and, with some training, the animal learned to choose the brighter light at the same level of performance achieved before surgery. Then came the test for equivalent stimuli. When the area of the brighter light was decreased so that the total amount of light energy coming from each member of the pair was equated, the discriminatory habit broke down. The animal had not learned the brightness habit in the strict sense of the term *brightness* and was in fact reacting to the total luminous flux. Whereas the normal animal has the concept, so to speak, of brightness, the monkey without the visual cortex was reduced to the level of a photoelectric cell capable only of registering light energy.

Klüver's studies of the visual cortex were characterized by the meticulous analysis of the deficit. In his equally influential studies of the temporal cortex, the symptoms were more bizarre and much more difficult to interpret. This study was published in collaboration with the neurosurgeon, Paul Bucy, in 1938 (Klüver & Bucy, 1938). First, it is necessary to call attention to the fact that the entire temporal lobe was removed bilaterally, with the result that the hippocampus on the medial wall was extirpated bilaterally as well as the neocortex on the lateral wall of the temporal lobe. Among a number of distinguishable symptoms that resulted from this lesion, the animals showed a strange placidity and an absence of fear in circumstances which would provoke intense distress in a normal animal. For example, normal animals show a marked fear of snakes, whereas an animal deprived of the temporal lobe tries to put a snake in its mouth. Further, the animals deprived of the temporal lobe had a tendency to examine every small item in their environment, picking them up one at a time and putting each in their mouth. Klüver showed the bizarre nature of this trait by presenting one animal with an endless number of objects such as nails, nuts, bolts, marbles, etc. The animal's desire to examine each object with its mouth seemed to be insatiable. In addition to these oral tendencies, the placidity and the compulsive examination of the environment, all of the monkeys showed heightened sexual activity.

A final symptom seemed to be unrelated to the emotional changes, but could be related to the tendency to pick up all small objects and examine them. Several animals were trained to discriminate between a number of pairs of visual stimuli, e.g., to select a circle and avoid a square. These animals lost the habit as a result of the operation but were able to relearn. In one case, training was started only after the removal of the temporal lobe. This animal learned finally to discriminate between a circle and a square, but only with great difficulty and after hundreds of trials. All operated animals showed the same generalization or equivalence after achieving the habit. For example, in the case of the circle and the square, any curved shape or pattern was preferred to an angular pattern. While Klüver viewed this symptom as "psychic" blindness, he recognized the practical difficulty of trying to separate a pure memory loss from a sensory disturbance. He felt it was especially hard to tell to what extent the deficit could be attributed to memory and to what extent it could be attributed to scotoma. In a similar vein, Klüver argued that the diagnosis of agnosia or memory loss in the neurological clinic should be viewed with some skepticism.

> A review of the clinical literature indicates that the more carefully a case is studied the more difficult it may be to decide whether there is really an "agnostic" or merely a "visual" defect, that is, whether the variety of "agnostic" symptoms can be reduced to disturbances of "elementary" or "higher" visual functions. (Klüver & Bucy, p. 61)

Klüver recognized that the full set of symptoms did not appear to constitute a single syndrome and probably were the result of removing separate areas of the cortex. The subdivision that comes first to mind is between the olfactory cortex on the medial wall and the neocortex on the lateral wall. The psychic blindness or loss of memory for visual habits seemed more likely to be the result of ablating the temporal neocortex than the temporal old cortex. But why a lesion of the temporal lobe would produce "psychic" blindness was not readily explained, the issue being the connection between the temporal lobe and the visual cortex. Klüver would expect to find cortico-cortical fibers from the striate area to whichever area was responsible for visual memory and association. We now know, chiefly from the studies of Mortimer Mishkin (1972), that there is a discrete part of the inferotemporal cortex, the ablation of which produces deficits in visual learning and visual memory. Since 1937 considerable research has been devoted to uncovering the nature of this deficit and to determining the exact locus of the lesion required to produce the deficit. Again from the work of Mishkin and his colleagues, we know that the striate cortex projects to the inferotemporal lobe by a series of relays. If this path is sectioned, the deficit is produced.

Klüver attributed the bizarre changes in sexual behavior and the emotional placidity to the removal of the hippocampus and pyriform cortex. This conclusion initiated an inquiry that continues to thrive to the present day. For our purpose it is imperative to consider how the symptoms would fit with the concepts of Papez. Since Papez's circuit was interrupted, we might expect that there would be a loss of emotional feeling, and perhaps the absence of response to stimuli normally evoking fear reflects just this sort of deficit. At the same time, Klüver's results are difficult to reconcile with studies of Bard and Mountcastle (1948) at Johns Hopkins University. These researchers, using the cat as a subject, found evidence that the cortex serves to *inhibit* the hypothalamus and, thus, the expression of emotion. That is to say, when cortical influence on the hypothalamus had been removed, the cat showed an excessive and inappropriate rage reaction, referred to as "sham rage." Since the hippocampus is the source of the most conspicuous tract that descends from the cerebrum and terminates in the hypothalamus, it was reasonable for Bard and Mountcastle to expect that removing the hippocampus alone would increase emotional expression by releasing the hypothalamus from inhibitory influences. Bard and Mountcastle found some support for this idea in their experiments published in 1947. At the risk of oversimplification, while Klüver found placidity after removal of the medial wall in the monkey, Bard and Mountcastle found just the opposite.

The issues raised by the differences in results of Bard and Mountcastle and those of Klüver have not been resolved to the present time, and it seems likely that there are species differences especially between the primate and the cat.

ELECTROPHYSIOLOGICAL STUDIES OF THE CORTEX

That changes in voltage reflect nervous activity was discovered many years ago, and this relation between electrical and neural activity has provided neurophysiologists with their principal method of study. This section will be divided according to the different electrophysiological methods for study of the cortex.

The Electrical Excitability of Cortex: The Discovery of Motor Areas

The discovery of sensory pathways that relay in the thalamus and terminate in areas of the cortex provided the first definition of sensory areas. The concept of a second kind of cortex, the association areas intercalated between sensory areas, was derived from the ideas of Flechsig and Campbell that they did not receive any fibers from subcortex, but only cortical fibers. In the traditional view of cortical areas there is still another class: the motor areas. I shall now return to the middle of the nineteenth century to the discovery that electrical stimulation of cortex results in bodily movements.

It is important to recall that Bell relied on stimulation as a way of revealing function. He was able to induce movement by touching the cerebellum, but not

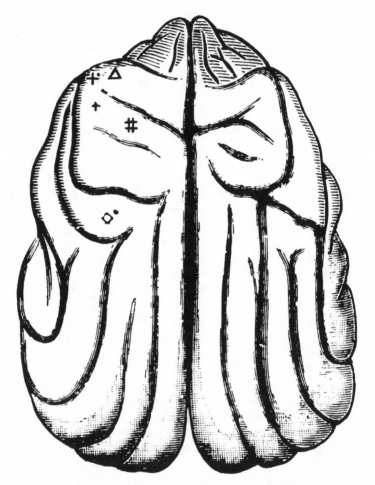

FIG. 8.22.   Dorsal view of dog's brain taken from a paper by Fritsch and Hitzig (1870). The signs (Δ, +, etc.) stand for various parts of the body which move when the locus in question is stimulated electrically. The Δ represents the center for the muscles in the neck; + represents the center for muscles of the front leg; # represents the muscles of the hindlimb; ◇ represents the muscles of the face.

by touching the cerebral cortex. Touching is, of course, a crude way to stimulate, and physiologists in the nineteenth century recognized the superiority of electrical stimulation. Still no evidence was found that fibers leave the cortex to reach the muscles of the face, arms and legs until the studies of Fritsch and Hitzig published in 1870. In the first experiments, dogs were simply restrained, a procedure that is utterly unacceptable today. In later experiments the dogs were narcotized and the cerebral cortex was exposed by removing the bone and the dura. Two flexible platinum wires were placed on the pial surface about 2 mm apart. With a suitable voltage difference between the two poles, the current flowed from one to the other pole even though the resistance of the tissue was considerable. The wires were flexible so that they followed slight movements of the cortex (e.g., those rhythmic movements produced by breathing) and did not penetrate the soft cortical tissue. In this way a region of the frontal cortex was discovered in which stimulation led to movements. Figure 8.22 shows a dorsal view of the dog's cortex with various symbols to designate movements and body parts.

This line of experiments was extended to the primate by the British neurologist and physiologist, Ferrier. Ferrier (1886) confirmed Hitzig's conclusions that movements vary as the locus of the excitation is shifted, and that stimuli at a given locus will elicit the same movement with great reliability. He depicted the topographic organization of the motor cortex by circular areas, each designating the effect peculiar to it. However, there was no sharp border between areas, and stimulation where areas adjoined sometimes produced both movements. Ferrier discovered that the motor areas of the monkey extended forward almost to the frontal pole and around the medial wall. Stimulation of the frontal area produced eye movements, while stimulation of the medial area led to movements of head and limbs similar to those produced by stimulating the lateral area.

Sherrington continued the inquiry with the chimpanzee as the subject. His results, first published with Grunbaum, are shown in Figure 8.23 (see Sherrington & Leyton, 1917). Note first the most frontal area labeled "EYES" and second that the principal area constitutes a strip lying rostral to the central sulcus. What cannot be shown in a lateral view is that much of the electrically excitable area lay hidden in the depth of the sulcus. The general topographical organization of this strip is suggested by diagramming the parts of the body and head that are affected. Sherrington made no effort to depict in the diagram the extent to which the arm and chest areas overlap. In general, he found considerable overlap. It is important to note that stimulation of the post central gyrus failed to elicit movement; in this respect, Sherrington's results differed from Ferrier's.

Sherrington combined the method of stimulation with lesions. A lesion of the hand area produced a severe paresis of the hand on the contralateral side. The fingers of the affected hand were "kept helplessly semi-extended, the wrist being dropped." These symptoms "diminished quite rapidly, and in six weeks' time the animal had in large measure recovered the usefulness of the limb"

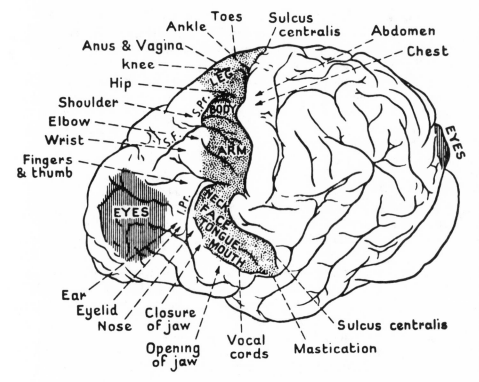

FIG. 8.23.   Brain of a chimpanzee, *Troglodytes niger,* taken from Sherrington (1906) showing the left hemisphere viewed from side and above so as to obtain as far as possible the configuration of the *sulcus centralis* area. The figure involves, nevertheless, considerable foreshortening about the top and bottom of *sulcus centralis.* The extent of the "motor" area on the free surface of the hemisphere is indicated by the black stippling, which extends back to the *sulcus centralis.* Much of the "motor" area is hidden in sulci; for instance, the area extends into the *sulcus centralis* and the *sulcus precentralis,* also into occasional sulci which cross the precentral gyrus. The names printed large on the stippled area indicate the main regions of the "motor" area; the names printed outside the brain indicate broadly by their pointing lines the relative topography of some of the chief subdivisions of the main regions of the "motor" cortex. But there exists much overlapping of areas and of their subdivisions which the diagram does not attempt to indicate.

The shaded regions, marked "EYES," indicate the frontal and occipital regions respectively the portions of cortex which, under faradization, yield conjugate movements of the eyeballs. But it is questionable whether these reactions sufficiently resemble those of the "motor" area to be included with them. They are therefore marked in vertical shading instead of stippling (as in the "motor" area). (Abbreviations: I. Pr., inferior precentral sulcus; S. F., superior frontal sulcus; S. Pr., superior precentral sulcus.)

(Sherrington, 1906, p. 278). In a similar way, lesions of the leg area caused temporary paresis of the leg on the opposite side. No doubt this line of inquiry contributed to the high honors that Sherrington received, including the Nobel Prize.

After the physiological experiments had been completed, animals were sacrificed and the brains were studied by Sherrington's colleague, Campbell. Campbell noted first that the cortex in the strip in front of the central sulcus corresponded to a discrete architectonic area characterized by huge pyramidal cells in the deeper layers of the cortex and the absence of a layer of small "granular" cells above the large pyramids—thus, the name dysgranular. In contrast, the region behind the central sulcus had a conspicuous layer of granular cells. It was reasonable to hypothesize that deep pyramidal cells sent their axons all the way down the spinal cord to the ventral horn cells that innervate the muscles. Sherrington himself noted that there was fiber degeneration in the spinal cord after lesions of the motor cortex and deduced that these fibers projected to the ventral horn cells.

The discovery of a cortical area that projects to spinal motor neurons took on added significance in the light of Sherrington's analysis of the simple reflex arc: The reflex pathway begins with the afferent neuron, whose cell body is in the dorsal root; the dorsal root cell sends a branch to an internuncial neuron that crosses to the ventral part of the cord and synapses on the ventral horn cell; the final path to the muscle is the motor neurons in the ventral horn. A comparable pathway can be pictured in the cortex: The sensory path terminates in the sensory area of the cortex where the stimulus is "sensed"; cortico-cortical pathways to the association areas provide the mechanism for interpreting the significance of the stimulus; finally, the association areas project to the motor area and the appropriate action is taken. The motor area thus became the motor area of the cortex and not just the cortical area connected to the spinal cord. The difference between these definitions is significant: The former implies that pathways from all sensory areas converge on the motor area, which is the final link in conditioning and learning. I will come back to this crucial distinction later when I discuss whether or not there is anatomical evidence for a massive flow of information from sensory areas to motor cortex.

Sensory Areas of the Cortex as Revealed by Recording Electrical Effects with an Electrode on the Surface

It was not until the invention of the cathode ray oscilloscope that the method of recording potentials was sensitive enough to record from the cortex and define the topographical projections of the sensory pathways. Credit for the application of the electron beam to neurophysiology goes to two American physiologists at Washington University in St. Louis, Erlanger and Gasser. The reward for their success was the Nobel Prize. While their studies were focused on the peripheral nerves and not on the cortex, their discoveries mark the beginning of present-day neurophysiology, and in only a few years their methods were applied to the cortex.

The first achievement of the cathode ray oscilloscope was the discovery in 1927 that the speed of the nerve impulse is a function of the size of the axon (Gasser & Erlanger, 1927). This was not accomplished by recording from single axons—the electrodes were far too big, and it required many more years to develop the technology for "microelectrode" and so-called single unit recording. Instead, Erlanger and Gasser recorded the action potential of an entire peripheral nerve. The action potential took the shape of a wave that could be regarded as an envelope covering the sum of a number of separate potentials. The early part of the wave could be attributed to impulses traveling at a faster rate, and successively later portions to impulses traveling at increasingly slower rates. Erlanger and Gasser hypothesized that impulses travel faster in large fibers and then measured the diameter of all the axons in the nerve. On the assumption that the bigger the axon the greater the potential and the faster the rate of conduction, they were able to reconstruct the actual shape of the wave.

In 1929 they reported the results of experiments with sensory nerves from the arm and leg of a cat (Gasser & Erlanger, 1929). The cathode ray was sensitive enough to show three separate waves which they first named A, B, and C. These three waves corresponded to three types of fibers: the A wave to large diameter myelinated fibers, the B wave to small diameter myelinated fibers, and the C wave to very small diameter unmyelinated fibers. The next step was ingenious. Recognizing that cocaine injections into skin at first reduce pain without causing a reduction in touch, they injected the experimental animal and observed the three waves. The C wave began to wane and eventually disappeared without significant changes in the A or B waves. Next they eliminated touch, first by a pressure block. (You are getting the experience of a pressure block when your arm or leg "falls asleep.") Once again the records showed a diminution of one wave—in this case, the A wave. Thus, they argued that pain is carried by the C fibers and that touch is carried by the A fibers.

Since small fibers enter the lateral columns while large fibers enter the dorsal columns of the cord, Erlanger and Gasser concluded that the somatic system is divided into two pathways: (1) the dorsal column system: the dorsal columns project to the cuneate and gracile nuclei, which, in turn, give rise to the medial lemniscus that crosses to the opposite side and terminates in the ventral posterior nucleus of the thalamus; and (2) the lateral column system which seems more complex—only some fibers project directly to the ventral posterior nucleus, while others synapse in the brain stem. Whether or not the latter path ever reaches the cortex was unknown at the time.

A few years after the methods of Erlanger and Gasser had been widely adopted, several laboratories in the United States and Great Britain succeeded in recording electrical potentials in the cortex with surface electrodes. The pro-

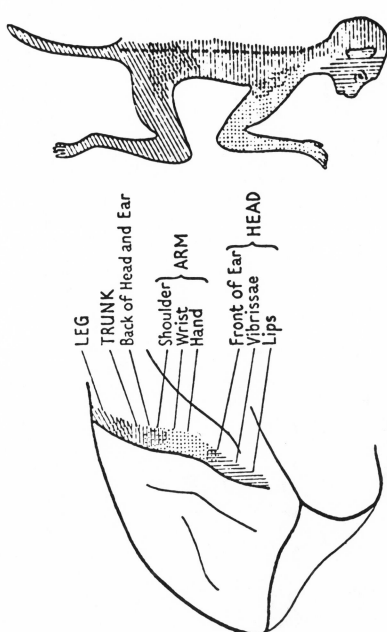

FIG. 8.24. A diagram from Adrian (1941) of the sensory area, or "somatic receiving area," in a monkey (*Rhesus*), showing the large area connected with the hand and face.

cedure involved the following steps: First, a deep anesthesia was induced; second, the cortex was exposed and electrodes were placed on the surface; third, the eye, the ear, or the skin was stimulated while the electrode was moved from place to place. No response was found in some areas of the cortex, and these were called the silent areas. You can anticipate that in some species, such as the monkey, the silent areas were extensive, while in other species, such as the rabbit, the silent areas were restricted. However, in the sensory areas the stimulus evoked a change in the potential that occurred with a very short latency.

The main accomplishments of these early studies were significant. First, they provided another way of defining the borders of a sensory area. For example, the area responsive to light coincided with the area defined as visual sensory by architectonic criteria. Incidentally, the name of the visual area as defined by architectonic criteria is the "striate" cortex; this area was also called area 17 by Brodman, who used a numbering system that remains popular to the present day (see Polyak, 1957). The area responsive to the touching of the skin corresponded to the cortex which earlier had been described as the somatosensory koniocortex. Koniocortex was a general term used by early German researchers in cytoarchitectonics to designate those areas that show the most conspicuous granular layers. Since the striate cortex coincided with the target of the lateral geniculate body, and since the somatosensory koniocortex coincided with the target of the ventral posterior nucleus, the method of evoked potentials provided a third way of defining sensory cortex: (1) thalamic connections, (2) cytoarchitectonics, and (3) evoked potentials. In the case of the auditory cortex, where there was some doubt of the exact border of the projection of the medial geniculate body, the method of evoked potentials did more than confirm earlier consensus. It had the potentialities of resolving earlier conflicts.

In general, this method of evoked potentials provided a map of the receptor surface more precise and certainly more dramatic than was possible with anatomical degeneration methods. For example, a map showing the representation of the body surface of the monkey was published by Lord Adrian in 1941 (see Fig. 8.24). Adrian, a Cambridge neurophysiologist, received the Nobel Prize for his achievements, most notably in the use of microelectrode recording to measure the action potential of single neurons. When Adrian mapped the somatosensory area of a variety of species, he found that different parts of the body had a relatively greater or lesser representation depending on the importance of the information coming from them (Adrian, 1947). The hand area is relatively large in primates, who normally use their fingers to pick up objects. In contrast, the representation of the limbs of a horse that serve simply for locomotion is relatively small. Where the snout is very sensitive and used for tactile purposes, as in the case of a pig, the representation of the snout is very large (see Fig. 8.25, left side) as compared to body and limbs.

The topographic representation of the retina as revealed by evoked potentials showed that the zero-vertical meridian which divides the retina into two hemi-

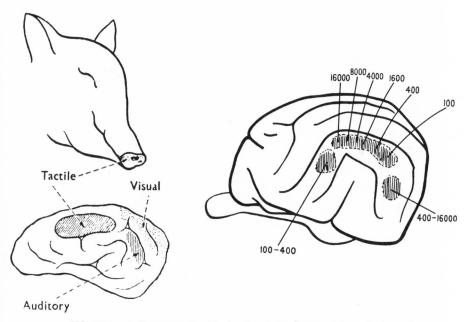

FIG. 8.25.   A diagram to show the functional significance of the projections of
the receptor surface to the cortex according to Adrian (1947). On the left is shown
the cortex of a pig. The chief point is that a large proportion of the tactile area is
devoted to the representation of the snout because that part of the body is the most
sensitive. On the right is the drawing of the auditory cortex of the dog to show the
representations of various frequencies of sound. Note that there are three representations of a 400 Hz sound. The most significant point is that the distance between
octaves in the primary area is about the same, suggesting that distance in cortex
reflects the capacity to discriminate pitch.

fields is represented at the rostral border at the cytoarchitectonic striate area. The
representation of central vision is proportionally much greater than the representation of peripheral vision, reflecting the same representational system found in
the somatic system.

Since the ear does not contain a map of outside space, you may question the
functional significance of a spatial representation of the basilar membrane upon
the cortex. The answer is that high tones have their greatest effect on the apex of
the cochlear. Clinton Woolsey, of the Johns Hopkins University, pioneered the
study of evoked potentials in the auditory cortex. Woolsey later moved to the
University of Wisconsin where he established one of the most important and
influential laboratories of neurophysiology, and his group became identified with
the use of the electrical recording method for studying the cortex. In an early
experiment published with Walzl, Woolsey stimulated directly various turns of
the cochlea in the cat (Woolsey & Walzl, 1942). The results showed that the
apex was represented rostrally in the auditory cortex and the base was repre-

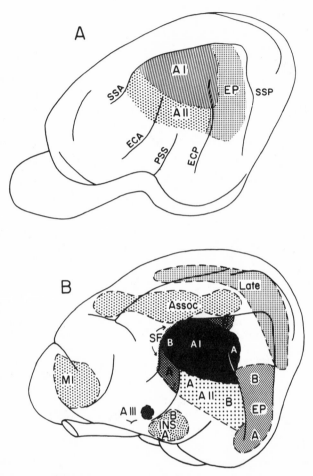

FIG. 8.26. Two diagrams of the auditory cortex in the cat to show how the number of subdivisions increased from 1949 to 1958. Diagram A shows three architectonic subdivisions each of which corresponds to an evoked potential map of the cochlea (Rose & Woolsey, 1949). In diagram B you can see that several additional representations had been discovered since 1949. Notice that each area is a complete representation of the cochlea from the apex (labeled "A") to the base (labeled "B").

sented caudally. Figure 8.26 shows the auditory cortex as this area is defined by evoked potentials. The letters "A" and "B" stand for apex and base, respectively. As more auditory areas were discovered the first area was named A I.

Woolsey also discovered a second representation of basilar membrane lying just below the first representation. In this ventral area the base was represented rostrally and the apex was represented caudally. These maps are also shown in Figure 8.26. It should be clear that if it were not for this reversal in the rostral caudal order, it would have been difficult to argue that the second area is not simply a continuation or extension of the first area. Woolsey called the second area A II. Still other areas were called A III, the insular area (Ins), and the posterior ectosylvian area (Ep). The significance of these will be discussed later.

A second visual area was also found by Woolsey and his colleagues at Johns Hopkins, this time using the rabbit as a subject (see Talbot, Woolsey, & Thompson, 1946). The first visual area, or V I, represents one-half of the visual field, with the zero vertical meridian represented at its rostral border. Of course, the other half of the field is represented in the other hemisphere. When the animal was deeply anesthetized with a barbiturate, no potentials were evoked beyond V I; When the anesthesia was considerably lightened, a second topographic representation of the retina was revealed, and this area (V II) was organized as a mirror image of V I. That is to say, as the electrode was moved further forward and increasingly removed from the border representing the zero vertical meridian, the neurons represented points in space increasingly peripheral. Thus, the hemifield is represented twice, once on either side of the border between V I and V II.

Since we have come to expect the same principles underlying the organization of sensory cortex, it came as no surprise that the body surface also had a second

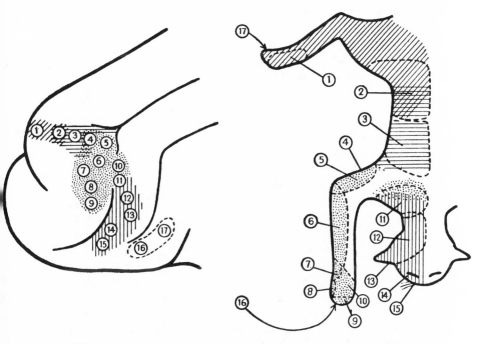

FIG. 8.27. A diagram from Adrian (1941) of the somatic receiving area in the cat, showing the additional posterior region for the digits (marked 16 and 17).

representation. This was also studied by Woolsey in the United States and by Adrian in England. One of the first signs of the second somatic area, or SII, was discovered by Adrian in 1940, and we reproduce an illustration from the 1940 paper (see Fig. 8.27). This illustration shows that each part of the body is numbered and that each number is then used as a code to illustrate the locus of its cortical representation. Thus, number 1 depicts the leg, 9 the arm, and so on. Now notice that numbers 16 and 17 correspond with numbers 1 and 9 and are represented in a second cortical area below the first area.

A demonstration of more than one representation of the cochlea was achieved by using pure tones to evoke potentials in the auditory cortex of the dog. Figure 8.25 (right side) illustrates the results obtained by Tunturi (see Adrian, 1947) and makes the point that a given cortical distance appears to represent about an octave; that is, the distance between 16 kHz and 8 kHz is about the same as the distance between 8 kHz and 4 kHz. Figure 8.25 also shows a second representation of tones from 100 to 400 Hz in the anterior ectosylvian gyrus and a second representation of tones from 800 to 1600 Hz in the posterior ectosylvian gyrus.

The EEG and the Reticular Activating System

A very different kind of electrical potential was discovered in 1936 by placing electrodes not directly on the brain but on the scalp in humans (Berger, 1929). Naturally, the distance from the skin to the cortex precludes the possibility that the very short latency and very small amplitude evoked potential could be recorded. The potentials recorded from the scalp were many times slower, an eighth of a second as compared to a hundredth of a second, and many times greater in amplitude. Also, the scalp potentials were rhythmic and were "spontaneous" in the sense that they were not induced by or evoked by a stimulus.

The record of these potentials was called the electroencephalogram (EEG, for convenience). The chief significance of the EEG is that these potentials vary in different states of health and disease. For our purpose there are two principal waves. With the eyes closed and the subject relaxed but not asleep, a high voltage, slow wave, called the alpha rhythm, is recorded. The peaks of the alpha rhythm repeat at a rate of 8–10 times a second. When the eyes open to look at something or when a loud sound startles a subject, the slow wave disappears and is replaced by low voltage, fast activity that is unsynchronized.

After World War II, two Northwestern University researchers, a psychologist, Donald Lindsley, and an anatomist, Horace Magoun, teamed to conduct a series of experiments that were destined to change the traditional view of the sensory pathways to the cortex (Lindsley, Bowden & Magoun, 1949). At various phases of their inquiry they were joined by other colleagues and notably by Moruzzi, who now holds the Chair of Physiology at the University of Pisa.

In the initial experiments, an electrode was introduced deep into the brain stem. I should add that aiming an electrode at various deep subcortical targets was made possible by a special instrument that provides coordinates in three dimensions for every part of the brain relative to certain key landmarks of the skull. While the animal is not deeply anesthetized with a barbiturate, humane treatment is assured by the use of chloralosane and certain surgical procedures that eliminate pain.

When the animals were left to fall into a drowsy, relaxed state with closed eyes, the synchrony characteristic of the alpha rhythm in humans was recorded on the EEG. Now I come to the major discovery: When the stimulating electrode was placed in the central core of the brain stem extending from the medulla to the midbrain, the EEG was desynchronized (Moruzzi & Magoun, 1949). This central core is diagrammed in Figure 8.28. These researchers discovered that electrical stimulation mimicked the effects of alerting drowsy, relaxed human or animal subjects. In general, the region of the brain in which electrical stimulation produces this effect corresponds to the reticular formation, so named because of its reticulated appearance resulting from the mix of cells and fibers. Figure 8.28 diagrams the reticular activating system.

Since the normal EEG record taken from the scalp in man reflects some kind of cortical activity (but not necessarily an activity that corresponds to the synchronous firing of cells), the reticular formation must be able to influence the cerebral cortex. The question then became, ''What is the anatomical pathway by

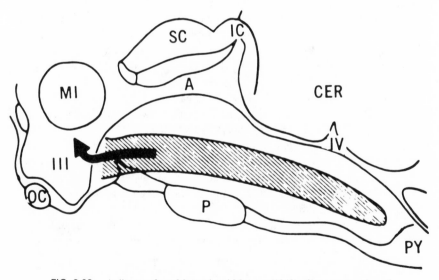

FIG. 8.28.   A diagram from Moruzzi and Magoun (1949) of a reconstruction of the midsagittal plane of a cat's brain stem upon which is projected (with diagonal shading) the distribution of the ascending reticular activating system. (Abbreviations: A, aqueduct; CER, cerebellum; IC, inferior colliculus; MI, massa intermedia; OC, optic chiasma; P, pons; PY, pyramidal crossing; SC, superior colliculus; III, third ventricle; IV, fourth ventricle.)

which the reticular formation can influence the cortex?'' First, the possibility was ruled out that there was an antidromic stimulation of the cortex through tracts which normally send descending fibers from the cortex to the reticular formation. Perhaps the currents delivered to the reticular formation spread to the medial lemniscus, which is a well-established pathway by which spinal cord impulses are relayed to the thalamus, or to the lateral lemniscus, which is a well-established path by which auditory impulses ascend to the inferior colliculus and are then relayed to the thalamus. To test this Magoun and his colleagues made lesions that transected the lateral and medial lemnisci; EEG responses to stimulation of the reticular formation remained unaffected.

Eliminating these possibilities left only the conclusion that the reticular formation has its own, as yet unknown, pathway to the cortex. The next step was obvious. Stimulate the reticular formation with single shocks and explore the cortex using the method of evoked potentials. That is, look for very short latency, stimulus-evoked responses of very short duration. These results were also negative. Magoun and his colleagues were led to conclude that the pathway from the reticular formation to cortex was very different from the traditional sensory pathways to cortex.

A clue to the nature of this pathway came from experiments in which stimulation of the reticular formation abolished the ''recruiting response.'' Before describing these studies, it is necessary to review briefly the experiments of Morison and Dempsey (1942). This team placed electrodes in the intralaminar nuclei of the thalamus and found that rhythmic stimulation of these intralaminar nuclei elicited a waxing rhythmic response, named the ''recruiting response,'' over much of the neocortex. The large size of area of cortex showing the response led to the name ''the diffuse thalamic projection system.''

The intralaminar nuclei had been defined earlier by LeGros Clark (1932) as the population of small fusiform cells that stream between and around the principal nuclei. These cells are embedded in the fibers that separate the medial dorsal nucleus from the ventral and lateral nuclei. The intralaminar nuclei are well developed in lower mammals, such as the opossum, and they regress in primate evolution. Further, inasmuch as they did not undergo retrograde degeneration after cortical lesions, they did not appear to project to neocortex. These findings led to the idea that they are a very ancient part of the thalamus. The new evidence that the reticular formation may utilize the intralaminar nuclei to reach the neocortex was at best puzzling and was regarded with great skepticism by most anatomists. (For more details on the locus and significance of the intralaminar nuclei, see Fig. 8.30 and text on pages 364–365).

One final point is required to relate the reticular system to the rest of the brain. Since an auditory stimulus can activate the EEG as well as electrical stimulation of the reticular formation, it follows that the sensory pathways somehow are able to convey their messages to the activating system. Magoun and his co-workers postulated that this was achieved by means of a collateral projection. It is important to emphasize that there was no anatomical evidence for these collaterals. For example, there was no known evidence of a collateral projection from the optic tract to the reticular formation. It remained for later anatomical work to support or refute the theory of the brain stem reticular activating system.

THE ORGANIZATION OF THE THALAMUS AND CORTEX: 1949–1959

The progress made in the 1930s and 1940s required a revision of the traditional view of the cortex as put forward by Campbell at the beginning of the century.

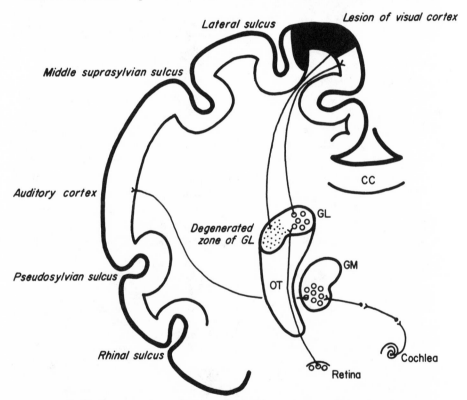

FIG. 8.29.   Diagram to show how retrograde degeneration can be used to trace the topographic projections of the thalamic nucleus onto the cortex. This drawing is a diagrammatic version of a frontal section in which a part of the visual cortex has been ablated. The lesion is shown in black. The lateral geniculate neurons that project to the lesion have been transected and they undergo retrograde degeneration depicted by dots. Normal cells of the lateral geniculate body continue to project to that part of the visual cortex that is spared. (Abbreviations: CC, corpus callosum; GL, lateral geniculate body; GM, medial geniculate body; OT, optic tract.)

First, the method of studying thalamic projections to the cortex by the retrograde degeneration of cell bodies in the thalamus showed that cortical areas hitherto regarded as "association" cortex in fact receive fibers from the thalamus. The technique requires first making a small cortical lesion which, of course, transects the thalamic axons that project to the area of the lesion. The animal is then allowed to survive at least 6 weeks. During this period, the cell body undergoes a series of changes which are apparent with a Nissl stain. Eventually the cells seem to explode and the fragments disappear. Retrograde degeneration is apparent then by the absence of normal cells and by the appearance of glial cells that proliferate during the degeneration process. Figure 8.29 is a diagram depicting retrograde degeneration in the lateral geniculate nucleus as a result of a lesion in striate cortex. The existence of retrograde degeneration was known as early as 1900, but it was not widely used to study the thalamus until much later.

Results of studies using retrograde degeneration confirmed many of the traditional ideas. For example, lesions of the striate cortex produced retrograde degeneration in the lateral geniculate body, and the locus of the degeneration varied with the locus of the lesion. However, large lesions of the temporal-parietal-occipital association cortex *also* produced retrograde degeneration in the thalamus chiefly in the pulvinar nucleus, and large lesions of the frontal lobe produced retrograde degeneration in the medial dorsal nucleus. These results were obtained in several laboratories about the same time. LeGros Clark was one of the pioneers in the use of the retrograde method to study thalamic projections; as early as 1932, he recognized the peculiar status of the pulvinar and medial dorsal nuclei. They are small in the lower mammals, such as the opossum and hedgehog, and grow very large with the evolution of primates. Other researchers using retrograde degeneration deserve mention. Walker, a neurosurgeon at the

---

FIG. 8.30. Diagrammatic representation of the various nuclei of the dorsal and ventral thalamus. Three sections are drawn and from the left to right they represent a rostral section, a middle section, and a caudal section. The anterior nuclei (AD, AV, and AM) are found in the rostral section. The middle thalamic section is divided into three parts by the internal laminae. First the medial dorsal nucleus (MD), dorsal and medial to the internal laminae (Int Lam); the lateral nucleus (Lat), lateral to the internal laminae; and the ventral lateral nucleus (VL), ventral to the internal laminae. There are cells within the internal laminae such as the paracentral nucleus (Pc). In the caudal section the lateral nucleus is replaced by the lateral geniculate nucleus (GL) and the pulvinar nucleus (Pul); the ventral lateral nucleus (VL) is replaced by the ventral posterior nucleus (VPL). The midline nuclei of the thalamus are present in all three sections and include reuniens (Re) and the medial ventral nucleus (Mv). In addition to the dorsal thalamus, these drawings show the location of the ventral thalamus: the thalamic reticular nucleus (Ret), zona incerta (ZI), and the ventral lateral geniculate nucleus (VGL). Other abbreviations are as follows: FR, fasciculus retroflexus; Fx, fornix; Ha, habenula; MTh, mammillo-thalamic tract; Pc, nucleus paracentralis; Pt, group of pretectal nuclei; Sub, subthalamic nucleus; TO, optic tract.

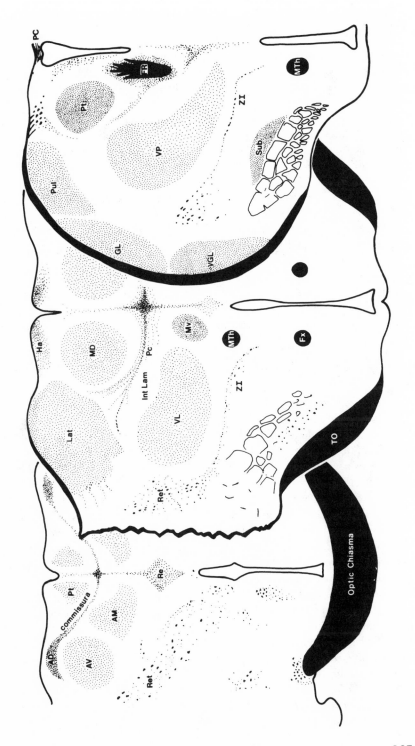

365

University of Chicago, studied the monkey cortex in 1937, and demonstrated the extensive cortical target of the pulvinar nucleus (Walker, 1938). Lashley (1941) studied thalamic degeneration in all of his cortical studies of the rat and amassed enough data to determine the pattern of thalamic projections in this species. Bodian (1942) published a retrograde degeneration study of the lowly opossum.

These studies of thalamic cortical projection in a variety of species failed to support the traditional idea that association cortex receives fibers only from other cortical areas. Instead, retrograde degeneration was found in the medial dorsal nucleus after lesions of the frontal association cortex, and degeneration in the pulvinar nucleus was found after lesions of the temporal-parietal-occipital association cortex. The location of the chief nuclear groups of the thalamus in a generalized mammal is depicted in the diagrams of Figure 8.30. The thalamus is divided into dorsal and ventral tiers and into medial and lateral sectors by the internal medullated laminae. The ventral group lies below, the medial dorsal nucleus lies above, and the lateral group lies lateral to the medullated laminae. A number of cells, usually fusiform in shape, are scattered throughout the medullated laminae. These cells constitute the intralaminar nuclei. Some of the intralaminar nuclei, such as the central lateral nucleus and nucleus centremedian, are well organized.

The results of the method of evoked potentials also posed a problem for the traditional view. How should the second sensory areas, V II, A II, and S II, be classified: Are they sensory areas or are they association areas? Note that V II, for example, since it lies adjacent to the striate cortex, occupies the area which Campbell would surely have called visuo-psychic. Finally, how can the results of Magoun be reconciled with the traditional view that each cortical area receives fibers from just one thalamic nucleus? According to Magoun, there is a diffuse thalamic projection system that overlaps with the projections from the traditional relay nuclei.

These questions were addressed by Jerzy Rose (Rose & Woolsey, 1949a), who was born and educated in Poland and then moved to the Johns Hopkins University in 1940 to begin a collaboration with Clinton Woolsey that continues to the present. Rose conceded that there may be some true association cortex in man—that is, areas that receive no thalamic input. However, for most and perhaps all experimental mammals, no area of the neocortex can be regarded as an "association" area in the traditional sense. To replace the distinction between association and sensory cortex, Rose proposed a classification scheme that depended upon the *type* of thalamic nucleus that is the source of the projections. Some thalamic nuclei receive fibers from outside the thalamus and this group, designated as *extrinsic* nuclei, includes the sensory relay nuclei. The second group of nuclei, designated as the *intrinsic* nuclei, receives its input only from other thalamic nuclei. The pulvinar and the medial dorsal nuclei are intrinsic. The evolution of the cortex can then be described by the relative size in an ascending series of mammals of the cortical targets of the intrinsic thalamic

Traditional View

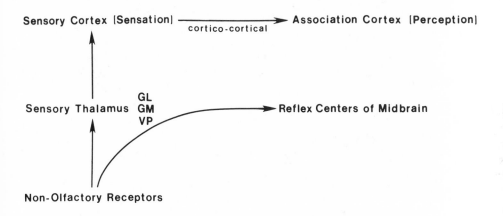

Revision by Rose & Woolsey (1949)

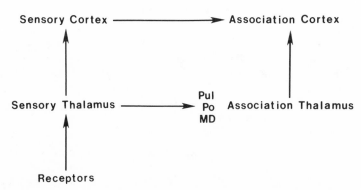

FIG. 8.31.   Diagram to show the connections of sensory and association cortex according to the traditional view and according to the revisions by Rose and Woolsey (1949). In the traditional view the association cortex did not receive thalamic fibers. The sensory cortex, of course, received fibers from the lateral geniculate (GL), medial geniculate (GM), and ventral posterior (VP) nuclei. It was found later that the association cortex also receives thalamic projections from the pulvinar (Pul), the posterior nucleus (Po) and the medial dorsal nucleus (MD). Rose and Woolsey believed that these nuclei received fibers only from the sensory nuclei of the thalamus.

nuclei, which Rose called secondary projection areas, and the cortical target or the extrinsic thalamic nuclei, which Rose called primary projection areas. The concept of secondary projection areas thus replaces the earlier view of association cortex. This resolution retains the idea that secondary areas are functionally more advanced, since (1) secondary areas depend on projections from extrinsic to intrinsic thalamic nuclei, and (2) secondary areas develop later in evolution. That is to say, the greatest development of the secondary areas occurs during the evolution of higher primates. The contrast between the proposal of Rose and Woolsey and the traditional view is diagrammed in Figure 8.31.

The question now became, "How are the primary and secondary projection fields related to the first and second sensory areas as these are defined by evoked potentials?" The first sensory areas, A I, V I and S I, posed no problem. These are clearly "primary," since they receive fibers from the medial geniculate body, the lateral geniculate body and the ventral posterior nucleus, respectively. It was not easy, however, to determine whether the second sensory areas, A II, S II and V II, are primary or secondary projection fields because small lesions restricted to these areas led to no retrograde degeneration at all. Rose concluded that V II *might* receive collateral projections from the lateral geniculate body, in which case it would be a primary projection area; or it *might* receive a sparse projection from the pulvinar nucleus, too scattered to detect retrograde degeneration, in which case V II would be classed with the secondary projection areas. In any case, the region intercalated between the sensory areas expand in the series: rabbit, cat, and monkey as depicted in Fig. 8.32.

Rose eventually established that A II was part of a primary projection area. In the course of this demonstration, it was necessary to subdivide the medial geniculate body to distinguish two kinds of projections from different subdivisions of the medial geniculate body. A projection is called "essential" if it is restricted to a single cortical locus, the destruction of which produces retrograde degeneration in the source of the projection (Rose & Woolsey, 1949b, 1958). A projection is called "sustaining" if it divides into collaterals that terminate in *two* subdivisions of cortex. The presence of either collateral, which amounts to saying either cortical subdivision, is sufficient to "sustain" the cell. Rose showed that only the rostral two-thirds of the principal division of the medial geniculate sends "essential" projections to A I. The caudal one-third of the principal division and the magnocellular division of the medial geniculate body sends "sustaining" projections to A II, as well as to A I and other cortical subdivisions surrounding A I and A II. Thus the target of the projections from the entire medial geniculate body includes a belt of cortex that would have surely been classed as auditory association or auditory psychic by Campbell. The meaning of this extensive sustaining projection was obscure at the time. The significance of the overlap in the projections from different divisions of the medial geniculate body was also obscure.

In the course of this inquiry into the auditory cortex of the cat, Rose restored the credibility of cytoarchitectonic analysis. Architectonic research had fallen

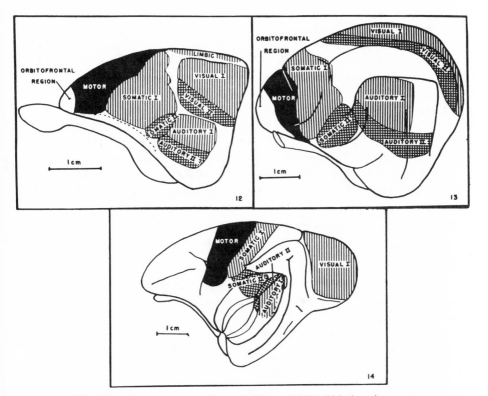

FIG. 8.32.   Three drawings by Rose and Woolsey (1949) which show the sensory cortex as defined by the method of evoked potentials in three species: the rabbit
(upper left), the cat (upper right), and the monkey (below). There are two main
points made by these drawings: 1) Each sensory field has a first and second area;
2) The region intercalated between the sensory areas expands in the series: rabbit,
cat, and monkey. This suggests that the association areas grow larger in primate
evolution.

into disrepute chiefly as a result of Lashley's devastating criticism published with
Clark in 1946 (Lashley & Clark, 1946). Several factors predisposed Lashley to
question the functional significance of the areas Campbell and Brodman had
established with such confidence and pride. First, Lashley had not been able to
show that the association cortex serves a higher level of function than the sensory
cortex, let alone localize intelligence in one particular subdivision of the association cortex. Second, architectonic research had made little progress since the
days of Campbell and Brodman; indeed, it was bogged down with picayune
matters such as how many features must change in order to establish a border
between areas.

Lashley eventually discredited the reliability of the method by showing that
borders could not be agreed upon by independent sophisticated observers. He
then went on to argue that differences in the layers of cortex in different cortical

areas had nothing to do with connections and that the number of architectonic areas did not increase in evolution.

When Rose showed that the essential projection field of the medial geniculate body corresponded exactly with A I as defined by evoked potentials, it only remained for him to show that this area was also an architectonic subdivision (Rose & Woolsey, 1949). As more auditory areas were identified by electrophysiologists, each of these areas turned out to correspond with an architectonic subdivision that had been defined earlier by Rose. In general, all of the areas defined by electrophysiology, such as V I and V II, correspond to architectonic subdivisions. Finally, more recent studies of cortical connections relying on the more delicate and precise transport methods also support the concept that the slightest differences in laminar organization reflect connectional differences.

The Nauta Method for Tracing Anterograde Degeneration of Unmyelinated Axons and Axon Terminals

Another technical advance was necessary for the next step in the inquiry into the sensory projections to the cortex. The traditional method of tracking fiber degeneration was restricted to myelinated fibers. Because terminating fibers are without myelin, the Marchi method provided neither a chance to visualize fiber termination nor the opportunity to study unmyelinated tracts such as the pathway taken by the C fibers. A method for tracing small unmyelinated degenerating axons was developed by Walle Nauta (Nauta & Kuypers, 1958). Nauta was born in the Dutch East Indies and returned to Amsterdam to complete his medical education. Not until after World War II did he move to the United States. His first position was Director of the Neurohistology Laboratory at Walter Reed Hospital in Washington, D.C.; later he moved to MIT.

One of the first achievements of the Nauta method was the demonstration that the lateral columns project directly and indirectly to the intralaminar nuclei of the thalamus. As late as 1950 there was no clue that the intralaminar nuclei received any fibers from an extrinsic source. Nauta showed for the first time that some fibers of the lateral column system project directly to the intralaminar nuclei; and Nauta and his collaborators also confirmed the accepted conclusion that some fibers of the lateral column system project to the ventral posterior nucleus (Mehler, Feferman, & Nauta, 1960; Nauta & Kuypers, 1958; Nauta & Whitlock, 1954). The relative number of these intralaminar projections decreases in an ascending series of mammals from opossum to primate, while the number of lateral column fibers projecting directly to the ventral posterior nucleus increases in this series. Many fibers of the lateral column also terminate in the reticular formation, and the reticular formation, in turn, was found to project to the intralaminar nuclei. Then Ford Ebner, one of Nauta's students, made lesions in the intralaminar nuclei and found evidence of terminal degeneration in the cortex. Thus the intralaminar nuclei project to the neocortex after all (Killackey & Ebner, 1972).

In sum, the methods of staining unmyelinated degenerating axons and axon terminals revealed that the lateral column pathway continues to the neocortex in parallel to the dorsal column-medial lemniscal path.

Fiber Size and Modality—George Bishop's Proposal in 1959

Shortly after Erlanger and Gasser began their Nobel Prize-winning studies of the peripheral nerves they were joined by a young physicist and engineer, George Bishop, who pursued the study of the distribution of fiber size in the peripheral and central nervous system and the neural basis of pain and touch until his death in 1977. This inquiry (Bishop, 1959) showed that the scheme of Erlanger and Gasser was an oversimplification, and that the quality of bodily sensation depends on some *pattern* of impulses in large and small fibers. A number of investigators not only opposed Erlanger and Gasser, but even took issue with the principle of "specific nerve energies," as Bell's Idea was later called. Bell, of course, was the first to explain differences in sensory qualities (touch, pain, color) by differences in sensory pathways. Weddell at Oxford was one of those who questioned the validity of the subdivision of the somatic senses into pain, cold, hot, and touch. An excellent review of Weddell's argument was published in 1955 by Sinclair, a member of Weddell's group (see Sinclair, 1955). While Bishop did not join this opposing camp, he was convinced that the function of the lateral column system was not independent of the dorsal column system and that touch could be conveyed by the lateral columns as well as the dorsal column system. Even more significant was the fact that the projections of the lateral column could hardly be described as a single pathway. Some lateral column fibers project directly to the ventroposterior nucleus, some project directly to the intralaminar nuclei, and some reach the intralaminar nuclei only after several synapses in the reticular formation. The discovery of parallel somatic paths reminded Bishop of Herrick's idea that only some of the somatic pathways in mammals have precursors in early vertebrates and others appear to have evolved with the origin of mammals.

However, it was not until his discovery that the fibers of the optic nerve vary in size and that only the smallest fibers project to the superior colliculus did Bishop question the accepted doctrine that *fiber size* is related solely to modality (Bishop & Clare, 1955). Bishop was struck by the fact that vision is not divisible into sub-modalities, so he sought some more general account for the variation in fiber size and looked to evolution for an explanation. In 1959 he proposed the idea that there is selective advantage for fibers to increase in diameter, the functional consequence being faster conduction. However, as larger and larger fibers evolve they do not replace smaller fibers, with the result that there are multiple pathways *in parallel.* The sequence of events leading to the formation of multiple pathways was pictured in the following way: Old sensory centers in the reticular formation developed new projections that traveled rostrally into the thalamus; as a result, new centers differentiated in the thalamus. Then, larger fibers evolved that bypassed the reticular formation and projected directly to the new thalamic centers. Thus, the so-called spinothalamic path which bypasses the reticular formation can be explained as a more recent achievement in phyletic history. The oldest somatic pathway is from C fibers to the lateral columns to the reticular formation, where several relays are made before reaching the intra-laminar nuclei. The last step in this pathway is from the intralaminar nuclei to layer I of the neocortex. Bishop attached importance to the fact that the site of thalamic termination in the cortex of reptiles, and presumably the mammal ancestor, is layer I. That some fibers from the thalamus reach layer I instead of layer IV (which is the terminus of fibers from the relay nuclei) had been known since Cajal. Also, the layer I fibers, inasmuch as they spread laterally along the cortical surface passing across borders between subdivisions, appear to be dif-fuse (see Lorente de Nó, 1938).

The newest somatic pathway is taken by large touch fibers that reach the ventral posterior nucleus after only one synapse and are relayed to layer IV of the somatic cortex. There may be other somatic pathways intermediate in phyletic origin that relay through other thalamic nuclei, and the posterior group is a good candidate for such a path. Note that impulses in large fiber paths reach the cortex earlier not only because nerve impulses in large fibers travel faster but also because those paths have fewer synapses.

Bishop argued that there is no need to postulate a collateral projection to the reticular formation from the newer dorsal column system since the reticular formation receives fibers directly from the lateral column system and relays the message to the thalamus in a pathway that is medial to the medial lemniscus. Finally, the diffuse thalamic projection system in Bishop's scheme can be re-garded as the last step in the old somatic pathway. In summary, Bishop viewed the various somatic pathways from the spinal cord as representing various stages in evolution. The oldest pathways are characterized by small fibers, by multiple synapses, and by a diffuse projection to layer I of the cortex. New pathways are characterized by larger fibers, fewer synapses, and more specific projections to layer IV of the neocortex (Bishop, 1959).

RECENT EVIDENCE ON SENSORY PATHWAYS AND SENSORY CORTICAL AREAS

The Electrophysiology of Striate Cortex: Hubel and Wiesel

The research reviewed up to this point has stood the test of time. It is not necessary for time to pass to make the judgment that the studies of Hubel and Wiesel on the visual cortex will make a lasting contribution whatever the future brings. (The reader should know that since the writing of this chapter Hubel and Wiesel were honored with the Nobel Prize.)

Their achievements depended first on technical advances in electrical recording. Instead of recording the synchronous activity of thousands of neurons from the cortical surface, they penetrated the cortex with a very small electrode so that the electrode tip lay close to a single neuron and a record could be made of the action potentials of that single cell. Second, by inventing imaginative ways of stimulating the cell, they were able to discover ''receptive'' fields that changed our view of the role of the striate cortex in perception.

To define the term ''receptive field'' it is necessary to go back to the Nobel Prize-winning studies of the retina by Granit (1947), Hartline (1938), and Kuffler (1953) that provide the starting point for the work of Hubel and Wiesel. When a microelectrode is inserted into the retina, a cell is first located by a record of its *spontaneous* activity. A very small light is then moved about in various positions of the visual field until a region is located in which the spontaneous rate of firing either increases or decreases. The receptive field is defined as that restricted area of the retina where illumination alters the spontaneous rate of firing of a given cell. In the case of the retinal ganglion cells, receptive fields consist of two concentric circles. Illumination in the inner circle excites the cell (i.e., increases its spontaneous rate), while illumination in the region surrounding the excitatory center decreases or inhibits the cell's spontaneous rate.

Hubel and Wiesel found that the receptive fields of neurons in the striate cortex were not circular in shape, but were elongated; they took the form of a slit. Further, the cortical cell was excited only when the slit was oriented in a certain way. Finally, in a given column of cells perpendicular to the surface, all of the cells were excited by the same orientation. In adjacent columns the orientation shifted gradually from vertical to horizontal back to vertical as the hands of a clock change with time. If a column is excited by a vertical line, for example, it might be inhibited by horizontal lines. Cells were also found to be sensitive to direction and could be excited by vertical lines which passed from left to right but not from right to left.

Finding that single cells are sensitive to line orientation and movement completely changes the traditional view that perception of a pattern is the result of cortico-cortical projections from the striate cortex to the visuo-psychic area. In the traditional view, the topographic projection of the retina to the striate cortex assures that a particular stimulus pattern will be represented by a mosaic of active cells isomorphic to the stimulus. For example, an inverted ''V'' produces a V in the retina and a V-shaped pattern of active cells in the striate cortex. According to the classical view, a still further projection from the visuo-sensory to visuo-psychic areas allows the shape to be perceived as an object—for example, ''a roof.'' The discovery of complex receptive fields of single cells in the striate cortex suggests the possibility that the perception of a roof as an object could be mediated by the striate cortex without the participation of the visual ''association'' cortex (Hubel & Wiesel, 1959).

The Auditory Cortex in the Cat and the Visual Cortex in the Tree Shrew

The history has now ended, but it would not be difficult to identify current research that will remain significant whatever the future of the inquiry will reveal. We are in the midst of rapid advances resulting from innovations in method and concept that are changing our view of the cortex. The retrograde transport of horse radish peroxidase (HRP) has made retrograde degeneration obsolete as a method of studying connections. The method of anterograde transport of radioactive amino acids promises to reveal every connection of the cortex. The method that Evarts (1968) has developed for recording from single cells of the cortex while the animal is awake and behaving promises to provide new insights into functional localization (see Evarts, 1973, 1982; Evarts & Tanji, 1976). The studies of Mishkin (1972) on the temporal lobe have revitalized the ablation method. Limitations in space prevent me from trying to review recent advances in method or from trying to summarize the present-day view of cortex. Still I feel it necessary to provide some closure on those issues which are left dangling and unresolved. In this section I will review my own research as propaedeutic to a final summary section.

In 1947 Neff came to the University of Chicago to begin a series of studies in the auditory cortex in the cat. To that inquiry he brought on the one hand a picture of the subdivisions of the cortex as defined by Woolsey and Rose and, on the other hand, a battery of objective tests to measure auditory discrimination. I joined his group shortly after his arrival.

The first results of this study showed, contrary to the expectations of the traditional view, that a cat deprived of the sensory auditory cortex would not suffer "cortical deafness" (Neff & Diamond, 1958). From the work of Klüver on the visual cortex we knew that the animal deprived of striate cortex is not absolutely blind but retains some crude ability to register the total energy of the stimulus. Perhaps the cat deprived of auditory cortex, while not deaf, retains just a sense of a change in sound energy. The results instead showed that cats with A I were able to discriminate changes in pitch and even changes in melodies produced by presenting the pitches in temporal sequences (Butler, Diamond, & Neff, 1956; Diamond & Neff, 1957). Some deficit in the ability to localize sounds in space was revealed, but the nature of this deficit proved hard to specify. The deficit certainly was not a simple sensory loss nor did it resemble the effects of abolishing the binaural mechanisms for localizing a brief sound (see Neff, Diamond, & Casseday, 1975, for review).

Perhaps the lesions were too restricted. We already knew of the existence of A II and we had hints that still other auditory areas lay beyond the borders of A II. Subsequent studies, however, showed that the size of the ablation did not explain the failure to produce cortical deafness. The symptoms that Schafer or Munk or Ferrier would expect to find were not produced by a lesion so drastic that all of the cortex of the temporal lobe was removed.

Given the results of Klüver's studies of the visual cortex in the monkey, it seemed either that the cat was peculiar or that the functional significances of the auditory and visual pathways to the cortex are not the same. I thought it was worthwhile to reexamine the effects of ablating visual cortex, even though this experiment had been done first almost 100 years ago by Ferrier, Schafer, and Munk. I chose the tree shrew as my subject for two reasons: (1) The striate cortex is extremely well developed in this otherwise primitive insectivore; and (2) the tree shrew may resemble the primate ancestor insofar as it has a strange mix of traits, some of which, especially the well-developed visual system, resemble primates. As contrasted with most taxonomic groups, there are living primates that are more primitive in the sense of being closer to actual ancestors—the Tarsius, the lemur, and the tree shrew all being examples of species that branched off the main trunk at different phylogenetic stages. Figure 8.33 contains drawings of the tree shrew, *Tupaia glis,* and the Galago, a prosimian primate whose brain is less well developed than the monkey's. There is now consensus that the tree shrew is an insectivore, but the fact that LeGros Clark, an outstanding paleontologist, made an error in calling it a primate only underlines the point that it is curiously intermediate between insectivores and primates (LeGros Clark, 1959).

In order to study the visual cortex of the tree shrew, we first trained the animals to discriminate between patterns and between different hues. Then we removed the striate cortex, the target of the lateral geniculate body. The animals showed no long-term deficit on any of these learned tasks and appeared to have normal visual capacity (Snyder & Diamond, 1968; Snyder, Killackey, & Diamond, 1969). They could avoid obstacles, they never bumped into a wall even in unfamiliar circumstances, they were able to follow moving objects, and they could jump accurately. If a much larger lesion was made, including the temporal lobe as well as the occipital lobe, then some sensory disturbance was evident although even these animals were not blind. We argued that if V II and the adjacent cortex of the temporal lobe were dependent on cortico-cortical fibers from the striate cortex, then the larger lesion should have no greater behavioral effect than the lesion restricted to the striate area. There must be a visual path to the extrastriate cortex parallel to the geniculo-striate path, and we predicted that this pathway probably takes a route first to the tectum and then to the pulvinar nucleus (see Fig. 8.34). We were not entirely unprepared for the concept of a tectopulvinar pathway and had earlier suggested that the pulvinar is probably not intrinsic (Diamond & Chow, 1962). This prediction was based in part on Bishop's view that every sensory system is composed of parallel pathways. In any case, such a pathway was found in the tree shrew using Nauta's method for tracing anterograde degeneration. This pathway has since been found in prosimians, monkeys, cats, and rabbits, and it probably is a characteristic of all mammals. Finally, the tree shrew is not unique in being capable of good vision in the absence of striate cortex. Recent studies of the cat show that removal of both V I and V II does not abolish pattern vision (Berkley & Sprague, 1979). These

FIG. 8.33.   Drawings of the tree shrew, *Tupaia glis,* an insectivore (above), and bushbaby, *Galago senegalensis,* a prosimian primate (below).

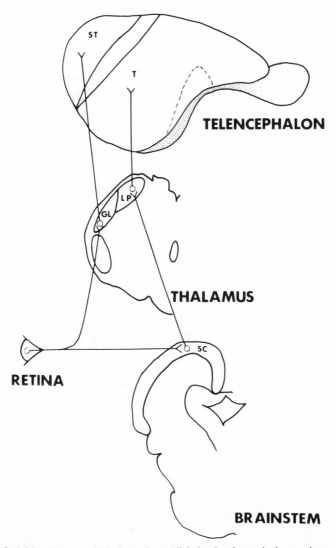

FIG. 8.34.   Diagram which shows the parallel visual pathways in the tree shrew. The chief point is that, in addition to the projection of the lateral geniculate nucleus (GL) to the striate cortex (ST), there is a second pathway that relays in the superior colliculus (SC) and the lateral posterior nucleus (or pulvinar nucleus, LP), and terminates finally in the temporal area (T).

results raise a question for a final and summary section. How can we explain earlier results of Schafer, Munk, and Klüver?

SUMMARY AND CRITIQUE: THE TRADITIONAL VIEW OF THE CORTEX IN THE LIGHT OF CURRENT EVIDENCE

Up to this point, my goal was to present each contribution in its own terms. While this does not mean that I tried to suspend all critical judgment, I did not think it would be fair to measure each author by discoveries yet to be made. For example, Bell's failure to recognize that each sensory pathway had its own cortical area does not detract from his "Idea." In this final section I want to reconsider the history of the inquiry, but this time in the light of current evidence.

Throughout the history, there is one principle that grows stronger with every new piece of evidence. The concept of "The Sensory Pathway" provides the key to understanding not just the cortex, but also the organization of the brain. I have tried to show that the origin of this idea can be traced as far back as the speculations of Charles Bell, who, of course, had little notion of a neuron or synapse. Without an understanding of a synapse a sensory pathway was hardly more than a primitive and vague approximation of the truth. Nevertheless, Bell's Idea was the beginning.

The lasting contributions of Cajal and Sherrington can hardly be summarized. Suffice it to say that the beautiful pictures of a cell body and its axon and dendrites, and the notion of a synaptic connection between axon and dendrite, provided the basis for the idea of a sensory pathway ascending to the cortex in a series of synaptic relay centers.

Campbell's chief contribution was identifying the target of each pathway in the cortex in architectonic terms. The striate cortex, for example, is unique, and every line of evidence—anatomical, physiological and behavioral, including the recent work of Hubel and Wiesel—points to a sharp functional difference at the borders of the striate area. Even Lashley conceded that the striate area may be the exception to the rule that architectonic borders have no functional significance.

It is another matter to assert that the striate cortex serves simple sensory functions and that the extrastriate belt serves visual memory and perception. The idea in the first place of what is simple and what is complex in the brain rests on philosophic distinctions. This is not to say that Hume was less than a great philosopher, or that he had no empirical evidence for his position. However, there are alternative philosophic views concerning what perceptions are innate and what are learned. There is even physiological evidence for innate neurological mechanisms for the perception of "objects." For example, in the visual system of frogs there are single neurons that respond to small, dark, moving stimuli. The description of these units as "bug detectors" seems to be justified.

In any case, Campbell was certainly wrong about the connections and functions of the extrastriate belt. We know first that this belt area receives thalamic fibers, so it is not an association area in Campbell's sense of the term. We also know that the pulvinar nucleus expands in primate evolution; even in prosimians, its projections to cortex extend across a vast area of the neocortex, including most of the temporal lobe. The pulvinar nucleus even projects to the striate cortex, thus overlapping the projections of the lateral geniculate nucleus. The extensive projections of the pulvinar nucleus and its great development in primates turned attention to its input. We now know that it is not intrinsic; it is not an association area receiving fibers from a number of other thalamic nuclei. At least a part of the pulvinar complex receives fibers from the superior colliculus. Further, those parts of the pulvinar complex that do not receive fibers from the superior colliculus, if such exist, receive visual input from the striate cortex. So all of the pulvinar nucleus can be identified with vision. It follows that as much as one-third, and perhaps one-half, of the neocortex in primates can be designated as visual cortex.

The question we now face is: How is this vast field organized? The *basic division* lies between the striate and extrastriate visual cortex. Thus, Campbell is vindicated in the most important sense, that cytoarchitectonics provides the starting point to an understanding of the organization of cortex. The extrastriate belt is the target of parallel visual pathways from tectum and pretectum relaying through the pulvinar complex. Very recent evidence shows that the lateral geniculate nucleus projects beyond the striate cortex in both primates and cats (Raczkowski & Rosenquist, 1980; Yukie & Iwai, 1981). This organization is found in such diverse species as cat and primate, and therefore appears to be characteristic of all mammals. For example, as many as 13 visual areas have now been defined in the cat by electrophysiological methods, and these extend to the border of the auditory field in the depths of the middle suprasylvian sulcus (Tusa, Palmer, & Rosenquist, 1981).

The auditory field, like the visual field, can be divided into a core area and an extensive belt. For example, the auditory field of the cat covers a vast extent of cortex which borders the visual cortex on one side and the somatic cortex on the other side, and even extends ventrally to the rhinal fissure. As in the case of the visual field, there is one area that can be singled out as a core of koniocortex that is the target of the essential projections from one special subdivision of the auditory thalamus. The belt areas around the core are recipients of parallel auditory pathways that are relayed through subdivisions of the auditory thalamus first identified by Rose. At least one of these pathways, the one that relays in the magnocellular subdivision of the medial geniculate body, projects to all subdivisions of the auditory field. There are at least four highly precise representations of the basilar membrane (Merzenich *et al.*, 1977). These maps depend on single unit recording and upon the definition of a receptive field as the "best frequency"; in other words, that frequency which can activate the unit at the lowest threshold. In addition to the four precisely tonotopic maps, there are several other areas with broader tuning neurons. This picture of parallel pathways in each major field, some very specific and some diffuse, fulfills Bishop's expectations as put forward in his paper on the evolution of fiber size. Whether or not each path reflects a different stage of evolution cannot be determined with certainty, but some pathways are more extensive and more diffuse. Clearly there is little or nothing left for "association cortex" in the cat. The extent of the visual and auditory and somatic fields in the cat and primate are shown in the drawings of Figure 8.35.

The idea that parts of association cortex are also targets of sensory pathways only serves to underscore the importance of the concept of the sensory path. But we must reject the idea that the pathway begins at a receptor and *ends* at the cortex. There is no evidence that visual sensation is achieved the instant impulses first reach striate cortex. Further, striate cortex sends descending projections both to the lateral geniculate nucleus and to the superior colliculus. The superior colliculus in turn projects to the striate cortex via relays in the pulvinar nucleus, so the visual pathway continues with a series of recurrent loops or circuits.

The discoveries of Magoun, Lindsley, Moruzzi, Morison, and Dempsey in the 1940s led to the idea that afferent pathways overlap in the cortex. If the intralaminar nuclei project diffusely to the whole of the neocortex, it follows that their projections must overlap with the projections of the classical relay nuclei. The fact that some sensory pathways project to several subdivisions and even to all of the subdivisions of a field implies that there is overlap in some, and perhaps in every, cortical subdivision. I have already belabored the point that the projections of the principal and magnocellular divisions of the medial geniculate body overlap in A I. According to the traditional view, going back to Elliot-Smith, each cortical area received fibers from just one thalamic nucleus. Thus, the striate cortex was thought to receive fibers just from the lateral geniculate body. We now know that, in addition to projections of the lateral geniculate nucleus, projections from the pulvinar nucleus and the intralaminar nuclei terminate in the striate cortex. We have recently found evidence that overlapping projections in the striate cortex terminate in different cortical layers. The lateral geniculate body projects to layer IV; furthermore, different layers of the lateral geniculate body project to different sublayers within cortical layer IV. Projections from the pulvinar nucleus as well as from the intralaminar nuclei terminate in layer I of the striate cortex (see, for example, Carey, Fitzpatrick, & Diamond, 1979; Ogren & Hendrickson, 1977).

To gain understanding of the behavioral significance of the organization into a core and belt and of the significance of cortical subdivisions in general, we must look again to the contribution of the oldest method—the method of ablation. Lashley's view of mass action does not seem to offer any hope for a solution. If

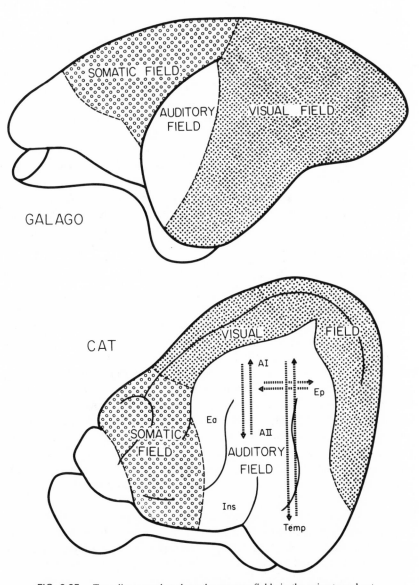

FIG. 8.35. Two diagrams that show the sensory fields in the primate and cat. The main point is that almost all of the neocortex can be assigned to one of the three fields, visual, somatic, or auditory, and there is little or no room for association cortex in the traditional sense. The broken-lined arrows in the auditory field of the cat are designed to show the reciprocal connections of the various subdivisions within a field. Thus, AI projects to AII and is reciprocated by a projection from AII to AI. Few, if any, fibers cross from AI to the visual field.

anything, the view that cortical subdivisions have functional significance is more strongly held today than 75 years ago. Each architectonic difference can be related to differences in connections. Yet the present picture of just three vast fields is not uncongenial to Lashley's criticism of localization of function. If there is no association cortex, Lashley was correct in concluding that the so-called association cortex is not special in learning and memory. Indeed, Lashley was the first to try to isolate sensory areas from motor areas by cutting cortico-cortical fibers. He believed he was cutting pathways from sensory areas to association areas which, in turn, project to motor areas, and he expected to find disruption of learned habits. He concluded that such projections did not play a role in conditioned reflexes. The study of cortico-cortical connections has also greatly advanced since the pioneering studies of Flechsig; i.e., rather than showing one-way projections from the core area to the belt, as was postulated in the traditional view, most of the subdivisions appear to be connected reciprocally. We now know that there are few if any cortical fibers which pass from the sensory areas to the motor areas of the somatic field. How then is sensory-motor integration achieved? The transport methods show that cells from layer V in every area of the cortex, including the striate cortex, send projections that descend to the brain stem and have the potentiality for making connections with motor neurons. Lashley is essentially vindicated, then, by the discovery that every area of the cortex is not only sensory, but also association and motor.

It remains to try to explain the results of Klüver's study of the occipital cortex in the monkey and the discrepancy between his findings and our results with the tree shrew. First, his lesions were much more extensive than the striate cortex and may have included the target of the tecto-pulvinar path in the monkey. The Pasiks (Pasik & Pasik, 1982; Pasik, Pasik, & Schilder, 1969) have evidence that monkeys with lesions restricted to area 17 can relearn pattern discrimination. Second, the extent to which the tectum depends on descending fibers from the striate cortex probably varies from species to species, and it is very likely that the function of the superior colliculus is severely disrupted by striate lesions in the monkey.

In conclusion, if I have selected the pioneers wisely, then every research described here has made some lasting contribution. I concede that the issue of the association cortex has not been settled once and for all even though the traditional view of association cortex has been disputed. In the cortex of man, language centers are found in one hemisphere and not in the other, even though the two hemispheres appear at first glance to be similar, even identical (see Fig. 8.1). How can the difference between the two hemispheres be explained? In what class are these language areas? Should they be classified as association cortex? Do they receive sensory input from the thalamus? The cortical basis for language and thought is one of the remaining mysteries of science, ranking with the question of the origin of life itself. We can only hope that the studies of the cortex in experimental mammals will contribute to the ultimate solution of this mystery.

ACKNOWLEDGEMENTS

I would like to thank Edna Bissette for her help in preparing this manuscript and Susan Havrilesky for preparing the illustrations. My own research cited in this chapter was supported by NIMH Grant 04849 and NSF Grant BNS 79-15780.

REFERENCES

Adrian, E. D. Double representation of the feet in the sensory cortex of the cat. *Journal of Physiology*, 1940, *98*.

Adrian, E. D. Afferent discharges to the cerebral cortex from peripheral sense organs. *Journal of Physiology*, 1941, *100*, 159–191.

Adrian, E. D. Sensory areas of the brain. *The Lancet*, 1943, *245*, 33–37.

Adrian, E. D. *The physical background of perception*. London: Oxford University Press, 1947.

Bard, P., & Mountcastle, V. B. Some forebrain mechanisms involved in expression of rage with special reference to suppression of angry behavior. *Research Publications of the Association in Nervous and Mental Disease*, 1948, *27*, 362–404.

Bell, C. Idea of a new anatomy of the brain. In *Medical Classics* (Vol. 1). Baltimore: Williams and Wilkins, 1936–37. (Originally published, 1811.)

Berger, H. Veber das Elektrenkephalogramm des Menschen. *Archives of Psychiatry*, 1929, *87*, 527–570.

Berkley, M. A., & Sprague, J. M. Striate cortex and visual acuity functions in the cat. *Journal of Comparative Neurology*, 1979, *187*, 679–702.

Bishop, G. H. The relation between nerve fiber size and sensory modality: Phylogenetic implications of the afferent innervation of cortex. *Journal of Nervous and Mental Disease*, 1959, *128*, 89–114.

Bishop, G. H., & Clare, M. H. Organization and distribution of fibers in the optic nerve of the cat. *Journal of Comparative Neurology*, 1955, *103*, 269–304.

Bodian, D. Studies on the diencephalon of the Virginia opossum. III. The thalamo-cortical projection. *Journal of Comparative Neurology*, 1942, *77*, 525–575.

Brodman, K. See Polyak, 1957.

Butler, R. A., Diamond, I. T., & Neff, W. D. Role of auditory cortex in discrimination of changes in frequency. *Journal of Neurophysiology*, 1957, *20*, 108–120.

Cajal, S. [The structure and connections of neurons.] In *Physiology or medicine: Nobel lectures including presentation speeches and laureates' biographies 1901–1921* (Nobel Foundation), Vol. I, pp. 220–253. New York: Elsevier, 1967. (Originally published, 1906.)

Campbell, A. W. *Histological studies on the localization of cerebral function*. Cambridge: Cambridge University Press, 1905.

Carey, R. G., Fitzpatrick, D., & Diamond, I. T. Layer I of striate cortex of *Tupaia glis* and *Galago senegalensis:* Projections from thalamus and claustrum revealed by retrograde transport of horseradish peroxidase. *Journal of Comparative Neurology*, 1979, *186*, 393–438.

Diamond, I. T., & Chow, K. L. Biological psychology. In S. Koch (Ed.), *Psychology: A study of a science* (Vol. 4). New York: McGraw-Hill, 1962.

Diamond, I. T., & Neff, W. D. Ablation of temporal cortex and discrimination of auditory patterns. *Journal of Neurology*, 1957, *20*, 300–315.

Diamond, I. T., Snyder, M., Killackey, H., Jane, J., & Hall, W. C. Thalamocortical projections in the tree shrew (*Tupaia glis*). *Journal of Comparative Neurology*, 1970, *139*, 273–306.

Elliot-Smith, G. Some problems relating to the evolution of the brain. *Lancet*, 1910, *1*, 1–6, 147–153, 221–227.

Evarts, E. V. A technique for recording activity of subcortical neurons in moving animals. *Electroencephalography and Clinical Neurophysiology*, 1968, *24*, 83–86.

Evarts, E. V. Brain mechanisms in movement. *Scientific American,* 1973, *229,* 96–103.

Evarts, E. V. Cortico-cortical and thalamo-cortical inputs to precentral motor cortex in monkey. In J. Orbach (Ed.), *Neuropsychology after Lashley.* London: Erlbaum, 1982.

Evarts, E. V., & Tanji, J. Reflexes and intended responses in motor cortex pyramidal tract neurons of monkeys. *Journal of Neurophysiology,* 1976, *39,* 1069–1080.

Ferrier, D. *The functions of the brain.* New York: Putnam, 1886.

Flechsig, P. Developmental (myelenogenetic) localization of the cerebral cortex in the human subject. *Lancet,* 1901, *2,* 1027–1029.

Flourens, P. *Investigations of the properties and the functions of the various parts which compose the cerebral mass* (G. Von Bonin, trans.). Springfield, Ill.: Thomas, 1960. (Originally published, 1824.)

Fritsch, G., & Hitzig, E. *On the electrical excitability of the cerebrum* (G. Von Bonin, trans.). Springfield, Ill.: Thomas, 1960. (Originally published, 1870.)

Gasser, H. S., & Erlanger, J. The role player by the sizes of the constituent fibers of a nerve trunk in determining the form of its action potential wave. *American Journal of Physiology,* 1927, *80,* 522–547.

Gasser, H. S., & Erlanger, J. The role of fiber size in the establishment of a nerve block by pressure or cocaine. *American Journal of Physiology,* 1929, *88,* 581–591.

Gaze, R. M., & Keating, M. J. The visual system and "neuronal specificity." *Nature,* 1972, *237* (June 16).

Goldstein, K. *The organism.* New York: American Book, 1939.

Golgi, C. [The neuron doctrine-theory and facts.] In *Physiology or medicine: Nobel lectures including presentation speeches and laureates' biographies 1901–1921* (Nobel Foundation), Vol. I, pp. 189–217. New York: Elsevier, 1967. (Originally published, 1906.)

Granit, R. Components of retinal action potential in mammals and their relation to discharge in optic nerve. *Journal of Physiology,* 1933, *77,* 207–239.

Granit, R. *Sensory mechanisms of the retina.* London: Oxford University Press, 1947.

Gratiolet, P. See Polyak, 1957.

Hartline, H. K. The response of single optic nerve fibers of the vertebrate eye to illumination of the retina. *American Journal of Physiology,* 1938, *121,* 400–415.

Herrick, C. J. The functions of the olfactory parts of the cerebral cortex. *Proceedings of the National Academy of Science,* 1933, *19,* 7–14.

Herrick, C. J. *The brain of the tiger salamander.* Chicago: University of Chicago Press, 1948.

Herrick, C. J., & Bishop, G. H. A comparative survey of the spinal lemniscus system. In H. H. Jasper (Ed.), *Reticular formation of the brain.* Boston: Little, Brown, 1958.

Hess, W. R. *The functional organization of the diencephalon.* New York: Grune and Stratton, 1957.

Hubel, D. H., & Wiesel, T. N. Receptive fields of single neurons in the cat's striate cortex. *Journal of Physiology,* 1959, *148,* 574–591.

James, W. *The principles of psychology* (Vol. 1). New York: Holt, 1890.

Karten, H. J., & Revzin, A. M. The afferent connections of the nucleus rotundus in the pigeon. *Brain Research,* 1966, *2,* 268–277.

Killackey, H. P., & Ebner, F. F. Two different types of thalamo-cortical projections to a single area in mammals. *Brain, Behavior and Evolution,* 1972, *6,* 141–169.

Klüver, H. *Behavior mechanisms in monkeys.* Chicago: University of Chicago Press, 1933.

Klüver, H. Functional significance of the geniculo-striate system. *Biological Symposium,* 1942, *7,* 253–299.

Klüver, H., & Bucy, P. C. "Psychic blindness" and other symptoms following bilateral temporal lobectomy in rhesus monkeys. *American Journal of Physiology,* 1937, *119,* 352–353.

Klüver, H., & Bucy, P. C. An analysis of certain effects of bilateral temporal lobectomy in the rhesus monkey, with special references to "psychic blindness." *Journal of Psychology,* 1938, *5,* 33–54.

Klüver, H., & Bucy, P. C. Preliminary analysis of functions of the temporal lobes in monkeys. *Archives of Neurology and Psychiatry*, 1939, *42*, 979–1000.

Kuffler, S. W. Discharge patterns and functional organization of the mammalian retina. *Journal of Neurophysiology*, 1953, *16*, 37–68.

Lashley, K. S. *Brain mechanisms and intelligence*. Chicago: University of Chicago Press, 1929.

Lashley, K. S. Thalmo-cortical connections of the rat's brain. *Journal of Comparative Neurology*, 1941, *75*, 67–121.

Lashley, K. S. *Brain mechanisms and intelligence: A quantitative study of injuries to the brain*. New York: Dover, 1963.

Lashley, K. S., & Clark, G. The cytoarchitecture of the cerebral cortex of ateles: A critical examination of architectonic studies. *Journal of Comparative Neurology*, 1946, *85*, 223–305.

Le Gros Clark, W. E. The structure and connections of the thalamus. *Brain*, 1932, *55*, 406–470. (a)

Le Gros Clark, W. E. A morphological study of the lateral geniculate body. *British Journal of Ophthalmology*, 1932. (b)

Le Gros Clark, W. E. *The antecedents of man: An introduction to the evolution of primates*. New York: Quadrangle Books, 1959.

Le Gros Clark, W. E., & Boggon, R. H. On the connections of the anterior nucleus of the thalamus. *Journal of Anatomy*, 1933, *67*, 215–226.

Le Gros Clark, W. E., & Northfield, D. W. C. The cortical projection of the pulvinar in the macaque monkey. *Brain*, 1939, *60*, 126–142.

Lindsley, D. B., Bowden, J. W., & Maquoa, W. H. Effect upon the EEG of acute injury to the brain stem activating system. *Electroencephalography and Clinical Neurophysiology*, 1949, *1*, 475–486.

Lorente de Nó, R. Cerebral cortex: Architecture, intracortical connections motor projections. In J. F. Fulton (Ed.) *Physiology of the Nervous System*. New York: Oxford University Press, 1938, 291–325.

Marchi, V. See Polyak, 1957.

Mehler, W. H., Feferman, M. E., & Nauta, W. J. H. Ascending axon degeneration following anterolateral cordotomy. *Brain*, 1960, *83*, 718–750.

Merzenich, M. M., Roth, G. L., Anderson, R. A., Knight, P. L., & Colwell, S. A. Some basic features of organization of the central auditory system. In E. F. Evans & J. P. Wilson (Eds.), *Psychophysics and physiology of hearing*. London: Academic Press, 1977.

Meynert. See Polyak, 1957.

Mishkin, M. Cortical visual areas and their interaction. In A. G. Karczmar & J. C. Eccles (Eds.), *The brain and human behavior*. Berlin: Springer-Verlag, 1972.

Mishkin, M. A memory system in the monkey. *Philosophic Transactions of the Royal Society*, 1982.

Mishkin, M., & Delacour, J. An analysis of short term visual memory in the monkey. *Journal of Experimental Psychology*, 1975, *1*, 326–334.

Morison, R. S., & Dempsey, E. W. A study of thalamocortical relations. *American Journal of Physiology*, 1942, *135*, 281–292.

Moruzzi, G., & Magoun, H. W. Brain stem reticular formation and activation of the EEG. *Electroencephalography and Clinical Neurophysiology*, 1949, *1*, 455–473.

Munk, H. *On the functions of the cortex* (G. Von Bonin, trans.). Springfield, Ill.: Thomas, 1960. (Originally published, 1881.)

Nauta, W. J. H., & Kuypers, H. G. J. M. Some ascending pathways in the brain stem reticular formation. In H. H. Jasper, L. D. Proctor, R. S. Knight, W. C. Noshay, & R. T. Costello (Eds.), *Reticular formation of the brain*. Boston: Little, Brown, 1958.

Nauta, W. J. H., & Whitlock, D. G. An anatomical analysis of the nonspecific thalamic projection system. In E. D. Adrian (Ed.), *Brain mechanisms and consciousness*. Springfield, Ill.: Thomas, 1954.

Neff, W. D., & Diamond, I. T. The neural basis of auditory discrimination. In H. F. Harlow & C. N. Woolsey (Eds.), *Biological and biochemical basis of behavior*. Madison: University of Wisconsin Press, 1958.

Neff, W. D., Diamond, I. T., & Casseday, J. H. Behavioral studies of auditory discrimination, central nervous system. In W. D. Keidel & W. D. Neff (Eds.), *Handbook of sensory physiology* (Vol. 5). New York: Springer-Verlag, 1975.

Nielsen, J. M., & Fitzgibbon, J. P. *Agnosia, apraxia, aphasia: Their value in cerebral localization*. Los Angeles: Los Angeles Neurological Society, 1936.

Ogren, M. P., & Hendrickson, A. E. The distribution of pulvinar terminals in visual areas 17 and 18 of the monkey. *Brain Research*, 1977, *137*, 343–350.

Owens. See Elliot-Smith, 1910.

Papez, J. W. A proposed mechanism of emotion. *Archives of Neurology and Psychiatry*, 1937, *38*, 725–744.

Pasik, P., & Pasik, T. Current concepts on the mechanisms of vision. In J. Orbach (Ed.), *Neuropsychology after Lashley*. Hillsdale, NJ.: Erlbaum, 1982.

Pasik, P., Pasik, T., & Schilder, P. Extrageniculostriate vision in the monkey: Discrimination of luminous fluxequated figures. *Experimental Neurology*, 1969, *24*, 421–437.

Polyak, S. L. *The vertebrate visual system* (H. Klüver, ed.). Chicago: University of Chicago Press, 1957.

Raczkowski, D., & Rosenquist, A. Connections of the parvocellular C laminae of the dorsal lateral geniculate body with the visual cortex of the cat. *Brain Research*, 1980, *199*, 447–451.

Revzin, A. M., & Karten, H. J. Rostral projections of the optic tectum and the nucleus rotundus in the pigeon. *Brain Research*, 1967, *3*, 264–276.

Rose, J. E., & Woolsey, C. N. Organization of the mammalian thalamus and its relationships to the cerebral cortex. *Electroencephalography and Clinical Neurophysiology*, 1949, *1*, 391–404. (a)

Rose, J. E., & Woolsey, C. N. The relations of thalamic connections, cellular structures and evocable electrical activity in the auditory region of the cat. *Journal of Comparative Neurology*, 1949, *91*, 441–466. (b)

Rose, J. E., & Woolsey, C. N. Cortical connections and functional organization of the thalamic auditory system of the cat. In H. F. Harlow & C. N. Woolsey (Eds.), *Biological and biochemical bases of behavior*. Madison: University of Wisconsin Press, 1958.

Sanides, F. Functional architecture of motor and sensory cortices in primates in the light of a new concept of neocortex evolution. In C. R. Noback & W. Montagna (Eds.), *The primate brain*. New York: Appleton-Century-Crofts, 1970.

Sanides, F. Representation in the cerebral cortex and its areal lamination patterns. In G. H. Bourne (Ed.), *Structure and function of nervous tissue* (Vol. 5). New York: Academic Press, 1972.

Schafer, E. A. Experiments on special localization in the cortex cerebri of the monkey. *Brain*, 1888, *10*, 362–380.

Sherrington, C. S. *The integrative action of the nervous system*. New Haven, CT.: Yale University Press, 1906.

Sherrington, C. S., & Leyton, A. S. F. Observations on the excitable cortex of the chimpanzee, orang-utan, and gorilla. In G. von Bonin (Ed.), *The cerebral cortex*. Springfield, Ill.: Thomas, 1960 (originally published 1917).

Sinclair, D. C. Cutaneous sensation and the doctrine of specific energy. *Brain*, 1955, *78*, 584–614.

Snyder, M., & Diamond, I. T. The organization and function of the visual cortex in the tree shrew. *Brain, Behavior and Evolution*, 1968, *1*, 244–288.

Snyder, M., Killackey, H., & Diamond, I. T. Color vision in the tree shrew after removal of posterior neocortex. *Journal of Neurophysiology*, 1969, *32*, 554–563.

Spearman, C. *The abilities of man*. New York: Macmillan, 1927.

Talbot, S. A., Woolsey, C. N., & Thompson, J. M. Visual areas I and II of cerebral cortex of rabbit. *Federation Proceedings of the Federation of American Societies for Experimental Biology*, 1946, *5*, 103.

Thorndike, E. L. *Animal intelligence.* New York: Hafner, 1911.

Tichener, E. G. *A textbook of psychology.* New York: Macmillan, 1916.

Tunturi, A. R. Audiofrequency localization in the acoustic cortex of the dog. *American Journal of Physiology,* 1944, *141,* 397–403.

Tusa, R. J., Palmer, L. A., & Rosenquist, A. C. Multiple cortical visual areas: visual field topography in the cat. In C. N. Woolsey (Ed.), *Cortical Sensory Organization Volume II: Multiple Visual Areas.* Clifton, NJ.: Humana Press, 1981, 1–31.

Walker, A. E. *The primate thalamus.* Chicago: University of Chicago Press, 1938.

Woolsey, C. N. Patterns of sensory representation in the cerebral cortex. *Federation Proceedings,* 1947, *6,* 437–441.

Woolsey, C. N. Organization of somatic sensory and motor areas of the cerebral cortex. In H. F. Harlow & C. N. Woolsey (Eds.), *Biological and biochemical bases of behavior.* Madison: University of Wisconsin Press, 1958.

Woolsey, C. N., & Fairman, D. Contralateral, ipsilateral, and bilateral representation of cutaneous receptors in somatic areas I and II of the cerebral cortex of pig, sheep, and other mammals. *Surgery,* 1946, *19,* 684–702.

Woolsey, C. N., & Walzl, E. M. Topical projection of nerve fibers from local regions of the cochlea to the cerebral cortex of the cat. *Johns Hopkins Hospital Bulletin,* 1942, *71,* 315–344.

Yukie, M., & Iwai, E. Direct projection from the dorsal lateral geniculate nucleus to the prestirate cortex in macaque monkeys. *Journal of Comparative Neurology,* 1981, *201,* 81–98.

Zukerman, S. The scientist and the man. In S. Zukerman (Ed.), *Grafton Elliot Smith: The concepts of human evolution.* The Zoological Society of London. London: Academic Press, 1973.

Name Index

Volume I and Volume II entries are listed following the designations I and II.

A

Adler, A. II: 163, 332, 337, 367
Adorno, T. W. II: 379, 404
Adrian, Lord, E. D. I: 17, 199, 202, 236, 253–255, 355–357, 359–360
Agnew, H. W. II: 206, 217
Ainsworth, M. D. S. II: 140, 146, 149
Al-Kindi I: 167
Alberts, E. II: 15, 18, 138, 146
Alecemon I: 3, 221; II: 200
Alexander the Great I: 137, 223
Alhazen I: 167–169, 293–294
Allderidge, P. II: 280–282, 293, 305–306, 327–328
Allee, W. C. II: 54, 59
Allen, F. II: 235
Allport, F. H. II: 100–101, 373, 375–376, 404
Allport, G. W. I: 286–287, II: 99, 107, 125, 146, 345, 347, 367, 379, 404
Alpert, R. II: 134, 149
Altrocchi, J. II: 275, 293
Amark, C. A. II: 46, 58
American Psychological Association (APA) II: 106, 107
Ames, A. I: 289
Anderson, J. E. II: 94–95
Angell, J. R. I: 12, 27, 33, 96, 266

Ansbacher, H. L. II: 99, 107
Appel, S. H. II: 56, 61
Appley, M. H. II: 5, 17, 157, 162, 167, 169, 175–179, 182
Aquinas, T. II: 152
Aries, P. II: 116, 146
Aristophanes II: 226–227
Aristotle I: 3–4, 63, 137–139, 148, 166, 168, 221–225, 227, 250, 263, 271; II: 2–3, 20, 65, 191–195, 200–201, 215, 237, 333, 392, 404
Aronson, E. II: 399, 404
Arrhenius, S. I: 230, 255
Artemedorus II: 195
Asch, S. E. II: 16, 391, 397, 404
Aserinsky, E. II: 206, 215
Ash, P. II: 104, 107
Atkinson, J. w. II: 179–180, 368
Aubrey, J. II: 281, 293
Augustine, St. II: 222
Avicenna I: 4, 224; II: 270, 326
Avogadro, A. I: 243
Ayllon, T. II: 244
Ayres, C. E. II: 165, 186
Azrin, N. II: 244

B

Back, K. W. II: 380, 387, 389, 404–406
Backer, R. II: 173, 188

Subject Index

Alfred Binet

Hermann von Helmholtz

Charles Darwin

Emil Kraepelin

Sigmund Freud

Karl Lashley